BEING THERE

An autobiography by arguably the most successful
all round international rider in the history of
New Zealand motorcycling

Hugh Anderson MBE

Pitstop, an imprint of
Woodslane Press Pty Ltd
10 Apollo Street
Warriewood, NSW 2102
Email: info@woodslane.com.au
Tel: 02 8445 2300 Website: www.pitstop.net.au

First published in 2014
This edition published in Australia in 2015 by Pitstop, and imprint of
Woodslane Press
© 2015 Hugh Anderson

Australian CiP data available from the publishers

Cover design by Troy Major and Hugh Anderson
Proofing by Eva Chan
Typesetting by DIY Publishing Ltd
Printed in Australia by McPherson's Printing Group

Motorcycle racers aren't like other sports people. When they enter the arena they are taking their lives in their hands. When they are on the racetrack, if they are not there in every sense of the word they are more likely to be at risk of serious injury or death.

Very few champions can explain exactly what it takes to compete at the highest level. What makes them tick, how they cope with the challenge and what the science is that makes them so dominant in their chosen sport.

Hugh Anderson is one who can. From humble origins as a lonely teenager on the family farm in New Zealand, to the heights of world domination, he explains in his own words the motivation, racing strategies, psychology of winning, heartache and triumph that helped him deliver Suzuki its first major Grand Prix successes in the 1960s. This was a golden age, when Japanese and European factories battled for supremacy on the world's most dangerous circuits. When technological changes saw two-stroke and four-stroke motorcycles compete in 50cc, 125cc, 250cc, 350cc, and 500cc classes.

Hugh Anderson's career continued for decades after winning four World Championships, with motocross and then classic racing affording him two more showcases for the talent that has made New Zealand's most successful racer.

This book demystifies the motorcycle Grand Prix scene that seems so 'sanitised' on television. It takes us inside the mind of one of the most resourceful, brave and analytical riders in the history of Grand Prix racing.

Hamish Cooper, Journalist

I had the impression that the track surface and surrounds had magnified. Larger to a much sharper, more clear version of normal. All motion had slowed, giving me more time and allowing my speed to be ever faster. Within all this lies the glue of rhythm on which my concentration is based; this synchronises every movement and gives me complete control. The product of perfect form, my true reward. This state of mind and place of perfection cannot be imagined or explained. Only those that have been there and have experienced it, know it.

These sublime experiences are my greatest memories, a time when I was completely right, perhaps the only time in my life when I was free of self-doubt and all other human frailties. If, at these times, had my concentration failed me, the price to be paid, in injuries, was awfully high.

Hugh Anderson

ACKNOWLEDGEMENTS

Peter Beazley — friend, photographer and sportsman. Without your guidance, enthusiasm and support, *Being There* may not have passed the starter's flag, or, in fact, finally arrive at the finish.

Linley Deane. Dear Linley, thank you for offering your computer skills and putting my hours of dictation on paper. And through difficult times, never being too tired or busy to continue the work. Your contribution and unfailing belief in the story encouraged me to carry on. Husband Barry too was always constructive and ever patient with the frequent, at times inconvenient, phone calls.

Hamish Cooper — who carried out the first edit and reduced a basic script to a manageable 130,000 words and made numerous valuable contributions.

My wonderful children, Caroline, Hugh and Michelle, who have collectively spent many hours advising, contributing and supporting our family throughout this journey. They have each brought their own unique skills and perspective to this project and for this I am very fortunate and grateful.

And then there is my love, Janny, whose unselfish patience and support through what seemed to her a never-ending process. She nursed me through an incapacitating brain tumour, being hospitalised by a blinding migraine and later a duodenal ulcer.

Ainslie Talbot. Thank you, Ainslie, for your time, skill and advice.

Bruce Weeks, Roy Long and Peter Beazley — what are mates for? Walking through the chapters with you guys made the road less lonely.

Rhys Jones. Thank for your hurried, last-minute overview.

Many thanks to all those photographers that I was able to contact and who so willingly gave their permission to use their images.

While every effort has been made to establish and contact the copyright holders of some images used in this book, in some cases this has not been possible.

DEDICATED TO MY EVER HELPFUL, LOVING WIFE, JANNY

'It is easy to give if there is someone willing to take; it is easy to take when there is someone with so much to give. She has made me into something approaching the man I once hoped to be. She came into my life at a turning point during that exhausting, terrifying and magnificent journey we call life. And for that I am eternally grateful.'

— *Peter Ustinov*

CONTENTS

4 fois Champion du Monde
(circuit de vitesse)

Hugh Anderson
New Zealand
4 fois Champion du Monde
(Circuit de Vitesse)

Les Graham

The World Championship Series as we know it was introduced in 1949. That year, when leading the Senior TT in the Isle of Man, in the last lap Les's factory AJS suffered mechanical failure just two miles from the finish. Les dismounted and, determined to finish, pushed the bike, to be joined for the last 500 metres by Jock West, Sales Director of AJS Matchless, who ran beside him, encouraging the exhausted rider to continue to the finish. Les finally crossed the line, still able to raise a smile, a hero of the press and public alike.

Les went on to win the 500cc World Championship that year, a feat sufficient to gain the attention of a schoolboy 12,000 miles distant. Later I became aware that he had been a bomber pilot during the war, rose to the rank of Flight Lieutenant and was awarded the Distinguished Flying Cross for his courage. To me this was an indication of his skills and the human qualities that enabled him to succeed in two fields that must rank near the ultimate of human endeavour.

When I was 13 years of age, he became my complete hero; his courage, dashing, determined riding and sportsmanship had considerable influence on my life.

His death, due to mechanical failure at the bottom of Bray Hill during the second lap of the Senior TT on the 12th of June 1953, was received with profound dismay and came as a deep shock to the followers of road racing in all parts of the world. The staff of the *Motor Cycling* magazine saw it as 'a stark, hideous, tragedy'. Les was exceptionally popular, not only because of his engaging character, but also because he had battled for many years against uncommonly bad luck.

A page from *Motor Cycling* contained a remarkable tribute to Les in the form of an ode. I took it from the magazine dated June 25, 1953, and kept it on my bedside chair for some time. Eventually, it accompanied me to Europe where it would play a crucial role when I was confronted with my own mortality at the Isle of Man TT.

Few photographs portray greater determination, commitment and will to win so vividly as this, taken during his dashing ride that finished in such a disheartening way.

Stuart Graham

Despite losing his father, Les, 1949 World Champion in a fatal accident during the 1953 TT, Stuart Graham has also enjoyed a successful racing career, racing motorcycles from 1961 to 1970, progressing from a 250 Aermacchi to a 7R and G50 in World Championship GPs in 1966. Impressive performances in the early GP of that year, including second to Agostini in the 500cc Belgian GP, earned him a place in the factory Honda team as team-mate to Mike Hailwood on the fabulous 250cc Honda 6. Quite an achievement for his first year in GPs. Several good rides included second to Hailwood in the TT and in Finland; a very promising start to his works career.

For 1967, Stuart joined Suzuki to ride their amazing 50 and 125cc two-strokes, adapting well to these complex machines. Highlights included a wonderfully emotional victory in the 50cc TT, after narrowly losing out to Phil Read in the 125 TT, and also winning the Finnish GP, and the final GP in Japan saw Stuart second on the 50 and taking the all-new V4 125 to an excellent second to Bill Ivy. Third in both 50 and 125 World Championships was a reward for a successful first year with Suzuki and things looked very promising for 1968.

Unexpectedly, Suzuki and Honda withdrew from GP racing, leaving Stuart's World Championship ambitions remaining unfulfilled. Stuart retired to start a garage business. However, having achieved TT success to emulate his late father, raced for the Honda and Suzuki factory teams on amazing machinery, and winning races and GPs during a special era, he can look back on a satisfying and rewarding career.

By 1973, Stuart had embarked on a second very successful career driving touring cars and winning races in his first season. By 1973, Stuart's big V8 Chevrolet Camaro, sponsored by Brut aftershave, which Stuart had introduced to motorsport, was the car to beat in the British Championships, and when he won the prestigious RAC Tourist Trophy race, he became the first person since Freddie Dixon pre-war to win both bike and car TTs. To repeat the victory in 1975 achieved a unique record. Throughout the 1970s Stuart continued to win touring car races, titles and awards in UK, Europe and overseas in Camaros and then as a Ford works driver in Capris.

Stuart retired in 1980 to concentrate on his expanding motor business, including a Honda car dealership. However, the offer of a sponsored Lola T70 GT in selected historic events in the UK and overseas proved too tempting. More wins and successes followed and as the international historic racing scene grew, so the opportunities continued.

Now into his seventh decade, Stuart still enjoys invitations to race some wonderful cars at prestigious events such as Goodwood, Silverstone and Le Mans, recently adding the RAC Historic TT to his list of wins, and relishes the occasional opportunity to demo/parade on a bike, especially a multi-cylinder gem from Japan.

Only a select few have made a successful transition from two to four wheels and winning TTs in both disciplines; Stuart has achieved a pretty unique record. I am sure his dad would have been proud.

Percy Coleman. Riding an Indian on the one-mile horse-racing grass tracks of the time,
Percy set Australasian records for:
10 miles in 9 minutes 13 seconds
15 miles in 14 minutes 28 seconds
1 mile in 55 seconds.
Percy was just 17 years old.

Percy Coleman as I knew him, at a grass track meeting with his two outstandingly
successful sons, Rod and Bob.

PROLOGUE

After sleeping fitfully I finally wake at 7am feeling very uncomfortable. Damn the bad luck of being in the wrong place at the wrong time and having an out-of-control rider crash into me at the beginning of practice for the New Zealand Classic two-day TT event at Pukekohe in late October 2008.

At 72 years of age I had made my fastest lap ever at the previous meeting there, beating the New Zealand and Australian champion Dave Cole on two occasions, and was looking forward to another enjoyable contest. But no, this unnecessary incident put paid to that. My 500cc Manx Norton, which I had purchased new in 1961, is now heavily damaged in my workshop and I have three broken ribs and am quite unable to get out of bed. It will be a long day.

I wait for Janny to help sit me up. She emerges from the en suite showered and groomed. Though in late middle age, she remains as beautiful to me as in the flower of her youth, still wearing that special rather cheeky mischievous smile I first saw when hospitalised after suffering severe injuries during the 1961 Dutch TT, 47 years ago.

My mood lightens, a feeling of wellbeing drifts over me and I grit my teeth as Janny helps me into a sitting position, steadies me as I slide my feet to the floor and gingerly stand up. Janny is amused at my temerity and relative helplessness; normally it is me who is 'gung ho, here we go', but not this morning. Janny helps me undress and prepares the shower; the warmth of the water is soothing, her hands gently soaping me in a manner more akin to a caress than the task of washing. Far too soon it is over, I step from the shower and am gently dried off. I feel more comfortable now that the painkillers taken earlier are beginning to take effect. I finish off my ablutions, apply aftershave and take Janny in my arms, hold her and thank her for loving me, caring for me and never having criticised my career in motorcycle racing.

During our 45 years of marriage, there have been two occasions following race accidents when she had been told that I was dead. After one of those incidents, our son conveyed the bad news to Janny who was track side and advised her not to go to the scene of the accident. Brushing aside the well-meant advice, she arrived just as I began to regain consciousness.

There have been many less dramatic, non-life-threatening incidents including a broken back, shoulders, legs, arms, feet, hands, dislocations, a fractured skull and other things including what are now hurting, ribs, lots of ribs. Whilst Janny is not always pleased about it, being a trained nurse and a person of courage, character and common sense, she copes well and would never ask me to give up the sport I love. And so following breakfast, I made a commitment to write this book; choosing our coffee table on the terrace, surrounded by luxuriant roses on a warm sunny spring day, seems like an inspirational place to begin this arduous task.

But first I must revisit all those special moments now etched in history, to travel again that rocky, emotional road of, at times, destructive self-criticism and soul searching as I strove to enhance and develop the natural abilities with which I have been gifted. Nothing can be omitted. The despair when head injuries leave vegetables in the place of intelligent, energetic, life-loving mates, sifting through the seemingly never-ending trail of deaths that lie behind you, but at the same time recognising a responsibility to your childhood dreams, your club, sport, country and contracts, a sense of abiding commitment that drives you on.

There is no place in old age for 'If only', 'I should have' or 'I could have' to haunt me through the years to come. I always wanted a clear conscience, the satisfaction of knowing that I have done my best at all times, never having taken an easier, less productive route, and seldom taking a backward step.

The need to race, the search for and retention of perfect form, an addiction to that strange ethereal state where silence and perfection, the product of total concentration and immaculate execution, in itself was my reward.

We have few opportunities in life. As a 10-year-old I hoped that this dream could be mine, driven by an all-consuming need to gain the skills required and hopefully join those gifted god-like men I worshipped as a child. That this was in the end achieved and I too became a multi world champion still leaves me a little in awe of the person international motorcycle racing allowed me to become.

The World Championship series as we know it today was introduced in 1949. Les Graham and Freddie Frith became the first 500 and 350cc champions.

These two great men were to me the epitome of dignity and courage. I could never hope to be the man that each was, but just to tread the same path, ride the same roads, and to be part of what they had made their own, to be there and share the air, the danger and excitement would be sufficient.

Above: Freddie Frith.
A photograph of another hero from my youth. This portrays the skills of a master craftsman at work. While descending Bray Hill with his wheels well off the ground, his balance and poise remain perfect as he holds the throttle of his factory Norton wide open.

Left: The original caption from a Japanese magazine was 'The Thinker', as I was known by the Suzuki team.

FOREWORD

Hugh finally tells his story. Many have encouraged him to do so for several years, but being a typically reserved and modest New Zealander, his amazing life and achievements have remained undocumented in full until now. A life now brilliantly recalled in a very perceptive and insightful way, and well worth the wait.

Personally, it is a privilege to write the foreword to this great story. Hugh and I have remained friends since our 1960s racing days. It was as a result of his recommendation that Suzuki invited me to join their factory team in 1967 following his retirement and I am ever grateful for his support and guidance at that time.

Until I got to know Hugh better, I was unaware that one of his boyhood heroes was my late father, 1949 World Champion Les Graham, helping to fuel his dreams of becoming a successful motorcycle racer, and even a World Champion. An interesting and pleasing coincidence how our lives and careers worked out.

Hugh was one of the finest motorcycle racers in the world during the 1960s, and Suzuki's first and most prolific World Champion, helping to establish the company's global reputation. Whilst known as one of the fastest and most determined riders on the circuit, Hugh's meticulous technical and mental preparations, as well as thoughtful attention to details, were legendary.

Away from the pressured and stressful environment of the circuits, Hugh often sought peace and solitude and was happiest with his own thoughts, or spending time quietly with his devoted wife Janny and their family.

This story is also a wonderfully detailed, personal and fascinating account of Grand Prix motorcycle racing and its extreme highs and lows, during possibly its most golden era. Racing ever more exotic and difficult, experimental machines for ambitious manufacturers engaged in an unrestrained technological power struggle, on some of the world's most terrifyingly dangerous circuits, was not for the faint-hearted.

This was an era when sadly death and injury were commonplace, and to have survived is an achievement in itself. To also win multiple World Championships and honours is a racer's dream fulfilled.

Stuart Graham

Stuart, Margaret, Joanne and Gullwing Mercedes.

'Life is either a daring adventure or nothing.' — *Helen Keller*

The first:
Ohinewai School Calf Club 1947

The finest:
Isle of Man TT winner 1963

CHAPTER 1

Spine tingles and goose bumps and I was only age 10

I stand in the farmyard outside the sheds admiring three months of rebuild work on my BSA Gold Star. Ginger Molloy, the previous owner, had painted it red, but I've resprayed it in the same trendy pale blue as my elder brother Gordon's Ford Zephyr convertible. The 350cc engine has been carefully overhauled by top engineers. I've made a new seat and then rebuilt the bike using all new fasteners. The one item that still needs replacing is the carburettor, as the screw-on cap is damaged. My friend Dave Kenah is due back from Europe after a season of long-distance road trials and will bring a new carburettor for me. As I'm only going to run it for a short time, it doesn't seem necessary to wire the top down.

I push-start the gleaming "Goldie" and it runs beautifully. As the engine warms up it gives off the sweet smell of the washing powder that I had boiled the cylinder head and barrel in to make them look factory-new.

Like most young men, I can resist all things except temptation. So I ride off down to the front gate of the farm, turn, and as the revs soar past 7,200rpm, I drop the clutch. The first run of the new season is a gallop back towards the sheds. In deference to the rebuilt motor, I shut off earlier than usual but nothing happens — the throttle is stuck wide open.

I jam on the rear brake, lock the wheel and stall the engine. Still travelling at speed, I hit a series of potholes that punch me off the seat and my foot slips off the brake pedal. With a mighty roar the engine restarts. Suddenly, Mum's empty garage appears to double in width and I can't avoid it. Again, standing with all my weight on the brake pedal, I stall the engine. Now with both wheels locked, we skid at speed into the shed, striking the back wall so hard the front wheel smashes through the timber. The bike is embedded up to the handlebars with the front wheel protruding into daylight on the other side.

Massive relief is being replaced by concern as I dismount and walk around to see how things look on the other side. One vertical weatherboard has been sprung off its nails and two are broken, but the damage is easy enough to repair. After freeing the Goldie I wheel it back to the workshop, light up a calming cigarette and check for damage. The front wheel has not been buckled, the tyre is okay and the forks move freely. With a saw, hammer, nails and a suitable piece of timber I quickly repair the garage wall leaving it looking as 'good as gold'.

My passion for wheels began when I was quite young. At eight I finally mastered the rather difficult task of riding brother Gordon's full-sized bicycle. I grabbed the handlebars, then slid my right leg under the top bar to reach the right pedal and operated the left pedal with my left foot — gaining any sense of balance seemed quite impossible. I fell on top of it, under it and got entangled in it and became resigned to failure.

Some weeks later, when home alone on a Sunday morning, I made real progress managing to rotate the pedals several times before falling once again. Finally, I gained sufficient confidence to leave the safety of the grass in front of the house and pedalled off in this clumsy, awkward fashion, down to the front gate and out onto the road. The bike rolled so freely on the hard seal, it seemed so easy and I relaxed, but then my right foot slipped off the pedal and my toes hit the road hard, ripping the ends off three of them as I fell heavily on the sharp, course stones. My left elbow, knee, hand and severely stubbed toes were bleeding and hurt a bit but without hesitation I scrambled up and got pedalling again. The distant shop was my goal and the pain seemed to sharpen my focus. I reached that shop and returned home. There was a large couch on the veranda — I lay down on it physically and mentally spent but I could ride a bike, my greatest achievement so far. When the family returned I was fast asleep. Mum bathed the abrasions and damage toes in disinfectant and bandaged me up. My siblings had the last words. Serves you right, that will teach you, when will you learn to listen to others?

My passion for motorcycling began when I was very young. In 1943, Gordon turned 17 and with his friend Stan Johns, from Huntly, they enlisted in the New Zealand Air Force and were based at Ardmore, south of Auckland, a two-hour drive from our home in Ohinewai near Huntly in the Waikato region. When on leave, Stan's New Imperial was their transport home.

Meanwhile I was on my own fantasy road trip. There were the remains of an old Norton motorcycle in the shed. Using what controls it had and verbally imitating the exhaust note as I changed up and down through the gears, I cruised the countryside, covering many enjoyable miles, and visited countless imaginary places.

Stan and my older sister Valerie soon became more than friends. As a nine-year-old I was itching to experience the thrill of riding a real bike and Stan was good enough to give me that opportunity. Being completely conversant with the controls, I took no time at all to safely circulate around the home paddock. It seemed so easy to balance, guide and control. The engine pulse of this living thing and its response to my every action, clutch, brake and throttle was the most moving thing of my life. Stan signalled me to stop. Being immersed in the depths of this wonderfully moving experience, I stopped beside him, dismounted, and with a stumbling gait walked wordlessly away.

Mum, Laurel, me, Valerie and Gordon. Taken in 1945 before Gordon was demobbed from the Air Force.

16

Early in 1945 Gordon was demobbed from the Air Force and soon after began a subscription to Britain's *The Motor Cycle*, one of the world's first specialist magazines first published in 1903. As a nine-year-old it became my window to the wider world. I found the text difficult to follow at times, but the photographs told their own story and I was introduced to new, quite different countries; I was fascinated by them all. While the motorcycles were central to my interest, the picturesque villages with thatch-roofed cottages, ancient ivy-covered houses and towns where all the houses were joined together were alien images to me. As were the narrow, tarsealed country roads with stone fences and humpback bridges. Every page contained a new experience, much wider than just motorcycling itself.

The world's first major post-war road race was the 1946 Manx Grand Prix held in early September on the famous Isle of Man TT Mountain Course.

Eventually, *The Motor Cycle* issue covering this arrived. The journalists seemed enthralled by the occasion. With emotive language, every facet of this inaugural meeting was described in detail. Enthusiasm and excitement leapt off every page. After carefully reading the article twice, I sat and reflected on it. Then the thought came to me that I would like to go there one day. Immediately, a strong physical buzz rushed up my spine. I shivered and became covered in goose bumps. It was nine months after my tenth birthday and the beginning of my road race dream.

After some weeks had passed, I could no longer keep what I had experienced to myself, and during an evening meal I boldly stated, "One day I am going to the Isle of Man." My siblings' reactions were universal and predictable. I was laughed at, told I was foolish and said such stupid things. Being by far the youngest, I had no verbal authority over them and was forced to accept their regular hurtful commentary and criticism as the truth. For many years that first realisation of "I would like to go there one day" was always close and when it came to mind, I invariably sensed a buzz of excitement. But to imagine or dream of actually being there seemed like many steps too far.

Soon after leaving the Air Force, Gordon bought a Norton; other motorcycles came and went. He was keen on all sports and excelled at rugby and tennis. Before the war, speedway or dirt track racing, incorporating midget cars and motorcycles, had been very popular in isolated New Zealand. International riders had visited, competing in well-promoted meetings that drew large crowds. A new track in a park near Newmarket in Auckland had been opened. Gordon was tempted. To test his skills, he

bought a 1927 EW 350cc flat-twin Douglas. The rear tyre was worn to the canvas so wet grass gave him a suitably slippery surface to practise on. That old bike seemed to be indestructible and served its purpose well.

Laurel, Gordon, Joan and Morrie Goord, Norton mounted in 1949. Archives.

17

Gordon making a winner's speech.
Archives.

Gordon riding 'our' Douglas in a
trial 1948. Archives.

Gordon then bought a speedway Rudge, which ran on methylated spirits, relegating the Douglas to the back of the shed and leaving an opportunity for an eager 12-year-old. From time to time when no one was at home, Roy Foster, a local lad with whom I shared many common interests, and I would bring the Douglas out and take turns riding it around the paddock. No one seemed to notice. As with all new projects, new skills are required, learned and developed. In this case it was siphoning petrol out of a car, which was more difficult than it seemed. Once, after too many sucks on the hose, I got a mouthful, which was not unusual. But in this case petrol was running out of my nose. No wonder I became a petrolhead. Obviously, the affliction is sinus related. The next step was gaining formal permission to use the Douglas. After considerable grovelling and agreeing to clean his speedway Rudge each time it was used and promising to ride the Douglas slowly and sensibly, I was allowed to ride it for half an hour on a Sunday afternoon. Such semi-loose arrangements are never meant to be utterly inflexible, and it soon became (virtually) mine. Roy and I made a skid pan near the edge of the river. Feet up, full lock slides became the goal, the pleasure and learning never-ending. Near our skid pan was a ridge. It began as a gentle slope, graduating to a steep bank. It didn't take long to adjust the speed to the size of the ridge and experience the much anticipated 'lift-off'. With speed and height the landings became ever more dodgy, leading to my first big fall, requiring a visit to Mum and her first-aid kit. Nothing too serious, just my right leg burned on the hot exhaust, my chin cut on something and my left thumb swollen and painful. My dear mum was 'sort of amused'. "You and that blinking motorbike," she said, but to her great credit, she never stopped me riding it. After Roy and I had been using it for 18 months or so, Gordon sold the Douglas. He claimed he wanted his money back before I destroyed it.

My cousin Fred Anderson lived close by on an adjacent farm. He was several years older than me and purchased a 1947 350cc Velocette. It wasn't very fast but utterly reliable so he rode it flat-out all the time. Fred often rode it around a track he had laid out in a field. Whenever I heard him riding around it I was off on my bicycle and onto his pillion seat. Fred then bought a 1950 BSA Gold Star and successfully competed in miniature TT grass track events and road races. This was a step up and certainly gave a more lively ride than the Velo. Before Fred rode in his first road race a certain amount of testing was required; I didn't miss many of them. Sitting behind and hanging tightly on to Fred with the bellowing open megaphone ending at my right foot allowed me, for the first time, to experience the excitement, speed and noise created by a road-racing motorcycle.

Roy and I used our bicycles to mimic the motorcycle trials portrayed in the British magazine. Riding around muddy, slippery tree roots on the riverbank taught us balance, observation as to the best route and the ability to guide the bike by lifting the front and rear wheel over obstacles. Racetracks were built on the river bank. We were forever sliding around corners at the railway station, the tennis courts after sand had been scattered on the surface, and anywhere else. Learning how to ride down near-vertical banks then encouraging less experienced kids to try. Not very sporting perhaps, but the results could be pretty amusing.

My mother, Daisy, tolerated our motorcycling obsessions. Mum's life had not been easy. My father, Hugh, was killed in a truck accident in 1938, during the transition from a small holding and milk round in Auckland to a larger farm, when I was 18 months old. So Mum moved four young children, the contents of a house and livestock to a new dairy farm. Then she had to cope with all the difficulties and long hours associated with it. You could say that she was often in survival mode. In our situation at that time and for many years to follow all the family had their before- and after-school jobs. No one worked harder than Mum. At 13 when a new tractor arrived, I was the driver. At 14 I knew how to handle guns. Using my father's old shotgun and with Pippy, a fox terrier and my constant companion, we kept the rabbit population down on our farm and the neighbouring farms.

It was at this time that the World Championship series, as we know them today, was introduced. In 1949 Les Graham and Freddie Frith were the winners of the 500cc and 350cc titles. These two great men were, to me, the epitome of dignity and courage. I could never hope to be the kind of men that they were, but just to tread the same path, race on the same roads that they had, to be part of what they had made their own, to be there and share the air, the danger, excitement and success, would be sufficient.

Roy, Ian Lumsden, another local lad, and I built a swimming hole on the bank of the mighty Waikato River. The river was seven hundred metres wide, deep and with a swift current, and tugs towing a string of barges had replaced genuine paddle steamers; it held no fears for us. We had a substantial diving board pinched from somewhere and mounted on the bank then laboriously attached a rope high in a tree to swing from. The hardiest of us, of which I was reluctantly one, began swimming as early as October when the water consisted partly of snow melt. Up to 15 children enjoyed summer Sundays there. Roy, Ian, Pippy and I would often walk upstream, lever a large log free and, encouraged by perfect echoes, yell and yodel as we rode it home then slip off it and swim ashore.

After my 14th birthday I started negotiating with Gordon about riding his 1947 Triumph Speed Twin. As with gaining permission to use the Douglas, it took weeks before I caught him at a weak moment and he finally agreed. But first came an in-depth team talk about my responsibilities, followed by two long rides with him behind me on the pillion seat. Initially, I was apprehensive, but within a short time I felt relaxed and comfortable. As I had on the stationary Norton six years before, I had also gone on many imaginary journeys on the Triumph. I was perfectly aware of how it worked, but never expected it to give such a smooth and effortless ride. For a week, each evening I only rode it up and down our long driveway, and Roy too was able to take his turn. Finally, I was out on the road alone, one of so many motorcycling highlights in my life. Often on a Sunday Roy would join me, and Pippy would sit on the tank as we enjoyed long rides on the quiet country roads.

Roy Foster, neighbour Robin Wilkins, Pippy and I with Gordon's Triumph 1950. Archives.

I had looked forward to starting school and excelled for the first five or six years. However, after learning to read, having gained a basic understanding of maths, a different teacher and with that life-changing report of the 1946 TT races, my interest waned. Gordon was a voracious reader and having access to his never-ending supply of fighter pilot autobiographies, prisoner of war escapes and what appeared as adventures of so many, I felt well informed regarding human endeavour. Added to that was the world news contained in our daily national paper and the motorcycle magazines that carried reports of the sport all over the world. Touring adventures through Europe, North Africa, America, South Africa, Australia and not forgetting New Zealand. Then there were the intrepid adventurers who rode around the world, all lessons on history, geography, mechanical engineering, human ambition, courage and resourcefulness. I felt quite well informed and passed all my exams. In my last year I was head boy, captain of the rugby team and selected to take part in trials for one of the country's oldest national rugby competitions. This catered for boys up to 13 years of age who attended a school in the Auckland Province. At stake was the Roller Mills Shield. On the Friday evening before the trials began I accidentally cut my right foot and was unable to play. I had no illusions of being a successful rugby player, but I found it terribly disappointing that after having been recognised as someone of value I was denied the opportunity to repay that confidence.

I muddled through secondary school, doing well in what I was interested in and basically ignoring the rest. My reports invariably carried the words 'Hugh is capable of much better work'. Yes, but not in that environment. I left the day I was 15, being wished good luck by just one teacher. He shook my hand and said, "Hugh, you will succeed at anything you set your mind to. Good luck."

I first worked at a large local country general store and delivered the rural mail. On Saturdays after finishing the 70km mail run, I cut gorse and blackberry on a neighbour's farm. The meagre wages paid at the time allowed me to buy a 125cc Royal Enfield, a terrible thing that I pushed home time and time again. Next it was Gordon's Triumph, what luxury and power compared to the Enfield. Oddly enough I seldom if ever exceeded 100kph (the speed limit was 70kph) but it was out in the paddocks on land we leased where I amused myself in full lock wheel-spinning slides. Not at great speed but it was a buzz controlling it. Then there was the challenge of using the brake to lock the front wheel then see how far I could continue riding it. With practise it became 20m plus. As always happens to the young there came a day when travelling at speed, on rough ground I lost control of it, one of those times when you keep opening the throttle when you are desperately trying to close it, and buried it deep in a block of ancient 4m-high gorse. It took a good hour to get it out and, being perforated as a pin cushion, a further three weeks for all the dried hard thorns to fester their way to the surface.

Having been handicapped by other hobbies, mainly along with Roy I became an extremely enthusiastic bird fancier. Encouraged by Fred Rix, the President of the Huntly Cage Bird Club, we busied ourselves trapping, exchanging, selling and buying a great variety of finches, canaries and budgies. When I was 13 we each built large aviaries to accommodate them. Finally, at 17 I made the decision to purchase a bike suitable for grass track racing. One Sunday when window shopping in Hamilton I met Dave Kenah, a like-minded young man whose interest tended towards the mechanical side.

A new Francis-Barnett was chosen. After enjoying the newness of it on long day trips running it in, I stripped it of all but the basic requirements, fitted aluminium guards, mildly tuned the engine and used a competition knobbly tyre on the front wheel only. I couldn't afford two, and felt that it was easier to control a rear-wheel slide than a front. I was nervous all week before my first event, fearful that sickness or some form of injury might deny me my entry into real motorcycle racing. This major, well-supported Miniature TT grass track event was held at Gees Farm, near Hamilton. The grass was short, the sun warm and the track dry, giving ample grip for my rear road tyre. From the beginning of practice to the programme's end, I was truly inspired. With fierce concentration, riding to the limit and constantly improving, I won all five races I was allowed to enter.

The Francis-Barnett was a converted road bike, and its build strength couldn't take the pounding I gave it. The forks broke and the rear suspension regularly flew to pieces. At the November 1953 London Earls Court show the first significant purpose-built lightweight scrambler, the D.O.T. (Devoid Of Trouble), was on display; I had to

21

have one. A slightly vague deal was carried out by correspondence with the importer Len Perry, 'The rider agent', a well-established motorcycle dealer in Auckland. He valued my bike, unseen, at between 85 and 120 pounds. Delivery was to be in May 1954. The day finally arrived with my Francis-Barnett restored to standard condition and highly polished in the hope of disguising the ravages of the many races and the 16,000 miles it had covered in 15 months. I arrived at Len's shop on a Friday morning and there standing on the footpath leaning against the wall, with its chrome-plated petrol tank and polished alloy guards glinting in the sun, was the D.O.T. Of no interest was the fact that Russell Wright's Vincent Black Lightning that went on to set world speed records, using a long straight on the Canterbury Plains, was parked beside it.

The D.O.T. may appear humble today but it was state of the art in 1954. Archives.

Len said he was a man of his word and offered me 85 pounds. I really wasn't in a position to refuse. No purchase made in later life has given me the pleasure, excitement, satisfaction, joy or thrill in use as that D.O.T. With its low gearing, latest four-speed close-ratio gearbox, raucous exhaust note and good power from the factory-tuned 197cc two-stroke Villiers engine, at last I had a handsome, rugged motorcycle built for its intended use. The special Earles leading-link front forks were a revelation compared to the telescopic forks of the time. Like in all small towns, the main street of nearby Huntly was crowded with shoppers every Friday evening. To me it was an absolute delight to accelerate up and down the short main street, popping it through the close-ratio gears with its poorly silenced exhaust blaring away for all to hear. It was difficult to establish how many shared my pleasure of it. I continued to range far and wide, using all my favoured roads and tracks. At 3am I pushed the D.O.T. in through the front door of our house, up the passage to my bedroom, placed it on its stand, slid into my bed and lay there. No one could have been more happy.

I won numerous races on the D.O.T. 250cc and 350cc, scratch events and on occasion the main 15–20 lap race of the day, typically an all-in handicap event.

Although I tried, it was totally indestructible, an excellent machine of its day.

While I was riding to Auckland 18 months later to trade it in on a BSA Gold Star, the prop stand retaining spring failed allowing the prop stand to lock in a forward position. Not being able to lean it into the next left-hand corner, I ended up sliding under the rear wheels of a fully laden truck. I regained consciousness in time to hear an ambulance siren and talk to the badly shaken, pale-faced truck driver, who thought I was dead. The D.O.T. was a mess but apart from a severe headache and a sore back, I was okay.

Over time I rebuilt and sold it. Meanwhile I had bought a well-used 1948 350cc BSA B31 in a dozen boxes. Rebuilding it with a high-compression piston, for use with alcohol fuels, a race carburettor and special camshafts transformed a docile commuter into a very competitive grass track racer. It was totally reliable, allowing me to win every 350cc race, some 500cc events and numerous race of the day open handicap miniature TT races. In November 1955 the Auckland Motorcycle Club ran a road race meeting at Seagrove, a disused wartime emergency airfield, where the 1951 New Zealand TT had been held. I fitted a pair of well-used old road tyres that Gordon had discarded, fitted special road race camshafts to the engine while Roy, now a welder, made up a racing megaphone exhaust.

Again time dragged, but race day eventually arrived. There were many more entries than I expected, ranging from New Zealand Isle of Man TT team members all the way down to me, a first-timer with little more in his favour than barely controlled enthusiasm. The circuit was about 3km long in a rectangular shape. The start-finish was on the main landing strip, some of the corners on the side, or perimeter, roads were covered in loose stones and there was even a long, grassed corner back onto the landing strip. It was a very simple layout that suited my experience, skills, and the B31, perfectly. All the road race bikes were set up for, and the riders expected, fast, smooth and cleanly swept sealed surfaces.

Practice went really well. The B31 had a standard touring gearbox that gave a much lower first gear compared with those fitted to a road race bike. When accelerating away from the slow corners the rear wheel would spin in the loose stones then hit a clean patch of seal, gain grip and leap forward. Lovely stuff. I literally flew past much more sophisticated and expensive motorcycles and not having a rev counter I was warned by the rattle of valve bounce when to change gear. The first race was a 350cc handicap with about 30 entries. Pumping with enthusiasm, I left the start, valve bouncing through the gears and utterly inspired. Gaining a powerful rear-wheel spinning drive out of the second corner into the back straight saw me rushing past numerous real road-racing bikes. Man, this is great, I thought as I headed into the long grassed section. The ground was quite dry and as this was the surface I had ridden on for years, it held no fears. I rode around the outside of several competitors. Then I was away down the straight with the speedo needle nudging 145kph. I hit the brakes again, only just managing to slow enough to get around the first corner. Now there were just four riders in front of me. Then suddenly there was no power, just the rush of air and I slowly wheeled it back to the trailer. The engine had no compression, and apart from a very light scraping noise, the motor turned over freely. Not to worry, I can fix it. But what a hoot this road racing is. Man, nothing, just nothing, has ever given me this kind of a buzz before. I had felt confident and in complete control.

Back at home I dismantled the engine. The cylinder barrel had been fitted with a new sleeve, which had slipped down and been smashed by the con rod and flywheels. It now lay in thousands of small pieces in the bottom of the crankcase; mystery solved. With a clear vision of the direction my motorcycling future was going to take, I began a complete makeover of the B31 to Clubman road-racing rules that were at the time petrol-burning, non-Grand Prix bikes. Engine modifications were made. My objective was the Rotorua Motorcycle Club's New Year's Day meeting. All the work was carried out in time. I worked through Christmas Eve, finishing the rebuild at first light on Christmas Day.

It started easily and ran nicely, and soon after sunrise I left on a steady running-in session. With a vibration-free, effortless lope and a sharp crack from the straight-through muffler, it cruised effortlessly at 110–120kph.

An American rider was once quoted as saying that "Heaven is some place attached to the end of a motorcycle twist grip". There had been something very special attached to the end of mine that morning. For 12km it ran superbly then suddenly the engine rattled and lost all power. That took the feel-good factor out of the day; the modified valve from a J.A.P. speedway engine had broken above the valve spring. Luckily, no serious damage had been done but with all businesses closed for two weeks over Christmas, I wouldn't be racing at Rotorua.

I was now working as a moulder at a small foundry in Huntly where, due to customer demand, an increase in production was required. Instead of an hourly rate we were paid for what we made; 'piece work' was introduced. I had been on a youth's hourly rate but with the new system I was put on adult rates. In the manager's own words, "Around here if you do a man's job, you get a man's pay", and my income increased rapidly. Naturally, I had met all the local lads who owned motorcycles. There was as many as 15, all good guys who rode a variety of late-model bikes. We went on day trips frequently on the shingle country roads. On occasion the mufflers were removed and it was all on. There was the occasional unintended get-off, sometimes with the bike and rider ending up down a bank buried in blackberries. All rather hilarious for a group of rather carefree young men.

Ginger Molloy and I met in our early teens; his elder brother Barry also rode motorcycles and a friendship evolved. After I began working in Huntly we saw more of each other. Ginger excelled at rugby league. He encouraged me to join the under-19 team of the United Rugby League club, one of three in Huntly. We won the season's series and played games in other areas. Graham Farrar was our captain and Roger Tait, the fullback. These two outstanding players went on to play for the New Zealand Kiwis, with Graham captaining the side in 1966 and Roger gaining that honour in 1968. It was quite remarkable how four lads, members of a 13-man team, from the small town of Huntly went on to represent their country at the highest level.

The next big meeting was on the Auckland Provincial Anniversary Weekend at the end of January 1957 on the Te Puna circuit near Tauranga. This time the valve modifications were a success. On a long straight in the main road near our home I had seen 165kph on the speedo. I tried different carburettor settings, spark plugs and, full of hope, looked for an even higher speed, all to no avail. Actually, it started blowing smoke out the exhaust and oil out of the crankcase breather so I fitted a larger oil tank.

In motorcycling, Ginger and I went on to become team-mates, sharing our meagre resources. Ginger wasn't as interested in off-road riding as I was, so it was for the first time that we competed together here, at Te Puna, in our first real road race. Ginger had a 250cc Tiger 70 Triumph, apprentice wages limiting his choice. Barry would take us there in his car, using our farm trailer for the bikes after the animal excrement had been removed.

After our machines passed scrutineering Ginger and I went through the entry list of the 350 Clubmans class. He felt he should be able to finish about 22nd out of 32 entries. There were 16 of the latest BSA Gold Star models that were far superior to what we had. I hoped for perhaps 14th place. The circuit was 6km long, the first half being tarsealed with mainly fast sweeping corners. The rest had a very thick loose and dusty shingle surface where the road snaked along the banks of a stream, then back to the start-finish straight. During practice on the sealed section, a slightly uphill, never-ending, flat-out sweeper bothered me. What are the indications that your tyres are reaching their limit of grip? Do they just let go and you are off or are there some early warning signals? Mine were still those old worn touring tyres, so I was concerned. John Anderson, a successful and approachable rider, was parked nearby. Rather humbly, I put these questions to him. John's advice was that normally on fast corners the tyres lost traction in a slow, gentle way. He said it was a matter of lifting the bike up a little or easing the throttle and this would allow them to grip again, but don't overreact. Take care on the slow corners as the engine pulls much harder in first gear so the rear tyre can slide suddenly and flick you off.

I checked over my bike, topped up the oil tank with more Castrol Grand Prix 50-weight and, with John's advice in mind, pushed out to the start of the 10-lap race. They slotted us into positions that had been drawn from a hat; they put me on the third row. I was very nervous and wished I had gone to the toilet earlier. We were the first race of the day and a large crowd had formed. The loudspeakers clattered out information about the top riders and instructions to the trackside spectators to stand well back. Finally, the flag dropped for the push-start. The bike fired up easily and off I went. Being among a bunch of riders doing unexpected things was a whole new experience and I wanted to finish, so I tried hard to restrain myself. However, interestingly the pace was less than I expected, with some riding rather erratically. I passed four riders then one passed me. I hit the shingle behind two other riders and got hammered with flying stones and enveloped in dust. They braked quite early as the circuit left the wider main road to dive down a lane to the riverside section. I passed them and tore off through the winding maze. I was straight-lining the corners as much as possible by just missing banks on the left and washouts on the right. There was dust well ahead. I had no idea of what position I was in but it didn't matter; this was pretty exciting regardless of position! I rode on lap after lap, trying to do better each time. The first slow corner after the start was a left-hand bend where we turned off the main road. Each lap I had been braking later, but this time when I sat up and hit the brakes not a lot happened — they had overheated and I wasn't going to stop for the corner. Spectators were standing across the slip road that I desperately needed to use. I squeezed the front brake harder and stood on the rear brake, but it didn't help. Don't these people know I can't stop? When will they realise? Someone's going to get hurt here. Then slowly their demeanour began to change. At first their faces showed no expression, all frozen. In what seemed like very slow motion they began to move. Their pace increased, their arms flailed, they grabbed hold of each other and finally I stopped among them, turned around, regained the circuit and tore away. That was amazing! So much had happened in such a short time. I passed bikes abandoned by the roadside. There was Bill Dempster, the Waikato man who had won numerous grass track championships, pushing in. I just kept going as fast as I could. I never looked behind, couldn't see anyone in front and buzzed around in my own little bubble. At last the white flag came out. One lap to go. You beaut! Then the chequered flag and back into the paddock.

What a relief I had finished. Taking off my gloves and helmet, I found myself chuckling. Bloody hell, I've finished, it was brilliant. The BSA was dripping in oil. I looked in the four-litre tank and there was precious little left, but enough. Ginger had retired but was happy enough with the experience. Where on earth had I finished? At last the positions were announced. Hugh Anderson third. Can you believe it? Fantastic, unbelievable. Then the announcer spoke about the sealed handicap and how it was formulated and so on, something I knew nothing about. Hugh Anderson first. Motorcycling had provided many highlights in my young life but this was right off the scale. It was not only the result but the sheer pleasure of riding the race. Eight weeks later another third place at the Hamilton 100 confirmed that with a suitable machine I could do well and my course was set.

Following a disagreement with the manager at the foundry, and with the help of Ginger's father, I gained employment at a private coal mine at Pukemiro, a 20-minute train ride from Huntly. The work could be hard but was well paid, especially if you were given maintenance work on a Saturday.

Later, in 1957 I graduated to a five-year-old ZB34 500cc Gold Star. It was in excellent condition but dated. The latest 350 models were as fast. However, it filled in a season by successfully acting as a road racer, grass tracker and ride-to-work transport. Ginger had purchased a near-new 350cc Gold Star and we rode these bikes hundreds of kilometres to meetings, always way, way over the legal speed limits and survived, and slept where we found a place to lay our heads. This included under the stars and the luxury of hay barns. We revelled in the freedom and the thrills of this new life.

Ginger was riding his rare 'road race' Gold Star extremely well, regularly gaining first three placings, and won the New Zealand Clubmans TT. My best result was winning the Clubmans race at the prestigious New Zealand Grand Prix at the Ardmore aerodrome just south of Auckland. This was the big International Grand Prix car event of the year with several national car races and three motorcycle supporting events. Up to 70,000 spectators attended and many more listened to the radio broadcast commentary.

Another new experience at the time occurred when Gordon and friend Len Jelaca, one of our top speedway riders, bought a speedway bike for me to ride at a new track in Hamilton. Speedway had gained a substantial following and many towns had their own tracks, which were packed every Saturday night. I enjoyed an occasional Wednesday evening's practice when, on a smooth slick track, I was as fast as Len. However, on race nights the midget cars tended to cut up parts of the track and while I did well enough, it wasn't that much fun. On this Saturday Gordon had taken part in a tennis tournament. I had milked the cows, called the dogs, realised that Pippy was missing, and had got on the tractor when Mum hurried out the front door waving her arms. I waited. Auntie Gladys, our neighbour, had phoned, Pippy had been hit and killed by a car outside her home. How do you value a pet that has lived with you through those important formative years of your life? To have enjoyed so many adventures, to have participated in our games, to have ridden on my push-bike and motorcycles. To have known my next move before I did, who had protected me when attacked by a very angry pig and slept with me. Was that creature but an animal and when does friendship transpose species and who is it that would ridicule the belief that your best friend is a dog? Okay, Mum, I will pick him up after I feed out the hay. I gently lifted his still-warm body and placed it in a bed of hay on the trailer. Toby, the cattle dog, ears drooped, moved away, flopped onto his belly and laid his head between his outstretched front legs. He too knew he had lost a friend. Time was short, so I wrapped Pippy in a bath towel and with his head protruding, laid him on the pillow of my bed; he was so lifelike that I expected him to open one eye as was his way.

We drove silently to speedway that evening and with a clear-headed resolve, I won all four of my races. The last from a handicap of 80m. At the after-race function I was congratulated from all quarters; they weren't to know that I had decided that scrambling and road racing was where my future lay. Speedway was fun but it wasn't me. I had ridden for the last time at Forest Lake Speedway. Next morning beneath my bedroom window, I dug Pippy's carefully measured grave. I then drove to Sloan's Farm, where we had spent countless happy hours catching small crayfish in a stream and cooking them. Pippy had often chased hares, unsuccessfully, and from the native bush where we had spent so many happy hours dug out a young lancewood, a singular tree that grew tall and straight and planted it above him. Many weeks passed before, on hearing a noise outside the workshop, I no longer called his name or had to check myself on the way home from work from calling at the butcher's shop for his small parcel of meat.

A tow car was required. I found a 1928 Ford Model A. With Ginger's help — he was an apprentice at a Ford dealership — we overhauled the engine and brakes. It may have been humble but was a major step up from the 1939 Ford Ten we used on one occasion last year. We had removed the front wheels and bolted the race bike's forks to a purpose-built frame that replaced the rear bumper. It was almost undrivable, the steering box was worn out, it had little in the way of brakes and the lights indicated where you were but not where we were going. It took all night to travel 200km.

In early October 1957 I bought an alcohol-burning, speedway J.A.P.-engined special, built for our many Miniature TT grass track events. Far from being intimidating, the power, brakes and handling all seemed in balance. It was just what I wanted. At my first two meetings, held over the three-day Labour Weekend, from a total of nine races, I won seven, finished second in one and slid off in another. They were a mixture of scratch and handicap events. Les Wilson, a noted motorcycle journalist from Auckland, wrote: "The leading rider during the weekend of racing was Hugh Anderson of Ohinewai; young, light and apparently fearless." Against strong opposition I went on to win North Island and New Zealand championships. Soon after I bought the grass tracker, Ginger decided to buy a 7R AJS from Len Perry and I bought his Goldie. This little bike and I gelled from our first meeting.

I led the 350cc Clubmans class comfortably on Boxing Day at the Wanganui Cemetery Circuit until a mix-up in pit signals with Dave Kenah had me slow too much and I was passed just before the finish. Third place in the 500cc class was some consolation, there were no more mistakes, and I was never beaten in the 350cc class again. Occasionally, I added a win in the 500cc Clubmans and frequently gained high placings in the Grand Prix categories.

Securing Ginger's AJS 7R before leaving on a major motorcycle adventure. December 1957. Photo Barry Molloy.

With the shared optimism of youth and a 1928 Ford tow car, how could we fail. Ginger, me and Ginger Singer. Note the two spare wheels. Photo Barry Molloy.

The Marton road race on December 27, 1957 was a simple, straightforward, country road circuit of a rectangular form, with a tricky bumpy approach to a bridge at one end and a sweeping S-bend at the other connected by two straights. The 350 Clubman class practice was followed by the 350 Racing class that I had also entered.

Some famous riders with wide international experience were entered. There was Rod Coleman, who won the 350cc class at the Isle of Man in 1954. Peter Murphy, who had achieved star status in Europe. Bob Coleman was an Isle of Man team representative. Unfortunately, he was seriously injured there but recovered in time to gain fourth place at the Ulster Grand Prix. John Anderson was another Isle of Man TT representative who, with Noel McCutcheon and Peter Pawson, won the much coveted team prize in both the 350 and 500cc classes there in 1958; and John Hempleman, who at 21 years was the youngest rider to be selected to represent New Zealand. I set off following this leading group, and to my surprise I had no difficulty keeping pace. Being a novice I was more than content to follow and learn.

Above: Dressed in our best, at the Wanganui after-race social. Ginger, Judy Hempleman, Ginger Singer, Jenny Hempleman and me. Archives.

Left: Posting a letter at Marton. Archives.

The strange thing was that our little world appeared to be functioning in slow motion. Sure there was a sensation of speed, but not 160ks, more like 80. There was no haste or hurry, just a smooth, effortless progress. For the first time I had experienced, was aware of, and understood form. In the 350 Clubmans race I simply rode away from the field — there seemed to be no more haste involved than riding down the road to post a letter — a major breakthrough in understanding the very essence of road racing. This awareness combined with well-developed concentration levels and a burning desire to succeed were to become my strong points.

Winning on the Lon Higgins-built special. Archives.

Being a newcomer I was placed towards the rear of the grid for the 350 Racing class but reached sixth place before red flags were frantically waved to stop the race. Something serious had happened. With others I rode slowly back to the pits. A horse lay dead in the middle of the road. A motorcycle and rider were lying nearby. It was Maurice MacDonald. I had met Maurice and his older brother Ramsay in 1954 at a Miniature TT in Rotorua. We were parked together in the race paddock that day. Ramsay had accompanied Maurice to the start. As Ramsay stood at the road edge looking back beyond the competitors' car park, he noticed a thoroughbred racehorse acting in an agitated way, tossing its head from side to side and cantering around its paddock. When the 350 race started, the noise created by the 30 open exhausts was sufficient to cause the now terrified animal to escape its enclosure. Just after the leading riders passed through the start to begin their second lap, the horse came galloping through the pit area, scattering people to its right and left. With a shower of stones it turned out onto the racetrack and continued its desperate flight up the middle of the road in the opposite direction to the riders. Maurice was closely following another rider. He pulled out to pass him and hit the horse front-on at 140kph. Maurice fell heavily virtually at his brother's feet. Ramsay was the first to reach him; Maurice lay still and silent. Though he did not have a mark on his body, the impact of the collision had ruptured his heart. Understandably the meeting was cancelled.

Soon after, I won the Taranaki Grand Prix, run on a short circuit at the New Plymouth aerodrome, beating, for the first time, the Isle of Man TT winner Rod Coleman. It was my first major victory and featured in a substantial report in the *New Zealand Herald*. Two national meetings on Auckland's anniversary weekend followed. The Bay of Plenty Grand Prix on Saturday at Whakatane and on Monday once again the Te Puna event at Tauranga. Practice on Saturday morning had not gone well, I was unusually nervous, I could not develop a rhythm and had never been so uptight. I had become the favourite and wasn't handling it well. Previously, I had been the underdog and revelled in it, but now I was the rider with a lot to lose. The first race was the 350 Clubmans. I got away in the lead, made a mess of the first corner and got pushed back to third, and had difficulty holding my place. For the second time I overshot a corner and managed to avoid the high roadside kerb by riding up the car entrance to a house onto the footpath, almost becoming buried in an overhanging hedge, then through a planting of shrubs and flowers and bounced back onto the road. That was enough to jolt me out of my nervous rigidity. Think of Marton; you must relax and let it happen, I told myself. Use your head, smooth out your ride. For the next three laps I rode with the leaders, gained that elusive rhythm, took over and won. Just to make it another excellent day, I won the 500 race too. A good lesson learned in controlling my nerves and perhaps a touch of conceit. Monday at Te Puna was fine. I had learned my lesson well, won the 350 race and gained second in the 500, when a faulty spark plug caused a consistent misfire.

Winning the Clubmans TT and coming second to Rod Coleman on his NSU Sport Max at Levin ended a very successful season. Then in the spring of 1958, with the assistance of a welder and panel-beater friend, we completed on our third attempt a copy, in aluminium, of a Manx Norton steering head front number plate cowl. I carefully painted it and fabricated suitable bracketing. It looked great and a test run was justified. As always, I lined the Goldie up, as it hit 7,200rpm I dropped the clutch and with the usual shower of stones it took off like a robber's dog. Suddenly, a young cow, panicked by the noise, appeared from behind the sheds. As she swung in front of me, the front wheel went under her belly and she was tipped neatly onto her back while I was thrown onto grass. A cow on its back, lying on your most treasured possession in a terrified, hoof-thrashing state is a scary sight. She rolled away from the bike, regained her feet and with a blood-curdling bellow and with a massive bowel-evacuating effort, from a standing start cleared a 1.5m fence. Then with intermittent bellows, her tail curled over her back and head swinging from side to side, she continued her leg-flailing gallop to the far corner of the large field. A not terribly impressed Gordon claimed she gave little milk for some days.

While the pursuit of motorcycle racing was definitely death-defying, strangely enough it was a major car accident on a Thursday night that nearly ended my life. When attending a Hamilton Motorcycle Club general meeting in October 1958, Dave and I became a little bored and left for a meal of peas, pies and potatoes at the local pie cart. On the road home a large petrol tanker was stopped on the road without lights and I hit it. The impact was such that it wrecked the truck's rear axle. My head hit the top of the windscreen surround of Gordon's Zephyr convertible with sufficient force to knock it forward away from the hood. My knees put great dents in the dashboard parcel tray and the steering wheel broke several ribs. I regained consciousness in the Huntly medical rooms. It seems I had laid a carpet of pie, peas and spuds wherever I went. I was suspected of having internal injuries and a very wise Dr Willoughby sent me off to Waikato Hospital where I spent five days under observation. I was about to be discharged when, during visiting hours on the following Tuesday evening, I was hit with severe stomach pains. My spleen had ruptured, and had I not been in hospital I would have died. I was opened up from my chest to my pubic area. The after-effects had me vomiting and coughing in agony. Ask anyone who has experienced broken ribs how that would feel, without the effects of the massive operation. Later it was discovered I had a broken vertebra as well. Finally I was given morphine painkilling injections. Wow, they were great; finally some relief and with a surprising side effect: beautiful dreams. One concerned the fitting of a Ford V8 engine into my old 1928 Ford tow car. Do you know that the bolt holes of the clutch bell housing and the engine mounts were all identical, so it fitted like a glove?

As time went on, food became a priority. I had not eaten for 10 days and again these fabulous meals were laid on by my drug-assisted imagination: steak, eggs, chips, tomatoes, onions, the lot. But I couldn't even keep a glass of orange juice down. Then I asked if I could suck a barley sugar and slowly things improved. After

18 days I began eating and at three weeks I was allowed to shuffle around my bed. When I was released from the hospital I had lost 13kg.

Four weeks later I won at Wanganui on Boxing Day. Then, on New Year's Day 1959, I took the Clubmans honours at the Rotorua Grand Prix and a close-fought third in the 350 Grand Prix class. A highlight of that race was challenging Forrest Cardon, who was well thought of as a rider, for second place. He was riding the importer's ex-works Norton with a dustbin fairing, fully enclosing the front wheel. After having passed Forrest my challenge was satisfied and I slipped back to third. Soon after at the Taranaki Grand Prix, where I had been so successful last year on a circuit where the use of very low gearing (I had the required sprockets made) helped me overcome the power advantage of the proper race bikes, I won the 350cc race beating, for the first time, the vastly experienced and very successful international rider John Hempleman. Another milestone.

However, there was a price to pay for my success. Late in January was the annual holiday double-header of Saturday's Whakatane Grand Prix and Monday's Te Puna road races. Having entered every race on both programmes, I fronted up to the secretary's tent to sign on. Race secretary Graham Ross gave me some unexpected news. Local officials had decided that the Clubman classes were for newcomers and those finding their way into road racing. As I had, in their view, progressed way beyond that standard, they had, without any previous correspondence or notification, decided to accept my entries only in the Grand Prix classes. Perhaps other riders had complained; I was more than a little miffed. At the time Motorcycling New Zealand did not have such a ruling, but clubs could add or introduce their own rules to suit their particular situation. Definitely a 'bugger this one' as both events paid good prize money and I would have, in this case, won close to 50 pounds. There was nothing to lose now. A fresh start really, an unexpected, unwanted upgrade.

I went to the start of the 350cc Grand Prix race with serious intent. I led from the drop of the flag, immediately finding a fluid, fast form, and pressed on with confidence. Just 100m from the finish John Hempleman rode by me on his more powerful Manx Norton leaving me to claim second ahead of Forrest Cardon on his special importer-entered works Norton. In the 500cc race I made a flyer of a start again, but by the end of the third lap both 'Hempo' and Cardon, now on the importer's 500cc Manx, had got by leaving me to a lonely ride into third place. Monday's meeting at Te Puna was another showdown. The only chance I had of beating Hempo here was to get to the long, winding, dusty, shingle section first. He was well aware of that, made a great start and went on to win the race. I duly buzzed around for 10 laps and gained second in both classes. Cardon had fallen breaking a collarbone.

Now that I could ride with them, I required equal machinery. The fastest route was to fit a full frontal fairing colloquially known as a 'full bin' that, like Cardon's, also enclosed the bike's front wheel. These were reputedly able to turn a 170kph motorcycle into a 190 to a 200kph job. Hope it works, I thought. I phoned the owner of one who to my delight agreed to sell it for 25 pounds. I first tried it at the Ardmore Grand Prix but it ground on the track surface on every corner. The fairing was too low but how to mount it higher? We did what we could but realised there were limits to how hard I could ride it. I found the streamlining gave greater air penetration but this made it difficult to stop. The Goldie brakes were not up to the task and

Whakatane. Saturday. Precocious youth, anger and some skill. Leading John Hempleman, a lapped rider, and Forrest Cardon. Archives.

Te Puna Tauranga, Monday. Making my mark in the road-race classes. Archives.

October 1959 winning the Northland Grand Prix by almost a lap. Archives.

after just two laps they were fading. Having limited options I rode the 500cc race steadily in the company of a friend John Farnsworth, also on a 350 Goldie. John would pass me during braking and in the corners but I'd breeze by him up the straights, all very peaceful and civilised. John Hempleman lapped us, then Noel McCutcheon and later Peter Pawson, all on their 500cc Manx Nortons. As Peter entered a very fast left-hander at the end of the back straight, he laid it over until his footrest was almost touching the track and his back wheel slid away. Strangely, what happened next seemed quite graceful and played out in slow motion. The bike and Peter gently hit the track. Puffs of smoke came off his leathers, and sparks flew in the air as the Norton slid up the road. On and on they skated horizontally, off the tarseal, on to the grass and out of our sight. So that is what a 200kph 'get-off' looks like. Not a good scene. Peter lost quite a lot of skin and suffered friction burns but no more than that.

The New Zealand TT at Mangere, in February 1959, was the next challenge. Dave and I fitted a high-compression piston to take advantage of the race fuel that we were now allowed to use. Dave lightened the rocker arms and we fitted special American valve springs to allow for higher revs. Stronger sidecar springs were fitted to the front forks to counter the extra weight of the dustbin fairing, along with a powerful 7R AJS front brake and new stronger rear suspension units. One lap of the Mangere circuit was 10kms with 7ks sealed and the rest shingle. Early-morning rain made the track damp in patches so I rode with caution, getting the feel of the new suspension and brake setup. I sped up considerably during the second practice and began sorting out my braking markers and cornering lines.

Heading the entries were a group of riders with international experience: John Hempleman, Noel McCutcheon and Ken Mudford, winner of the 1954 Ulster Grand Prix on a factory Norton. Then there was Australian champion and successful international Eric Hinton. All of them were riding the latest Grand Prix motorcycles. I was positioned on the second row beside Eric Hinton but my carburettor flooded and the engine was reluctant to start. I left in a fierce, clutch-slipping, must-catch-up mode. The Goldie was pulling hard, really hard; I braked as late as I dared for the first slow corner, rushing past several up the inside, including Hinton. As we blasted out onto Ascot Road there were only three in front of me — Hempo, McCutcheon and Bob Newbrook, on a Norton, another top New Zealand rider. When braking at the next slow corner I gained on Bob and we accelerated off on the shingle section reaching top gear before a gentle left turn. The Goldie wriggled about on the loose surface in protest and stones thrown up by Bob's rear wheel rattled against the aluminium shell enclosing me and the bike, adding an extra dimension. This was real racing.

I slipstreamed Bob down the start-finish straight. The Goldie was showing 8,200rpm on its 5.28 top gear, which was 190 to 195kph. I reached my brake marker, counted one and braked past Bob then scooted off towards the shingle section. Round that flat-out left in the shingle again, chin on the tank, I was faster this time. The bike was writhing underneath me. The rear swung out and back then out again, more this time, but I just kept the bars pointing straight ahead and the rear wheel came back into line again. Pretty good stuff was going on here and I was closing on Noel McCutcheon. I braked later on the downhill dry clay area before the narrow Oruarangi bridge, then left in a wheel-spinning slide and a shower of stones. Great game this, I thought. With the fairing crunching on the road as I swung through a left, two rights and a left flat-out, I closed on Noel. I waited until he braked for the slow church corner and braked later but only just managed to get around it. First the front, then the rear tyre slid. What's wrong with this thing? But all those years in wet grass paddocks came into play and I controlled it. Now I was in second place, 11 seconds behind Hempo. The Goldie had never performed like this. The front brake was fantastic. I had not experienced this level of inspiration and enjoyment before in my life. On the start of the fourth lap the gap was down to nine seconds. On the start of my fifth lap the gap was just three seconds.

The clay downhill section is turning black with rubber. I brake later, brush the side of the bridge, lift the clutch and at 7,500rpm release it and leave again in a wheel-spinning shower of stones. The rear wheel drifts to the right on the slight left turn up to the brow of a rise and then a slight right turn over the rise. I correct the drift to the right and the violently spinning rear wheel swings sharply to the left. I swing the bars and front wheel to the left to correct it and bang, the steering hit the lock stops. A huge belt of adrenalin runs through me. This is unreal, absolutely fantastic. Nothing, but nothing, can be as good as this. I turned the bars a little to the right off the lock stops and banged it against them again, just for the hell of it really. Never before had I felt so much in my element. With a spinning rear wheel you have full control. The bike straightened up, I changed into second gear and was off, closing the gap to one second as we passed the start. Adrenalin was turning to aggression.

I continued the charge and decided to brake into Hempo's slipstream, then he would never get rid of me. At my marker I counted to four and slammed on the brakes; the front wheel locked and began turning to the left, I was going down. I released the brake and the bike stood up. Now I was rushing up on Hempo, I grabbed the lever, the wheel locked and again it began to fold under. I was in strife and released the brake, again it stood up. As John turned left, I missed him by a whisker, crossed the road up the specially cambered kerb at speed, leapt into the air onto the grass lawn of a church and buried the bike in an overgrown elaeagnus hedge. On impact I let go the bars and sat up; when we stopped I was pinned to the rear hump of the seat by the baggy crotch of my leathers, supported by the tentacles of the hedge. I couldn't move and laughed. I don't know if it was from relief that I had not hit Hempo, the silly predicament I was in or the stimulation from the risks I had been taking. Marshals lifted me up off the seat. Only part of the rear wheel of the Goldie protruded so we hurriedly started pulling it out and branch by branch, vine by vine, extracted it. No damage was obvious, so I ran with the Goldie back to the track, pushed it into life and was off again. Riding with a fraction less flair but enjoying it, at the beginning of the eighth lap I was in third place, 49 seconds behind Hempo and 44 behind Noel, but still six seconds in front of Bob Newbrook. Well, things could be worse and suddenly they were. The engine revved freely and there was no drive. The primary chain had broken and disappeared. I parked the bike and sat beside it.

I felt okay, no worries, just exhilaration from the high-speed on-the-edge experience. The Goldie had never gone that fast before and I certainly hadn't ridden with less concern. A spectator walked up carrying my chain. Ironically, he was the Norton Dominator rider who had given me a lift home after the B31 dropped a valve one early Christmas morning three years ago. Anyway I gained consolation in having broken the lap record by three seconds.

I went to Noel McCutcheon, who was nearby in the pits, to buy a riveting link to fix the chain. Noel gave me one, refused payment and then offered some advice. Having seen me sliding about after I passed him he felt that in my best interests it would be wise to slow a little. Gain more experience over more racing miles. You are young and have time, he advised. Going too fast too soon can be a serious mistake. He didn't question my ability, but he had seen other young riders with excessive flair and dash come unstuck and get badly injured. I took it all in and thanked him.

As we prepared for the 500cc race, Dave said, "Stop sticking your knees out, it looks terrible." As it wasn't a conscious thing I said, "I'm not", and so began a change of riding styles that was about to happen all over the world. A misfiring engine hampered me but when it ran properly I lapped just one second slower than in the earlier race. Then an engine cooling aluminium air duct shook loose from its rivets in the streamlining and dragged on the road. Exit number two. With two retirements, some might think it was a disappointing day, but for me it had been the best in my life. Just three riders had made faster lap times and they were all on the latest 500cc Manx Nortons and all had years of successful international experience. I'd achieved this on a four-year-old sports bike, which Dave and I had prepared, on a fast circuit that suited more powerful engines. Where else in the world did a Gold Star BSA hold the lap record, at 4m.19 secs,against world class opposition, on the circuit that was used for the national premier event of the year? To emphasise that performance: Len Perry, winner of a myriad of national titles, fastest 500cc lap was 4m.31secs and Peter Pawson (probably still suffering from his Ardmore injuries) who had finished in the top 10 in the 1958 Isle of Man senior TT lapped at 4m.25secs. Both were on late-model 500cc Manx Nortons and Hempo, riding the same 350cc Norton, went on to finish sixth in the 1959 350cc world championship.

As I often did, when I woke next morning, away from the hype and adrenalin, I thought through the previous day. I became a little alarmed at how close I had been, on several occasions, to doing serious damage to the bike and myself. In place of exhilaration I felt chastened in my foolhardiness. Things came back into perspective at the following meeting, where I felt confident in my abilities and wins kept coming. After effortlessly winning the Northland Grand Prix by almost a lap in October I suffered another painful operation due to a bowel adhesion, which left me with health problems that affect me to this day. Ten days after leaving hospital, I rode at Levin, New Zealand's only purpose-built track, as did Ginger. After the usual overnight drive in a mate's car and trailer and between vomiting sessions — I was still a sick lad — I managed two thirds behind Ginger, now back on a Gold Star, who, riding to his potential, almost beat Hempo.

The opportunity to buy two Manx Nortons late in 1959 ignited my long-held ambition to go to Europe and the Isle of Man. John Hempleman returned to New Zealand in October. Soon after, he broke a leg at a grass track event and was out for the rest of the summer. His bikes were very good, though well used; I bought them for 640 pounds. Not having sufficient cash to take the pair I first took delivery of the 500 and collected the 350 after selling my Gold Star. Dave Kenah too was pleased as he admired the engineering associated with a Manx Norton much more than a rather mundane BSA. His enthusiasm was very welcome as I knew less than bugger all about them. Dave, being a tool maker, was in his element and played a major part in maintaining the two bikes, showing me the basics, and over time purchasing, on my behalf, the special tools required, Any idea of waiting to be selected for the official three-man Isle of Man TT team, which had successfully represented New Zealand since 1950, wasn't in my make-up. What if they didn't send one? Having come so far I intended to do this journey on my own. Now the time was right and the decision was made easier when Gordon decided to employ managers, to run his farm and butcher's shop, and come with me.

Wanganui's tricky street circuit wasn't the place of choice to ride a 500cc Manx Norton, the most powerful Grand Prix machine available to a private owner, for the first time. It had short straights, mainly slow corners and was very bumpy. Compared to my Goldie the Manx frame was stiff and taut, the suspension was on the hard side, the brakes had extreme bite and the power of the motor, on the low gearing we were using, gained instant respect. There was little basis on which the two bikes could be compared. Steering was light and seemed to overreact to my input. So much of what I did when riding the Goldie did not suit the Norton. With limited practice I had little opportunity to identify what I needed to change or adapt to, let alone learn how. After a super ride on the Goldie, I gained a good close second to Rod Coleman on his 7R. At the start of the 500cc race a case of determination to win, overtaking the ability to achieve it, led to an unpleasant, aggressive ride. I was braking too late, entering corners too fast and not able to open the throttle early enough to get a fast exit. This had me braking even later to make up ground that I'd lost leaving the previous corner. During the first few laps everything I did seemed to only make my problem worse.

My seminal racing experience at Marton came to mind: ease back just a little, recalculate my braking distances, enter corners a little slower, open the throttle a little sooner and smooth out the ride. It took a couple of laps to do this. From that point I was able to make marginal adjustments to every aspect, lowering my lap times. I began gaining on leaders Rod Coleman and Bob Newbrook and eventually won the race. The lesson I had learned at Marton had paid off, although it would have taken many more laps on that headstrong Norton before it would be anything like riding down the road to post a letter. However, in no time I was as comfortable riding those Nortons as I'd ever been on my Gold Star and was never beaten for the rest of the summer.

By March, Gordon and I were ready to leave. I had completed what at the time was the best racing apprenticeship a young rider could ever hope to serve. The New Zealand Shipping Company ran a regular service via the Panama Canal to England. We chose the *Rangitoto*, sailing out of Wellington on Tuesday, March 8, 1960, arriving at Southampton on Friday, April 8. We would join the overnight Auckland-to-Wellington express train from its Huntly stop. Our pair of Manx Nortons, tool boxes and cabin trunks would be stowed in the guard's van at the rear of the train.

On my last pay day at the Pukemiro mine the union president, Fred Rix, stood outside the pay office with his miner's hat in his hand. Over 50 pounds was placed in it. On presenting it to me, Fred said, "Hugh, you are one of us and we want to help you." From Europe I wrote regularly to Fred, who read my letters to the mine employees at the monthly union meetings.

On the Saturday night before we left a farewell was held in the large, full-to-capacity local hall; it was a night to remember. After the traditional supper, speeches were made, and I paid special thanks to Mum for the help she had given me, and the many others who had assisted me on my way. The dance ended at 1am on Sunday. Later, back in our house along with numerous extended family members, Mum said, "It wasn't true what you said tonight, was it?" I asked her what she meant. Her reply was, "I haven't helped you at all." Being surrounded by family was not a time or place to discuss the matter.

Once seated on the train later that Sunday, I reflected on Mum's words: "I haven't helped you." I took a pen and pad from my briefcase and began a long letter. Through illness, sprains, fractures and spills off motorcycles and serious operations she had always been there, as mothers who care tend to be. She had known only hard work, there had not been time for sport and precious little for any form of recreation. She may not have understood this burning need I had to compete in New Zealand and now Europe, but to her great credit, she never at any stage tried to stop me. And that, in those conservative times, still coloured by Victorian Protestant ethics, was seen by me as the greatest help of all. I posted the letter to her, but being a woman of her time, when personal emotions, love even, were not spoken of, it was never mentioned.

Flat on the tank and loving it. Archives.

Gordon and I ready to leave for Wellington, England and beyond.

CHAPTER 2
No place to hide
SURVIVING IN A FOREIGN ENVIRONMENT

I pop my head over the fence to be hit by an explosion of noise and blinding speed as a group of sidecar outfits hurtle through a 160kph corner in front of me. Wow! Although travelling just centimetres apart they are drifting and sliding alarmingly, the rasping exhaust notes of their highly tuned BMW flat-twin engines rising and falling as the rear wheels lose and regain traction. Then they are gone, leaving the smell of burnt rubber and castor-based racing oil floating in a draught of disturbed air.

Although I consider myself a veteran of racing in New Zealand, I am totally gobsmacked.

I look at others around me, expecting surprise, amazement and admiration to be written all over their faces, but no. One fellow is nonchalantly rolling a cigarette, another checking his programme while others chat and laugh, showing no reaction. I gain the attention of an elderly chap holding a stopwatch and comment how fast I thought the group had passed. "Oh," he says, "that was only the second lap of practice; they will be going much faster later on."

Welcome to British short-circuit 'scratching'.

The *Rangitoto* docked at Southampton, as scheduled on Friday, April the 8th. Gordon and I took the especially laid on 'boat train' to London. As we travelled through the countryside I realised I had left a young, colourful and vibrant country for what seemed to be a tired, rundown old motherland. I wasn't surprised to notice ancient stone farm buildings but rather their neglected state. As we passed villages and towns, we could look down into the backyards of rows of grey, slate-roofed terrace houses. They seemed unloved with unkempt hedges, overgrown gardens and fences falling apart. A different world.

I had come from a productive land. Britain's insatiable demand for all our agricultural products allowed New Zealanders to flourish, enjoying the world's third highest standard of living. Every working man had the opportunity to own his own home, usually a wooden bungalow painted in the colour of his choice, set on a large section where his family nurtured colourful flowers and a productive vegetable garden. It was so different to what I was seeing here. I was to learn that the true beauty of the English countryside slowly reveals itself in May, and then bursts forth into the confidence of full flower in June. An amazing transition.

As arranged, John Hempleman met us at the Waterloo station and took us in his van to a hotel in Woolwich, south-east London, home of the National Arsenal. A huge storage and weapons manufacturing facility, more importantly to me it was the home of AMC Motorcycles, manufacturers of AJS and Matchless machines.

After dinner, Gordon and I went exploring and found our way to the AMC factory. Another shock for the new arrivals from 'Down Under' was that apart from the large sign above the main entrance of the multi-storey brick building, there was little to indicate that up to 300 motorcycles a day were produced here.

Next morning Hempo arrived early to give us the first taste of short-circuit racing in England, an international meeting at Silverstone, on a disused airfield. It took two hours to cross London. Auckland was no more than a village in comparison. On arrival I was shocked by the sheer speed of the sidecars. Back home our sidecar champion had thrown together a racing chair one weekend, bolted it to a 1000cc Ariel Square Four road bike and gone racing, and we laboured under the illusion he was fast.

Soon after, the pit gates opened and we could drive on to what had been the main landing strip of a World War II bomber base. Race transporters were parked in long lines on both sides of the strip with bikes being ridden up and down, warming up for their practice session. I wandered off to observe some of the star riders, their machines and mechanics. I wanted to see how they went about their work, the equipment they carried and what modifications they had made. There was much to learn.

After years of reading race write-ups in the English motorcycle magazines and studying photographs and rider profiles, I could recognise all of them instantly. Their race bikes were beautifully engineered. Everyone seemed in good humour as they went about their jobs of changing tyres, gearing, fork oil, rear suspension units and on occasion attending to more serious issues. Two sidecar crews seemed to have structural problems and were industriously cutting and welding. Slowly, the feeling of awe gave way to one of intense cold. We had left a hot summer and travelled through the tropics. It was a freezing eight degrees with a strong breeze.

I made for the warmth of the restaurant. Having been shaken to the core by the speed of the sidecars and chastened by the sophistication of the top riders' equipment and support crews, I now felt very much the awkward, unsophisticated country boy that I was.

I rejoined Hempo and Gordon in a stand overlooking the top-gear, take-it-as-fast-as-you-get-to-it right-hander that entered the start-finish straight. The 125cc and 250cc races had given the young British star Mike Hailwood, riding superior machinery, easy wins. It would be the larger capacity classes that would be hard fought. In the 350cc race Hailwood made a cracker of a start, gaining an early lead. At the end of the first lap he hurtled into view at 190kph, his AJS heeled over to the limit with his chin still on the tank and his right foot scraping the tarmac. He used every centimetre of the track plus a narrow concrete strip on the outside. As impressive as that was, he was followed by the wily Scot Bob McIntyre, who was travelling even faster. He in turn was closely followed by a bevy of sponsored riders led by brilliant newcomer Phil Read. Then came a horde of some 30 riders, all nose to tail and separated by centimetres, not bike lengths.

The depth of ability was staggering. So many were riding impeccably, with the rider in 15th place appearing to be as fast as the rider in fourth. I had hardly recovered from that spectacular first lap when Hailwood reappeared. McIntyre was closer now and three laps later he took the lead. Hailwood fought back and overtook him but at the end McIntyre rode over the finish line first. What an introduction to the cauldron of British short-circuit racing!

With a host of circuits dotted around the UK and practice sessions often twice a week, riders and tuners had a chance to hone their skills and their machines to the finest edge of perfection. At that time foreigners did not win on UK soil; the competition was far too tough.

Gordon had noticed that I was uncommonly quiet. "You'll be all right," he said cheerfully. "I would say you'd be twelfth or fourteenth at least." And pigs might fly, I thought. I cast my mind back to New Zealand where I had mainly ridden on closed public-road circuits, the laps being five to eight kilometres in length. Frequently, we were allowed just one short practice session per class; this was never sufficient to learn the track well enough to ride like these guys. There would be several changes of surface, including long sections of dirt, as many of our side roads were shingle. I enjoyed the loose surfaces and had found the most effective method of braking was to lock up both wheels until the bike became wayward then release them, and once it had settled, lock the wheels again. This tended to create a lot of dust and flying stones, some bouncing off my helmet. No one out-braked me and it was safe, as you knew exactly what your wheels were doing. The joy of it for me was leaving slow, dirt-surfaced corners with an engine screaming and the rear wheel spinning in a controlled drift. These were recognised skills in New Zealand but absolutely of no use here. I had a lot to think about.

Before leaving home I had written to Mick Vinson who was the honorary manager of the New Zealand Isle of Man team. Mick managed a large mixed vegetable and fruit producing farm in Swanley, North Kent. Mick's enthusiasm for motorcycling, and due to his friendship with Jock West, sales director of the AJS and Matchless factory (Associated Motorcycle Ltd, known as AMC), had led Mick to make a large storage shed at the farm available as a base for New Zealand riders. He was extremely helpful, especially so when a New Zealander was hurt or suffered fatal injuries. Having access to the farm's facilities, which included a fully equipped workshop, was a boon and helped New Zealanders overcome some of the never-ending problems they faced. I phoned Mick, a fine, pleasant outgoing man who invited us to join him, his wife Eileen and children Judith and Guy for dinner. He also passed on the good news that New Zealand Motorcycling was considering entering a team in the TT after all. Meanwhile Gordon found a newspaper advertisement for a van.

The next day, dressed in my suit and tie, I left Gordon to check out the van and, by bus, train and taxi, made my way to central London and the offices of the Auto-Cycle Union to apply for an English national and international licence and the relevant insurance policy. Then it was on to an important meeting with Lew Ellis, Shell's competition manager. During the train ride I received another culture shock. I thought I would start a conversation with a chap sitting next to me, as you do. He gave me a withering look and moved to another seat. What had upset him? I looked around to find no one in conversation. Most were reading papers while others just sat staring into space, with no eye contact. Then it dawned on me that the guy must have thought I was trying to 'pick him up'. Perhaps I was lucky that he was 'straight'.

I arrived at Shell UK's head office, Shell Mex House on the Strand, feeling awkward, apprehensive and out of place. Lacking negotiating skills was going to make the next two hours difficult. I walked through a doorway you could have driven a truck through and found a uniformed attendant seated in a small office. I was told to wait for Lew, who would come down and take me to lunch. Lew was a tall, pleasant, chain-smoking warrior of the London business world who had a penchant for red wine and posh restaurants. This sure as hell wasn't me. Seated in a private booth and handed a menu, I glanced through it, recognising nothing that was familiar. For example there were three types of spaghetti but up to now I knew only one, and that came out of a tin. Noticing my obvious vacant stare, Lew announced what 'we should have'. With sweat trickling down from my armpits I agreed and drained my wine glass.

Over a cigarette he asked how things were coming together. With a confidence I didn't feel I spoke glibly of having received good start money offers from the Austrian, French and German GPs, also from the top internationals at St Wendel, Germany; Madrid International; and Mettet, Belgium. He was impressed. The sweat began to trickle again. Our meals arrived and when we were into our second bottle of wine Lew began explaining how most of the fuel companies had withdrawn support for car and motorcycle racing. "Last year I would have been happy to pay you one thousand pounds but this year I have had to turn away good riders that we have been supporting for years. My job has never been so hard," he said with a benevolent look and his hands opened and spread wide. That amount of money would have paid for a new van, a new race bike and spares. He was succeeding in softening me up so I would accept anything he offered.

"What type of van will you be using?" he asked.

"A Ford," I lied. "We checked it out yesterday and will pick it up on Thursday." The Ford Thames was larger and much faster than a Bedford or Austin but as they had only been in production for two years they were not easy to find second hand. Lew must have been impressed with our progress in such a short time.

"All right, Hugh," he said. "You are obviously capable of organising yourself so I'll give you a cheque for two hundred pounds and a further fifty when you have our Shell X100 motor oil sign painted on the back of your vehicle, and of course all the lubricants you will require for the season." I agreed instantly, drained my glass and stood up. I needed to escape the claustrophobic confines of the restaurant and bank that cheque.

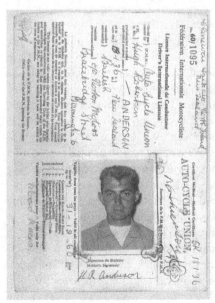

My first international racing licence.

Later that week a basket of mail was delivered, which had been forwarded on from my contact address at Norton Motors. With the impatience of a child at Christmas I ripped open the 22 envelopes. I couldn't understand a word but numbers are universal: 3000 schillings from the Austrian GP; 100,000 lire from Imola, Italy; 700 deutschmarks from the Saarlands GP; 450 francs from the French GP; 10,000 pesetas from the Premio Internacional de Madrid, Spain; 600 guilders from the Dutch TT; 3000 francs from Mettet, Belgium; 4000 francs from Chimay, Belgium; 30 pounds from Mallory Park, England; then 5000 francs from Aix Les Baines, France; plus start money from Tubbergen, Holland; Silverstone, England; Dreikenrennen, East Germany; and Hockenheim, West Germany.

AMC race shop staff Jack Emmet, Derek Dixon and Tommy Mortimer wheel out a batch of new Matchless G50s. Archives.

New trials bikes on test. And they get paid to do this!

There were enough starts to choose from to take me through to the end of June, and I had an oil contract. The ever-present weight of self-doubt was pushed, at least temporarily, aside. I had been accepted. There was a place for me in the fabled 'Continental Circus'. I may not get rich but I would survive. An average of 50 pounds a meeting would be sufficient to maintain the bikes, cover travelling expenses and leave enough for two meals a day. No Christmas had been as good as this. Fourteen years of dreaming had become a reality. It took another two weeks to navigate the jungle of paperwork required to enter these meetings and get documentation to travel to the Continent. There were carnets for the bikes and international insurance for the van that for a young 'colonial' was very difficult to obtain. I was given the essential Green Card on the morning we left for the Austrian Grand Prix. We worked all hours to prepare the bikes and find all the basic equipment required.

We did find a Ford Thames van, at Dagenham Motors in Woolwich. It was two years old, had covered 40,000 miles and seemed okay. Yeah right. How that decision would come back to haunt us over the next few months. The *Rangitoto* was now berthed at the London docks where my two Manx Nortons were unloaded. Down on Mick's farm we began working on them with enthusiasm. We drew up a wish list of all the things that had to be done and a few more that we would like to get done. That list was long but not impossible to get through.

Easter weekend heralded the beginning of the frantic English season with seven major events around the country. Thruxton, Hampshire; Brands Hatch, Kent; Crystal Palace, London; Snetterton, Norfolk; Oulton Park, Cheshire; Cadwell Park, Lincolnshire; Thornaby, Middlesbrough; and at Errol in Scotland; a real weekend of racing.

Friday was Brands Hatch just 20km from the farm but we were too busy to attend. It seemed that most lap records were broken with the 'King of Brands' Derek Minter winning both the main events with Mike Hailwood hard on his heels. Mike won the two lightweight classes. The Oulton Park International Trophy meeting in Cheshire was a 'trade-supported' event, a meeting that many of the major accessory manufacturers attended. It was a chance for me to meet the various representatives and stock up on tyres, chains, spark plugs, oil and so on. We intended to take all four Norton wheels with us to have the brakes relined and new tyres fitted.

Our spirits were high when we left London early on Sunday morning but it took us much longer to get to Oulton Park than we expected. Finding our way across London was far from easy and negotiating the country roads a challenge. There was more than one rather heated, in a brotherly way, discussion about how to read a road map. We arrived at the circuit late in the evening.

At 6am next morning the chilly paddock was filling fast with riders and mechanics on a mission. At first I felt embarrassed asking the trade representatives for supplies. They were quick to notice and all were very helpful. The amount I received was invariably more than I had intended asking for. They seemed to be a very pleasant, sociable group of individuals who enjoyed being at the centre of activities.

During the afternoon's main events I went to every point of the circuit that I could gain access to. Fifty thousand spectators attended and they were not disappointed. In the two main races Derek Minter and Scott Bob McIntyre, who was the first rider to lap the Isle of Man at over 100mph, in 1957, had terrific tussles, setting new lap records then promptly breaking them as they fought for supremacy. McIntyre won the 350cc race by .02 of a second. Minter won the 500cc class after McIntyre's engine slowed. Bob Anderson, Alan Shepherd and a young Phil Read battled away over third place.

On Monday evening we drove to Birmingham, the hub of British motorcycle manufacturing, and found a quiet street to park up and sleep in the van. Soon after we stopped there was a tapping on the window on Gordon's side, which he chose to ignore. The tapping became more urgent.

"What do you want?" asked Gordon when a woman with a heavy northern accent started asking about something he couldn't understand. He told her to go away but she persisted, and soon after was joined by another woman. They spoke together for a while then the other woman said, "You can have it for a pound."

Having no idea what she was on about and thinking they were on their way home from a pub and amusing themselves, Gordon thought he would go along with what appeared to be some kind of joke. "No, that's too much," he said. They shouted, banged on the van and left. They only thing I understood them saying was "that cheeky bastard wanted a f--- for nothing". Only then did we realise what they had been attempting to sell.

The next day we met up with Hempo, who took us on a tour of some of the major factories. He drove us past the Dunlop tyre factory. It was huge, a multitude of three- and four-storey brick buildings connected with full-width roads. Norton had created a sophisticated, high-profile image based on its overwhelming success in road racing, so I assumed the factory would be housed in a grand building. But it took us some time to find the entrance to the spares department, which was through an ordinary door leading into one of many large brick buildings in the street. Beside it was a small brass plate stating 'Norton Motors Ltd'. The plate was corroded from the weather and neglect, and the wording was barely discernible. Hempo arrived and introduced us to the spares manager and we secured some more parts.

The Amal carburettor company was next. We were again made welcome. An hour later we received a box containing the parts I had requested plus an assortment of screws and small fittings for the racing carburettors. All this for three pounds 10 shillings! Great. Our afternoon ended with a quick visit to Terry's where once again we were well received and given several sets of valve springs. Hempo was going back to London so we arranged to meet at New Cross speedway to spend time with some of the New Zealand riders, including Eric Williams, whom we had met on the *Rangitoto*. It was one of those great nights. The stadium was full of supporters, with Wimbledon being the visiting team. Both were equal until the last two heats when Wimbledon gained a two-point lead. We all went off to a local pub. Some of the New Zealand riders present were notorious, party-loving characters. One was so renowned that a shipping company refused to have him on their ocean liners. I don't know when the bar closed; perhaps it didn't. At that time speedway riders were well paid, had a good time, were very good company and seemed to write their own social rules.

The drama and excitement the start of an Isle of Man TT creates. In a matter of weeks my life's ambition will be realised.

CHAPTER 3

Facing the fears of Silverstone and enjoying
what became a very productive lunch

I ride through an avenue of spectators, who reach out to touch me as I inch my way past. Bathed in sweat, my throat parched from 45 hairy, 60-second laps through a park in Madrid, my first victory on European soil hasn't sunk in yet. My 500cc Manx Norton has to be revved to keep the race-tuned engine running but it doesn't drown out the cheering of the fans. This is so different from winning in New Zealand. Back in the pits Gordon asks why I've been going so fast at the end of the race. "You had more than half a lap lead," he shouts. Really. He should have seen the view from where I was sitting.

Total silence had descended as the starter raised his flag, then a massive firework exploded, the flag dropped and we all pushed off, creating a wall of noise from our megaphone exhausts. Passing was made difficult, especially on the back straight. Every time the lead riders appeared the unrestrained crowd would surge forward from both sides onto the track to gain a better view. Only when the leading rider charged into the narrow corridor of fans would they melt back to the track edge. I wasn't receiving any pit signals, as due to the large crowd we hadn't been able to find a convenient position, but having passed the leaders I was aware of their speed and felt that by turning slightly faster lap times my lead would steadily increase.

I regularly lapped slower riders, narrowly missing one who literally crashed under my front wheel. Just when I was beginning to wonder when this race would end, I noticed some of the spectators had begun waving handkerchiefs. Next lap there were even more. I assumed a rider was catching me and the fans were encouraging him, so I lifted my pace. Now arms were being waved and mouths were opening in shouts I couldn't hear. As I rushed past so very close to them they appeared not to be looking at me but behind me.

There must be a rider closing on me. I snatched a brief look back. A rider was there, but surely that was the one I'd just lapped. Now people were moving farther out onto the track, jostling and gesticulating. As I rushed into the long, difficult corner near the start I almost lost control of a vivid slide, but then at last the finishing flag was waved. Later we learned crowd animation is simply the Spanish way of acknowledging and congratulating the winner.

Now a marshal is guiding me to the officials' stand. Speeches of congratulations are made in a language I don't understand. Feeling slightly dazed, I'm presented with a bunch of roses. For the first of many times to come, I stand to attention as the New Zealand national anthem is played. While the Premio Internacional de Madrid isn't rated as a major meeting on the international calendar, it is the win that confirms I'm a fully paid-up member of the 'Continental Circus'.

My first taste of life in the Continental Circus began with the Austrian Grand Prix on May 1, 1960. Held on a track near Salzburg, it was known as 'the autobahn circuit' and encompassed several motorway on and off ramps and an overpass. The surface ranged from concrete to cobblestones. The event had yet to gain world championship status but was an important international meeting. Many of Europe's top riders had entered, including Englishmen Dave Chadwick, Dickie Dale, John Hartle and Peter Ferbrache, Australians Bob Brown and Tom Phillis, Rhodesian Jim Redman, New Zealander John Hempleman and most of the Continent's national champions. Fresh from my shock introduction to the speed and skill on show at Silverstone, I was desperate not to make a fool of myself in such exalted company.

When practice finally began at 1.30pm, I discovered the 350cc Manx Norton lacked power and vibrated at high revs. Confident that it wasn't a mechanical fault and at times hearing a vague rattle led me to believe that the special American valve springs needed replacing. Fortunately, the 500cc Manx was running well.

Typically, grid positions were established by your fastest lap in the final practice session. I pulled the pin on the 500. Entering at high speed the circuit's two ever-tightening corners, one on concrete, the other on cobblestones, at 170 to 180ks, was definitely stimulating. It was here that I got a little loose at times and, as I always had on New Zealand gravel roads, enjoyed the bike moving about. It may have appeared a little wild to some, but having gained a feel for the surface I was perfectly comfortable and enjoying myself.

The pleasure of being back on my bikes again and feeling as fast as anyone raised my enthusiasm. I was cleaning the bikes when Gordon returned with the official lap times. I was fourth fastest. What a relief! The lingering doubts hanging over me since Silverstone were cast off. Gordon put the kettle on. It was time for a cup of tea and more of our usual stimulating diet — bread and jam. I turned to be confronted by two riders in leathers and one of their helpers. They all began talking loudly at once; I didn't understand a word. I smiled and offered my hand but that only seemed to aggravate them. One chap used precise arm movements, obviously a skill honed by practice, to indicate that I'd passed at speed, missing him by a few centimetres and causing him to wobble dangerously. Another seemed to be blaming me for pushing him onto the grass verge. The helper made a silent protest. Whilst nodding his head he kept tapping the side of it with his index finger.

Gordon was taken aback. I explained that, when getting on the pace, I had caught a group travelling relatively cautiously and taking up most of the road so had chosen the largest gap. It must have been wide enough as I didn't touch them. Being blown off by a newcomer in a hurry could bruise egos; it had happened in New Zealand and would probably occur again here. I soon found some of the continental competitors enjoyed wearing the best riding apparel available. These 'pit posers' seemed prone to bluster despite producing average on-track performances.

Shrugging off that minor confrontation I prepared for Sunday's race programme beginning with the 125cc event at 1pm, the 350cc at 3pm and the 500cc at 5pm. To control my nerves I kept busy checking and rechecking the bikes, answering correspondence from race promoters, writing letters home; anything to keep my mind off the races.

Mindful of its valve spring problems, I kept the 350's engine revs to a minimum and rode steadily into 11th place. Starting from the front row in the 500cc race allowed for a fast, unobstructed getaway. An excellent start had me busily disputing fourth place with Bob Brown and Dickie Dale. For the first half of the long race I rode with them, learning a little more each lap and making up for my slower engine by clinging to one of their rear wheels to slipstream them up the straights. Occasionally, I'd pass one or both of them under brakes only to be re-passed on the fast straight. This was early in the season and both these very experienced campaigners were riding into form on their brand new Manx Nortons. Eventually, they tired of a wild kid from Down Under in their midst and sped up. I tried to stay with them but my clutch began to slip and I was forced to ease up and nurse the bike home in seventh place. The finishing order was Dave Chadwick, Dickie Dale, John Hartle, Bob Brown, Tom Phillis, Peter Ferbrache and Hugh Anderson.

After the race Bob and later Dickie took time to have a chat with me. The main piece of advice offered was 'never forget your next meeting', meaning contain your dash and ambition as it's a long season and you don't get paid lying in a hospital. Or perhaps they were thinking of their own wellbeing — if this guy is going to ride with us let's make him safe. As I sat with a contemplative cigarette taking it all in, I had no inkling that 1960 would become a year of tragedy. Two weeks later Dave Chadwick would die at Mettet in Belgium due to non-existent crowd control, five weeks later Peter Ferbrache would go at the Dutch TT when possibly trying too hard, Bob Brown would be lost in August, at the West German Grand Prix at the Solitudering near Stuttgart when riding the new 250cc Honda four, and an international meeting at the Nürburgring would claim Dickie Dale virtually 12 months to the day after I rode with him in Austria. There seemed to be nothing in common regarding these accidents and to my knowledge there was seldom any form of inquiry as to what caused them.

Top: I spent what little money I had on the bikes. Decent leathers could wait. Artur Fenzlau.

Above: Leading Japanese Champion and friend Fumio Ito. Artur Fenzlau.

Dickie Dale was a man of vast experience who had ridden for the Gilera, Moto Guzzi, MV Agusta and BMW factories. Bob Brown had ridden a Gilera to third place in the 1957 Isle of Man TT and had repeated it on Nortons in 1958 and 1959.

Dickie and Bob were two of the elders of the Continental Circus. The 1960 season was Dickie's 11th of international racing and Bob's seventh.

Our next stop was on the other side of snow-covered Pyrenees in the sun of Spain at the Premio Internacional de Madrid. The Ford Thames van had given trouble from the time of purchase. Fitting new driveshaft universals in Salzburg to cure an ever-worsening transmission vibration only seemed to spark new mechanical problems. As we passed through Switzerland one of many front wheel shimmies suddenly became violent, tossing us about in the cab. A steering arm had broken, but luckily a garage was close at hand.

After the owner ordered the required parts, we retired to a local café for a few hours then returned to find two collapsible camp beds laid out in a side room for us. Another example of the hospitality encountered all over Europe. When the parts arrived they didn't fit, but a cut and weld job had us on the road again. We had travelled only 500km and there were still 1300 to go. Pressing on over the Spanish border into a country that at that time under dictator Francisco Franco was of Third World status, we found ourselves dodging potholes on some of the worst roads we'd ever driven.

A loud clatter announced a broken shock absorber mount; we removed it and bounced on. Then at 10pm as we arrived on the outskirts of a village, the engine temperature gauge soared ominously high. A strong swirling wind carried light rain, matching our grim mood. We looked at each other, then Gordon said, "You've got overalls, and you're smaller than me so you will slide under easier." Why wasn't he my younger brother so I could 'guide' him? I slid under the van to investigate. It wasn't hard to find the leak; the lower hose had split. Luckily we had a roll of high-quality adhesive tape to wrap around it.

Gordon set off to fill our 20-litre water container. He reappeared out of the gloom complaining that people had slammed their doors in his face. I went farther afield and knocked on a door at which an elderly, crow-like woman appeared. Having no knowledge of Spanish except "Gracias, amigo" learned via cowboy movies, I pointed at the container and said "aqua" several times. She looked at me as though I was several sausages short of a barbecue and cruelly slammed the door shut. This may have had something to do with the fact that I had used the masculine form 'amigo'. I got the same response from her neighbour. I carried on down the windswept street to another light, knocked on the door and stood well back. An unshaven, robust, no-nonsense-looking man opened it. Again I went through my miming routine. His countenance lightened and he joined in my make believe by pretending to wash his hands and face.

With relief I offered my hand. He shook it and invited me to enter. He sat me down, took the container and filled it at an outside well. His teenage son had a little understanding of English and luckily I managed to convey to him that I was from New Zealand, raced motorcycles and was competing at Madrid on Sunday. When his father returned the lad explained my situation. He was hugely impressed and insisted I have a small glass of a very strong brew that I sipped timidly being careful not to choke. "No," he laughed, indicating that it should be flamboyantly tossed back and swallowed in one gulp. Oh dear. The good man then insisted that I had bread and salami followed up with a wickedly strong coffee. By the time I got back to the van, Gordon was more than a little agitated. Cold, wet, hungry and worried, he had become convinced that I had suffered from some form of foul play. Revved up by the coffee and brandy,I drove on to Madrid, arriving at the pits in the sprawling Parque del Retiro at 2am on Friday morning.

Practice started late in the afternoon, after the traditional two-hour siesta. I was troubled by rear-wheel slides. Thinking the tyre was partly deflated, I stopped and checked, but it was okay. I then realised that some of the corners had been polished smooth by the thousands of vehicles that used the road each day as a short cut between suburbs. The key to success here seemed to be a long, 180-degree sweeper. After giving it some thought I began fitting drive sprockets that would allow me to enter it in second gear with the engine at 4,400rpm to 4,700rpm. This created a satisfactory balance between speed and power. After making several adjustments to the settings of the notoriously fickle Amal Grand Prix carburettor, I made the fastest lap in practice just 1.4 seconds slower than the record set the previous year by motorcycle legend John Surtees on the fabulous four-cylinder MV Agusta.

Flowers, and for the first time our flag and national anthem. Archives.

After the on-track formalities at the finish we cleaned the bike and had lunch; it was only one o'clock. Following the siesta a bullfight was being held with the prize giving later in the evening. The prize giving was a lavish affair held in an impressive building that I believe may have been the city council chambers. We were assigned an interpreter who quietly translated the formal speeches as they were being made. To have been the winner and treated with such respect was as humbling as it was rewarding to receive that impressive trophy. To assist my recall of that moment, I have the handsome cup standing on my desk top.

Our next meeting was Mettet, in Belgium. After having new front wheel bearings fitted in France, the van reluctantly got us there but the bikes now gave us trouble. After replacing the American valve springs with standard British ones, just a few laps into practice a valve spring retainer broke, bending the valve. We fixed that but I retired from the race while in seventh place with a front-tyre puncture. I also retired from the 500cc race after a disastrously slow start and a nasty near miss when passing a slower rider on a very fast corner.

I joined Gordon to watch the race unfold. Dave Chadwick led followed by Dickie Dale and South Africans Paddy Driver and Jannie Stander. Dave was missing when the chequered flag came down. Rotten luck to break down when leading, we thought

Giving a 'possum in the headlights' impersonation as I accept the magnificent trophy. Archives.

as we walked back to the van. When the riders returned to the paddock we were told that a horrific crash had occurred involving Dave, another rider and spectators.

During the last lap when comfortably in the lead, Dave came up to lap two riders, who were deeply involved in a dice of their own. One rider moved sharply to his left to make a pass on the other, hitting Dave, who was in the process of passing him. Dave was forced off the road, striking two spectators walking along the verge. Dave and one spectator were killed instantly. The second spectator lost a leg and another rider, with whom Dave's cartwheeling motorcycle came in contact with, received a broken leg.

In those days spectators could move about as they wished and often walked along the edge of the circuit and were frequently seen crossing it. On such a fast track, with average speeds in excess of 145kph, a serious accident was just waiting to happen.

The season's first world championship Grand Prix at Clermont-Ferrand in central France was next. As we drove through a town in southern Belgium I saw a high-class restaurant. Not having eaten any fruit and vegetables for some days, a real meal would be a necessary treat. After combing our hair we entered the establishment. Not recognising anything on the menu, I asked the waiter, "Parlez-vous anglais?" He looked to the heavens. Obviously, another test of my ability to mime, much practised of late, was required. Allowing my hands free rein I indicated a large plate piled high adding cow-like moos and an elaborate pulling of plants from the soil and cleaning and trimming them, not forgetting a convincing display of needing a knife and fork to deal to the feast. The longer it took, the more confident we became that we were going to be delivered a real meal. Eventually, three waiters appeared in line. The first two were each carrying a large plate stacked high with sandwiches, the third with two plates and knives and forks. Knowing that "No, no, you have got it all wrong" wasn't going to work, I did my best to sound like I meant "Merci beaucoup". The fillings were beef and celery.

Apart from another burst radiator hose, then having to remove and repair a leaking radiator, we had a trouble-free run. At the circuit we met Gary Hocking, the brilliant young rider from Rhodesia who was now a member of the all-conquering MV Agusta team. He invited a group of us to the MV marquee to view the bikes. An unforgettable sight greeted us: seven immaculate, state-of-the-art Grand Prix-winning motorcycles. There was a 280cc twin cylinder for Gary to ride in the 350cc race, two 350cc four-cylinder models for John Surtees, one a new lightweight version, and two 500cc fours for John and his Italian team-mate Remo Venturi. They sat there in a glow of factory-red livery, very much works of art.

During the third lap of the first 350cc practice, my Norton engine suddenly locked solid in the middle of an S-bend. On occasions such as these a rider's reaction time can be the difference between serious injury or just a nasty moment. At 130kph, time stood still as the fingers of my left hand appeared to ever so slowly stretch out and pull in the clutch lever, allowing the screeching rear wheel to turn free again. The tyre regained grip, instantly lifting me out of the seat with a vicious shake of the handlebars. I left an ugly, 3m-long black tyre mark that remained all weekend. It was a vivid reminder of what could have been as on my right was an unprotected drop of some 4m into a riverbed of massive boulders. An experimental top bevel bearing had collapsed. In contrast the 500 went well and I found the beginning of a rhythmic flow.

Rhodesians Willie van Leeuwen, Shaun and Tommy Robinson and John Hempleman. Archives.

Saturday afternoon was qualifying time. After mechanical difficulties, crashes or other problems, riders would use their 350cc machine in the 500cc class or their 500cc into the 350cc class so they could qualify for their start money. For some of the riders that start money would allow them to eat for a week and pay for fuel to attend the following meeting. There was an unspoken rule that when riding a machine that didn't qualify for a particular event, you did not interfere with the progress of others or finish in a prize money-earning or trophy-winning position. Normally, you would do several laps and 'retire' in a pleasant spot and spectate.

We fitted the 350 fairing to the 500, as this carried a different number and colours to the 500, and hurriedly joined the 350's out on the track.

On that first lap I felt a slight drop in performance, slowed and returned to the paddock. Gordon removed the spark plug and as we turned the engine over there was noticeable resistance. The new top bevel bush fitted at Mettet had nipped up.

As 'Shaun Robinson' of Rhodesia, I hold sixth place at the French Grand Prix. Archives.

Time was short, so we dismantled the housing, tapped the bevel free and began relieving the minor galling and damage. Reassembling it, we flooded the housing with oil and crossed our fingers. Gordon warmed the engine as I quickly pulled on my racing leathers. As I walked to the bike the engine stopped. The bevel had nipped up again so that was that. Our first Grand Prix and unable to qualify in either race.

During the 500cc qualifying session, one of our new friends, Rhodesian Tommy Robinson, crashed heavily and was taken to hospital. As soon as the track was opened to the public, with his brother Shaun we drove to the crash site to collect Tommy's bike. His Norton lay several metres down a bank at the base of a tree. A spectator pointed high up its trunk to where it was heavily scored. The bike had hit it hard. The situation had us feeling very uneasy about Tommy's condition.

On returning to the pits two officials came and asked us to take Tommy's bike to the police station, adding that Tommy wasn't expected to live. Another death so soon. Luckily, Shaun hadn't heard the bad news. How do you handle this? I called Shaun over and said, "These people can be over-dramatic when there is a serious crash; it seems the police have to be advised. We have been asked to deliver Tom's Norton to the police station. It seems that Tom has been hurt but should be okay." The colour drained from Shaun's face and we hurried to the hospital.

We found Tommy in a very uncomfortable state. He didn't recognise our voices or answer us but moaned incessantly. "What are his injuries?" we asked the nurses, but no one spoke English. They were very busy and with five fingers indicated how many injured riders had arrived from the track that day. Gordon, who had been at the scene of more than one serious accident, was less concerned. He felt that frequently the noisy patients are okay; it's the silent ones you worry about.

Due to Tommy's situation, Shaun lost all interest in taking part in the races but decided to do several laps in the 350cc event for the start money and then retire. It was agreed I would take his place in the 500cc race and we would share the start money equally. I rode in my first world championship points-carrying Grand Prix race as Shaun Robinson from Rhodesia.

As Gordon warmed the 500 I pulled on my riding gear. It was an exciting moment, a major milestone, regardless of whose name was in the programme. I made a good start from near the back of the grid and by the end of the first lap was among the leading group of privateers.

As *The Motor Cycle* magazine described it: "A fierce struggle raged over sixth place between John Hempleman of New Zealand, Jannie Stander of South Africa, Australian Bob West, Shaun Robinson, Rhodesia, Fumio Ito of Japan, and Jacques Insermini, France."

Later in the race *The Motor Cycle* went on to say: "At half distance Hempleman became embroiled in a desperate cut and thrust with Robinson and Ito." As the race progressed I passed Ito, Hempleman and West to find myself in sixth place. Being concerned about the ramifications of gaining world championship points in Robinson's name, I drifted back, allowing Ito to pass. I finished in an inconspicuous seventh place. Surtees won, followed by Remo Venturi, Brown, Driver, Laddy Richter, Austria, Ito, 'Robinson', West, Hempleman and Insermini.

As we hadn't received any news regarding Tommy's progress we were anxious to visit him. This time he knew who we were but wasn't very talkative and seemed to have considerable pain in his shoulder, back, left leg, an elbow and a hell of a headache. However, he could move all his limbs so he was okay.

Silverstone Saturday, a major international, followed with practice beginning in the Isle of Man in just 12 days. We had work to do. Back in London a large amount of mail awaited us. One letter was from Motorcycling New Zealand, confirming a team would be entered in the Isle of Man TT races. Peter Pawson was to be team captain. Australian Trevor Pound and I would make up the required three entrants.

Another piece of excellent news was that New Zealand AJS importer Percy Coleman, father of Rod, was in the UK having discussions with Jock West, sales director of AMC, and Jack Williams, manager of the race shop, regarding the possibility of them supplying a new 7R for me to use in the 350cc class at the TT. Percy's letter stressed that demand always exceeded supply. Whether one became available or not, it was gratifying to know that a man of Percy's standing was out there batting for me. Another letter was from the Dutch TT organisers offering reasonable start money. I completed and returned the entry form. My cup may not have 'runneth over', but it was full enough.

The priority now was to get the van sorted out once and for all. We gave a long list of faults to the workshop manager of Dagenham Motors. It was jamming in gear, the brakes were bad, radiator and hoses leaking, it had a noisy differential, needed all the steering gear renewed, front suspension totally overhauled, the list went on. Their avoidance of responsibility was the last straw. Gordon had a short fuse. Words were said. We had paid serious money for the thing, 345 pounds when a new one was only 500. There seemed little doubt that we had been given a raw deal. When we added that we were convinced that it had done 140,000 miles and not the 40,000 claimed, the manager's face reddened. He blustered and apologised but the end of next week was the earliest they could book it in. He then appeared to remember he had an urgent appointment elsewhere and hurried off. We tried to locate the salesman we had bought it from but he seemed to have business off the premises and could not be found. Londoners were a sharp bunch; we weren't. If we were going to get to the Dutch TT, scheduled to begin immediately after the Isle of Man races, the van had to be repaired now, leaving us without a van for the TT. We now faced the very risky business of sending the two Nortons and locked boxes of spares by train from South London to Douglas on the Isle of Man. This plan, with its chance of damage and theft, was bordering on foolishness but we had no option.

Time was running out. We were due to officially sign on at the important Hutchinson 100 race at Silverstone in just 20 hours. I phoned the organisers to advise I could only start in one class. The response was "never mind, come along and enjoy yourself". We finished preparing the 500, loaded up and finally hit the road north at 2am. The left steering arm, repaired in Switzerland, broke as Gordon inadvertently nudged a kerb as we did a U-turn before driving into the pits.

Things took a brighter turn when after signing on I visited the Avon tyre enclosure. The manager, who had been so helpful at Oulton Park soon after our arrival in the UK, welcomed me warmly and asked how our season was progressing. He was aware that I had won the race in Madrid and was amused at how I had managed to gain a start at the French GP and why I had finished in seventh place under the name of Shaun Robinson from Rhodesia. He offered his congratulations, gathered two pairs of tyres and, as he needed to call at the Hailwood équipe, accompanied me back to the van. Noting that its tyres were worn out he asked for an address to send a new set. Brilliant!

I had always enjoyed New Zealand's aerodrome-based circuits at Ardmore and Ohakea, but remembering how impressed I had been on the day after we arrived when Hempo brought us here, I was bathed in apprehension as to my ability to compete. After lining up near the front of the dummy grid I rode with a mid-race finishing group staying with them for the eight laps allocated to us.

While I was changing the gearing Percy Coleman called. He was in good spirits and obviously enjoying the heady atmosphere generated by one of the most prestigious events held in England at that time. Gordon offered to finish my work while Percy and I retired to the restaurant. Over a late lunch he explained that while he had been pulling all the strings possible at the AMC factory, he wasn't confident a 7R would be available for the TT. We enjoyed each other's company. How age and youth are united with respect and a common interest, when the experience of one is combined with the youthful energy of the other to create a vibrant meeting ground of ideas. As I rode back after my next practice session, after having started with and hung on to a group of the top riders, I caught sight of Percy hurrying along pit lane towards me. He was obviously impressed with my riding and said so. When he left, his parting words were: "I'll be at the factory first thing Monday morning knocking on doors."

We woke up early next morning. Race day always creates nervous energy from the moment you open your eyes and the start of the 500cc race was 4pm, a long wait. As this event was run by the British Motor Cycle Racing Club, the world's biggest club formed solely for motorcycle racers, bikes of all ages and capacities were catered for. From pre-war Rudges, Triumphs and Velocettes to late-model ex-factory Ducati, Benelli, Moto Guzzi and MV Agusta models, there was a vast array and a huge crowd.

To be conversant with the pre-race procedure we watched the start of the 350cc championship event and the first few laps. Just the same as the day after we arrived in the UK, they rode nose to tail, shoulder to shoulder, at what appeared to me an astonishing speed lap after lap. I found it hard to believe I could compete in that intensely competitive environment and turned and walked back to the van. From that time on I seldom watched a race anywhere. To think that I was travelling at a similar speed unnerved me.

It was late in the afternoon when the starters for the 500cc championship race, the main event, assembled on the dummy grid. I had qualified 17th and was hoping for a steady ride. The Norton fired up instantly allowing me to pass several riders. Then I hung on to the rear wheel of the guy in front as though my life depended on it. At the end of the first lap the race was described as "41 starters roared past in a frenzied procession never more than a bike length apart".

After seven laps I was 13th, the lowest position I'd filled in my life. Bob McIntyre was eighth followed by Phil Read, who 12 months later would win the 350cc TT, and John Hartle, who had finished second in the earlier record-breaking 350 event and was team-mate to the great John Surtees in the MV Agusta team, was in 11th place.

We travelled in very close formation separated by little more than a metre. Our field of vision consisted mainly of a rider's backside. Suddenly, on the ninth lap at Stowe a rider shot out of the speeding procession in a shower of sparks and a cloud of fibreglass dust. No one eased their throttle or showed any reaction. They knew full well that had anyone closed their throttle, a massive pile-up would have ensued, so they just continued over the slightly uneven concrete sections in their head-nodding, foot-scraping way.

Soon after that excitement John Hartle retired with a split oil tank, and ex-scrambler and brilliant all-rounder Ron Langston came unstuck at Club Corner. I was now at the tail of a group dicing for ninth place but suddenly my goggles flew off my helmet, bringing a rather educational ride to an early end. I found out later that it was Bob McIntyre who had crashed at Stowe when his Norton's engine seized. He suffered bruises and a cut nose. A young Mike Hailwood won, setting a new lap record of 160.6kph, the first over 100 mph lap, followed by Derek Minter, Tommy Robb, Bob Anderson and Dickie Dale.

Back at the farm in Kent south of London, we prepared the bikes and packed parts and equipment into our ex-Army tool boxes ready for the rail journey to Douglas on the Isle of Man. We left the van at Dagenham Motors and made our way to the Bank of New Zealand in Central London. I had an arrangement with the New Zealand Norton importer, Bill White, who was based in Auckland, that allowed me to buy Norton spares directly from the factory at the healthy dealer discount of 33 per cent. First I had to deposit a substantial sum of money in the importer's London bank account, and then mail the deposit slip to Bill White, who would then notify the Norton factory spares department to supply me with parts up to that amount.

After converting all the various currencies we had into English pounds I deposited 115 pounds into Bill White's account. The payment I would receive from being a team member, and provided I qualified for and started in both TT races, would pay our hotel and return fare to Liverpool with money to spare.

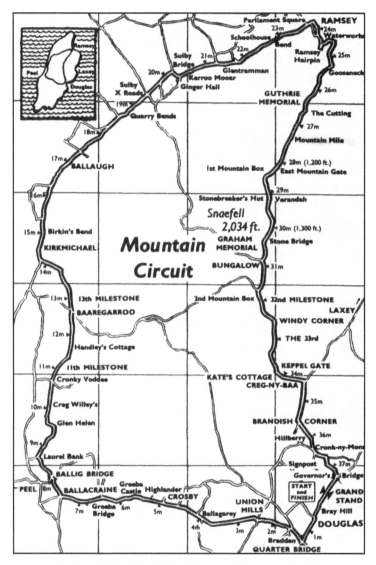

The formidable Isle of Man TT mountain course. Archives.

CHAPTER 4

Risk stimulates your very core and the courage it carries sharpens the knowledge of ourselves

THE ISLE OF MAN – THE GREATEST CHALLENGE OF ALL IN A ROAD RACER'S LIFE

As I plunge at full noise down frightening Bray Hill, my eyes are forced shut as I hit the bottom of an evil dip in the narrow tarmac. Then as I crest the next rise the AJS 7R wobbles a little and the engine revs blare louder from the open megaphone as the rear wheel leaves the ground. When it lands and grips again, the pounding jolt pushes me back into the seat.

Every mile of the legendary 37.7-mile Isle of Man TT course is lived. Not ridden, but lived, as I sense and assess every movement of the machine, feel its pulse, and get to know it as well as I know myself.

Building a relationship between a human and a mechanical device is vital for survival on this unforgiving course. Crashing isn't an option and can be caused equally by human error or not reading the signs of imminent mechanical failure.

Both man and machine are functioning on the very edge of their ability and design. It's a brutal, intensely personal experience.

My chest and chin are raw from the constant buffeting, forced into the sponge rubber on top of the petrol tank in an attempt to keep my head and vision steady on the long, bumpy, flat-out sections. This mild discomfort is insignificant. It is all part and parcel of riding here, yet another badge of honour displayed as a distinctive chafed red, unshaven jaw.

Strangely, as the lap unfolds I feel relaxed, focused and with a sense of freedom. Finally, I am without self-doubt, anxiety or even fear.

The miles fly by quickly and, as I pass fewer riders, now the road is mine. I feel comfortable. I do not need to do more — a top-10 finish in this, my first year, would be superb. It would justify all the effort, expense and sacrifice I have experienced in an amazing week of soaring highs and desperate lows.

For 14 years I had been waiting. Step by step I had followed the prescribed career path and, with each passing year, the long-awaited moment had drawn closer. Finally, at 2.20pm on June 1, 1960, I stepped on to the wharf at Douglas, the main town on the Isle of Man, to begin the most challenging stage of an adventure conceived in childhood.

During the four-hour ferry voyage from Liverpool my emotions had fluctuated between excitement and worry about the task ahead. Would I be good enough? Then a smudge appeared on the horizon and gradually took the shape of a mound, which would almost certainly be the mountain the TT course climbed and descended.

Within a surprisingly short time Douglas came into view, basking in sunshine. Its half-moon curve of a hotel-lined promenade had been etched into my mind by those wonderfully descriptive motorcycle magazines that I had read with unbounded enthusiasm for the past 14 years.

In my imagination I had ridden many a race here. I knew the names of the corners, the history of the races from the first in 1907, who the winners were and the make of motorcycles that they rode.

The time had come for me to ride a real race. If before I had been a little intoxicated by a vivid imagination, finishing in the position that suited my imagination, from today on it was reality and I was a very sober young man.

TT fortnight brought the island to life and was the beginning of two weeks of motorcycling mayhem.

We left the ferry and took a bus to Rose Villa, the hotel that had become the traditional TT home of the riders from the Commonwealth. Our hosts, Roy and Gladys Gilbert, gave us a warm welcome and showed us to our room, which was on the top floor and shared with John Hempleman.

Next was a visit to the garage, a large building that normally housed several buses but made available each year to the rider guests of Rose Villa. This year they would be Canadian Mike Duff, Australians Tom Phillis, Ron Miles and Trevor Pound, and fellow New Zealander Peter Pawson. Just as we arrived we met Tom Phillis, who was preparing to leave on a refresher lap of the circuit. He invited us to join him.

Tom pointed out some pitfalls that newcomers faced. Going too fast too soon, knowing where the slow corners are, as the track is made up of so many fast blind corners that a slow one can catch a newcomer out. If you become disoriented or at all confused, slow down until you recognise a familiar landmark and cautiously speed up again. Sit up during the early laps and treat them as a high-speed tour. Don't follow anyone who passes you going much faster — you'll be concentrating on him and not the circuit and learn little. At some stage he will suddenly rush into a corner you hadn't seen and you'll frighten yourself silly scraping around trying to miss a kerb, promptly forgetting most of what you have learned during that lap, if not for the whole practice session. Take note of areas where sun strike occurs during early morning and evening practice sessions, or where the track remains wet under trees, long after rain has stopped, or where an unseen kerb juts out.

As informed as I thought I was, I knew little more than five per cent of the corners. There were no straights, just corners leading into curves and curves into sweepers that took you into kinks, more fast blind corners and then a hidden tight bend. It seemed amazingly fast; most of the lap was ridden in third and top gear. How else could a rider with just 40bhp and 200kph available to him average speeds in excess of 140kph?

Through the towns there were kerbs, footpaths, concrete walls, houses built almost on the roadside, power and phone poles, banks, trees and wire fences. The sun could be shining at the start but rain could have fallen a few kilometres up the road or anywhere else. A blanket of fog frequently lay over the high country, bringing vision down to 20 metres.

That was quite enough information to digest. I began to feel like an adult, going back to a place he had enjoyed as a child. A lot seemed familiar but so much was not.

Finally, on Friday afternoon, the Nortons and spares boxes arrived. Happily, we set off balancing the boxes on the seats as we pushed the bikes the 3km around Douglas Promenade from the ferry to the garage. What a relief it was to start making progress towards getting out on the track. We intended to do the first practice session on the 500 and hoped that the notification from Bill White, giving Norton Motors instructions to supply spares, would arrive in time to rebuild the 350cc engine and use it for practice, while I overhauled the 500cc engine.

We quickly stripped the loosely assembled 350 engine and Gordon ran off to the Norton service department to fit a new big-end bearing that we had bought when we first arrived in the UK. I went to the office of the Auto-Cycle Union to sign on, have my riding gear checked and collect my race numbers.

Mr Cornwall, who had been very helpful when I called at the London office of the ACU soon after our arrival in April, welcomed me with a warm smile and congratulations on my success so far. Once he'd sorted through the paperwork he checked my helmet. "I'm very sorry, Hugh, but we can't allow you to use this here. I appreciate that you have had the strapping repaired, but it's so old the padding has collapsed and the shell is cracked. Look," he said, showing me the defects I was well aware of but had hoped would be overlooked.

Obviously, the disappointed look on my face affected him. "I'm very sorry, Hugh, but I have no option. Please, for your own protection, buy a new one." He placed the battered old thing under the counter. I picked up my gear bag, struggled to thank the well-intentioned man and set off on the long walk back to the garage. There was no need for a pen and paper to work out my financial position. It was just 15 pounds, including all the small change, less the price of a helmet at five pounds 10 shillings. Hopefully Gordon had more than me. Finances were going to be tight. Breakfast and dinner were supplied by the hotel. We had to buy our own lunches but were often too busy to bother so we could do without them, wash our own laundry and hope no other unexpected expenses arose.

Needing to get out on the track as soon as possible, I started to prepare the 500 for the first practice session, being held late tomorrow evening. Gordon returned with the new bearing fitted to the 350 flywheels so we reassembled the lower half of the engine and, together with the gearbox, refitted them into the frame. I carried on preparing the 500 while Gordon thoroughly cleaned and laid out the remaining 350 engine parts on paper ready for reassembly when we could get more parts from Norton Motors.

That evening Hempo offered to take me around the track so I joined him with a pen and exercise book. This was an opportunity to create written race notes in a form that I could study and learn from.

Without transport there was no other way. Not for me the 100 laps and 14-day study many riders boasted having done on a road bike before official practice began. I felt fortunate to have been given the opportunity to cover just three laps of the 61km course and actually be on the island for three days before practice began.

John drove slowly, relating in detail where he positioned himself for Bray Hill, where he braked and which gear he used and the lines he took on every corner, what to avoid, to know where the slow corners were and to make haste slowly. He also pointed out landmarks from which it was safe to ride flat-out until arriving at a large tree, a big house, a protruding power pole, a gate entrance and so on, but don't try it on your first few laps. Sit up and just roll the throttle off and on and leave the brakes alone. There are so many minor curves and kinks that appear major turns, but as you approach them they open up and can be ignored, but only if you know them.

That took us three hours and the exercise book was more than half full. Those notes were my key to unlocking the mind-boggling complexities of this ultimate racing challenge. I stayed up late going over and over what I had written until finally I began to make sense of it. I made up tests to challenge my memory and by 2am I felt less tense. The short time available was going to be a problem, but thousands before me had learned it, so why couldn't I?

Early on Saturday evening we rode the Norton up to the race paddock, with me sitting on the petrol tank and Gordon clinging on tight, carrying a few spanners. We weren't going to be late for the most important appointment of my life. Avon checked our tyre pressures and Reynolds riveted the joining links on the chains before we moved into the machine examination bay where all the bikes were carefully checked before gaining access to the track. This pre-practice procedure was followed all week. We then joined the queue of riders waiting to start their first practice lap for the 1960 Isle of Man TT races.

In 1949 and again in 1950 I'd seen photographs taken, during early morning practice, of New Zealander Sid Jensen walking out onto the circuit. Each time he had been pushing a new AJS 7R and how grand it had looked in the early light. I would read those magazine articles time and again, while taking in every detail. Now, on a well-used and rather tired Manx Norton, it was my turn. With a rather confusing mixture of apprehension and excitement, I waited my turn.

I ran a few paces, released the clutch lever, it fired up instantly, and as I swung into the saddle and opened the throttle I felt a strong sense of the rightness of it. To at last be on the circuit that had made up the driving force of my ambitions since I was just 10 years old. Finally, it was my privilege to hear, for the first time, the deafening exhaust echoing off the roadside houses as I sped off, towards Bray Hill, at the beginning of my first lap.

Keeping my speed down to a steady 130–140ks, I approached Bray Hill, where the road suddenly disappeared and a distant horizon is all that is visible. From the time of my first road race four years ago, at Te Puna near Tauranga, I had disliked travelling at speed over the blind brows of hills. I knew the road curved slightly to the left, but how much? I leaned a little in that direction but then, with confidence wavering, leaned a little to the right and, wham, the road and rows of houses suddenly reappeared. With relief I bounced my way down the steep, bumpy incline, hitting the bottom with an unexpected jolt, and travelled cautiously towards Quarter Bridge.

I cruised along, concentrating on each corner as it appeared. Being able to use the entire road allowed me to see much farther around or into them, giving a quite different view to that from a vehicle, using only the left-hand side, when the roads are open to the public. Riding these historic miles for the first time was precious to me, and after completing that lap, the serious business of learning began. The advice of Tom Phillis and Hempo was not discarded. The higher speed of my second lap helped me place the order of towns and groupings of corners more realistically than was possible from a slow-moving van. This gave me a clearer understanding of what my notes related to and a 29-minute, 77mph (125kph) lap was okay under the circumstances. Actually, I was over the moon; I'd done two laps of the magic isle, and for a fleeting few hours I enjoyed that experience. The reality of learning the course, the lack of money and the major task of rebuilding and preparing the bikes had been forgotten about.

I woke early on Sunday morning and, as usual, thought through the activities of the previous day. The circuit was my main concern. In places it was very bumpy. I couldn't see most of the holes and bumps and when concentrating hard on where I was on the track, without warning, whack, you could catch a good one. It was disconcerting to say the least, and worse than any other circuit I had ridden on. Never mind that, I thought. It's out of bed. I've got nearly three hours' solitude in the empty lounge before breakfast. To try to learn the 37.7 miles all at once was too great a hurdle, so to make the task more manageable I split the lap into several sections, bracketed between slow corners. Painstakingly, I worked through them, here and there rewriting and adding new information. Writing and rewriting certainly helped me memorise the detail, as all school teachers know only too well. (I am staying with miles here in the island, as it fits with the history of it. The word 'kilometre' seems out of context, at least to me it does.)

By the time the guests began to come downstairs for breakfast and distract me, I felt conversant with the first seven miles out as far as Kirkmichael. During the day we cleaned and checked the 500 ready for the early start on Monday morning. We were able to do little more to the 350 and decided to send a telegram to Bill White informing him of our plight and for him to notify Norton Motors at the earliest. Late in the afternoon I slipped away to our bedroom and continued working on what had become my pace notes; just like an actor, learning the script. By chance and circumstance Hempo had allowed me to learn not only the sequence of bends but also the braking points, optimum gear for each corner, the engine revs to use and the approximate entry points. This information virtually gave me the cornering lines to use, and with that I buried my head more deeply in the huge task.

After dinner I went up to our bedroom to continue my 'study'. Hempo and Gordon were ready for bed at 10.30pm so I used a chair in the neighbour's room until midnight when they arrived back from a good time in a local pub.

Roy Gilbert, our host, banged on our door a few hours later. All three of us slid reluctantly from our beds, splashed our faces with cold water and made our way downstairs. It was first light and practice began at 4.45am. We needed a good hour to have our cup of tea and toast, ride up to the start, have the tyres and chains checked, and then pass through scrutineering before joining the queue waiting for our turn to push off. By then it was full daylight, a pleasant calm morning with clear skies. Now was the time to put into practice the results of my hours of study.

Off towards Bray Hill. Man, it was a weird feeling cresting the top of this notorious rise. Now that I had a better understanding of the sequence of the corners for the first half of the lap, things flowed quite well and tensions eased, allowing me more fluency, but no lack of concentration. My knowledge of the area from Sulby Bridge to Ramsey needed to be improved, however as there were less blind bends to worry about, I thought my speed over the mountain was okay.

I gave the Manx full throttle leaving Governor's Bridge at the end of the lap. With my chin on the tank I rushed through the start-finish area flat-out, and why not? But I sat up and closed the throttle well before the brow of that dreaded Bray Hill.

The Union Mills sequence of corners fell into place and then after sitting up and closing the throttle through the terribly fast 120mph Glen Vine right-hander, I continued carefully through the flat-out section to Greeba Castle. Here I was able to take the first two lefts followed by two right-handers in two steady sweeps, a thrilling experience. I began to feel that my judgement of speed, angle of lean and understanding of the corner sequences learned from my notes was working and I was riding a steady smooth passage through the Laurel Bank and Glen Helen areas and on to Kirkmichael.

I rode on, allowing my knowledge to dictate my speed in an attempt to maintain that flow. It worked well until I mistook Kerramoor for Glentramman. The first is a slow, blind, just-over-a-rise, second-gear left and right while the second is a fast third-gear left and sweeping right. I crested the rise a good 50kph too fast and had to hit the brakes as hard as I ever had in my life. Then I bullied the barely controllable bike to the left, hit the wall a hard glancing blow with the handlebar and my right shoulder and finally came to rest at the entry to the right-hand corner breathing heavily. The engine had stalled and was still in third gear, a very untidy experience, but I guessed that is why this area is always swarming with spectators. Now feeling very wide awake, I carried on to the start-finish and began my third lap, but disaster struck just five miles out.

With a terrible rattle the engine lost all power. I coasted to a stop feeling a little sick. When the roads were opened a policeman picked me up in his car and took me to our garage. I borrowed Tom's van and brought the bike back to the garage. Hurriedly dismantling the 500cc engine we found the exhaust valve had broken, badly damaging the piston and the cylinder head.

I had no need for any breakfast; food did not appeal. I sat on a tin beside the bike swamped by self-pity. That the average speeds of the two laps I had completed were 83.5mph and 85.2mph, despite clouting the wall, didn't help my mood. The reward was two broken bikes, no money and time fast running out. I had only four days to get a bike going and qualify. If that didn't happen I'd be denied a start, would not receive the 120 pounds team payment from the British ACU, and would be unable to pay our hotel bill. That would look just great in the papers back home! "A promising young rider, selected to represent his country and expected to do well, failed to qualify." Say no more. Even if I got one of the Nortons going it would hardly be at its best; add in the few laps' practice I'd get and any chance of making a respectable debut was zero.

With unbounded enthusiasm I had dreamt of being here, but in reality it had the makings of a nightmare.

By the time Gordon returned after breakfast I'd stripped the head and he set off on a borrowed bicycle to Norton Motors for a valve seat insert. They didn't have one but phoned the factory in Birmingham to send one over. Then, unbelievably, help suddenly was at hand. At midday, just when I felt I should remove my leathers and get cleaned up, a chap came into the garage asking after me. I answered him rather wearily, thinking, "What else could have gone wrong?" "I'm Jim Boughen," he said, "from the AMC race depot where I've just finished a new AJS 7R for you. It's ready to collect."

My feeling of relief and amazement was so strong it rendered me speechless. I stood there dumbfounded while Jim began repeating himself thinking I hadn't heard or understood him. Percy Coleman's efforts had borne fruit and I was the benefactor.

What good luck. If Percy has this much faith in me, I will never let him down. These thoughts would become my mantra over the next few days. Whenever more energy and effort were required, I would repeat it over and over again.

We set off to collect the 350cc 7R. I sat on the crossbar of our borrowed bike and Gordon pedalled, as he liked to be in charge. Jim Boughen, the race shop foreman, who was to become a lifelong friend, was amused by our novel mode of transport, then went through the various details that he felt I should be made aware of regarding the new bike. After buying a new helmet and a fairing for the 7R, I had just five pounds left in my pocket.

Tuesday passed quickly as we mounted the fairing to the AJS, a time-consuming job, and had new tyres fitted on all four wheels of the Nortons and the brakes relined by Ferodo. Obviously, the Nortons needed to be made as race ready as possible, so we could begin building two engines the minute we had the okay to access the parts required. Now that we had the 7R we only had to have the 500 ready for Friday's Senior TT. The AJS was ready for Tuesday evening's practice, but I was loathe to go out on it until I'd spoken to Percy, partly to thank him, but also to establish what he expected of me and have a general chat about the rest of practice week to make sure we were thinking on similar lines. It was his bike, so I wanted him involved.

On Wednesday evening I decided to practise on the 7R, as I had no idea of Percy's whereabouts and time was running out. Then, quite like Syd Jensen had done 11 years before, I pushed a brand spanking new AJS 7R out onto the start line — another special moment. I rode off steadily and noticed immediately that it gave quite a different ride to a Norton. It was much lighter and reacted more to the road surface, was decidedly twitchy and very much alive. It turned into corners faster, the brakes were savage and the suspension seemed oversprung with insufficient hydraulic dampening, so I carried out a steady lap to become accustomed to it. The engine was reluctant to rev over 7500, when its limit was 7800–8000rpm, but I completed three laps, learned more about the circuit and enjoyed the bike sufficiently to cover the third lap at 86.3mph, my fastest lap so far.

Percy called after we had returned to the garage. We were pleased to meet up again and he felt that the 86mph lap first time out was excellent. He wasn't happy regarding the unwillingness of the engine to rev out freely and advised us to return it to the factory depot. On Thursday a factory mechanic fitted new valve springs, suspected of causing the poor engine performance, while Gordon and I removed the wheels and had the Dunlop race tyres replaced with Avons. The Dunlops had a different feel to the Avons that I had always used, then while out again on Friday morning the gearbox began giving trouble. I managed to carry on at a reduced pace.

As I left Parliament Square, Ramsey, I sensed a strange feeling in my stomach. It was difficult to diagnose when riding fast but it persisted. Jeez, I needed a Jimmy Riddle, can you believe it? Here I am lapping the Isle of Man and have to stop for a pee. That's unheard of, surely. Having no option, I stopped on the Mountain Mile, leaning the 7R on a post and hurriedly fumbled with a reluctant zip. I felt a little foolish as the riders waved out as they raced on up the mountain. After practice we returned the bike once more to the factory workshop where they stripped the gearbox, but were unable to find the fault.

After lunch Jack Williams, the race shop manager and arguably the most accomplished engine development engineer in the UK at the time, used the factory transporter to take the bike, Percy and me out to Jurby, an emergency air field that riders were allowed to use for test purposes. Jack remounted the carburettor and altered various settings. This helped a little but the engine still showed a reluctance to rev. The gearbox was still giving bother so Jack took the 7R back to the race depot to fit a new one and recheck the engine.

The valve insert for the 500 Norton had arrived, so we took it to the engineering shop, which fitted it that day. Then another disaster occurred. The chap assigned to cut the valve insert at the correct angle relative to the valve, cut it at quite the wrong angle and completely ruined the head. Surprisingly, they still wanted me to pay for their work, so I gave the head back to them and walked out. The cost of a new cylinder head virtually equalled our 17-night stay at Rose Villa. I guess we will get to the end of our strife sometime, I thought.

Late on Saturday morning we called at the AJS race depot. Jim had been working on Percy's bike. A new gearbox had been fitted and he had found the ignition timing to be two and a half degrees too far advanced and that hopefully was the reason for its poor performance. My spirits were lifted considerably and the weather was good, so I planned to do four laps during the final practice session that evening.

Now was the time to put into effect my mantra of "This man has faith in me, I will never let him down."

A chap from Perth, in Western Australia, loaned me his BSA road bike to do a refresher lap and once more check that my much updated pace notes were absolutely correct and I had every detail committed to memory. Having circulated this complicated track with its over 250 corners just eight times, I had no right to think I could cover four fast, mistake-free laps but, believe me, I intended to give it my best shot.

I rode out to Ballacraine checking my markers and lines all the way. Then, sitting on the parked BSA, I mentally returned to the start and came forward visualising the road clearly in every detail. I didn't feel totally clear regarding two areas, so I rode back, checked them out and then felt secure. In this way I made slow progress around the circuit and it was four hours before I returned to the garage. Gordon had become concerned and the owner of the BSA a little agitated wondering how many times I had thrashed his BSA around the course. He was relieved to find it had only been one slow lap!

As I wriggled into my black leathers for the final practice session on Saturday evening, June 11, I had no idea what my lap times would be. I did, however, have a strategy based on maximum concentration and commitment. Speed would not be based on aggression but rather the application of hours of learning my race notes. I felt I was near the crest of a mountain, with the challenge to avoid falling off and still reach my absolute full potential. Percy's involvement demanded no less; he may not expect it but I knew he would appreciate it.

Watching the Shell fuel attendant pour 18 litres of 100 octane petrol into the tank and knowing I was going to use all of it in one run gave a strange feeling in my gut. If all went to plan I would be riding at race pace for nearly two hours. I knew the 7R would go well, there were no blanks in my circuit knowledge and at long last I felt a semblance of confidence returning. I tried hard not to break into an idiotic grin or shout out. That sort of thing was not done here, old chap, so keep it bottled up.

Later I was to learn that my best lap in this session, at a 93.3mph average speed, probably made me the 12th fastest rider, on a 350cc British machine, in TT history. In doing so, I also set the fastest lap of that session.

I'd scaled my mountain and here's how I did it.

Lap One, 25.15min, 89.3mph: To start with I tried to keep it smooth and gain a competent sweeping flow. Greeba Castle was the first test as I used third gear for the first time but surprisingly each corner fell into place and it felt good through to Glen Helen. Then I gripped the tank tightly with my knees, guiding the bike more with my body than the handlebars as I motored hard up bumpy, twisting Creg Willey's Hill. It worked well, the front wheel felt much steadier and I kept away from roadside banks. Flat-out down to the 11th Milestone, nailed through the first two rights, I eased off for the third, then back to third gear and through the blind left with room to spare. I snaked through the S-bend at Handley's Corner and managed the first sequence of Barregarroo well. Up into fourth gear, speeding down to the second part of Barregarroo known as the dreaded 'Hole in the Wall', I sat up and eased the throttle, taking a deep breath and diving through. It's okay, it's okay, you can do it, I told myself.

Placing my chin on the tank I headed for the 13th Milestone. A quick look at the rev counter showed 8000rpm so I sat up to use wind pressure to hold the revs back without releasing the throttle.

The 7R was going brilliantly and now it was into the fast third gear, long right and left that follows. Now when I got a series of corners reasonably right it was feeling fantastic. There were no bumps, no physical tightening up, taking perhaps three right-hand corners in one long sweep, then picking it up and doing the same again around a couple of lefts. Sheer exhilaration. Up and over the Ballaugh Bridge jump, I experienced a brief floating peace as both wheels left the ground, and then it was back to work. After Ramsey I tried hard to find the best way through the series of bends at the Water Works made up of three rights, a long bumpy left, a very bumpy right taken flat-out in third, back to second for a left, and on to the Gooseneck.

It was a case of position the bike well, then guide it more with my knees through these incredibly rough sections and relax my steel-like grip on the handlebars. It can be surprising if you allow the bike to find its way and don't force it. At times a major question of faith is called for, but it seems to work. Now if I could learn to breathe at the same time, real progress could be made. I swept past the Mountain Box in third gear with room to spare, then the Black Hut and on to the four rights that make up the Verandah, supposedly taken flat-out in third. This is where the road carves its way around the side of the mountain. The outer verge is marked by a straggly wire fence with unprotected posts above a sheer drop into a deep valley. It's the kind of challenge that makes you wish you'd paid more attention at school and qualified for some cushy, boring number at a bank or in an accountancy office.

The sequences of instructions for a 7R are: Flat-out in third at 100–110mph, ignore first right, take second right in the middle of the road, third right will fall into place, last right okay. 'Yeah, right.' The Bungalow was fine. Being able to see the road ahead allows you to relax for a whole 60 seconds before rushing into Brandywell and on to the very difficult three lefts of the 32nd Milestone. Doing the first well and then having the confidence to drift out wide to place yourself in the best position to take the two following lefts as one, doesn't come after just eight laps of practice. Sounds good, if you read this slowly, but I was supposed to be in top gear. So I shut off and went back to third, moved about to get that crucial line, lean and speed trio right, then braked for Windy Corner. From there it was just a matter of trying to do everything neatly while anticipating what was coming up next and relax into the riding of it all.

Lap Two, 24.45min, 91.4mph: Through the start flat-out and on to that Hill, I sat up before the brow and once more guessed the angle of lean required to go through the curve. Seeing only empty sky for a split second then there it was and I was placed just about right, so I nailed it all the way down for the first time. When I hit the bottom, the suspension flattened, the impact jolting both my eyes shut. Wow, yet another surprise as I bounced along the narrow road at near maximum speed.

This lap I wanted to capitalise on what I had learned during the first. I now knew what needed to be changed on every corner; the clever bit was making those changes. I went much faster through Union Mills than I thought possible. Then an odd thing happened. It seemed the faster I rode, the easier it became.

Up until now I had been leaning the 7R over too far, relative to the modest speed I had been travelling at. This had caused me to waver a little with uncertainty through most places, but now it was beginning to feel natural.

Greeba Castle went very well, with me changing back up into top gear before the last right-hander. Unbelievable. Yet it felt perfectly okay.

I tried to control my instincts to go ever faster. I'm fortunate in having alarm bells that ring, too early at times, and too often at others, and on occasion they remain silent. Here I'll reluctantly admit to having had a few frights, followed a few seconds later by a nervous tingle that rattles up my spine. Yet when it's more than a slight misjudgement but a real problem, there is no emotion at all. I just calmly go through all the procedures I know — there is no spine tingle — and so far it has worked.

I had decided to enter the top-gear right-hand corner at the entrance to Quarry Bends a little wider to give myself more room, as I had been brushing the cottage wall with my shoulder. The approach was perfect. I peeled off a foot outside my previous entry point but hit a savage bump that I'd never seen and it threw me wide. I changed back to third gear, laid the bike over as far as I dared with the outside kerb just three feet away. I tried to use a little rear brake but the back wheel slid so I eased off and it came back. In a flash, the exhaust pipe scraped the road and the footpath seemed to rear up at me. Just as I braced for a jarring thump of tyres on the concrete verge and all that would follow, the kerb turned away from me as it followed the curve of the left-hander exiting Quarry. Now riding straight at an eight-foot-high concrete retaining wall, I lifted the 7R upright and braked as hard as possible. I managed to turn the bike to the left a little, giving me a few more precious yards and finally came to a stop, once more against a wall. This time I had kept the engine running, found first gear and, after letting some rider pass, carried on. I had been too busy to notice the spine tingle.

The fact that this wasn't a mistake helped my battered confidence but beware of making a late entry, unless you've previously tried it at a modest pace. For the rest of the lap I was happy just to tidy up my lines through some of the most difficult areas and stifle the strong urge to try new ones.

Lap Three, 24.36min, 91.9mph: Now I was getting into a groove with just a few changes to be made. Rhencullen could be taken faster as could Milntown Cottage and the corners preceding it were all so fast, top-gear flat-out, some said, but I'd been happy with half throttle and changing back to third as I accelerated away towards School House Corner. We'd had a couple of 'moments' so steady up and concentrate on being smooth, safe and secure, and positioning yourself correctly, I told myself. This place demands that you do strange things, such as enter left-hand corners on the left-hand side of the road to position yourself for the unseen right that follows. Then stay in the middle of the next right that is followed by another right and then a left. It's a wonderful feeling when it all falls into place though.

Lap Four, 24.15min, 93.3mph: As I roared through the start the 7R no longer felt like a stranger. I had become accustomed to its sometimes apparently wayward behaviour. Really it was just a different motorcycle to ride and, once understood, it was allowing me to get through sequences of corners faster than I had anticipated.

One lap to go for the day. This was not the time to leave anything in the garage, without need for heroics, avoiding haste, but do everything as well as I now knew I could.

Flat-out down Bray, a piece of cake now. Brake later for Quarter Bridge and still gain a fast exit. The same at Bradden. Union Mills entry is breathtakingly fast but there is still room at the kerb's edge. Flat on the tank in top gear around Glen Vine and stay on the tank all the way to Greeba Castle. Brake later and go in faster than ever before. The corners were falling into place, two lefts and a right melted into two lazy sweeps then back into top gear.

An absolutely magic feeling enveloped me. I felt that I'd unlocked the door to the combination of tyre adhesion, speed, judgement, knowledge and confidence. Minor errors no longer inhibited me and progress was swift. Whilst very demanding mentally, physically it was almost effortless. Then I caught two slower riders approaching the humpback jump at Ballaugh Bridge. I passed one and lined up the second, who braked early but unexpectedly accelerated again. I was caught in no-man's land braking hard He took the middle of the bridge where the rise is less pronounced. I was forced to the left that rose at a much steeper angle. I got serious altitude, a very heavy landing ensued and a few nasty wobbles followed. I missed the house jutting out on my left and roared on. As I neared peak revs in third gear and prepared to change into top, I checked the rev counter. It had disappeared. I changed up anyway and then took time out to see if it had fallen into the fairing where it could jam the steering. No, it was still in its purpose-built bracket clamped to the front fairing support tube but due to the nasty jolt on landing it had slipped around and it was now hanging directly below the tube. If I got my head in the right position I could just manage to see the dial numbers from 7000rpm to 9000rpm, so that was okay.

Next challenge was Milntown Cottage. The fast guys say it's flat-out on a 500 so worth a shot on a 350. I had been practising my lines on this section, as it's bumpy as! On my earlier laps through here and several other rough spots, my vision had become blurred. I could still make out the walls and hedges but the position of the roadside kerbs wasn't always clear. Now it seemed they had adjusted to the situation and almost normal clarity had returned. So it was down the bumpy straight in top gear, chin on the tank pad, then sit up and go into an equally rough right-hander, exiting as far to the right as possible to be prepared for a left-hander, go through it and keep as far to the left as possible ready for the next right, which is the most important corner of that series. It was a struggle throwing the 7R from side to side, especially timing the entry for that last right. Phew, but there was room outside me, so it was back down on the tank. The front wheel lifted off the ground over a hump. I've not noticed that before so maybe I'm getting on the pace, I thought. School House was also bumpy and I needed to be faster, but I was very cautious of changing my lines now so I went into it faster and used the concreted 3m-wide bus stop on the exit. It was there, so why not use it?

Making good time through the difficult bumpy series of corners above the Water Works was very satisfying and then I was up on the mountain. Finally I had the confidence to get around the Verandah and the 32nd flat-out. The extremely fast 33rd had been a temptation — the road is very wide and the right line a little vague. Many experienced riders claimed it was easy to take it flat-out on a 350. I felt sufficiently confident to give it a go.

All tucked in with chin on the tank and toes on the footrests, I rushed into it. Immediately the rear tyre let go in a gentle slide. Not having forgotten John Anderson's advice given at my first ever road race, I lifted my head a little and ever so gently eased the throttle. As John said it would all those years ago, the tyre delicately reattached itself to the tarmac and all was okay. Talk about living on the edge.

After all that excitement, I entered the long slowish left of Keppel Gate much faster than before and felt both wheels squirming and moving. Careful now, laddie! Then I rode off to Kate's Cottage. Jeez, that place is bumpy, but it is taken flat-out. The next corner of interest was Hillberry, a case of get up real close, sit up, brake a little down to third gear and aim at a shrub farther up the road on the right to line up the long left of Cronk-Ny-Mona. Here you take three corners flat-out in a long sweep that feels very satisfying. All the rest are fairly slow and easily done and it was back to the start.

With a mixture of relief and satisfaction I closed the throttle, braked to a standstill and became stunned by the silence. After an hour and 40 minutes' riding, I felt a little strange. The demands of concentration had left me mentally drained and, with all the noise, almost deaf. There seemed no need to hurry back to the pits, so I took a little time to gather myself, regain my feet and push the silent 7R back along the narrow fenced path to the paddock.

No one was there to meet me, so I leaned the 7R against the fence, removed my helmet and gloves and bludged a cigarette off a bystander. I know these are not good for you but I'm quite sure that one did me no harm at all. The aluminium fins were pinging as the heat of 150 miles slowly dissipated. I was surprised to find the petrol tank had dents on both sides of its cutaways where my knees had hit it during that nasty landing at Ballaugh. I wonder how I'll explain that, I thought.

Hempo came running up in a highly animated state. "Did that feel fast?" he asked.

"What?" I replied.

"That last lap," he said.

Every lap I'd done here had seemed fast, so I said, "Well, yeah, I guess so."

My favourite section, Ballaugh Bridge, a second or two of floating peace. Archives.

Then he shouted, "You just went round faster than I have on a 500."

John had ridden here on four occasions so knew it well. As I was acting, feeling and, I suspect, looking rather dopey, John said: "Nah, you couldn't have gone that fast, it must have been a timekeeper's mistake."

Actually, I wasn't bothered what the lap time was. I'd done my best, experienced dozens of special moments, had completed four laps on a great little bike, qualified for the races and, most importantly, would be paid the 120 pounds expenses that would cover my costs until the next meeting!

Percy, Mick and Gordon arrived. Percy had a smile from ear to ear. "Well done, Hugh, great ride," he said as he shook my hand.

Then John Dale, the New Zealand Matchless importer, came up. "Hugh, you were going much too fast for your first time," said the conservative John. "You haven't been here long enough, you haven't done enough laps, and you're far too inexperienced to be safe at the speeds you're travelling at." Then they all started talking to each other, which suited me.

Percy broke away from the group, came over and said, "Don't listen to them, Hugh. I saw you go through Hillberry where you looked perfectly safe. I'm going off to insure the bike and will see you later." Perhaps the wise man knew more about my near bingles than I thought. Team manager Mick Vinson was looking rather serious and uncomfortable. Three New Zealanders had been killed in Europe during the past five years and others had suffered serious injuries. He didn't want to be associated with more.

No one had told me what the lap time causing so much fuss was, so I asked.

Almost in unison they said 24.15, which was 93.3mph. I'd succeeded. That lap time could not only be repeated, lap after lap, but improved on. For the first time since my Norton broke down I felt satisfied with what I'd done. The official practice lap times for that evening session were finally posted on the notice board.

International Junior 350cc: H R Anderson AJS 24.15.2, G Hocking MV Agusta 24.22.6, A Shepherd AJS 24.37.6, Tom Phillis Norton 24.55.0, L Carr AJS 24.55.2, R N Brown Norton 24.55.6.

The fastest five riders in that class during practice week were: John Surtees at 97.5 and John Hartle at 96.19 on MV Agustas, Bob McIntyre at 94.4, Mike Hailwood at 93.6, and Hugh Anderson at 93.3mph.

Tiring of the well-intentioned banter, we returned to the hotel and a much needed meal. While eating we were frequently interrupted by resident riders, mechanics and guests to compliment and discuss the surprising progress I had made. I was starting to become something of a focal point. Having benefited so much from the help that Percy gave and the results I had gained, I now knew much more about myself and the abilities I possessed. Perhaps it is only when you come under extreme pressure do you learn what you are actually capable of.

First thing on Monday morning we finally had a phone call from the Norton spares manager to tell us they had received confirmation from Bill White to supply me with parts. Hempo took us to the depot where I handed over the flywheels of the 500 to have a new big-end bearing fitted and also collected a new cylinder head, two valves, an exhaust cam, piston and the parts required to reassemble the 350. Finally, the difficult, time-consuming rebuild could begin.

The machine examination for the 350cc class began at 10am on Tuesday morning. Peter Pawson and I, in our pressed grey pants, tie and blazer with the fern leaf emblem on the pocket, complete with our immaculate AJS 7R racers, presented ourselves to the scrutineers. After coping with the hard work, long hours and demands of practice and final machine preparation, this was a cheery, chatty, leg-pulling, carefree moment. Autograph hunters leant over the picket fence pleading for riders to sign their books. Avon inflated the tyres to the correct pressures, Reynolds checked all the chain links had been riveted, Shell filled our petrol and oil tanks and the machine examiners carefully went over the race machines.

Tradition has it that they are then locked away under guard in a large marquee until 10am the next day. Riders regain access to them just one hour before the start of the race. The officials were sympathetic, helpful and considerate. God, what a wonderful experience it was to be here.

We worked on the Norton all Tuesday afternoon through to 2am on Wednesday. Being seriously occupied we forgot that the hotel locked its doors at midnight so we made ourselves as comfortable as possible in the garage. Not the best way to prepare for a 226.73-mile race of endurance that would take up to two and a half hours later that day.

We were up and about at 6am. While Gordon worked on the Norton I rode a refresher lap on my new Aussie mate's BSA. So much had happened in such a short time I needed the reassurance, self-belief perhaps, that this lap would give me. I enjoyed it. My memory proved to be spot on and left me feeling both exhilarated and relaxed.

Due to the lack of time and, under the circumstances, difficulty in concentrating on the technical complications of carrying out the valve timing and final assembly of the 500cc Norton cambox, we pushed it down to the Norton race depot with the understanding that we could collect it following the 350cc race.

As always before a race, I ate a big breakfast. Hempo took us up to the start. At exactly 10am the scream of a siren and the release of the side flaps of the marquee indicated we were free to collect our bikes. Those who had further work to carry out rushed in to retrieve their mounts, while we patiently waited our turn before collecting Percy's shining AJS. Thirty minutes before the start the siren screamed a second time, indicating riders could start engines. Within a few minutes there was an extraordinary cacophony of sound as 100 bikes, in a confined space and all with open megaphones, began to warm up. Ten minutes before the start, the 'Stop engines' sign was displayed. The spark plugs used to start the motors were changed for those to be used in the race and we all moved out onto Glencrutchery Road to take up our positions, forming up in pairs ready to start at 10-second intervals.

The starting positions of the fastest 15 riders were drawn from a hat, the remainder seeded as to their performances before the TT. Being number 74 meant I would be one of the last to start. Tensions rose as the second hand of the large clock, stationed at the start, moved slowly around the dial for the last time. It reached 11am, a large firework went off and the great, multi world champion Geoff Duke dropped the flag and Bob McIntyre pushed off alone, as Gary Hocking, MV Agusta, was a nonstarter. Next were Australian Bob Brown, and John Surtees, who *The Motor Cycle* magazine had described as the greatest rider in history. Slowly the field moved off and eventually it was my turn to start this great race.

Having agreed to ride the first lap at a 'steady' pace and then see what happens had eliminated all pressure and left me feeling surprisingly relaxed. I beat my starting partner away, rode off flat-out in top gear towards Bray Hill and calmly roared down to the right-hand curve at the bottom and bounced my way along the undulating road to first-gear Quarter Bridge. I was careful here as, being the first slow corner after the start and everyone with full fuel tanks, heavy braking could force petrol out through an overflow pipe and onto the road causing slides and spills. At Braddan Bridge I passed the two riders who had started 10 seconds before me. Then after Union Mills, on the long flat-out ride to Greeba Castle, I passed four more.

Overtaking on the TT circuit can be difficult, due to the never-ending corners. Having so little experience only added to the problem. But I was enjoying it, absolutely.

I was surprised how early one chap braked for a corner. Another had used very strange lines and yet another I actually brushed against, when he seemed to be having difficulty changing gear. This put me way off line for the following right-hand corner, resulting in one of those buzz-up-the-backbone moments.

Approaching Signpost Corner, near the end of the first lap, the line of the road was clearly marked out by hundreds of spectators. They were sitting on or standing behind the walls that line the road for the next two miles to the bottom of Bray Hill, creating a colourful, clearly defined avenue to pass through. A situation that could be likened to a guard of honour as all the competitors who compete here earn a large badge named 'Respect'. This, among all motorcycle-racing enthusiasts, they retain for life.

Having completed the agreed-to 'steady' lap I could now try and repeat the 93mph practice lap. With the perfect line I plunged down Bray Hill and as the lap unfolded I entered a mental state where I felt truly at one with my machine and my ability to ride it to the limit. All too soon I came to the end of the lap and my pit stop. Gordon poured 10 litres of fuel into the tank and told me I was placed 13th at the end of the first lap. I removed my fly-splattered goggles and took the clean pair from his head. Just as I dismounted to push-start the 7R, South African Robert Duffield, who was helping us in our pit and had been busy with his stopwatch, called out, "You are now up to eighth or ninth." Gordon snapped the tank cap closed and I sped off to begin what could be four of the most significant laps I would ever make at this home of greatness. A place in the top six was beckoning.

Suddenly, everything changed. Soon after leaving Union Mills, and travelling uphill towards Glen Vine, the engine began to rattle as it reached 6800rpm in third gear. Christ, what's that? I thought, hastily changing into fourth. The engine became quiet again until the indicator needle edged around to 6800rpm and the noise began again. Bugger, a valve spring has broken, I decided.

My stomach became a hole of despair, but hang on: there are two special springs to each valve; if I keep the revs below 6800 I might still qualify for a finisher's award. By sitting up in top gear and keeping a careful eye on the rev counter I was able to proceed at a reasonable pace until reaching Bishopscourt. There the engine lost all power so I released the clutch and coasted to a stop on the footpath. Leaning the silent 7R against the wall, an array of emotions flooded over me as I removed my helmet and gloves.

Broken bloody valve springs! Terry's have been making them forever and still they break. No wonder they give them to you free of charge, they aren't worth anything, I thought. I considered that to be denied a top-six finish on my first visit here had cost me recognition, credibility, respect and an opportunity to gain entries at more major events with better start money. Then there was the concern of how much damage had been done, and how would Percy feel?

I was jolted out of my misery by a voice from behind the wall. "What happened?" asked a well-dressed man.

"I think a valve spring has broken," I replied.

"What bad luck, and you were having such a good ride. Would you care to join us for lunch?" he asked. I was led through a gate into the beautifully kept grounds of a fine home. Some 20 family members and friends were seated at a large table on the lawn. With a sweep of his hand my host introduced me to the group who gathered here each year to enjoy the occasion. Bikes continued to roar past in ones and twos while a radio kept us informed of the race progress. Odd place this, I thought. One minute rushing around the most difficult course in the world living my dream, the next seated with a rather well-to-do group of strangers having lunch. The race commentator announced that "Number 74 Hugh Anderson from New Zealand has retired at Bishopscourt — rider okay". This caused some amusement and with that I relaxed and enjoyed yet another novel experience.

An older male member in the group clearly remembered the first TT held in 1907 when Rem Fowler won the twin-cylinder class on a Peugeot-engined Norton. I tried to hide my amazement but it seemed so long ago. Two world wars had been fought since then, a killer flu had travelled the world in 1918 and there had been a serious global depression. Meanwhile, motorcycles had developed from unreliable, skeletal-framed objects that appealed only to adventurers and eccentrics, to the fast, sophisticated, beautifully crafted machines of today. The knowledge of the TT races contained within the group was impressive, but what surprised me was the enthusiasm shown by the women present. They spoke with animation and authority about this sport that was dominated by men and mechanical things. Conversely, at that time, women in New Zealand seemed to think it was superior to claim to know nothing whatsoever about motorcycle racing, and felt that it was a foolish pastime. Understandably, I felt comfortable in their company, but was wise enough to say as little as possible. I may have been a font of knowledge at home in Ohinewai, but not here.

At race end, John Surtees, who was expected to win but had suffered gearbox problems, was led over the line by team-mate John Hartle. Bob McIntyre was next, then Derek Minter followed by Ralph Rensen in fifth. Ralph's fastest lap was 10 seconds slower than my best lap in practice. At the end of the second lap, before I retired, I had a lead of 12 seconds over him. Obviously, without the valve spring failure, fifth place had been a definite possibility. After thanking my generous and interesting hosts I rejoined the 7R, sat on the footpath beside it and waited for someone to collect me.

My thoughts returned to Percy. What would he say? Knowing a little about Percy's amazing youthful on and off the racetrack exploits, I felt sure he would understand my reluctance to stop.

I had not previously experienced a valve spring breakage and it seemed to me at the time that if I rode on carefully I might still qualify for a finisher's award. This was 'The Island'. To have turned a mental switch and stopped all the momentum that had been created, not just over the past 10 days, but also the build-up to this day, begun many years ago in childhood, and now when so much was promised, to have just closed the throttle and rolled to a stop. No. I couldn't have done that. Yes. Percy will understand.

It was late when I got back to the garage. Meanwhile Gordon had collected the 500 Norton from the factory depot and pushed it back. I removed my leathers and we began the final assembly and had it running late in the evening. Weigh-in for the 500cc class was at 10.30 the next morning ready for Friday's senior TT but the engine needed to be run in followed by a thorough check-over. I chose to pay the nominal penalty fee that allowed us to delay that formality until 10pm. Robert Duffield managed to borrow a van from one of his mates so we could take the Manx to Jurby airfield. We spent several hours there running in the engine and sorting out a few problems. By the time we left it was performing okay. Back at the garage we checked everything over yet again, gave it a final polish and rode it up to race control where it passed examination.

The 350cc Norton had to be made ready for Mallory Park for Sunday's post-TT meeting. There was still a lot to be done to it but at midnight we finally had it ready to run. I woke late on Friday morning feeling very flat. All the drama and late nights were taking their toll. The expected excitement of riding in my first Senior TT seemed to be missing. After breakfast Peter Pawson offered to give us a ride up to the start, but halfway there his van ran out of petrol. We pushed it to a petrol station, then the engine was reluctant to start. The tension rose and Peter, feeling the pressure, scorched off up to the paddock negotiating every corner on three wheels and screeching tyres. As we entered the vehicle park the siren screamed out and the bikes were available for collection.

Once more I started near the rear of the grid. When I had first ridden the 7R it had felt lively and unstable. Having grown accustomed to its ways, I now found the Norton felt clumsy, and the steering seemed slow with little feedback, as though the front tyre had lost pressure. By the time I reached Ballacraine I had become accustomed to the difference so rode on steadily with the aim of a top 20 finish. As in the 350 race, the more riders I passed the more optimistic I began to feel. Then towards the end of the second lap the engine emitted that all-too-familiar expensive rattle, lost all power and once more I coasted to a halt.

I pushed it two miles uphill back to the pits and found Gordon. We put our tool box on the tank and, with a strong sense of failure, pushed and coasted our silent way back to the garage. It was a relief to find that the problem lay in the cambox, so the Norton factory mechanics were responsible, not us. Gordon returned to London to pick up our van and meet us at Liverpool the following afternoon.

It was time to pack up. Even though their vans were heavily loaded, Tom Phillis and Jim Redman offered to take my boxes of spares, tyres and suitcases to Liverpool. Robert and I pushed the two bikes along the Douglas Promenade to the ferry. In a way, I was relieved to be leaving. The island challenge had been almost overpowering, the constant machine problems depressing and the late nights exhausting. I was looking forward to the future when my Nortons would be fast and reliable, the 7R repaired and available and the circuits relatively easy to learn. New adventures always raised my spirits.

Mrs Herbie and Leslie Quayle, with programmes in hand, peek from behind the door frame as I fly past, within two metres of them, at over 180kph.

CHAPTER 5
Lap records and world championship points

At the Mallory Park post-TT event, as we had at the French Grand Prix we took the only bike we had, in this case the 350cc Manx, through scrutineering then fitted the 500 fairing and had it examined at an alternative examination point. So popular were the 350cc and 500cc classes that 50 riders were eliminated from each during qualification. I qualified easily for the 350cc final but just managed to make the 500. My Manx wasn't the fastest taxi off the rank. I actually found the hustle and bustle of close-quarter competition at moderate speeds, compared to the island, invigorating.

A slipping clutch forced me out of the 350 final while I was holding a comfortable ninth place. With new clutch plates, stronger springs and the fairing from the 500 fitted I was ready for my next race, but competing against top riders on 500cc machines with a 350 was like taking a knife to a gunfight. That I was only there for the start money was forgotten — well, a flag had been dropped, hadn't it — and while holding 14th place I tried too hard entering Gerrards, a long never-ending 145kph right-hander with at least three changes of surface. Before I could think of World Speedway Champion Barry Briggs' famous words, "If in doubt, go flat-out", the front wheel slid away, the footrest dug in and I went down in a mass of arms, legs and motorcycle. The bashing and crashing went on for what seemed a long time before the bike hit an earth wall with a dull thud.

I lay there, my right leg trapped under it and my mouth and eyes full of dirt. Except for a decent-sized hole in my right calf muscle, I seemed to be okay. With friends we had met on the island, we drove down to London. Whatever happens when you are asleep? I woke up quite unable to get out of my sleeping bag. They thought I was joking at first but every limb I tried to move hurt like hell. With gritted teeth and help I managed to sit at the table, have a bite to eat and then left for the local hospital to have my leg cleaned up. The nurse was kind enough to arrange bandages, dressings and antibiotics to take with us. On Tuesday morning I saw a doctor about my very swollen left knee; he prescribed total rest.

Gordon and I then went to the AJS-Matchless race shop, our first visit. I entered hesitantly — you don't rush into what to me was hallowed ground, you wait at the door to be invited. These highly skilled men demand respect; riders come and go. The hopeful, the boastful, the light-fingered and the failures. They have seen them all. I am just another hopeful. The staff greeted us warmly. Unfortunately, Percy's 7R engine was quite badly damaged; the good thing was that my performance on the island had impressed them and I was welcome there.

Foreman Jim Boughen took me to one side. John Surtees had been trying to make contact with me regards joining Triumph factory tester Percy Tait to ride a Triumph Bonneville, entered by John's retail outlet, at the prestigious Thruxton 500-mile endurance race this coming Saturday. Jack Williams, the race shop manager and recognised as the leading development engineer in the UK at that time, invited me to use his phone. I spoke to chief mechanic Keith Arney and the arrangements he suggested were quite acceptable to me, so we drove directly to the Surtees shop.

Naturally, I had been pleased to have been accepted at the AJS-Matchless workshop. Now to have been recognised by no less than the great John Surtees as a rider of sufficient skill and character to represent his high-profile Motorcycle Agency was truly amazing. Had I really come so far in the nine weeks since we arrived? Suddenly, my shoulder, elbow and the hole in my leg were hardly noticeable and my knee no longer caused an exaggerated painful limp. Chief mechanic Keith Arney went through the bike with us. It looked great to me. Keith took it down from the work bench so I could try the riding position and placing of controls. A pointless exercise really, as I would have ridden it even if it had nails in the seat.

We were doing well, holding fifth place and second Triumph when during the third hour the primary chain broke. Of the 52 starters, several crashed including Bob McIntyre, Phil Read and Sammy Miller, and seven were taken to hospital; 26 finished. An AJS CSR won by a remarkable four laps, Triumphs were second and third, fourth a Norton, sixth a Matchless. All were 650s. The following week full-page advertisements were taken out in the two major magazines claiming an AJS CSR was "Undoubtedly, the fastest, safest and most reliable standard motorcycle built". The two positives from the event were I had met Keith Arney, who became a lifelong friend, and I was now fully conversant with the Thruxton circuit.

I took the advice of Tom Phillis and had my 500 engine checked out by Bill Stuart, who had been a mechanic in the Norton factory race team during the 1950s. Gordon and I used the time to very carefully go over both bikes ready for the International Commonwealth meeting at Thruxton on the 1st of August.

Meanwhile, on the other side of the world, Mum had sacked the farm manager and was doing the job herself, leaving Gordon no option but to fly home. His flight was paid for in New Zealand. We shared what little cash we had. I had entered three meetings on consecutive weekends: Thruxton; the Ulster Grand Prix in Dundrod, Northern Ireland; and the Leinster 200 in Southern Ireland. I arrived at Thruxton penniless, but I was there. Top English motorcycle journalist Les Wilson was to later write: "Dedicates like Hugh don't have to eat and don't worry about not rating a mention for elegance in the 'Taylor and Cutter'. When Hugh arrived at the Commonwealth meet he had had no breakfast. It had been that or petrol and petrol won."

Natural talent is the base on which you build. How you develop that base is your true ability. It is what you do with what you have.

If I were ever going to do well on an English short circuit and gain some credibility with the press and race organisers, this was the time. My main opposition would come from Tony Godfrey, Tom Phillis and Paddy Driver. Tony held the lap record and was one of the main contenders for the British championship. Tom had gained fourth place in the Senior TT and lapped just on 99mph. South African Paddy Driver always acquitted himself well, and Peter Pawson had done well here on previous occasions. On top of that stellar line-up there were 30 keen British riders, many of whom were on their home track.

Practice went well and as the races were only 10 laps, it was a matter of getting straight on the pace and hanging in there.

Tony led from the start of the 350cc race on his Norton, but I passed him on the second lap, pushing on as hard as I could. Just when I had begun to think I was going to win, Tom came slithering under me into the sweeper before the start-finish straight. I stayed in his slipstream, and we finished just a bike length apart. Paddy was third with Tony 50m back in fourth. Tom and I had jointly broken the brilliant Derek Minter's lap record. Okay so far.

As we pushed off at the start of the 500cc race the rider to my right lost his footing, fell against me and we both went down. With so little time to gain any kind of a result I was now in the right frame of mind to attack the pack! Initially, it looked like a solid wall of 30 black-leathered riders, but after bumping one or two aside and taking very wide or tight lines I managed to find a way through, then catch and pass Driver and Pawson. That got me up to third. I caught Tom after making the fastest lap of the meeting but Tony was two seconds ahead at the finish. Second place can never replace a win but that fastest lap was some consolation. Tony being English got the headlines.

As expected, Tom was gracious in defeat and after some leg pulling we cleaned the bikes, loaded the vans and joined the queue to collect our start and prize money. I was handed a cheque for 120 pounds. But I needed some cash for food and petrol. I whispered to race secretary Neville Goss, "I am broke and need some cash." He turned to his staff and loudly proclaimed, "Hugh's skint and needs some cash!" Forty pounds was found, a new cheque made out and with "Good luck at the Ulster" ringing in my embarrassed ears I left. I picked up South African Robert Duffield in Birmingham and drove all night to Glasgow to catch the Monday evening ferry to Ireland.

We shared the driving while learning about each other's adventures and life experiences. It was remarkable how quickly trusting friendships could be established, especially among fellow Commonwealth members. Robert and I still remain in contact.

The Dundrod circuit winds for 11km through the lush countryside of Northern Ireland. It is a very fast, undulating, demanding circuit and bears many similarities to the Isle of Man. We pulled into the paddock, unloaded the bikes, rearranged the van to create sleeping quarters, and then I went off with my pen and notebook to do my homework on the track. As the time for the first 350cc practice neared, I became ever more excited. It was going to be good to ride the 7R again.

After three laps I felt sufficiently confident to start passing a few. The race shop had done a good job of rebuilding the engine and it was going really well. When I went out on the 500 a following breeze was blowing along the slightly downhill starting straight. I hit a top speed of 225kph flat on the tank. When I sat up for the fast Rushey Hill bends, my cheeks blew back towards my ears and the disturbed air created by the riders ahead caused my head to wobble about disconcertingly, blurring my vision. Wow! I'd never gone that fast before.

As I prepared for another practice session, I lined up near Ralph Rensen, a likeable hard case from Liverpool. Ralph rode hard, played hard and had a great sense of humour, although he was selective with whom he shared it. He had been a member of the Continental Circus since 1954. Ralph turned towards me and with a glint in his eye said, "Follow me."

At first I struggled to stay with him, but it was the most exhilarating, educational experience of my life. On one lap we passed a rider on a Francis Beart Norton.

Soon after we returned to the paddock, Ralph came to our van, his face radiant, eyes sparkling and a wide grin.

"Where did you pass Ellis Boyce?" he asked.

"At the next right-hander," I answered.

"Great," he said, "that will put those Manx Grand Prix winners in their place."

Francis Beart was a famous English tuner with many race wins. He was sponsored by Shell and supported by the Norton factory. His machines were distinctive, painted green, with numerous holes drilled to lighten them and always immaculately presented. I qualified sixth, behind Ralph. John Surtees was on pole on his MV Agusta.

During the evening the paddock was open to the public. Sidney Grey, who lived locally, introduced himself. Over the years he had helped New Zealanders and continued to correspond with them. We invited him to join Robert in our pit for the races next day.

I got a flyer of a start in the 350 race. As I followed John Surtees' MV off Leathemstown Bridge I saw his exhaust pipes touch the track. He moved a little further to the side of the seat and accelerated hard enough to create a perfect rear-wheel drift. I had never seen it done before and was so fascinated that I lost momentum and was swamped by riders. What a bugger. First John Hartle, then Ralph, Bob Anderson, Dickie Dale, Paddy Driver and Peter Pawson rode past. What a plonker. From second place to eighth in 800m. I got my head down, re-passed Paddy and Peter in a risk-taking super-late braking effort at the bottom of Deer's Leap, and rode on. I out-braked Ralph at the hairpin and set off after Dickie and Bob. Could I catch them? Both had vast experience and the best Nortons available.

Searching for more speed, I reverted to the power gear-shifting tactic I had learned on my Gold Star back in New Zealand. Keeping the 7R's throttle wide open, I lifted the clutch just enough to change from third to fourth gear. It worked perfectly and I got a kick in the backside and an extra 100rpm. When leaving a second-gear corner I did the same into third and gained 200rpm more than before. Finally, I was in Dickie's slipstream.

I out-braked Dickie and slipped in behind Bob. We flew down Deer's Leap and I braked under him into Cochranstown; Bob made an early entry to block my pass, and our fairings touched. Later, *Motor Cycling* described our rivalry: "There was a first-class carve-up for third position between Bob Anderson, Hugh Anderson, Dickie Dale and, for a few laps, Peter Pawson. The battle raged with such fury that quite often the positions were completely re-shuffled between consecutive corners." On the last lap Bob and I rode through the left-right-left of Tournagrough as one, and down the hill to the crucial hairpin. Bob hit his brakes hard, I slipped up the inside of him and hit mine. The 7R's brakes are good. The front forks bottom out, the bike bounced about as the semi-locked rear wheel sways from side to side, but it doesn't bother me. Riding vintage bikes at speed around rough paddocks as a 12-year-old was more difficult than this. Leaving the corner with the engine screaming I burn the clutch to the max then power-shift into second; the 7R leaps forward then into third and taking the deepest breath of my life sweep flat-out into the last corner and under the chequered flag.

After stopping I feel quite strange and have difficulty balancing the bike. Excitedly, Robert came running to me, mouthing words I couldn't hear. My tongue is stuck to the roof of my mouth. Robert takes a bottle of drink from a stranger, and with relief I take a mouthful. People are patting me on the back. After having been concentrating so deeply for so long, emotions flood back. So much had taken place in that whirlwind 148-mile race. I am overwhelmed, mentally and physically disorientated.

A marshal tapped me on the shoulder — you are wanted. Crikey, I'd forgotten about that. I kick a well-wisher as I clumsily dismount. The marshal escorts me to what surely is the most important podium of a rider's career. The first at a world championship points-carrying Grand Prix. Winner John Surtees and runner-up John Hartle welcomed me with firm, honest handshakes.

Bob Anderson checking on Dickie Dale. My focus is elsewhere. The Nick Nicholls collection at Mortons Archive.

Proud as punch and why not? Archives.

The all-important first Grand Prix podium. Archives.

Finally, I made my way back to the van. With the curtains drawn I lit a cigarette and relived the race. Before the cigarette was finished I was chastened by the realisation that, as good as that ride was, I still had a lot to learn. Later two well-dressed men approached, introduced themselves as organisers of the Italian Grand Prix and asked if I would like to compete there. Assuming my worst possible poker face, with a large happy smile I said yes. They offered me 120,000 lire, which sounded like a lot of money so I signed on the dotted line.

After such a rewarding ride, I approached the 500cc race with less enthusiasm. Once more I made a good start and arrived with Alan Trow, a top-six finisher in the Isle of Man and a multi-winner at national events, and others at the slow Leathemstown group of corners. Too late, Alan realised the surface was damp from light rain. He slithered off, I just missed him and pressed on in eighth place close behind Dickie Dale.

While lying flat on the tank I noticed a reflection in the perspex screen. The sun has come out, I thought. I noticed it again and a couple of laps later the reflections became stronger. Soon after, my right foot felt hot, bloody hot, and I looked down to see sheets of flame streaming back from under the engine. I groped for the petrol tap, skidded to a stop and threw the Norton against a fence. The exhaust pipe had ignited felt material tied on to the frame to soak up engine oil.

No marshals with fire extinguishers were close by, so I was lucky that a spectator came running with his jacket to smother the flames. The jacket was plastic and melted rather easily, but the enthusiastic Irishman wasn't worried. He now had 'The Jacket' that had saved a Grand Prix bike from burning out at the 1960 Ulster Grand Prix. It would be a valuable souvenir and a great story to tell over a Guinness or two.

Sidney, who had manned my pit, invited Robert and me to dinner with his family. After a healthy Irish country meal we retired to the lounge to watch television. Sidney was keen to come to Italy with me, so that was arranged. When we were back at the van I asked Robert, an Afrikaans speaker, why he had been so quiet. "I couldn't understand a word they said," he admitted.

The Leinster 200 was a typical country circuit in a farming area. We decided to camp on a farm near the start so I knocked on the door and a pleasant woman in her mid-fifties opened it. I explained I was a New Zealand rider and my friend a South African. Hotels were too expensive and could we please live in the van here for a couple of days. "To be sure, you can stay. My son will show you where to park and he will clear a place in the shed where you can keep your bikes."

Every day is a good day, just some are better than others. We even ended up being allowed to use their toilet and join them for an evening meal. Robert couldn't believe our good fortune.

"How do you do it?" he asked.

"Robert, I am twenty-five per cent Irish, I'm one of them," I replied.

Each morning our hostess kindly recited a long prayer for my safety.

The circuit was easy to learn. I finished the 100-mile/160ks event in steady, very cold rain, behind John Hartle but well ahead of Ralph Rensen in the 350cc race.

The organisers started the 500cc race immediately because of the bad weather. I was freezing and soaked, and after only having time to change my goggles and gloves, I was off on another 160km ride in unpleasant conditions. John Hartle and

Ralph had good 500cc Nortons so I settled for third, which was fine until the 19th lap when the gearbox locked at 160kph. I was tossed up the road in front of it. The Norton followed closely, making a hell of a din. Fearing it would catch up to me, as soon as I had slowed sufficiently, I ran to the side of the road, tripped over the grass verge and fell head-first into a drain. My first thought was why is the water so warm? Hypothermia was well advanced.

I got out no wetter than before to find my Norton enveloped in flames and billowing clouds of smoke. Crikey dick, I don't like this! Luckily, marshals with fire extinguishers were soon on the job and with the strength of the desperate I dragged it out of the pool of petrol it had been lying in and the flames were soon doused. A gearbox lock-up is the worst mechanical failure you can experience, and quite rare. I was lucky to come away with minor abrasions. An article in a local newspaper carried the headline 'New Zealander Hugh Anderson crashed, his machine was burnt out'.

mes and smoke on the
iboyne Road after H.
derson's Norton, following
o skid, went on fire.

Rensen, Hartle
in
form

R ALPH RENSEN of Liver-
pool riding a Norton won the day's major event, the 500 c.c. class, in the "Leinster 200" meeting at Dunboyne yesterday.

Nortons were also ridden by Raymond Spence, of Belfast, and Ballymena's R. I. Ireland, who finished second and third, respectively.

SHOWERY WEATHER

Some keen sport was witnessed in showery weather which made the going very slippery and caused some competitors to retire. One of them, McConkey, spun and buckled his machine badly coming into Dunboyne Village.

Rensen engaged in an exciting struggle for second place with Noton in the 350 c.c. event. Anderson eventually fini' runner-up to Hartley, the record for the class an average of 83.96 m.p.

Dickie Carter, on a 249 1, took the 250 c.c. race, in v his expert control of a fas was favourably comp' upon.

HOW THEY FINISHED

500 c.c. SCRATCH
h. m. s.   m.p.h.
R. Rensen, Belfast (499 Norton) ... 1 12 13   83.08   (25 laps)
R. Spence, Belfast (499 Norton) ... 1 14 15   80.81   (25 laps)
R. L. Ireland, B'mena (350 Norton) 1 13 43   78.14   (24 laps)
W. McCosh, Ballymena (349 A.J.S.) 1 12 23   77.56   (23 laps)
F. O'Reilly, Dublin (349 B.S.A.) 1 12 27   72.88   (22 laps)
T. W. Holmes, P'down (499 Matchless) 1 15 36   72.70   (22 laps)

350 c.c. SCRATCH
h. m. s.   m.p.h.
J. Hartle, Surrey (349 Norton) ... 1 11 28   85.96   (25 laps)
H. Anderson (349 Norton) .... 1 13 20   81.52   (25 laps)
R. Rensen, Belfast (349 Norton) 1 14 53   80.58   (25 laps)
T. Pound, Surrey (349 Norton) 1 12 53   76.99   (24 laps)
W. McCosh, Ballymena (349 A.J.S.) 1 14 25   77.11   (24 laps)
K. Terretta, Cheshire (349 Norton) 1 12 45   78.88   (25 laps)

250 c.c. SCRATCH
h. m. s.
G. Carter, Dublin (249 N.S.U. 1h. 6m. 48s.   2
S. Hodgins, Belfast (249 N.S.U.) .... 1 12 41   73.86 m.p.h. 2
N. Orr, Belfast (349 N.S.U.) .... 1 14 52   71.45 m.p.h. 3
H. Dunlop, Ballymena (203 m.v. Augusta) 1 11 40   61.13 m.p.h. 4

OVERALL HANDICAP
h. m. s.
S. Hodgins, Belfast (249 N.S.U.) 1h. 5m. 11s.   1
H. O'Reilly, Dublin (349 Norton) 1h. 6m. 41s.   2
V. Carter, Dublin (249 N.S.U.) 1h. 6m. 48s.   3
J. Shannon, Loughbrickland (349 B.S.A.) ... 1h. 8m. 57s.   4
T. Pound, Guilford (349 Norton) 1h. 8m. 19s.   5
E. Oliver, Cookstown (349 A.J.S.) 1h. 8m. 50s.   6

**Fastest Laps—J. Hartle (349 c.c. Norton), 2m. 43s., 88.34 m.p.h.;
250 s.—G. Carter, Dublin (249 N.S.U.) 2m. 53s., 83.34 m.p.h.**

*I climbed out of a drain to be
confronted with this. Archives.*

Sidney and I enjoyed our drive to Italy and the Grand Prix at Monza. The Nortons of Dickie Dale and Bob Anderson were a little faster than my AJS, but I stayed in their slipstreams as we diced for fourth place. Unfortunately, when we began lapping riders I lost their tow and finished sixth. This, surprisingly, gave me seventh in the 350cc world championship. Seventh place on the 500 race was quite satisfactory.

I had been stony broke before Thruxton so had decided not to return to New Zealand at the end of the season. Even now when I could afford the fare, the thought of packing up my gear, spending 10 weeks on a return sea trip for a short New Zealand summer season seemed a costly time-waster. Better to stay in the UK and be properly prepared for next season. I was enjoying every day here where for so long I had wanted to be. Jock West, sales director at the AMC factory in Woolwich South London, offered me work in the view room, where the dimensions of all the major engine parts were checked. Then later Rose and Geoff Maynard, who had previously hosted New Zealand riders, offered me a comfortable bed in their townhouse at a fair price.

The temptation to ride at the last event of the season at London's Brands Hatch was too strong to ignore. After just five laps' practice on the 7R and three on the Norton, we were ready to race. A flying start on the AJS saw me involved in a dice with Tom Phillis and Alan Trow, who was a local ace, over fourth place. When chasing Alan hard up a left-hand corner that took us from the old to the new circuit, the rear wheel began drifting away, but I corrected it. This happened each lap, and as I gained confidence I allowed it to move more, helping me to take the corner faster. It was a new skill I was determined to develop. Tom took fourth, me next and Alan sixth. On the second corner of the 500cc race the gearbox locked again, tossing me high in the air to land at the feet of a marshal and, of all people, Jock West. The result: a dislocated right shoulder. A first-aid attendant tried to put the shoulder back in place. After several painful attempts he gave up and I was taken to St Mary Cray's hospital where all the injured riders from Brands end up. Doug Stead, Alan Trow's mechanic, loaded my van and dropped it off at the hospital and left the keys at the office.

On arrival at the hospital my leathers were expertly cut along the seams, I was then knocked out and the shoulder put back. After I came round and could talk sense, I left and drove to a farewell party for John Hempleman, who was retiring and returning to New Zealand permanently. We enjoyed a pleasant evening and my shoulder seemed okay. I stayed in a local boarding house. Next morning I was sore, geez, I was sore. Being unable to look after myself I put on a pair of pants, pulled a large jersey over my head and with my arm still in a sling, drove to Birmingham to stay with friends who took in boarders.

Days passed and as my shoulder didn't improve I felt I needed some form of physiotherapy. Lew Ellis, the Shell oil representative, had a myriad of contacts so I phoned him and he gave me the number of a competent chap in London. He wasn't impressed with what he found and sent me off for X-rays. Three bones had been broken and he was concerned the joint could become 'frozen'. In due course he sorted it out and with regular exercise, including swimming in a nearby pool at lunch time and attending the associated gymnasium of an evening, it slowly improved.

It was mid-October before I started work at the AMC factory and late in November when I began working on my bikes in the shed at the Vinson farm. Trying to work in below-zero conditions with no heating and poor lighting was not much fun.

Alan Trow, who had decided to retire from road racing, heard of my predicament and offered me the use of his personal workshop within his motorcycle and scooter retail business in Welling, near where I lived. Life could hardly be better.

At that time I became close friends with Alan Jones, a road tester of new bikes at AMC, and strengthened my relationships with the 'Race Shop' staff. Cockneys have a wicked sense of humour.

Roy Hewitt, one of the other road testers, used a sidecar outfit as personal transport that he always parked in the same place. As he rode off each evening he would take both hands off the bars and, with a flourish, take his goggles, stretch the elastic out over the peak of his helmet and carefully position them.

One day his mates painted over the lenses. As usual Roy reached up and placed them over his eyes. He immediately slammed on the brakes, spinning the outfit almost in its own length to face the opposite direction.

Jimmy King, the engine builder in the rectification department, was sometimes the butt of the road testers' humour. After he had assembled an engine they would discreetly place an oil seal or gasket on his bench and say, "What's this, Jimmy?"

"Oh Christ," he would say and start stripping the motor.

The testers and rectifiers were all issued with 12-pound hide mallets. If the cam gears whined, they would tap the screwed-on housings up, down or sideways to quieten them. Frequently, kick-start levers, when used for the first time, stuck down. Again a deft clout would move the engine casing and release it.

Sometimes staff would supplement their income by 'nicking' various parts. An expert could tell what a person was carrying by his stance, as most wore bulky motorcycle-riding kit. Standing very upright with the head held back meant handlebars or exhaust pipe. A stiff-legged gait was fork tubes down the trousers. Arms held close to a body could be hiding the bulging effects of a crankcase, cylinder head or even a gearbox. Doorman Ted Neahan attempted to catch the pilferers, but being old and having poor eyesight were disadvantages he couldn't overcome.

In mid-winter, alterations to the sewer/drainage system of the factory was being carried out. One day the factory personnel were told not to use the toilets or sinks between 2 and 3pm. Immediately, the word went out, watches were synchronised and sinks filled. Precisely at 2.30pm the toilets were flushed and sink plugs removed. A torrent of water rose to the workers' waists. Abuse filled the air; several furious, very wet mud-splattered men entered the building intent on killing someone. All part of the florid never-ending folklore of the AMC factory.

Having won national championships in off-road competitions at home, I was keen to try my hand at English scrambles, as they were then called. Jock West agreed to make a works 350 scrambler available but at a price. If I didn't do well, I wouldn't have it again. So, without any fitness training or practice and my shoulder far from being at full strength, I made my debut at Crawley on February 19.

The circuit slowly deteriorated into a sea of glutinous mud. I had never ridden in such conditions. Australian Tim Gibbes, who later retired to New Zealand, won all three races. New Zealander Ken Cleghorn was third in one and fourth in another, but failed to finish in the third event. My efforts were earnest if not successful. I fell off four times on the last lap of my first race. I had never been so buggered. The course was changed for the second race and I finished a steady 10th. I built on that to finish sixth in the last event without falling but was very tired.

For me, this scrambling was just a diversion from the real thing, another form of motorcycling pleasure.

The engine was surprisingly powerful for a 350cc at that time. Archives.

Totally buggered. Have they lost the chequered flag? Archives.

The works AJS 500. So much was expected of it. Archives.

CHAPTER 6

The hissing grew louder, we had to leave, and the frightening reaction of a clairvoyant

A CONTRACT WITH SUZUKI

Is this my moment of destiny? I ask myself as I stand in the Suzuki team enclosure at the 1961 Isle of Man TT. Before me are two motorcycles in the early stages of development. A few days earlier I'd signed up to the fledgling Suzuki race team. Now is my chance to ride one of these revolutionary motorcycles.

As I haven't even heard one running, I feel it's wise to start the 125 in the paddock before venturing onto the track. Two mechanics push me off and I gradually open the throttle to coax the engine into life. Nothing happens. I open it ever wider. It fires. I lift the clutch. In an instant the tachometer needle shoots around to 12,500rpm. I snap the throttle shut. It stops instantly. Jeez, I've broken it. Then we try again and get the same result and I look quizzically at the mechanics. Let's get this right, I think.

I point to the 12,500rpm mark on the tachometer. "Okay," says the mechanic. So finally, I just keep twisting the throttle in rapid, repetitive blipping. The needle flicks from 8,000rpm, the highest revs I had ever seen on the rev counter of a British bike, to 12,500rpm and back in an instant. I keep it screaming with my eyes glued to the rev counter. At these revs the warming-up process is short, so I soon cut the engine and the mechanics fit the racing plugs.

As ready as I'll ever be, I join the circuit and ride off down Glencrutchery Road. Surprisingly, I find that even running the engine at maximum revs through the lower gears doesn't produce a lot of power. I descend Bray Hill at a modest speed, continue to Quarter Bridge and stop. After checking for overheating, oil leaks, or any obvious reason why it isn't performing better, I decide the wise option is to return to the pits using a side road.

After a long, cold, wet English winter, France offered sunny spring relief, and Le Mans the first major meeting for the Continental Circus in 1961. Riders from throughout the Commonwealth, the Continent and UK had gained entries, creating a colourful mix of languages, accents and attitudes. Naturally, I gravitated towards the people I'd met during the previous year: a mixture of Australians, Rhodesians, French and Austrians. We were the new boys, all equals and ready to help and support each other by sharing our spare parts, skills and knowledge. Not only was this an act of friendship, but also one of survival.

Laurie Shephard had agreed to travel with me during the 1961 international season as an unpaid (although at no cost to himself) cook, confidant and, above all, companion.

We had become friends in early 1960 during the five-week voyage from Wellington to Southampton. Laurie was an outstanding athlete. During his university days he set new records when winning provincial sprint championships. His main sport was rugby union where his size, speed, strength and skill were well suited for the wing position where he excelled. Laurie had taken his education seriously, showing great ability as a school teacher. Eventually, he would become the headmaster of a private school in the north of England.

I believe that his success, in later life, was in no small way due to that rounding off, that essential worldly-wise edge he gained during the time he spent with me. Laurie has a different take on this and claims to this day that I was the worst 'pupil' he has ever been associated with and I remain a work in progress.

Le Mans was a mixed car-bike promotion. The motorcycle events were two 500cc races, with the points gained in each race totalled to give the overall placings. The full circuit was used, including the famous 7km Mulsanne Straight. I'd never ridden flat-out for so long and was surprised to feel bored by it. There was nothing to do except mould yourself tightly around the motorcycle and 'will' the rev counter to move on another 100rpm. I finished third in the first race. While again lying third in the second near the end of the last lap, the Manx Norton engine clattered loudly and I coasted to a stop and started pushing as fast as I could. The finish line seemed a long way off but the passing of each following rider rekindled my efforts. Only after riding at 220kph for the previous 30 minutes can you appreciate just how slow running with a motorcycle actually is!

The race officials and spectators entered into the spirit of the occasion, shouting encouragement. I finally staggered under an exaggerated waving of the chequered flag, threw the Norton at Laurie, who was waiting, and collapsed in a breathless heap on the grass verge. Finally, I regained some composure and, with Laurie's help and more applause, we made our way back to the pits. I'd finished 10th. That night all of the prizes were in various forms of French liqueurs. We enjoyed a noisy, at times hilarious, night around a fire. Next morning wasn't worth talking about really.

We dismantled the Manx and found the inlet valve retaining collets had pulled slowly through a Bill Stuart experimental aluminium retainer. Luckily, damage was minimal. Rhodesian Willie van Leeuwen, who was born in Breda, Holland, spoke Dutch fluently and told me about his friend with a motorcycle shop where he was sure we could sort out my Norton.

Jan Meierdres doing a fine job. Archives.

Jan Meierdres, son of the original Velocette importer to Holland, was a fine, steady, well-educated man and an ardent motorcycle-racing enthusiast. His wife Nel, an outgoing girl from Amsterdam, was a ball of energy and fun. Her father owned a large engineering business. We were in the right place to sort out the Manx so parked the Ford van on the grass verge, under trees, beside a canal, opposite Jan's shop

While we waited for the parts to arrive from England we helped in the workshop servicing 50cc mopeds and repairing punctures. I became lifelong friends with Jan and Nel, who named their second son Hugh, an unusual name in Holland where it is pronounced 'Huge'. Two years later Jan was best man at our wedding.

Our canal-side sojourn ended when the parts finally arrived and after an all-night rebuild we left for Salzburg and the Austrian Grand Prix. A surprising number of locals came to see us off. We had become minor celebrities during our stay.

The two bikes performed very well in practice on the fast autobahn circuit, especially the 500cc Norton, which was a huge relief. In the 350 race there were not only several successful international riders to contend with, but the rather special factory twin-cylinder Jawas. These were not the smoky, smelly two-stroke models but sophisticated double overhead cam racers that performed so well in Grand Prix events; Franta Stastny finishing as high as second and Gustav Havel third in the world championships that year.

From the start Stastny gained almost two seconds a lap on me but Havel much less. The race was long, so I kept working hard at lowering my lap times and eventually started to gain on Havel. The constant pressure had its effect and he slid off, unhurt, on a fast cobblestone corner, in an impressive cloud of dust..

A few laps later, when the chequered flag dropped, I was delighted to be told I had won. Unknown to me, Stastny had retired at the pits early in the race. You beaut! The first Austrian rider home and I set off on a lap of honour, but not before I had snatched a handsome Austrian hat from the head of the secretary of the meeting. All concerned seemed to enjoy the fun. That hat was worn at race meetings until Suzuki team caps became de rigueur.

Laurie couldn't understand my surprise at having won. "I'd been telling you that on our signal board," he said. "What's the use of me giving you all this information if you don't take any notice of it?" When fully focused, pit signals could be an unnecessary distraction. So why bother with them?

Ride to the limits of the grip. Ignore the surface. Artur Fenzlau.

Congratulations and I have acquired a hat. Artur Fenzlau.

I gained the holeshot from pole position in the 500cc race but fellow New Zealander Peter Pawson came by. I moved into his slipstream and got a tow to the first corner. It was a fast right curve onto cobblestones. I rode under him and went on to lead for the full distance. There were more celebrations. I gave a rather rotund clerk of the course a hug. He showed surprise but didn't resist.

Me, Frank Perris and Bert Schneider. When a large crowd lines the track, straw bales are hardly required. Artur Fenzlau.

The previous year I had met Wagner, a pleasant young man who became a close friend. He had been with us all weekend and was quite over the moon about our success. Being 'the guns' of the day, we needed to dress accordingly for the evening's social and prize giving, but we had left our formal clothes back at Jan's place in Breda.

Novel transport for a victory lap. Artur Fenzlau.

As Wagner was shorter than Laurie but taller than me, he offered to take us to his home for 'a fitting'. What followed was bordering on slapstick comedy. There were pant legs that didn't reach Laurie's ankles and jackets where my fingers hardly protruded from the sleeves. After each fitting we paraded in front of the family to gales of laughter. Neighbours became involved with more advice, more clothes and ever more laughter. Finally, we gained a semblance of respectability, even if Laurie had to wear his pants down around his hips with the fly partly undone and a large hunting jacket to maintain some modesty.

Prize giving was a full-house party in an upmarket hotel. A handsome genuine silver cup was the prize for first place in the 350cc class. A large gold-faced clock was presented for the 500cc race. I was pleased to find a bonus had been added to my start and prize money and asked if this was for hugging the clerk of the course, which again brought roars of laughter.

I have donated the silver trophy to the New Zealand Classic Motorcycle Racing Register, where it is competed for annually in the 350cc Clubmans event — the class in which my road-racing career began with a winning ride in the handicap section at Te Puna in 1956, followed by many more. The clock is now with my good friend Kevin Grant, owner of the 500cc Norton I bought new in 1961.

The Saarland Grand Prix at St Wendel in West Germany was next. It was a true 'road race' circuit, like the ones I had cut my teeth on in New Zealand, with narrow, steeply cambered streets. There were cobblestones worn smooth on a left under a railway bridge and a right-hand uphill climb with occasional patches of modern tarmac. This was definitely my kind of racetrack.

At the welcome dinner we met Karl Recktenwald, a local policeman who was an experienced national rider. As the evening passed the subject of motorcycle hire was brought up. Karl wanted to take part in the 500cc race and the organisers were prepared to pay a substantial hire fee to have him ride. Could I help? This was all a little new to me, so I asked if I could consider it. Laurie was very keen on the idea as when we had arrived at the Austrian Grand Prix I was broke yet again and we had been dipping into Laurie's pocket money (actually, his total wealth).

The following day we changed the gearing, checked every nut and bolt on the two bikes and started the engines. The AJS felt fine but the Norton was a little harsh and the engine noisy. We hurriedly removed the head and barrel and found the big-end bearing was worn. Strange, I thought, as during the winter I'd given an engine builder a new bearing assembly that should have lasted much longer.

German oil companies provided impressive mobile workshops at these events so I approached one and handed over the flywheels and a new big-end bearing to a large gruff man of few words. An hour later the flywheels had been reassembled and the engine rebuild began. Another all-nighter ensued.

We decided to hire it out; I wasn't happy with the gearbox as it had seized twice the previous year, even though Norton Motors had rebuilt it on each occasion. Later I found a bent main shaft had not been detected. We needed the money so I did the deal with Karl and the organisers paid us the agreed 50 pounds. Laurie hurriedly changed the race numbers, all hand-painted back then, and I fitted a large main jet in the carburettor to act as an engine rev limiter.

After a few laps of practice it was obvious the 7R with its less tractable engine and harder suspension wasn't suited to the circuit. I took out the 350cc Manx. With its steadier handling and softer power delivery it gave a better platform from which to attack the demanding track. Later, Englishman Ralph Rensen, who had become a good friend and my main competitor for the honours of being the top rider competing in the Continental Circus that season, came over. "I'll beat you this time, you little bastard, now you're not on that fast AJS." He was always a boisterous, happy sort of person, but tough as they come when he wanted to be.

Again, I was asked by the promoter August Balthazar if I would hire my 7R to another friend of his, a pleasant man in his mid-thirties. He had escaped from Czechoslovakia and had a car-wrecking business. We agreed. Steady light rain was falling on race day, ideal conditions for me, but not popular with many riders. I lowered the gearing, to better suit the slower race pace, and eagerly awaited the start.

Ralph led from the drop of the flag, which was good as I followed and learned. He was trying very hard, dragging his foot speedway style on the road to help hold the bike up when his tyres lost grip. His body was full of tension but he was very determined. I followed feeling quite relaxed, gaining a feel for the surface and managing to get the back wheel moving into a controlled drift on the extremely slippery cobblestones.

As I passed over each fresh patch of seal the tyres would grip aggressively, pulling the wheels into line, then start sliding again as we moved back to the slippery old stones that covered a few hundred crucial metres of the circuit. Within that short distance was the winning and losing of the race. I found by shifting gear where there was good traction, changing lines to allow for rear-wheel steering and finding the best braking points, I gained an easily maintained rhythm. I passed Ralph and motored on to lap all but the first three riders.

After the post-race celebrations Ralph approached silently from behind, wrapped his arms around me, lifted me up and loudly proclaimed, "There are old bastards and there are bold bastards but there are no old bold bastards." Then he put me down, we shook hands and carried on the usual banter of "Did you see me slide on the second lap?", "Man, I was lucky under the bridge", "Did you see that guy and the bike up the bank — how did he get there?" and so on.

Above: Lapping #67 with Ralph #82 not far behind. Walter Trager.

Below: The ultimate result for a private owner. All your own effort. Walter Trager.

Late in the evening at a post-race party, Karl and I found a quiet corner and discussed how he could buy a new Manx Norton. Karl had ordered one from the importer but it was sold to his rival. Understandably, there was a little angst in the air. After competing in the German Grand Prix at Hockenheim the following weekend, I intended to return to England and collect a new 500cc Norton and offered to take him to the factory where we would be able to discuss his situation with management.

The Hockenheim racetrack had just three corners: a flat-out curve, a medium-fast and a slow one. On the 500 during early practice I'd almost got to the point of taking the left-hand curve at full noise (all the fast guys claimed they could), but again eased the throttle before entry. With a bang, the motor blew. I quickly lifted the clutch and freewheeled dangerously fast through the curve, but managed to stay on track and survive.

First a big end and now a piston, whereas both should have lasted at least 10 meetings. Much later I learned the engine builder had sold my parts to another rider, given my engine a quick check-over and handed me a hefty bill. I qualified on the third row of the grid for the 350cc race but at the push-start the rider next to me fell heavily and we both went down. Two of the following riders couldn't avoid us and also fell. It took time to disentangle ourselves and the pack had long gone before I started my engine. After a token number of laps I gave up and returned to the paddock to prepare the 350 for the 500cc race.

I made a good start and rode aggressively just centimetres from the rear wheel of any rider who came past. At each corner I would pop out from behind them, pass three or four and brake very late, then slip in behind any other rider who came past for another tow. When I felt I'd done enough to qualify for the meagre start money being paid, I returned to the paddock.

I collected Karl and we left for England and Laurie stayed with Willie.

Karl and I formed a close friendship during that long overnight drive. Though being of a similar age, we had vastly different childhood experiences. At age 12, Karl was conscripted into the Hitler Youth Movement, where the training was harsh and exhausting. For all Europeans, but particularly Germans, the post-war reconstruction period, the shortages of food and accommodation were difficult and the problems well documented. In 1950 Karl joined the police force and became a keen motorcyclist and started racing in 1955. Showing promise, he went on to gain his international licence. Understandably, he now wanted the best bike available.

When driving I often sang popular songs to pass the time. Karl joined me. I sang 'Lilli Marlene', a popular German song from the war period that was also translated into English. He sang it in German and so we passed the time. The noise of the van, driven at close to its maximum speed, gave us confidence in our rather average voices.

We crossed the Channel with Skyways, on a Bristol Freighter cargo plane. Karl took a window seat, eager to see England for the first time. Southend, a town built post-war, came into view and there was a long silence as he observed the scene. "But it's so clean, tidy and modern," he exclaimed. No doubt quite the opposite to the propaganda of his youth.

At the Norton factory on Wednesday morning, Karl produced the documentation confirming he had placed the order for a Manx at the beginning of the year. The sales manager was disappointed with the actions of the German importer and gave his assurance he would do his best to resolve the matter.

We called on the builder of my engines. A heated discussion followed. He claimed that the only reason I was doing well was due to the superior performance of his engines and I would never win on the new bike. I bet him the 36 pounds I still owed him that I would.

Karl and I arrived at Tubbergen, Holland, at 6am on Friday morning. The race paddock was dead quiet. I snuck into where Laurie and Willie were sleeping, dug Laurie hard in the ribs, he yelled, then pulled Willie out of bed and got out of there. They later joined Karl and me for an early breakfast. We learnt that Berti Schneider and Rudi Thalhammer, Austria's best riders, were using the first six-speed gearboxes manufactured by their brilliant engineer friend, Michael Schafleitner.

Tubbergen was a fast circuit incorporating two long straights, a group of medium-fast curves through a heavily wooded area and three very slow corners. It would be a perfect track for Berti and Rudi to take full advantage of their new acquisitions.

After a good start in the 350cc race I settled into third, then at half distance moved up to second place behind Rudi. His very good Norton, assisted by the six-speed gearbox, was faster than my well-used 7R. On the last lap, I passed him through the curves under the trees, then got into his slipstream as he overtook me down the long following straight. But my AJS wasn't good enough and Rudi beat me by a wheel. I gained the consolation of having cracked a new lap record. As we toured back to the paddock acknowledging the large animated crowd, I patted him on the back. He acknowledged my congratulations. Close races can make and cement close friendships.

I didn't leave anything to chance at the end of the 500cc race, slipstreaming Berti on my new Norton. I won the braking battle at the last corner to reach the chequered flag first. During those modest times we were not encouraged to stand on the footrests, wave our arms in the air and play to the crowd. No, you kept it inside, a hugely warm feeling of relief, of respect, and admiration for the skill, determination and daring of all involved. This was life on the edge, what a gas!

Berti and I clasped hands momentarily then cruised around the track side by side, quietly acknowledging the rowdy crowd with an occasional raised hand and nod of our heads. With slightly shaking hands I lit a cigarette and sat silently alone. Man, if life gets better than this, I'm not sure how I'll cope, I thought with a wry grin.

There were major celebrations at the prize giving that night as this was the biggest event of the year in this small Dutch town. Having been paid well and awarded several trophies, I felt I owed some of my rivals for one or two fairly 'heavy' passes. I shouted and Laurie, the consummate host, kept glasses topped up. He met a fine-looking girl named Albertje, who joined our group. At about 10pm the party-goers started a snake dance through the streets and we joined using my van. The Austrian riders climbed up onto my roof rack, others stood on the rear bumpers and more hung from the open doors. Someone had a trumpet and blew the horn, all good fun. Laurie walked Albertje home and while leaning against the front door enjoying a farewell hug, one of them was unwittingly pressing the doorbell button. Suddenly, the door flew open with Albertje and Laurie falling on top of her screaming mother. The light came on and there was Dad brandishing a large steel poker. Laurie hurried off.

Then sadly we later learned that a German rider had crashed at high speed in the 500cc race. His machine cartwheeled into the crowd, injuring three adults and killing a young boy.

After confirming my win by telegram to the errant engine builder, it was then a 2,500km odyssey to Madrid where, much to his delight, Ralph beat me. I had been comfortable following him, waiting until five laps from the end to have a go but lapped riders got in the way; at times there was as little as a metre between us but Ralph intended to win it. The crowd loved it. When the circuit was opened they swarmed into the paddock area trampling over our gear and knocking bikes over in the crush. To our collective relief, police arrived and with loudspeakers and waving threatening batons took control.

In late afternoon a group of us attended a bullfight. The idea of wounding and humiliating an animal was foreign to us so we cheered the bull and booed the matador. The Spanish seated near us were far from amused as the first bull's life was slowly ended. A pair of gaily high-stepping, decorated horses entered the ring, a strong leather strap was attached to the dead bull's horns and, with a fanfare of trumpets, the horses galloped out of the arena with the bull's body swaying behind them.

The next show consisted of an almost totally blinkered horse protected by a coat of chain mail. The rider was wearing what appeared to be a light suit of armour, and carried a long pole with a wide cutting blade attached. The bull came out of its pen at speed. It caught El Dicko on the horse by surprise. With a hurried jab he missed cutting the muscles at the base of the bull's neck, limiting its ability to lift its head to defend itself. The bull hit the horse at speed and tossed it effortlessly onto its side. Several decoys ran out waving capes, desperately trying to attract the bull's attention before it ripped the horse apart and dealt to the rider.

The arena became deathly silent while we cheered. Those seated around us glared and hissed. The bull was doing grand work chasing the decoys. He caught one by surprise who, with his face distorted by fear, began sprinting to the wall. The bull was gaining. The decoy leapt at the fence, clinging to the railing while the bull buried his horns in a gap between the rails, millimetres beneath his feet.

The decoy escaped. We booed again. The bull extricated himself from the fence and trotted majestically around, head and tail held high, blowing heavily from extended nostrils and foaming from the mouth. It was indeed a handsome animal. The horse, now back on its feet, with rider in position, was definitely nervous and not keen on a rerun. Boof. The bull attacked the horse again. With his cutting tool, the rider managed to partially complete his job and left.

Out strutted the matador. We booed him. The crowd hissed at us. The matador waved his cape. The bull, with his head high, eyed him ferociously, then lowered his head and charged. The matador deftly used his cape to gain the eye of the bull, which galloped through it, brushing him as he passed. It skidded to a halt and turned quickly. The matador continued to wave his cape about playing to the crowd. He turned just as the bull arrived, tossing him high in the air over his back. We leapt to our feet cheering and clapping loudly. In their excitement someone knocked over a large bottle of beer and its contents ran down the terraced concrete seats. Each recipient leapt to their feet shouting and shaking their fists. The hissing grew menacing. It was time to leave. Back at the race paddock we had another cultural experience. This one was extremely confronting.

Laurie tells the story. He fell into a discussion with a Spanish sidecar racer. His partner turned up and a few more people joined the circle around his large table. She was a typical Spanish gypsy beauty with long black hair, fiery dark eyes and bright clothing. She started on at us about the crazy lives we were leading; the racing danger, the risk in our travels over Europe; in general the very pointless existence we were living. Ralph Rensen had joined us and had plenty of forceful views to offer.

After a while things mellowed out a bit with the fine Spanish wine. Somehow the conversation drifted around to what we were all going to do in the future. The woman then offered to tell us our fortunes. It was fairly light-hearted stuff. We had to sit opposite her while she held our palm and we looked straight into her eyes, a pleasing though somewhat unnerving experience. I seem to remember that she said my fortune did not lie with motorcycles (considering the vast amount I have spent on them in the intervening years, she was correct). Ralph plonked himself down in front of her, thrust out his hand and stared into her face. She took up his hand and looked at it, then up into his face. Her whole demeanour changed in a flash. She dropped his hand, buried her face in her hands, turned and ran crying to her caravan. We were left a little shocked to say the least. Ralph tried to laugh it off as rubbish, but we were all fairly taken aback and sheepishly went back to our vans. This was a fortnight before the Isle of Man TT race where Ralph lost his life.

The 1961 Isle of Man organisers had received a record entry of 366 riders from 23 countries. One of the newcomers was Kiwi John Farnsworth, from Auckland. After we'd taken him on a slow sighting lap, he asked, "How the hell can anyone learn this in a week?"

"You can't, but if you break it up into manageable sections you will," I explained. "Why go beyond Ballacraine, seven miles from the start, if you are not fully conversant with every corner or sequence of corners up to that point? Break the circuit up into manageable sections, and learn them individually, that's not so hard." John agreed.

A knock on the door at 3.45am on Saturday heralded the beginning of another demanding week. Out of bed into my leathers, including a thick jersey as it was cold, and down to the kitchen for a quick cup of tea and piece of toast. We heard an MV Agusta drone past the front door. It was time to join the cavalcade to the paddock on the 7R. The first two practice laps passed all too quickly. The only problem was the cold. With an awkward, stiff-legged gait I joined Laurie and a huddle of shivering riders who were enjoying a hot cup of chocolate in the Cadbury tent, a TT tradition. This is where you heard about the close calls, near misses and surprises, interspersed with how they had managed to get around the Verandah, the 33rd Milestone, or the bottom of Bray Hill flat-out. There seemed to be as much action in here as there was on the track. Most were on a high, thrilled to be back on the island again. Later, when the times were posted, I was surprised to learn I had made the fifth-fastest lap.

On Sunday, June 4, Shell boss Lew Ellis called at our garage.

"Are you free for the next hour or two, Hugh? Mr Okano, the Suzuki race team manager, would like to see you."

"Sure, Lew, give me a few minutes to wash up and I'll be right with you."

As I left to join Lew in his car, others sharing the garage offered their congratulations and promised to still speak to me even when I was rich and famous.

When we arrived at the Fernleigh Hotel, where the Suzuki team was staying, Lew introduced me to Mr Ishikawa, the secretary-interpreter for the team. He ushered us into the lounge where I met Mr Okano, the team captain-manager and Mr Shimizu, the chief engineer. Ishikawa explained that a considerable amount of engine development had been carried out since last year and the team hoped to gain better results. Ishikawa went on to explain that their race schedule for 1961 included just three Grand Prix — the Isle of Man TT, Dutch TT and the Belgium GP.

They congratulated me on the progress I'd made in developing my skills during the short time I'd been in Europe and hoped I would agree to join them so together we would achieve our mutual ambitions. At that time I hadn't formulated a long-term plan or had any great ambitions other than 'being there', but was well aware of my current short-term financial pressures; the need to increase my income and avoid living from hand to mouth. Knowing they had a lot to learn and aware of their current lack of competitiveness, they were, as a group, humble, self-effacing and wanting to please. After they carefully explained the terms under which I'd be employed and went through the simple two-page contract with me, I agreed to join them and signed on the dotted line. There were no restrictions on my riding my own machine. Messrs Okano, Shimizu and Ishikawa all added their signatures. We then enjoyed a cup of Japanese tea, the first of many.

Later we gathered in the workshop where I was introduced to the mechanics, trying very hard to remember the names of those I'd be working with. I sat on both the 125cc and 250cc twin-cylinder, air-cooled two-stroke machines that had been allocated to me. They appeared fairly basic without any indication that they would be race winners. Minor lever and footrest adjustments were made, then long discussions were entered into regarding engine characteristics and performance. It was a pleasant, light-hearted occasion. They seemed happy to have me with them and I was pleased to be there. I mentioned to Ishikawa that I thought the exhaust pipes seemed rather low and may hit the road. He interpreted this to the team, who all laughed and, chorus-like, replied: "No. No. Okay. Okay." We agreed that during practice the next evening, after I had completed two laps on my Norton I would do an exploratory lap on their 125cc.

On returning to my garage, I was barraged with free advice regarding investment opportunities and how I could capitalise on my future. Had my fellow racers known my contract figure was a mere 100 pounds a meeting, they would have been underwhelmed. As far as I was concerned it was a foot in the door, and 300 pounds in my pocket, at the time, was a substantial amount to me. Actually, I now felt quite relaxed about the situation. There was little reason to believe this was anything more than the beginning of a new challenge. I had no expectations of success in the immediate future, as Honda and Yamaha had a head start on Suzuki. As always, I would just do the best I could and see what happened. The next day, after completing two trouble-free laps on the Norton and recording the fourth-fastest time in the 500cc class, I made my way to the Suzuki team enclosure for my first test ride.

My slow descent down Bray Hill was a disappointment and I turned off the circuit and returned to the pits via some back roads. The Suzuki team were surprised to see me so soon. With tact and in the nicest possible way I explained that perhaps we should go to Jurby Airfield later in the day where I could become more familiar with the bikes. Hopefully, altering various engine settings would find more power. To make progress I needed to quickly gain a new skill, based on patience, good humour and well-reasoned advice diplomatically presented in tune with an engineer's beliefs. A rider wanted the fastest engine, a technician wanted to produce the most reliable. A rider's value was judged by his lap speed, the technician by the finishing order. Compromise was negotiated with a smile, not always in the rider's favour I might add, thus avoiding bruised egos.

After a short test session at Jurby the team agreed that the 125cc RT61 needed further development to be competitive and my entry would be withdrawn. The 250cc RV61 showed more potential. When we finally found the optimum carburettor settings, many of which they had not used before, the engine felt strong enough to give a competitive ride. I learned a great deal that day and not only about these new bikes. Perhaps, more importantly, I gained an insight into the people that I was destined to work with for the next seven years. Back in 1961 Europeans' knowledge and understanding of Asian cultures was almost non-existent. During my time with Suzuki I don't think we ever completely overcame the gap in the knowledge of race craft, the understanding of it and the subtle need to have the bike set up in a way that allowed the rider to perform on the extreme edge of his ability. Engineers are guided by what they see as facts and figures. A question of 'if we can measure it, we can master it'. I tried to find a compromise by working with my mechanics in the Suzuki workshops.

A lightweight practice session was scheduled for the following morning, Wednesday. This was the ideal opportunity to evaluate our 'improved' machine. We were disappointed to find that while warming the engines we were again experiencing inconsistent fuel flow and flooding carburettors. Not wanting to forgo this opportunity of a ride in racing conditions, I decided to go anyway.

Before joining the circuit we lifted the front wheel of the 250 Suzuki to empty the fuel that had pooled in the fairing's belly pan. Then, armed with a spanner and a selection of spark plugs, I set off. Riding at a steady pace, I hoped to complete two laps. Engine performance was inconsistent, at times dying through a lack of fuel, when it was sensible to ease off to avoid seizing a piston. When it was flooding I used less throttle to avoid fouling the plugs. At times it ran cleanly and produced surprisingly good power but after a few kilometres the engine would hold back, giving every indication a piston seizure was imminent. On the approach to Kirkmichael the engine died completely. It had run out of fuel.

I pushed it into the village where an older chap was watching from his front garden. After leaning the Suzuki against his fence I removed my helmet and engaged him in conversation. Being from New Zealand and riding one of these new Japanese jobs he found me of interest and invited me in for a cup of tea that developed into a full breakfast. His father, who had owned the house before him, had clear memories of the 1911 TT when Canadian-born American Jake De Rozier crashed out on his Indian while leading the race. Eventually, the Japanese mechanics arrived full of apologies for not filling the petrol tank correctly! I reassured them by saying that without fuel the bike was very light and easy to push. They appreciated the tension-relieving joke. We were okay.

Back at the garage I asked if we could inspect the float chambers as I thought there must be an obvious reason for the carburation problems. The two float bowls were carefully dismantled and inspected. They contained traces of a fine fibre-like material, causing the simple fuel-regulating cut-off valves to stick, sometimes open, other times shut. Strands of fibreglass were leaching from the fuel tank, probably caused by an additive in the British petrol that had not been present in Japanese fuels. To overcome this, the tanks were drained and dried out after use.

We visited Jurby again and, to our collective relief, for the first time my 250 performed well. With consistent fuel flow we were now able to tune the carburettors properly. Our next opportunity to test the bike was dawn practice on Friday and clearing showers greeted us. I left the start with confidence as, for the first time, throttle feedback seemed normal. As the lap unfolded I found it ran best on three-quarter throttle openings as the main jets were set too rich. By pushing the cut-out button occasionally, with the throttle wide open, I gave a cautionary blast of cool air through the engine to help avoid any tendency to seize. At the end of the lap I stopped at the pits to 'read' the spark plugs. It was obvious that smaller jets were required. These were fitted along with colder spark plugs.

As I left the pits the change in performance was encouraging so I decided to attempt a brisk lap. It went well until a minor gearbox problem arose and there was still a feeling of the engine holding back. Again, keeping the throttle wide open on long fast sections and pushing the cut-out button to kill the engine momentarily helped. The steering and suspension was quite adequate relative to its performance.

At the end of practice the official times for all the competitors were made available. To the delight of the team I had made the third-fastest lap that morning. I had heard a distinctive scraping sound on several fast corners. Sure enough, the exhaust pipes were heavily scored where they had hit the road. When the mechanics saw this they were initially concerned but then large smiles lit up their faces. They now knew I was serious, had gained some of the skills required to get the best from the engine and was sufficiently confident to test the bike's limits.

The very much a prototype 1961 250cc Suzuki. Archives.

Later in the day the engine was stripped and it looked good. The high spots on the pistons were carefully eased with fine abrasive paper and the gearbox problems rectified. The team asked questions of me, made notes and took my opinions seriously. I was careful not to say too much as the beginning of mutual respect was emerging. That evening we all went out for a team dinner and my first experience of what was to become a regular occurrence in the years to come. We were seated at a long table. Mr Okano was at the head, Shimizu on his right, with me to his left and Ishikawa beside me.

After Mr Okano praised the team and me for our efforts, I was asked to speak. I thanked Mr Okano and his staff for seeing in me a rider who was capable of producing the performance they expected. I added that I was a team person and firmly believed that, provided each member developed his skills and worked to his potential, was patient, kept an open mind and listened to what others had to say, we would all make progress. I felt confident and respected so added that I excelled in the company of positive people and thrived when surrounded by enthusiasm. Then I remained standing until Ishikawa had finished interpreting what I had said. They were impressed, stood, and with large smiles clapped for some time.

During the meal the general discussion covered the early days of the Suzuki Motor Company and my history as a young man in New Zealand. They were particularly amused about my journey through the rear wall of Mum's garage on the Gold Star with the throttle stuck open. The anecdotes continued and so began the most successful factory-rider relationship in the history of Suzuki's Grand Prix racing.

Before returning to the garage, I stopped and sat on one of the many seats positioned along the Douglas Promenade. It was dusk, a time when you could feel alone, unseen even, but clearly make out Douglas Bay and its surrounds. A sense of acceptance, at last, and satisfaction washed over me. A feeling of completeness I had never known before. If Mum could have sat with me here, now, in this environment, she would have understood at last and been proud of me. Reality returned with a thump. Laurie would be working on my 1958 Manx, as it had to be totally stripped. So I replaced my suit with overalls and helped complete the job.

Despite the numerous side issues and heavy workloads, practice had gone well. The following best positions are what I achieved from a total of 12 completed practice laps: Saturday, June 3, am session, 350cc, fifth fastest; Monday, June 5, pm, 500cc, fourth; Wednesday, June 7, pm, 500cc, third; Friday, June 9, am, 250cc, third; Saturday, June 10, am, 350cc, fifth, and 500cc, second. Due to damp patches at various points of the circuit and mist on the mountain, during that final practice session on Saturday morning, 10 riders crashed: seven were hospitalised and one died.

Now it was time for that grand TT tradition, the weigh-in. Today only a document check and machine scrutineering, but in the 1907–10 period of the TT a machine, its engine capacity, weight and fuel use was part of the race formula. In those days and for years after, the trade 'barons', as the representatives of accessory manufacturers, and oil and fuel companies were known, would set up behind a line of chairs and tables. As the top riders passed, then referred to as the 'fancied runners', they would literally bid for their services, offering substantial financial inducement to use their products, such as chains, tyres, spark plugs, oil and petrol. I explained this history to the Japanese and also pointed out Rem Fowler, the 1907 TT winner. In excellent health, he attended the TT every year and appeared little older than late middle age.

Top: Leaving Parliament Square and the crowds of spectators. T.C. Marsh. Middle: The start of the 500cc race. Tommy Robb to my right front, Ron Miles, Australia right rear. Archives. Bottom: Signpost Corner with dried mucus showing on my face shield. Archives.

They were amazed. It was remarkable to think he spanned a 54-year gap between basic, single-speed, spindly motorcycles and the sophisticated racing machines we now rode.

The start of the 250cc race on Monday brought an extra tension to the Suzuki team. They were well aware that their future reputations were on the line. To finish the five-lap, two-hour, 188.65-mile race was the first priority; it was easy to ride with that in mind. For the first lap the bike ran very well, averaging 88mph, the seventh-fastest lap of all the race finishers. Gear selection problems returned during the second lap, and the need to use the kill switch frequently to keep the engine internals cool cost me time. We fitted new spark plugs during the refuelling stop at the end of the third lap. With gear selection becoming more a matter of luck, and after enduring an attack of cramp, I nursed it home in 10th place for a bronze replica.

Team members Alistair King and Paddy Driver retired on the first lap and the only other Suzuki to complete the full race distance was ridden by Michio Ichino, who finished some six minutes after me. Mr Okano had a wide smile. His phone call to Japan later that evening would contain some reasonably good news.

Under 'Good Old Days' on the Team Suzuki website there is a piece 'Reminiscences about Hugh Anderson'. The paragraph covering that 250cc TT follows: "Result was four Suzuki riders retired, Ichino came 12th and Anderson 10th. Suzuki management appreciated and put a high value on Anderson's 10th place. This was his first ride on a two-stroke machine. He willingly worked closely with his mechanics and had good control of the unstable Suzuki RV61 machine over the five-lap 188-mile (305km) race."

With my main focus diverted to Suzuki, and having had limited practice, I was not in a position to excel on my own bikes. I finished seventh in the Junior, just 4.5 seconds behind a factory development Norton, and was the first privateer (owner-rider) and first AJS rider home.

In the Senior race, as my bike was not fast, the engine had been reluctant to rev from new; I used the highest gearing available. In theory this gave a top speed of over 135mph at 7,000rpm. Suffering from a brain-numbing cold, I lined up for the Senior. My bike, in Kiwi vernacular, "Wouldn't pull the skin off a rice pudding." Aussies would say, "You could kick your hat down the road faster." That dishonest engine builder had been correct.

I'd never started a race feeling ill before, but it seemed a great cure for start-line nerves, as I had none. There was no emotion at all. After a steady start I picked up the pace and on the fourth lap was getting into the zone. When passing through the fast corners at the 11th Milestone, I noticed some movement on the right of the track. Someone had crashed heavily, debris was on the road, a bike under the hedge and a marshal was holding a rider down. I pushed on, totally focused without a blip in concentration, until, on the fifth lap, I high-sided leaving the Gooseneck. Only then did I realise how sick I was. Unable to get to my feet, I crawled off the road on my hands and knees and lay on the grass verge.

Mucus had been running from my nose and blown back around my ears. Spectators helped me to a safer place, cleaned me up and gave me soup, sandwiches and a cup of tea. Apart from a sprained ankle and general bruising, I was okay. When the roads opened Laurie came with the van to pick me up. We reviewed the past two weeks and agreed that we had definitely come out of it ahead. The relationship with Suzuki was excellent, we had gained a good result on the AJS and finished rebuilding the 1958 Manx, blown up at the German Grand Prix. I could now deliver it to the buyer in Birmingham, and make the final payment on Percy Coleman's 7R AJS.

We returned to the garage and learned that Ralph had fallen. We loaded the van, showered and for the first time went out for a high-class steak meal, washed down with ample wine. We returned in high spirits only to be told that Ralph had died. He had been enjoying his best TT results ever. Sixth on a factory 125 Bultaco, third in the 350 class and was contesting third place at the time of that fatal crash. We were told that during the spill the plastic screen on the fairing had broken. Ralph had suffered a severed main artery in his neck and died in the marshal's arms.

While waiting for the ferry at 5.30am next morning, feeling rather sad, sore and depressed, I wrote in my diary, 'Ralph, my good friend and pirate from the past, is dead. Yet another mate to fall foul of the many traps that lie in our daily path.'

The Dutch TT at Assen in the north-east of Holland attracted up to 150,000 spectators from all over Europe, a very special celebration of motorcycle racing. Farmers give up their fields to campers and Friday night is parade night. Many shops don't close, the central park is transformed into a huge fairground and a carnival atmosphere continues until dawn. The crowds are so dense that movement though the narrow streets is reduced to a shuffle where every language of the Western world can be heard. This celebration is shared in complete safety by youngsters and pensioners alike in an atmosphere of good humour and respect, typical of that found when motorcyclists gather anywhere in the world.

I was again riding the 250cc Suzuki, plus my AJS 7R and the 500cc Manx. The first few laps on the Suzuki were used to run in a new engine, and then gradually increase speed and engine revs. When I felt secure in knowing what changes needed to be made, I called at the pits where my two mechanics quickly altered carburettor settings and as always changed the spark plugs. Immediately, the engine felt happier, allowing me to make several fast laps, which resulted in smiles all around. The team was still on the back foot, however, and not in the same performance ballpark as Honda or Italian manufacturers such as Morini and Benelli.

During the afternoon practice session I began pressing on with the 7R. There was a very fast right-hand kink at the back of the track. It was a challenge, one I had been perhaps a little too ready to accept. Could I get through it at near-maximum speed in third gear, without backing off? After three attempts, each faster than the previous, the rear tyre let go. We went skating up the road balanced on the right-hand footrest and megaphone, but with luck and a little skill I got it all back again via a long slide on the grass verge. Later I found that I needed to brake for that corner, and still be faster than most. Perhaps this virtual obsession stemmed from the belief that I wasn't good enough through the fast stuff, but perhaps irresistible challenge and that ever present excitement of risk played their part.

The Suzuki performed well during the early laps of the 250cc second practice but when the clutch cable broke I felt it wise to stop at the pits, as I didn't want to abuse the fragile gearbox that had played up at the TT. The mechanics apologised profusely, as was their way, but I wasn't concerned. I was confident we were growing stronger with every small step taken.

Another tradition of the Dutch TT was that on Friday afternoon a pre-race machine and documentation examination was carried out in the centre of town at the marketplace. Entrants were encouraged to ride there. Up to 150 racing motorcycles with open megaphones made a spectacular entrance. The only thing conspicuous about the police was their total absence. Laurie insisted on taking the Manx on a long detour back to the paddock. He arrived windswept and bright-eyed with exhilaration. He had taken it to maximum revs in first, second and third gear. At the time a pretty exciting experience.

At the start of the 350 race I was at the tail of a group contesting fourth place. Gary Hocking, Rhodesia, on an MV Agusta, was dicing with Bob McIntyre, Scotland, on an Italian Bianchi, for the lead. They were followed by Franta Stastny, Czechoslovakia (Jawa), Ernesto Brambilla, Italy (Bianchi), Paddy Driver, South Africa (Norton), Junior TT winner Phil Read, England (Norton), me (AJS) and then Silvio Grassetti, Italy (Benelli).

The dice is on for fourth place. The spectators have a box seat. Archives.

Phil moved over on me when I tried to pass and put me on the grass. When it happened again I knew it was intended. I passed him under brakes and pushed him wide on a right-angled corner, then accelerated away in pursuit of Paddy. I slipped past him. Ernesto was in my sights. It took two laps of intense concentration to catch him. Finally, he made an error at the end of the start-finish straight, allowing me to get under him and push on as hard as possible. Third-placed Franta was the next target. My full throttle obsession kicked in again.

For several laps I had been very tempted to keep it wide open through a left-hand second-gear corner. Obviously, I would pick up precious time but when I did the rear tyre let go. Once more I got it back but was doing 130kph in the grass heading for another corner. There was no chance of getting around it, so I laid the AJS down. After sliding on the grass for a short distance, the tyres again came in contact with the track surface. The instant grip caused the bike to shoot upright in a dramatic high-side that catapulted me up the road to land on my shoulders and head. I came to a rest in a large drain. The AJS flew through the air, its engine screaming, and landed heavily on me, adding to my injuries.

The track marshals removed the bike, ambulance staff did their best to lift me gently out of the drain, with a dislocated and fractured hip testing my pain threshold. I was placed on a stretcher and carried to a first-aid station. The staff checked out my injuries then, to support my hip, bound both legs together before lifting me into an ancient ex-military Chevrolet ambulance where I was strapped firmly to a wooden bench. For some reason, known only to the manufacturers, this vehicle appeared to have no normal working suspension. The only exit route from the circuit was along very rough farm tracks. Occasionally, the staff stopped the vehicle to give me a break from the pain.

Honda's magnificent 250cc six-cylinder engine.

CHAPTER 7

I fell off my bike and landed in the arms of the finest person I have ever met

On arrival at the Assen hospital the staff were efficient and understanding. The orthopaedic surgeon explained they would, under anaesthetic, put my hip back in place, then fit a full body cast from my chest to the toes on my right leg and to my knee on the left leg.

"How long for?" I asked somewhat anxiously.

"Six weeks," he replied.

I told him I was a fast healer and four weeks would be okay so he compromised with five. My injuries were a dislocated and broken right hip joint, a broken left collarbone and three broken ribs on my right side caused when the 7R landed on me.

As the plaster was being applied I felt uneasy, a little like being buried alive. The thought of not seeing or moving most of my body for five weeks took some adjusting to. As they encased my upper body I kept expanding my chest to gain as much 'freedom' as possible. Even so, there were moments when unease became suppressed panic. When the job was finished I was left cold, shivering and 'set' in a half-sitting position with my feet at chest height, legs spread by a piece of wood, with appropriate openings where required.

Laurie visited me as soon as the race meeting was completed and the roads opened. After establishing that I was reasonably okay and giving what little of me was protruded from the plaster cast a bear hug, he began, as he had in Austria, something of a tirade about ignoring his signals board. As always he had diligently offered information and advice. During the first few laps it was only my ever improving race position. In due course he added 'steady'. By the time I had gained fourth place and was going for third he had added and underlined 'slow down'. When he realised his signals were being ignored he threw the board to one side and left the pit signalling area. Laurie claimed my aggressive, single-minded riding attitude and the determination displayed could lead to only one thing. Sitting next to a hospitalised, fully plastered, helpless rider, he felt his opinions totally vindicated.

Not having seen his messages I couldn't argue if they were pertinent to my current situation or not, and suggested his display of pique was more to do with his cost-free tour of Europe coming to an end than my welfare. He laughed. With my broken ribs I couldn't.

Next day a group of my fellow Continental Circus riding friends called. As usual in these situations there was constant leg pulling, wisecracks and advice on how to establish a good nurse-patient relationship. Most of them had had some experience of long hospital stays and were quite willing to relate the tales of success they claimed to have had. Others preferred to recount their less pleasant experiences. The arrival of the Suzuki team leaders waiting in the corridor was a signal for them to leave. Even though my ribs were killing me it had been good to see them. Their leaving brought home the fact that I'd be leading a lonely existence for some time.

Mr Okano, Mr Shimizu and Mr Ishikawa showed real concern about the extent of my injuries and the discomfort I must be suffering. They were surprised and relieved to be told the pain level was low and that I would be riding at the Ulster Grand Prix in six weeks. They discussed in broad terms their plans for 1962 and hoped I would be available to join them. I assured them I had no intention of crashing regularly and I looked forward to the time when Suzuki produced Grand Prix machines capable of winning races and I wouldn't have to try so hard on my British bikes to gain a podium finish. This was typical of the team humour. They said my faith in them was appreciated, but asked me to be patient for another two years. Before leaving they thanked me for my co-operation, patience and the contribution I had made towards the overall benefit of the team.

Soon after they left, a member of the Dutch TT organising committee arrived with a handsome fruit basket and a bundle of flowers. This show of concern, generosity and recognition was unexpected and appreciated. In fact my day ended on something of a high. In time, bones would heal and life would carry on.

The following week an eyesight problem arose and gradually worsened. I felt it could be serious so kept it to myself, hoping it would go. My vision had become blurred and every time I looked at a wall picture I could clearly see three images of it, all at different angles. I tried to ignore it but couldn't. I stared at it trying to will the thing to revert to the singular but it wouldn't, so I reluctantly reported it. Wires were attached to all parts of my skull at the X-ray department and several 'photos' were taken. The verdict was that I had a fractured skull and, because of that, nerves to my eyes were damaged. I again enquired what would be the expected recovery time. "Oh, not so long, maybe six or seven weeks, no longer" was the reply.

A postcard from fellow competitors.

The positive side was they had diagnosed the problem and it would heal, so best to lie back and avoid looking at that damn picture.

After several days, during which I had eaten three meals a day and taking into account the normal digestive procedure, I began to wonder when something was going to happen down below. Another concern was how the process was going to be managed. Feeling that my situation wasn't unique, and having faith in the well-trained nurses, I relaxed. Eventually, it became apparent that a 'movement' was imminent so I pressed the help buzzer hard and long. When the nurse realised why I'd called, the smile left her face. She hurried off and returned with four helpers. With two on each side they raised me, slid the bedpan under me and left the room. Good so far but I was left wobbling and rocking about, due to my left collarbone being broken, the shoulder being strapped back and my arm in a sling. I only had mobility and strength in my right arm and, to a degree, my left leg. However, due to the position I was in, the top edge of the plaster was pushing hard against one of the broken ribs, which reduced the movement and strength in that arm.

I pressed the buzzer again. Someone had to support me. The pretty young nurse soon realised the problems I was experiencing were not conducive to 'doing the business' and put her arm around me as support. Now, as you all know, after a period of inactivity, it can, even in the privacy of your own home and complete with your favourite magazine, take considerable time and focus to get the plumbing working again. Under the circumstances, while balancing on an unstable pot with one foot in the air, ribs hurting like hell and held in the arms of a female, I didn't believe anything worthwhile could occur.

Just when I thought all the preparatory work had been wasted, and without any prompting from me, there was a totally unexpected and thunderous explosion followed by a rapid evacuation of generous proportions. Eventually, it was over. The nurses were called back and I was lifted up and the pan removed. This process was carried out regularly for the duration of my confinement.

A friend had loaned me a transistor radio that I tuned into Radio Caroline, the first 'free' station in Europe. To escape regulations, controls and taxes the station operated from a boat anchored in the English Channel and played the latest pop hits 24 hours a day with few interruptions for advertisements. Each morning at 6.30 a nurse came and all my accessible parts were thoroughly sponged and dried. Being a fairly normal, fit and healthy young man this sponging and drying could activate activity in the sexual department. So to avoid embarrassment for both parties, mainly me, actually, I would listen intently to the music, blocking everything out. Some days it worked, some it didn't.

One morning I woke with a start to see the most striking girl I had ever seen. She smiled in amusement at my startled expression. Then carrying herself with pride and confidence she walked to the side of my bed and said, "I'm Janny, I've come to wash you." Christ, I hope there are some good songs on the radio, I thought, as I fumbled in panic with the control dials.

Janny washed and dried my top half then threw back the blankets to scrub up the other bits. I concentrated as never before on the music, not daring to look, but despite my efforts an erection began.

"I'm sorry," I said.

"Oh, that happens often," she replied casually. I believed her.

I couldn't read due to my blurred vision and there was little to do to amuse myself other than listening to the radio. Later in the morning, while wondering when I'd see Janny again, an idea sprang to mind. I poured my jug of drinking water directly into the urine pot and pressed the buzzer.

In walked Janny. "Could I have some more water, please?" I asked. She silently took the jug and soon returned. Yes, she was indeed a gorgeous girl.

Obviously, if the water jug had been emptied, it was only a matter of time before the urinal was full, giving another excuse to press the buzzer. I waited expectantly and in walked a straight-faced stranger. Damn, I hope I haven't lost her, I thought. Then I noticed movement at the door and heard muffled laughter. Janny and her friend had set me up. What a relief to know she was aware of my 'interest'.

At midday a straight-faced Janny delivered my lunch.

"Could you help me please?" I asked.

"What is wrong?" she replied.

"My back is very painful," I said.

"Where?" she asked.

I did my best to indicate and took the tea towel covering my lunch and suggested she should pack it in where the top of the plaster was digging into my back. For the first time in 10 days I was comfortable. I thanked her profusely.

When Janny came to collect the empty lunch plates I took the opportunity to play the helpless card and asked if she would be kind enough to buy me some sweets.

"What sort?" she asked.

"Oh, I don't know, anything will be good," I replied.

"Maybe," she said, and walked out.

Several days passed and Janny hadn't returned. I grew concerned and asked each nurse who came to my ward if they had seen her. Many didn't speak English, some thought she was working at nights or in another ward, others didn't know her. I became convinced I had lost her.

Eventually, there was a knock on my door. Janny glided in — tall, slim and elegant in a black and grey Chanel-style suit, with perfect make-up. Blurred as my vision was, there was no question about it. This young woman had presence and maturity beyond her years. Janny gave me a large packet of sweets, then eased herself into a chair at the end of my bed. After gracefully crossing her legs, she placed her hands in her lap and, with a faint smile, fixed me with a steady gaze.

Now what do I do? I thought. Making small talk, especially with girls, had never been a strength of mine. But I desperately wanted to communicate, to amuse, entertain and interest her. Struggling to keep my voice steady and speaking slowly, with the utmost sincerity I thanked her for coming, thanked her for the sweets and commented on how beautiful she was. Being confident and totally without conceit, she shrugged off the flattery and said, "Try a sweet, they are rumbonen."

They seemed to have a strong taste of alcohol. "What are they made of?" I asked.

"Rum and chocolate," she said. An odd combination, I thought, but very welcome.

Janny had taken English, German and French at school but had little opportunity to practise them. She wasn't sufficiently confident to express herself in detail and often answered me in Dutch.

Suddenly, the door burst open and in strode Laurie. Without realising I had a visitor he cheerily asked, "How are you going, young fella?"

Janny rose out of her chair and Laurie stopped in midstride. She walked towards him, offered him her hand and said, "I'm Janny and you are Laurie, I think." Laurie seemed undecided as to who he was, and then agreed he was indeed the man in question and shook Janny's outstretched hand. Janny then walked to my bedside and after adjusting my pillows said, "I must go now", shook my hand and walked out.

"Come back soon," I called.

At the door she turned and with an impish smile said, "Maybe", and was gone. I still knew nothing about her, not even her surname.

Laurie was caught completely by surprise by Janny's demeanour and it took some time before he was able to exclaim, "What a stunning girl!" He then began his daily ritual of lunching from 'our' freshly filled fruit basket. After the crash, Laurie had made his home in the paddock at the TT course, where showers and toilets were available. Using a collapsible bed in the van, life was quite comfortable. The reason he gave for staying was that as I was in such a sad and sorry state I needed his intelligent conversation, humour and excellent company to help pass the time. Actually, he had met the daughter of a local racing enthusiast and each day joined her family for an evening meal.

Finally, Laurie had to leave his comfortable and carefree lifestyle to return to London and find work. Before leaving he offered to assist me at the Ulster Grand Prix, although he was convinced I didn't have a snowball's chance in hell of recovering in time. His attendance was reliant on my agreeing to read his pit signals. 'It won't worry me if you don't take my advice, but for God's sake read them,' he said. With a cheerful "See you, young fella", he left.

On Wednesday, July 28, five weeks after the accident, the orthopaedic surgeon gave the long-awaited instruction to remove the plaster. Excited about getting up and about and on with my life, I was put on a trolley, wheeled to a workshop and advised that I would be attended to shortly. My thoughts of 'How is this going to be removed?' were interrupted by the arrival of a 1.9m, 110kg grim-faced woman. I thought she may use her bare hands, but from a small selection of appliances she chose an electrical device with a saw-like cutting blade. It managed to efficiently chew through the plaster, as there was a guide attached to the machine that slid along between the plaster and my skin. It buzzed away, doing the job well, until she reached the inner thigh of my left leg. Somehow part of the machine started removing a slice of flesh.

I grabbed her now lethal little machine and pushed hard against her to halt its progress while she in turn continued to push even harder. The struggle continued but I was the most motivated. It was hurting and while she may not have understood my verbal instructions, there was no mistaking the volume. Eventually, she gave up and in total disdain glared at me. "Men," she said, "out of bed so big", indicating a 2m specimen, "in bed, so small", indicating a dwarf-sized version. You have had some disappointments in the bedroom, I thought, as I tried to explain that her clever little device had somehow attacked my leg. She mumbled something incomprehensible, which I took as an apology, but who cared. I was free and sat up — only to faint and fall back on my pillow.

Without the support of the plaster cast my right leg went into spasms. I sat up only to faint again. I then tried to relax and once back in the ward I slowly bent and straightened my knee trying to regain control. Finally, the spasms decreased so I slowly started easing myself into a sitting position to the point where light-headedness began, held it as long as possible, and then lay down again.

By late evening I was feeling much better and sitting up. After some moments of dizziness my head cleared and for the first time I was able to look out of the window only to be confronted with a dense fog. Will I have to stay another month? Slowly, as my eyes focused, my vision cleared. I turned back into my room. Again, everything was a foggy blur, but slowly my vision became normal. Obviously, the nerves to my eyes were still damaged. I will need to leave as soon as possible; I'll never pass that eye test booked for Friday afternoon. Later that evening, using the bed as support, I shuffled, time and again, from one side around to the other. What a sense of achievement! Gradually, I was feeling stronger and more confident.

I would be riding at the Ulster Grand Prix in Ireland! I felt my life was back on track, albeit a rather wobbly one for the moment. Knowing I would make a full recovery and having met and gained the friendship of a special person brought back that essential sense of excitement.

The following morning, Thursday, I was given a pair of crutches and after the most refreshing shower of my life walked up and down the passageway. My hip and ankle, sprained in the Isle of Man crash, were not too uncomfortable and soon I could manage with just one crutch. During the day I phoned Bert Schuurman, who had taken care of my van, and asked him to bring it to the hospital car park with the keys and my clothes to my room. After waking early on Friday, I carefully stood by my bed and walked around it gaining confidence. With concentration I would manage okay. I got dressed and walked unsteadily out the front doors. By focusing just a few metres ahead I found my van and scrambled up into the familiar seat. Looking into the distance while waiting for my vision to clear, I inhaled the unique heady aroma of the special vegetable engine oil we used and the race gas. Petrolhead? Yeah. One hundred per cent!

I had arranged to meet Janny. Though still reluctant to talk about herself, after coffee we were able to spend a very pleasant hour together in a local park. I spoke about swimming in the river, camping in the bush, the freedom youth had in New Zealand and why I had come to Europe to race motorcycles. I doubt if Janny shared my outdoor interests, however, as I've said, small talk with girls was not my forte.

It was time to go; there were no signs of sadness at our parting. I avoided the handshake and went for the hug. We laughed. Why be sad? We both knew this was but the beginning. I watched as Janny walked away. At the corner she turned and waved. I could see her arm but not that mischievous grin.

My good friends Jan and Nel Meierdres spectating on the Isle of Man. Archives.

112

CHAPTER 8
I couldn't lift it onto the stand, or start it, but I qualified sixth

Laurie and I ride through the streets of Belfast in a convoy of motorcycles. Any hospital stiffness or discomfort is being soothed away by the familiarity of riding a motorcycle, any motorcycle, even at commuter pace. But my vision is still a bit of a worry. Thing is, I'm not on a road motorcycle, I'm on my 7R AJS. If this sounds bizarre it's easily explained. I'm just one of a group of penny-pinching racers who'd pushed their bikes on to the ferry to Ireland for the Ulster Grand Prix, the real jewel of the Emerald Isle's road-racing season.

Canadian Mike Duff had offered to take my suitcases, tool box and spares in his van. So this was a chance to save some of the start and prize money on offer. A few moments ago, we'd simply pushed the bikes down the ferry gangplank, gathered in a group, and then coaxed them into noisy life with a quick sprint along the dock. Now we are riding through the centre of Belfast.

Police are on duty at most intersections. When we arrive, rather than stopping us they quickly bring all other traffic to a halt with a big hand in the air and an impenetrable glare. Having got the commuters' attention they wave our noisy group through with a cheery smile and a friendly wave.

No problems, this is Northern Ireland.

The bike transport to the Ulster Grand Prix may have been makeshift but the accommodation was top shelf.

Sidney Grey, who had travelled with me to Monza last year, had invited Laurie and me to stay with him at the family home. His uncle had a garage adjacent to the pits, an ideal arrangement.

On Wednesday, after looking into the distance for some time to allow my eyes to focus, I was late to go out for the first 350cc practice session. As I rode onto the circuit I could see a plume of smoke rising from a sequence of fast corners at the end of the start-finish straight. When practice was over we learned that Australian Ron Miles, who was sharing the garage with us, had fallen and been taken to hospital. We helped Ron's travelling companion to load his equipment and second bike into his van and hoped he would be okay.

Yes, Laurie, I promise, hand on heart, to read your signal board. Archives.

Impatient with the pace, I pulled the pin. The Nick Nicholls collection at Mortons Archive.

I've only been out of hospital for eight days, give me a break. The Nick Nicholls collection at Mortons Archive.

My eyesight gradually improved and during the final practice session I managed to surprise an awful lot of people, and myself, by qualifying sixth fastest on the hastily repaired AJS and 10th on the 500cc. Even so, after having been out on the bike it took some time before I could read a programme.

As my legs were still weak, following five weeks in hospital, I made a poor push-start in the 350cc race, but managed to slip past several riders over the next five laps.

Then I closed in on a tight formation led by Tommy Robb and Mike Duff, both of whom later became factory riders and Grand Prix winners, Ron Langston, who had finished fifth in the Isle of Man, and Franta Stastny, on the works Jawa who would take fourth place in that year's world championship.

I managed to pass a couple of them but could make no further progress. After another lap or two I became frustrated; I felt that I could brake later at a medium-fast left-hand corner. So I moved out of the line, waited for them to brake, then much later hit mine hard and passed them to move into seventh place. Feeling stronger every lap, and while I was gaining on the fifth- and sixth-placed riders, the engine began to vibrate. It got so bad I was forced to retire at the pits. A crankshaft bearing had failed and we also found that the frame had broken.

The 'wise old heads' of the paddock had a tough saying in those days: "Let's see how good the young up-and-coming riders are after their first big one." They considered a strong comeback after a major spill would be the ultimate test of commitment to road racing. I felt the ride that day on the AJS, against some of the world's best riders, proved mine.

There was minor mayhem at the push-start of the 500cc race when two riders tangled and both lost control. One hit me and we both went down. There seemed little damage to my Norton, but I had a jagged gash in my right lower leg. I'd had enough action for one day, so we returned to our garage and packed up.

Next job was to visit the race secretary's office to collect my start money. He wanted to reduce it, as he said I hadn't started the Senior race. Expecting this, I claimed to have been doing 130kph, then removed my boot and lifted the leg of my leather race suit, showing him a blood-soaked sock and holding the gash open to add effect. He was impressed, said no more and paid me the full amount.

Having no option, I borrowed a length of rope to tow Laurie on the AJS with my Manx back to Belfast and the ferry across the Irish Sea. Before we left the paddock, Laurie made me promise not to exceed 60kph or pass any cars. As we entered Belfast it was difficult to beat the lights and we ran a few reds. When we reached the docks Laurie, using quite positive language, claimed my eyesight had worsened and now I had become colour blind. He would be doing the driving tomorrow, thank you very much!

As usual, by the time we got on board, the returning spectators had occupied all the seats and most of the floor area. They were described as cattle boats for good reason. We retreated to the bar where a group soon gathered. After an hour or so the stories had become less true and more blue.

Then the boat became quiet as news filtered through that Ron Miles had died. We looked at each other helplessly. Was it rider error? Mechanical failure? Who knows, perhaps it didn't matter now. The beer became sour and we all moved off to find a piece of vacant carpet and tried to sleep.

On Monday I had my leg stitched up and a few days later, at Brands Hatch, fellow New Zealander and mate John Farnsworth and I enjoyed a dice in the 500cc race. The contest began on a wet track when we were in fifth and sixth place. As it dried, four local circuit specialists passed us but we benefited from another light shower and re-passed them to finish sixth and seventh.

The following week my Continental Circus tour resumed. I won the race in the suburbs of Bilbao, the capital of the Basque country in north-west Spain, after taking my stitches out with my fingernail scissors and long-nose pliers. They had grown in, so it wasn't a painless operation.

I spent 10 days swimming, walking and finally jogging as I regained a semblance of fitness while staying at St Raphael on the French Riviera with French champion Jacques Insermini and his delightful partner Nanou, who was multi-lingual, ever helpful and 'matriarch' of the race paddock. Ten days later I was waiting impatiently, in the early morning, for the race office at the Monza circuit, home of the Italian Grand Prix, to open. I was hoping to receive a letter from nurse Janny. Finally, the office opened and there it was.

Dated August 26, 1961 it was in reply to one I'd sent from England. It read:

Dear Hugh,

Thank you for your letter that came yesterday. Yes I am well, thank you, and everything here goes good. What you wrote is correct. We know only a little about each other. Are you sure it will help to know more? It's OK. I am joking. If you can come again to Assen I would be pleased to see you. I hope you come in your van and not an ambulance next time.

Yes we did enjoy our short times together. That was a nice time in the park, the first time we were properly alone. It wasn't against regulations so that made it much easier for me. I could speak without worrying about the matron. She was always a big shadow over me and made me a little afraid. You must understand that, Hugh.

It was good that you rode so well in Ireland. I don't know how you could do that because you couldn't see or walk well when you left me.

I wonder what you will do after Italy. You said you would like to come to Assen. That would be fine. I would like to see you again and you will meet my family.

Goodbye for now, Hugh,
Janny.

If only she could have known how important to me that letter was.

After a good start in the Italian Grand Prix and gaining a slipstream tow from many of the fast factory Bianchi twins, I made a break on all the other private owners on my old 1958 ex-Hempo 350cc Norton holding on to gain sixth place. The 500 Norton was too slow on such a fast circuit so I 'retired' early, packed up my gear and steered the van towards the Alps and the long haul to north-eastern Holland.

It was late Monday evening when I arrived at Assen hospital and called at the enquiry desk. I was recognised immediately, no doubt a result of gossip, and after an internal phone call, was advised that Janny wasn't available. Her friend Pieta was finishing her shift soon and would accompany me to Janny's home. As I hadn't sent a telegram informing the family of my arrival, there were going to be a few surprises in store.

We parked outside 31 Schaperstraat and knocked on the door. Janny let us in. The look on her face showed much more than surprise. We were taken into the lounge where I met her mother, Tinie, who showed all the signs of mild panic: "Who is he? Where did he come from and what is he doing here?"

I was asked to sit in a chair and then totally ignored for the next 30 minutes while Tinie, Janny and Pieta carried on a very serious, animated, non-stop discussion of which I understood absolutely nothing.

Finally, I was consulted. The van can't be left all night on the street in front of the house. It must be taken to a garage. It turned out this wasn't for safety reasons, but a case of what would the neighbours think! Father not home and a TT rider's van parked outside made for a scene that didn't fit the social standards of the time. (During the Dutch TT week it was a classic case of lock up your daughters, the TT riders are in town.)

Tinie guided me to a garage and the van was safely locked away. On our return I was told once more to sit while the three continued their noisy debate.

I began wishing I hadn't come, but Janny's letter was so clear, mature and friendly. What had I misunderstood? I'm a good judge of people and the words used in the particular way Janny had expressed them showed a calm, articulate person with integrity, character and more than a little affection towards me. So what had gone wrong?

After another hour decisions had been made. I was shown to a room and told, "You can sleep here." I lay there, totally convinced I'd made the biggest blunder in my life and planned to make profuse apologies and leave first thing in the morning.

Then the door opened and Janny entered, the diffused light from the hall highlighting her blonde hair that fell to her shoulders. Wearing a babydoll negligee she looked drop-dead gorgeous — and lay on the bed beside me. After an unexpected cuddle, she patiently explained the reason for the prolonged discussions.

The annual bird-shooting season had begun. Janny's dad, Gerrit, was staying with his parents an hour away. Both men took their shooting hobby seriously. Gerrit was a sergeant in the Dutch Army and Janny explained that he was a positive man who saw everything in black and white. She also knew that a young man who happened to be a TT rider, and a total stranger at that, would not be seen as a suitable companion for his daughter or be welcome in his house. Tinie intended to set off by bus first thing in the morning to explain the situation to Gerrit and his parents. We were to follow after lunch, by which time Tinie hoped she would have managed to diffuse any explosive tendencies Gerrit might have.

Janny's grandparents' home was imposing, built back from the road and surrounded by a well-kept lawn. I parked some distance away, feeling that under the circumstances a little space was a good thing. Tinie, Gerrit and his parents were gathered on the lawn to meet us. I stayed by the van while Janny walked briskly up to them, hugging her grandparents and talking animatedly to her father.

She waved me over to join them. I nervously noted the grandparents were bright-eyed and cheerful. Obviously, young love excited them. Tinie was rather pale and nervous and Gerrit, dressed in his bloodied shooting apparel and with a spread-legged stance that clearly stated "You've got this far, laddie, but you won't be going much farther if I can help it", offered me his hand.

Looking him directly in the eye I took it and, during the firmest of firm handshakes, said: "I'm very pleased to meet you, Mr Oeseburg." I was then introduced to Grandad, who gave me a warm smile, a wink and a vigorous handshake. Grandma gave me a spontaneous hug and even Freda the dog was rubbing against me seeking attention.

As we approached the house I noticed a flourishing vegetable garden. I directed Janny to it and expressed my admiration of it. Grandad quickly joined us and seemed delighted with my knowledge of gardening. My questions and general vocabulary concerning plants and their cultivation stretched Janny's knowledge of English, but was sufficient to indicate that, like him, I was a man of the soil.

During afternoon tea, Janny's grandparents made it clear they were pleased to see us together. Tinie became less tense and even Gerrit managed the occasional tight smile. I was to learn later that Gerrit had every intention of sending me on my way, but his father advised him to be patient, meet me and then make a decision. Tinie, Janny and I returned to Assen in high spirits, feeling a major hurdle had been overcome.

Eight days later I wrote the following letter to my mother:

Dear Mum

Trust you received my last letter written soon after the race in Bilbao in Spain. My results at Monza were fair, gained sixth place and first private owner in the 350cc class on my Norton, only covered a few laps on the 500cc Norton, it is not quick enough on these fast tracks.

After Monza I drove up to Holland and have been staying with an extremely pleasant family here in Assen, namely the parents of the nurse I met in hospital. I will be returning to England via an overnight ferry from Rotterdam on Friday the 15th in preparation for Brands on Sunday. Enclosed are photographs of Janny and her parents. To cut a long story short, I have fallen in love and have intentions of marrying, perhaps as early as next year.

Mrs Oeseburg is anxious to hear from you, Mum. Would you as soon as convenient put pen to paper please. Gordon and Laurel might also write. They would like to know about us, as a family, about my character and reassurance that Janny, pronounced Yanny, would be welcomed into our lives. I'm sure you would like her.

Janny is handsome, dresses very well, as the photos show, and is quietly confident without conceit. Whilst being of a serious nature, Janny has a spontaneous, fun side. An indication of her intelligence is that she speaks three languages fluently and has a good working knowledge of a fourth. I have written to Mr Coleman and others asking them to provide character references as well.

Janny's father Gerrit, the equivalent of George in English, is a sergeant in the Dutch Army overseeing maintenance at various vehicle parks in the north-eastern region of Holland. Gerrit is a highly skilled mechanical engineer, who in his youth owned motorcycles, so we have something in common. They are a Christian family belonging to a Protestant based church. Gerrit is an elder and Tinie sings in the choir.

Gerrit and his father are avid hunters of game, namely partridge, pheasants, rabbits, hares and ducks. They lease the shooting rights over various tracts of council land and do very well; they are allowed to sell what they shoot. They both have superbly trained retrievers. I've never seen dogs so well disciplined or as faultless in going about their work.

On Saturday last, Gerrit took me and another English-speaking chap duck shooting. After he had shot two he gave his gun to me. It wasn't expected and, by very good luck, I shot one as it came in to land. He enjoyed that.

I am quite sure I'll be on a Suzuki next year. I had dinner with their representative at Monza. He is very keen, and why not indeed? I was their best performing rider this year. They don't appear to be in a position to pay a substantial contract fee due to overseas currency restrictions but I will wait and see how things unfold.

When I arrived here in Assen I was well tanned and one of the locals called me a 'klein black mannigan', a little black man. Really! I don't mind being called black, but little!!!

Will close, wishing you all the best from Janny and her parents.

Yours, Hugh

Janny decorating the Christmas tree with Gerrit's mum and dad and mother Tinie. Archives.

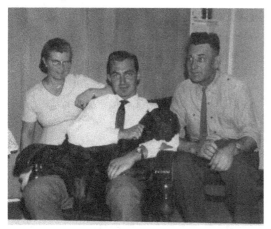

Before leaving for Zaragoza and New Zealand. With Tinie and Gerrit, and Freda the retriever in my lap. Archives.

I returned to England to begin packing my gear and prepare for the exciting few months ahead. I would be sailing back to New Zealand with the van, race bikes plus a stack of parts for fellow racers.

These were my worldly possessions and the plan was to cash them in after the New Zealand racing season to fund another year on the Continent.

After leading the 500cc race at Brands for two laps in the rain I finished fourth, then set to work gathering and packing parts, ordered by competitors at home, and overhauling my bikes ready for the New Zealand season.

To travel to Spain for one meeting did not make economic sense. However, it gave me the opportunity to see Janny, in Assen, for the last time, and as Peter Pawson had also entered we could travel together and share expenses. All up a 3600km round trip. Understandably, when the time came I was loath to leave Janny; she made the decision for me really and sent me off at 10pm. Peter was to cross the Channel with his Norton and I would meet him at the ferry terminal in Calais at 10am. Unfortunately, the generater packed up 100km into the journey. Switching to parking lights only and following trucks, I arrived in Breda and drove to Jan's shop. After a short nap I had the generater in my hand when Jan arrived at 7.30am. A local garage overhauled it while I waited, then I hurried south to meet a rather agitated Peter who had been waiting for sometime.

Fishermen always talk about 'the big one that got away' and that happened at Zaragoza. I gained pole position on the tight, part-cobblestoned parkland circuit, ahead of Mike Hailwood on his MV Agusta. In the race I clung to Mike's back wheel, not finding it too difficult to match his pace. A few laps later the clutch cable broke and I was out, a legacy from the Ulster pile-up that had gone unnoticed.

We had just five days to get back to England, finish packing and deliver two vanloads of bikes, tyres and God knows what to the docks. After having slept in a bed for just one night in five, finally my turn came to step on to the deck of the *Ruahine* and follow instructions to my six-berth cabin on the bottom deck, the cheapest fare available.

I hung up my clothes, sorted out storage for my personal effects and, with a total release of anxiety and tension, gratefully stretched out on my bunk and fell into a deep sleep.

The largest and most effective bicycle brake ever. As used on a 1965 50cc Honda.

CHAPTER 9

Having a contract with two factories realised ambition but terminated a dream

A long-missed panorama spread out in front of me as the *Ruahine* slipped into Waitemata Harbour in November 1961. The Auckland landscape was covered in multi-coloured houses. No two were the same shape or size and all were resplendent in colours that far exceeded a rainbow. The very boldness of the chosen roof colour glared back at the viewer as a declaration of Kiwi individuality.

The air was warm and humid with heavy, dark clouds. Suddenly, rain hissed down, drenching the unwary in seconds. This was not the New Zealand I remembered. It was more like Singapore and the Far East. I had no inkling that my own country would appear so foreign.

Back on the farm after 21 months away, I slowly readjusted. I stood on the front veranda to gain a better view of the scene I had enjoyed from my youngest days. In the next paddock a large gum tree dominated the skyline. Its thick, white branches thrust starkly upwards; it had always been there. When young, I had been convinced that the shadows clearly seen on a full moon were a reflection of that tree.

Then there was the distant view. Our farm was in a valley perhaps 30km wide. Looking to the east was a line of hills running from north to south as far as the eye could see. Unlike me, with my young dreams and hopes, they were solid and unchanging. With my dog Pippy I had walked and climbed many of them and camped in the foothills with friends. This was indeed my home, my base.

Once again Dave Kenah assisted me in preparing the Nortons for the Boxing Day Wanganui Cemetery Circuit street race. Motorcycling had brought world recognition to little Wanganui, home of the brilliantly successful Coleman family of father Percy and sons Rod and Bob; and to the Cemetery Circuit, where each year since 1951 a major national race meeting is held. A fast, exhilarating S-bend takes racers through the middle of an old cemetery. That's right, you can't miss them, the headstones are trackside.

The competition looked as hot as the melting tar on Boxing Day 1961. Peter Pawson was back after several successful seasons away. He had consistently finished in the top 10 in the Isle of Man TT and won and gained many top six results in the Continental Circus. He was a member of the remarkably successful New Zealand team that won the Isle of Man TT team prize twice. Back also was John Farnsworth. He was another New Zealand team member, backing that up with top-three results in Ireland. His European season had ended with a brilliant fourth at the East German Grand Prix.

Then there was Ginger Molloy, New Zealand's top Clubman rider and competitive in any company on his fast 500cc Gold Star. He would be destined for greater achievements overseas. For the first time for several years, a strong group of Australian riders, led by Ron Robinson, would keep the Kiwis honest.

In the 350cc race, I made a flyer of a start in the blistering summer heat, rushed past the headstones and cranked into the next corner only to see, too late, loose

Being interviewed by Tim Gibbes while relaxing in the Wanganui sun. Archives.

Fully focused and winning. Photo Peter Beazley.

stones on the track. I lost my front wheel and skated off unhurt onto the grass. Before I could restart, the whole field of riders went through. I did not consider retiring and chased off after the leaders, passing more than 25 during the eight-lap, headlong dash to the flag. I crossed the finish line beside Ron Robinson to gain third place. Peter Pawson won comfortably.

Again I made a good start in the 500cc event and maintained a handy lead throughout. Peter was second and Ginger third.

The traditional Rotorua Grand Prix on New Year's Day used a 2.5km track that encircled a horse racecourse. The sting in the tail being a fast, sand-surfaced bend, each year this was given a liberal coating of waste oil to dampen the dust and help compact the loose surface. A light shower passed over just before the 350cc race. The flag dropped and as I rode off the sandy stretch, around the very sharp left-hand corner, back onto the tarseal and began to accelerate away, the bike slid sideways. The road was as greasy as the proverbial. During practice our tyres had been carrying oil onto the sealed part of the track. The light dressing of rain had made it lethal. On the second lap I didn't bother turning on the tarseal. Instead I rode directly across onto the dirt on the right-hand side, turned and wound the throttle wide open. When the rev counter hit 7,500rpm, I dropped the clutch and, as I had done so many times on our driveway at home, in a shower of dirt and stones, accelerated away, gaining a considerable advantage on the field.

In some ways the 500 race was easier. The roads were dry, though still greasy, and the more powerful engine could spin the rear wheel in second gear, which helped increase my speed on that sandy corner. Slides are more easily controlled with a spinning rear wheel. Conversely, if it grips, it tends to push the front wheel, a more uncomfortable situation. I came away having won both major races.

Our travelling circus moved on to downtown Tauranga on January 2. Virtually every rider competing in this summer series knew each other well. It was a big happy family, including the Australians. Spectators felt very much part of the action and at times it was difficult to get on with the pre-race preparation required, as everyone wanted to have a chat.

Treating the oil-slicked surface with respect. Photo Peter Beazley.

John Farnsworth made a good start in the 350 race and gave every indication he was going to pull off a win. But when lapping a group of riders I slipped through to reach the chequered flag before him. The 500 race went my way too. Prize money was quite substantial. A rider could earn up to 60 pounds by winning both main races at most meetings, which was equivalent to four weeks' wages in the early 1960s.

As we had after the Rotorua event, riders gathered at an enthusiast's home. Over a few beers and a mountain of fish and chips, the stories of the day were told and near get-offs re-enacted. As an endorsement of the camaraderie and mateship that existed, these evenings were priceless.

The New Zealand TT was now held at the Ardmore aerodrome in South Auckland in conjunction with the Grand Prix Car Association, which ran a highly successful series of international events that attracted many of the world's best drivers and their exotic Formula One cars each summer. Usually over 70,000 spectators attended, the largest crowds ever assembled in New Zealand. Long queues formed on the narrow approach roads. Thousands of young people camped overnight on the verges to gain early entry to the circuit and their favoured viewing spots. These healthy young adults found ways that were not unique to pass the time; having a few beers was one.

The conservative *New Zealand Herald* newspaper ran an article about the experience. A local farmer, whose property had a long road frontage on one of the main routes, was interviewed. He congratulated the motor racing enthusiasts for leaving the roadside clean and tidy. As far as the overnight activities were concerned, he said what he'd observed would make his Jersey bull jealous.

The 7R was running very well, allowing me to win the 350cc race unopposed. The 500cc race was always going to be the hard one. Peter Pawson had a very good Manx Norton and he knew how to ride it. We started together and I stayed in his slipstream. It was too early to think about taking the lead, even if I could, so I waited to see what might evolve. On the third lap we sped down the back straight where we were timed at 192kph. Just before entering a long left-hand top-gear bend, the fastest corner on the track, I noticed Peter's rear tyre was nearly flat. He had a puncture. I quickly backed off and gave him plenty of room. It was the same corner where he fell during the 1960 event.

The tyre almost rolled off the rim when he leaned into the corner. Peter corrected the long frightening slide but he was running out of road. He laid it over again. Another great slide. He picked it up and rode onto a grassed area where he laid it down in textbook fashion and slid for a very long way. He was unhurt but it must have been a nasty experience, allowing me to ride on and win.

I returned to England in early March. Having posted start applications to the European organisers, from New Zealand and in Panama, en route, a mountain of mail from sponsors and organisers was waiting for me. Start money offers had increased considerably and even Lew Ellis of Shell seemed likely to loosen his purse strings.

England suddenly felt like home and everything was coming together exactly as planned. I picked up my brand new red Ford Thames van in London and lunched with Lew. He was still as difficult as ever and my negotiating skills had not improved, but I managed to get 50 per cent more than last year. When I placed my large order for Shell oil products on the table, he paled just a little but didn't refuse. There was more than enough oil for my van, and race bikes for speedway friend Barry Briggs, my young mate Dave Downer, a promising rider who I was helping, myself and still have stock left over to sell on the Continent. I had no hesitation in drinking much more than my share of two expensive bottles of wine.

I had a contract pending with Suzuki and another, unexpected, offer on the table. Tom Arter was a big player in UK road racing. He was the principal of Arter Brothers Limited, Barham, Kent. They were agents for AJS and Matchless motorcycles, Morris cars and vans, and an array of farm equipment that ranged from a humble plough to huge, state-of-the-art combine harvesters. He was very well connected within the AJS Matchless factory, and had been a major sponsor for many years.

Peter Pawson rode for Tom in the Isle of Man in 1961, finishing eighth at 96.56mph in the Senior. In February I'd been told that Tom had mentioned my name as one he was considering for sponsorship during this British season. Now it seemed that

Tom's interest in me had attracted the possibility of full support by the AMC factory, using their special experimental-development machines.

Jock West invited me to meet Tom and Jack Williams at the AMC race shop behind the main factory building. I had every intention of accepting whatever conditions were suggested, as money wasn't an issue; being accepted into the British motorcycle racing fraternity at such a high level was.

I found Tom to be a well-built, pipe-smoking man of few words. As always, Jack was enthusiastic about engine development. A larger inlet valve had been fitted to the 1962 G50 racer and the frame changed to give more ground clearance. Finally, Tom and I were able to retire to a local cafe. Not being one to beat about the bush he promptly outlined his proposal. We would use the works bikes at selected meetings and his own at the remainder. We would compete at all the main national and international meetings in England that did not clash with world championship events and my Suzuki contract, and in the Isle of Man and at the Ulster Grand Prix. He would transport the bikes and pay all accommodation costs. I would negotiate my conditions of entry and retain all prize and start money.

Without hesitation I said, "That seems very fair to me, thank you, Tom."

After shaking hands on the deal he said, "Well, that's that then, what's for lunch?"

No contract paper in sight. Just a firm handshake and a direct look in the eye.

Feeling that sandwiches were not up to our celebratory mood, Tom suggested beans, bacon, eggs, chips and fried bread were called for.

"That should see us through to dinner," he said.

I was invited to Sunday lunch to meet his wife Gladys and children. After a game of tennis it was time for a tour of Tom's garage. Very few people entered here. It was his private domain.

The centrepiece was a perfect running example of the fabulous twin-cylinder 500cc AJS Porcupine. This was the rare factory racing model that my childhood hero, Les Graham, won the inaugural 500cc Grand Prix world title on in 1949 and Rod Coleman continued to ride and develop to the point that it was frequently beating riders on factory-entered Manx Nortons. He also had more than one G45 and G50 Matchless and 7R AJS racer. Wall shelves were cluttered with racing carburettors, magnetos, cylinder heads, pistons. He had a huge stock of spares.

From the time I had left Janny in October last year I had written daily. I had promised to come and see her as soon as possible after arriving in England, but there was so much to do and the agreement to ride for Tom brought a lot of unexpected responsibilities, work and testing. I did not have the courage to tell sales director Jock West, a former squadron leader in the air force, or tough-as-they-come Tom that, "Look, lads, I'm off to see my girlfriend in Holland, be back in ten days." Riders had a certain reputation regards flirtations of short duration and I'm sure questions would be raised as to my attitude. I was as motivated as them and wasn't going to squander this opportunity. Meanwhile, with continuing apologies I wrote to Janny every day, hoping a window of opportunity to visit her would arise.

My first ride on the works bikes was at Silverstone on April 7. From the start of practice the position and responsibility I had been given gave me the inspiration to ride to my full potential. As was normal then, Tom had not taken my lap times.

As the riders in the 350cc class pushed their bikes out onto the start line, officials called out names and grid positions. The words "Hugh Anderson, Number One" rang out. Bloody hell, I couldn't believe it! I had lapped faster than Hailwood, Minter, Read, Shepherd, Godfrey, King; the cream of the British crop, the best short-circuit specialists in the world. Now what do I do? During that strange pre-race silence and tension that descends on riders, officials and spectators, the well-known voice of race commentator Murray Walker boomed out: "Anderson has obviously made a mistake. He's in the wrong grid position and the officials will sort him out in due course." Later, on several occasions, Murray apologised profusely for his gaffe.

How I wished I had been told earlier and had time to come to terms with what I had done. From a boy I had held the UK's top riders in awe. They were such gifted, special people, the best. Never brimming with confidence off the bike, I felt I had no right to be sitting on pole. No time for logic. Obviously, if I felt comfortable in practice, I was capable of the speed required. But being in a trying-hard-not-to-pee-in-my-pants situation, it didn't enter my head.

The flag dropped, the bike started instantly, but feeling well out of my depth I convinced myself that I was a crash looking for somewhere to happen. At the end of the second lap Minter came past, his Ray Petty Norton really flying. A few laps later Read came alongside but couldn't pass. I felt fairly comfortable riding at his speed and slowly gained confidence. Next Mike Hailwood swept past on the inside, braking for Copse Corner, but he entered too fast, was laid over to the max, his foot and fairing grinding on the track surface.

What followed was a brilliant display of throttle control and limits of tyre adhesion. When his front tyre began to slide, he gently opened his throttle. This lifted the pressure off the front wheel transferring it to his rear wheel, causing that tyre to lose traction. As he gently wound the throttle back a little, his front tyre slid. I had the faster line and, with my rear tyre drifting nicely, re-passed him and pressed on as hard as I dared.

Crashing during my first ride for Tom and the AMC factory was not an avenue towards making friends and impressing people!

Motor Cycling magazine had this to say later: 'By the fifth lap, Minter had a 50m lead and a terrific six cornered dice had developed for second spot between Anderson, Tony Godfrey, Shepherd, Hailwood, Read and Alistair King.' Two laps later Mike came past again with the same result; my confidence increased — perhaps I was capable of riding with these guys?

On the 12th lap I was still holding second place, but the engine began vibrating badly at maximum revs. I had to lower the limit from 8,000rpm to 7,000 rpm and hope it would finish. Mike got past and, with just two laps to go, Alan Shepherd, also on an AMC factory bike, slipped by and I came home fourth.

Mike was parked close by and came over. "You were going bloody well," he said, "but there were bits and pieces of metal dropping off your bike. I was hoping it would stop and save me having to scratch past you."

Tom and I hurriedly checked the bike over. Several cooling fins had broken off the cylinder head and barrel. The engine was old and the last of the genuine works specials. It was never used again.

Following a poor start in the 500cc race, I pushed up to fourth place and a relatively steady ride to the finish. The finishing order was Hailwood, McIntyre, Shepherd

Tom Arter. Tough but fair. Archives.

and me. New lap and race records were created in both classes. Tom Arter was happy. We had made a promising start.

Meanwhile I continued writing a letter each day to Janny, explaining my position and what I was doing. So far I had not received a reply and my concerns were mounting. Finally, on Tuesday, April 10, the long-awaited letter arrived. To my utter dismay Janny, as gently as she could, informed me our romance was over. She had been waiting more than five months for me to return and I had been in England for three weeks and not come to see her. If I were serious about our relationship, I would have made Assen my main priority.

"I will wait no longer," she wrote. "I have told my family and friends that you would be again in Assen soon, but Hugh, you haven't come. I feel a fool. Words are no longer enough. Janny." Janny had no idea how busy I was in a situation I hadn't expected.

I sat up late writing what I thought was a most eloquent, caring, loving, heart-and-soul-on-the-table letter to Janny. After reading it I was sure that there was no way she could ignore my love and sincerity. But Janny had made a statement and that was that. She did not reply. Being a beautiful, popular woman, I was sure she had more than one prospective suitor knocking on her door.

I had clearly envisaged the life we may have had together, even the children we would have. Her dismissal of me certainly left a hole. Distance and time, try as you might to overcome it, does dilute, soften and reduce love.

There were just 14 days before Easter weekend when we would be at Brands Hatch on Good Friday and Thruxton on Monday. The AMC race shop had built a new 350cc engine for me and Jack wanted me to run it in and test it as soon as it was ready. The brake specialist Ferodo was no longer offering its services at national race meetings. Tom had eight wheels that needed their brakes relined and Ferodo were based in the north of England. He asked if I would take them up.

Of course I said yes, drove to his home, removed them and began the long drive

Read, Hailwood and I at Brands Hatch. Perhaps I can win this. The Nick Nicholls collection at Mortons Archive.

I tried and learnt a major lesson. The Nick Nicholls collection at Mortons Archive.

north to Chapel-en-le-Frith arriving early the next morning. Ferodo were busy and I had to wait for a day and half, drive back and refit them all. I didn't have to do this but I was very grateful for the help that was being given to me.

By this time the new engine had shown good horsepower during runs on the dyno and in a day or two testing could begin. The Matchless G50 I had used had been fitted with a special five-speed gearbox and this also needed to be tested at Brands Hatch. I consoled myself with the fact that I was being employed by two factories, something I had never imagined, so get on with doing the very best you can.

Brands Hatch and Thruxton were two major meetings in the UK racing season.

The Brands organisers had received 465 entry applications, almost three times the number they could accommodate. Enthusiastic and knowledgeable crowds of up to 40,000 packed the stands. Motorcycle racing and motorcycling had never been more popular.

Before the start of the 350cc race, Tom casually offered me the following information: "Last year Fred Neville set the existing lap record here on this bike. It is set up exactly in the same way now as it was then. Have a good ride." Pressure, what gives you that impression?

The race went well, with the usual bunch of riders scrapping over the first five places.

On the fifth lap, Hailwood led from Read with me, Shepherd and Minter fighting for third. We caught Phil Read on the last lap and after a whole lot of leaning on each other, which I was not at all accustomed to, Derek Minter gained second with Read, Shepherd and me crossing the line together. But I drew the short straw and finished fifth. After the race I noticed tyre rubber marks on the front forks. Further investigation revealed traces of rubber on the megaphone and rear suspension covers. That this had happened was okay but not knowing when it did bothered me. It was this handlebar-to-handlebar riding, typical of UK racing then, that attracted the crowds.

Hoping to do better in the 500cc class, I got a good start, leading until Minter came by. I tried to hang on to his back wheel and got the hairiest, hardest ride I ever experienced, but I hung in there. Read came alongside as we approached the finish flag. We went under it together but he got the nod. The finishing order was Minter, Read, me, Shepherd and Hailwood.

The last solo race of the day was an open to larger capacity engines class. Read, Hailwood and I became involved in a tussle for first place. Just as I began to feel like I had a chance of pulling out the big one, I slid off. Up until this time my spills had been made up of a vigorous fight to the last and come off second best affairs. On this occasion, only when my backside started sliding up the track did I realise I had lost it. Not a bruise even. A life-saving lesson was learnt. From that point on when things looked nasty and I had basically lost control of the situation, I laid the bike down.

Tom was disappointed that I hadn't beaten Read, as I had at Silverstone. I later learned that he had loaned Phil a pair of bikes to use in the South African series. The idea was that he would become accustomed to them and ride for Tom in the 1962 season. Showing little appreciation, Phil returned a pair of worn-out bikes and then went off seeking sponsorship elsewhere. All to my benefit, as it turned out.

On Easter Monday at Thruxton I was surprised to find Hailwood had entered on MV Agustas. The weather was so intensely cold that I went for a pre-practice run complete with leathers and jacket. After winning my qualifying heat I was looking forward to taking on Mike and his 350cc MV. If I got a really good start on the 7R and took the bumpy Horizon Bend section absolutely nailed in third gear, which was very much on the limit, at over 145kph, I could be in front of him at the end of the first lap. I told Tom to stand on top of the van. "It could be interesting," I said.

Mike, having to do little more than go through the motions to win, would obviously be a little cautious and I hoped to be the glory boy. Sure enough on Horizon Bend flat on the tank, absolutely nailed, I rode around the outside of him with hopes of beating him to the chicane and then who knows what might follow. Unfortunately, I found that the 350cc MV had not only a lot more power than my 7R, but I was quite sure it was much faster than my 500cc G50 too. He blasted past me and carried on for an easy win.

However, Tom was delighted with my passing of Mike and gaining an easy second place. Again having won my qualifying heat in the 500cc class, I hoped to have a crack at local ace Tony Godfrey. I had beaten him easily in the 350cc class but as in the past he was more competitive on the 500. And that was how it turned out. The Matchless G50 felt a little flat and unwilling to rev even so Tony and I passed and re-passed several times. I was disappointed to finish third, a few metres behind him. *Motor Cycling* magazine was good enough to write that Tony and I had 'dominated the interest in the race'.

Following our success over Easter weekend, I left with my 50cc Norton for a five-week, four-meeting, 5,500km tour on the Continental Circus. It would start with my fourth trip to Spain, where I would be competing in the Premio Internacional de Madrid for the third time. This would be followed by the Spanish Grand Prix in Barcelona where I would meet the Suzuki team and our new bikes for the first time. Then I would carry on to the French Grand Prix at Clermont-Ferrand in central France, before travelling to St Wendel in Germany for the Saarland Grand Prix.

In many ways, travelling was the very essence of the Continental Circus. Sure, racing was important and the main attraction, but touring historic Europe had not lost its appeal. It brought to life all that I had explored through hundreds of books and magazines. The names of many villages, cities, towns and districts were familiar when studying maps to plan a route. Perhaps where a history-changing battle had been fought, an artist or writer had been born, or a martyr had lived and died. All my life Europe had been the main stage with New Zealand but a small player in comparison.

At Madrid, where well-performed Tommy Robb was my main competitor, the only change from previous races was that rain began to fall just before the start. When dry the track was dangerously slippery. Believe me, the surface would now be treacherous. You little beauty, I thought!

When the flag dropped it was obvious that a subdued, exploratory lap would be the sensible option. I rode off as if I were on a road bike going to the shops. Most of the others revved their engines and slipped their clutches in an orthodox, power-driven start and began sliding all over the road.

I arrived at the first corner, a left-hander, keeping well to the left of the track. Here there would be more traction and I would not get knocked off by the over-excited, out-of-control riders behind me. I gently applied the brakes. Almost immediately a rider without his bike went flying past to my right and careered into a barrier. I tensed, waiting to be hit by his machine or that of another crasher, but managed to slip around safely and carry on.

Riding a circuit 45 times, just 1.7km in length, in such difficult and treacherous conditions, demands intense and sustained concentration. One mistake, as many made, going by the number of bikes parked trackside, would have you on your backside. However, I won, lapping the entire field at least once.

Meanwhile, there had been rapid developments at Suzuki, as I found out a few days later at Barcelona.

At this time the big curse of racing two-strokes was piston seizures. MZ, the East German powerhouse of racing two-stroke technology, had been working on the rotary valve, boost port, expansion chamber principle for some years, but they still suffered frequently from piston seizure.

The main issue that caused our Suzukis to seize was incorrect carburettor settings. Usually teams managed to test in private before the season began. The worst possible initial test venue is amid the hype and excitement of a Grand Prix where a rider's mentality is geared solely for racing. The tight, slow, twisting, hilly nature of Montjuich Park, venue of the Spanish Grand Prix on May 6, 1962, was a nightmare in the making for Suzuki.

I saw the new bikes for the first time at Suzuki's Barcelona headquarters the day before practice began. They had been totally redesigned and bore little resemblance to those used the previous year. The 125 was a single-cylinder and the 250 a twin. We had two bikes for each class. The team was made up of Ernst Degner, Frank Perris and me with Mitsio Ito, Michio Ichino and Seichi Suzuki.

An opportunity to escape East Germany's draconian and rotten political system was presented to Ernst by a Suzuki Motor Company representative. Ernst had the boldness, planning skills and nerve to take it. Courage was required by the bucket load. It doesn't bear thinking about what would have happened if his wife Gerda and their two drugged boys, hidden in a sealed-off area in the boot of a friend's large American car, had been caught at the border.

The family escaped on the 17th of September the previous year, after the Swedish Grand Prix. Ernst was notified that his family had escaped to West Germany and that night took a ferry to Denmark and freedom. He arrived at the Suzuki factory late in 1961. As he had helped develop the MZ engine, he knew all its technical details intimately.

Ernst also had some good ideas for the future. Coincidentally, Suzuki development engineer Nakano-san had already made considerable progress down a similar design path to Ernst. Over time Ernst became my mentor, and we often worked into the night together on our bikes when other team members were out on the town. Even the fact that his help meant I was able to beat him on the track did not change his willingness to keep giving me advice.

Very few sportsmen are capable of such a selfless attitude. It was a sad day when injuries forced Ernst to retire and then he lost his life, far too soon, from a heart attack. To me he was a special person and a man who always seemed in good spirits.

On May the 4th at the Spanish Grand Prix the Suzuki's new engines were run in Europe for the first time. They sounded loud and lively as they were being warmed up in preparation for our first practice at Montjuich Park on the Friday morning. This was little more than an engine running-in exercise and an opportunity to learn the track and gain a feel for the bikes. The brakes and suspension were adequate, but nothing more. While the 125 was small and docile, the 250 was large and fast, but with power being produced from only 12,500rpm to 13,000rpm it gave a rather lively, unpredictable ride. Unfortunately, both were prone to the same old problem: piston seizures. Alterations were made to the 125 for the second practice, allowing me to increase my speed and begin to enjoy it. Unfortunately, the 250s suffered endless problems.

Overnight all the engines were totally dismantled and rebuilt. This meant we had to start from scratch and run them in and make various adjustments, mainly to the carburettors, to have them running well enough to qualify. At the completion of practice, I was the only rider not to have seized the 125 and had managed to qualify seventh fastest.

The problems with the 250s continued. So much damage was done that we ran out of spare cylinders. Mechanics worked all night modifying and fitting spares from the 125s to have them ready for the race.

Honda took the first four positions in qualifying for the 125cc class, with Mike Hailwood riding the Dr Joe Ehrlich 'made in England MZ lookalike EMC' into fifth and his team-mate Rex Avery sixth. I was pleased to be seventh fastest ahead of Ernst, Frank and a tight bunch of Spaniards and Italians on Bultacos, Ducatis and a Mondial.

During the 50cc race just one of our bikes got to the finish, in seventh place. My 125 had shown enough promise in practice to have me hopeful of a reasonably high placing. After gaining a good start I held fifth place for three laps behind the four Hondas but ahead of Mike Hailwood. Then the engine slowed and I was forced to retire joining Ernst and Frank. At least I had held the highest position and lasted the longest. All the Suzuki 250s stopped before the end of the second lap with ignition problems or piston seizures.

The French Grand Prix, on May 13, was a complete disaster for Suzuki. There had been little time to modify or even have new parts flown in from Japan. Frank crashed heavily when a piston broke during the first 250cc practice and mine seized. All the spare parts had been used, leaving team management no option but to withdraw our entries in that class. On a brighter note, the 50cc machines showed a big improvement, but our 125s still gave trouble. Frank fell in practice and again in the race when his seized. I lasted for several laps before the engine slowed. The quality of the material used in the pistons and the piston bore clearance was definitely suspect. Not unexpected when running prototypes for the first time.

I left the Suzuki team and drove off to stay with my German friend Karl Recktenwald at St Wendel to prepare for the Saarland Grand Prix. This year I was in the 500cc class. World champion Gary Hocking's entry on a 500cc MV Agusta put paid to any chances I had of winning, but I still managed to qualify second fastest on the difficult cobblestone street circuit. The meeting had attracted many of the world's best riders, including Mike Hailwood, Paddy Driver, Mike Duff, German champion Rudolph Glaizer and naturally Karl on the Manx Norton I had helped him purchase.

From the start the MV fired up instantly. I was close behind on my 500c Norton and, try as I might, Gary just pulled away. Chasing the leader hard helps you get away from the pursuing pack and at the end of the 30-lap, 55-minute race, I had a big lead on third finisher Mike Duff.

As always after these events, where the pressure to perform was less intense than at Grand Prix level, we formed happy, and at times hilarious, groups at restaurants, cafés and hotels. This camaraderie was at the heart of the renowned Circus.

For the next big event, the Isle of Man TT, Tom Arter had full AMC factory support and Canadian Mike Duff would be my team-mate. I had first met Mike when we shared a garage at the 1960 TT. We'd become close friends and had many interesting discussions about our future hopes. Mike declared he wanted to 'get there' in immaculate traditional style, so he turned himself into one of the most stylish riders in Europe. But to my mind, there was no time to hang about practising a style. 'Getting there' was reaching your full potential; I intended to try to accomplish that as soon as possible before talented younger riders arrived to breathe down my neck, and any style would do.

Riding for two factories in the 125, 250, 350 and 500cc classes would make this a busy TT. I would be out for every early-morning practice, often after sorting out mechanical issues with just three hours' sleep. An extra responsibility was being named captain for Motorcycling New Zealand's three-rider team in the Junior and Senior classes. The other members were John Gabites and Colin Meehan. Due to a booking error at Rose Villa, Colin took my bed and I moved in with Tom Arter.

During practice, my 500 was going so fast I was having difficulty riding flat-out in top through the fastest, nastiest corner ever, the bottom of Barregarrow. Part of the problem was a serious lack of self-belief. After three consecutive early-morning sessions, I had a nightmare that consisted of blasting down to that corner and careering at 220kph straight into the bank. I woke up sweating, kicking and screaming. Tom said nothing.

After lunch the next day he suggested I get a couple of hours' sleep; he had difficulty waking me at 6pm.

From a mechanical viewpoint, just about everything imaginable went wrong. My specially developed but experimental 7R factory engine was a failure and replaced by a standard unit. Then the big-end bearing failed twice on the G50.

Mike Duff, Alan Shepherd, Bob McIntyre and I were being paid by Dunlop to run an experimental rear, triangular profile tyre. It was designed to put more rubber on the road at extreme lean angles. They seemed okay.

The 125cc and 250cc Suzukis suffered from piston seizure and crankshaft bearing failure. The 250 was eventually withdrawn and I found myself monitoring engine condition more than concentrating on the circuit. A lock-up when running an engine in at 120kph left a 3m mark in the road. It reminded me not to take my hand off the clutch lever and from that time on, I never did.

My 350 times on the 7R were nothing to write home about. The Matchless G50 went better and I was fifth-fastest qualifier and the second-fastest rider on a British bike.

The 350cc race was always going to contain fireworks as Hocking and Hailwood were on MVs and Tom Phillis and McIntyre on Hondas. Hocking had survived a horror crash during practice week when he hit a slower rider at 200kph and his MV speared through a hedge, caught on fire and was burnt out. Two days later he went out and lapped at over 100mph. Those guys were tough.

Starting order was Tom Phillis Number 1, with Hailwood 10 seconds later at Number 3, and Hocking another 10 seconds back at Number 9.

Jim Redman accompanied Tom to the starting grid and they chatted for a while. Before leaving, Jim wished Tom well and added, "If you take it easy you can have this one away." Tom replied in his laconic drawl, "You can't have it both ways." They were to be his last words.

For some reason team orders denied Tom Phillis a high placing in the 125 and 250 classes. Although he was the current 125 world champion he was being used as a support rider only by Honda. His position, it seemed, was to develop a new 350. Following the first Grand Prix of the 1962 season at Barcelona, Tom wrote to his wife: "I won't be winning any world championships this season. In the 250cc race I had to be content with a lap record and leading the race until given frantic 'slow down' signals from the pits." Being a very determined and serious competitor, Tom was obviously out to prove a point in the 350cc TT riding a virtually untested, new, poor-handling 285cc Honda in its first race.

Hailwood caught Tom at Ballacraine just 11km out from the start. Then Hocking caught and passed both of them on the mountain. At the end of the first lap they screamed through the start as one. Just 2.8 seconds covered the three of them. Obviously, Tom was trying very hard to stay with the two brilliant MV riders. But they were on vastly superior machines compared to his experimental 285cc Honda.

Proof of Tom's effort was that Mike had made up 10 seconds on him in the first 11km yet only another 1.4 seconds over the rest of the lap. Was Tom doing this entirely for himself, or was this magnificent effort being made to prove to Honda management that they had underestimated his ability and were treating him unfairly?

Isle of Man Junior TT, Mike Duff is fifth, I am sixth and Ready seventh. The Nick Nicholls collection at Mortons Archive.

My race number was 16 so I started 1min 10secs after Tom, and being slower than him I would have been about two minutes behind him on the road. On the second lap I rode past an accident scene at Laurel Bank. The marshals had yet to arrive. It was Tom. He was still partially on the bike, his right leg draped over the seat and his head under the front wheel. A small puddle of oil had formed under the Honda's engine and a trickle of blood ran from under the front wheel.

Tom was dead.

At the end of the lap I stopped to refuel. Just 3km farther on, a badly damaged AJS 7R was leaning against a stone wall at Union Mills. It was Colin's bike. He will be very lucky not to have serious injuries, I thought as I sped past. I rode on concentrating as best I could. After leading until the last lap Hocking's engine gave bother and Hailwood won the battle by just 5.6 seconds.

At race end I found that what I had suspected was true. Tom and Colin were dead. After waiting for John Gabites to finish, and greeting him with "Thank God you are still alive", there was no need for me to stay in the paddock. My job was done.

With my duffel coat pulled over my T-shirt and shorts I drove down to Douglas Bay, a place I had previously retired to in an effort to find answers to problems.

Tom Phillis, a rider that so many admired. Archives.

CHAPTER 10

By accepting death, you lose the fear of it

'Any driver-rider who hasn't suffered from nightmares is a liar.'
— *Juan Fangio*

I had my life to sort out. With my duffel coat hood pulled over my head, I sat in a deflated huddle on Douglas Bay, hoping that time and a cigarette would allow me to find a way to cope with this situation and provide the answer as to where my future lay. First grief dominated all my thoughts. Tom Phillis, of all people, married with two young children, was dead.

A friendship had developed from the first time we had met. His disposition was such that it had not bothered him that his advice to me at one race meeting had me beating him at another. Actually, Tom saw humour in it. Following the 1960 TT races he told me where to get my troublesome Norton engines rebuilt. This had resulted in us racing together at Thruxton with such verve that we jointly broke the lap record in one race and I beat him in the other.

Tom was a confident, open, self-effacing person dedicated to our sport. A vibrant member of the Continental Circus, he was capable of stripping a Norton engine in the back of his van, repairing it, then rebuilding it overnight and winning on it the next day. A well-organised, experienced, intelligent man. A true champion no less, but he was dead.

And poor Colin. Imbued with a burning ambition to ride for New Zealand, he had worked industriously for many years to afford his dream and now, due to no fault of his own, he too was dead. During the past two and a half years there had been so many; some were close friends.

Since my first ride at the Austrian GP back in May 1960, of the six riders who finished in front of me only one, John Hartle, was still alive. Dave Chadwick, Peter Ferbrache, Bobby Brown and Dickie Dale had all gone. My pirate mate Ralph Rensen, Ronnie Miles too and now Tom. There had been many less known names who had copped it. Really, what chance was there of me staying alive?

Did I have to continue? No, I didn't. The first two years here were just a wonderful adventure, an amateur living a dream. But I was a professional now. Without realising it, accepting those contracts from Suzuki and Tom Arter had increased my responsibilities way beyond self-gratification. Suddenly, I was living in a different world. I was riding on the very edge in every race to satisfy my employers; a thrill in itself of course, but without room for the smallest error. Already the screaming, kicking nightmares of crashing to death had begun. Could I handle this? Did I have a choice? What were my options?

Retire. First there would be the ignominy of it. Then the stark truth of returning to the local mine; each day the same and a 20-year house mortgage hanging over my head. I had an idea, a vision perhaps, of the qualities a future wife might have, the style and standard of life I would like to lead. That was not going to happen. No. A life of boredom and frustration awaited me. Outside of racing my life had little value.

The ode written by Francis Gabuche to *Motor Cycling* after Les Graham had been killed in 1953 came vividly to mind. As it had done before, the answer to my troubled mind lay within his words:

> *It is an easy thing to blame*
> *Those who dare for dying*
> *And easier still to say they died*
> *For nothing, gave their lives for one*
> *High-flying moment on the heels*
> *Of Mercury. But how can those with wings*
> *Refuse to fly? And if they take that chance*
> *And die, who is to say they died*
> *And nothing was achieved? Life's not*
> *So precious if it is not worth a man's*
> *Endeavour, or is heavier in the balance*
> *Of right and wrong than the ideal*
> *Of those who try themselves and lose.*

I drew hard on a cigarette and added up what attributes I had that seemed to suit this sport. I understood it and could make sense of it. I fitted in and was accepted. Yes, I would continue on the same path. Hopefully what success I gained might bring balance to my life, see me qualify as an equal and set the childhood wrongs, criticisms and hurts to rights. If I were to follow my heroes then I had to face the risks they had faced and accept the consequences. There were no alternatives.

On Friday morning, before the Senior TT race, I rode around the circuit twice on a 250cc AJS road bike the factory had loaned me. It had a significant effect. It was early, the roads were empty, the circuit was mine and slowly the heaviness of the past few days eased.

After the siren screamed out on Friday morning Tom Arter wheeled the Matchless G50 out of the holding marquee and I helped him start it before going off to sit alone. As always I spent the time mentally riding the track, confirming each braking point, the gear to use and the line on each corner. The siren screamed again and we all moved up on to the Glencrutchery Road and lined up in our starting positions. Excitement and nerves were absent this day. There was a job to do and I would do it the best I could.

Tony Godfrey, whom I had often raced against, started 10 seconds after me. He made up that difference on the first lap, passed me approaching Parliament Square, Ramsey, and pulled away. Slowly, I began to gain enthusiasm, confidence and rhythm. As I started the second lap, I felt like pressing on at somewhere near my capabilities. I caught and passed Tony at Ballacraine but as I approached Quarry Bends the engine lost all power. I lifted the clutch and allowed the motor to clatter to a stop.

I had time to park the bike before Tony passed through. Not only had I caught him, regaining some five seconds, but I'd built a 10-second-plus lead. Tony's second lap average was 99.56mph. My second lap pace showed I could have joined the 'lapped at 100mph' brigade. However, as every Yorkshire man will tell you, "If my uncle had boobs, he would be my aunt."

Jack Williams and his race mechanics must have been dreadfully disappointed, as all their special G50s broke down. Alan Shepherd, lying third at the end of the first lap behind the MV Agustas of Hocking and Hailwood, went out on his second lap. Mike Duff then took over third place, but he broke down on his fourth lap. Both had lapped at over 100mph. Due to the number of retirements, Ellis Boyce, on a Francis Beart Norton, finished third at an average speed of just 96.27mph.

After retiring I was sitting on the bank at Quarry Bends and got a close-up view of what a crash looks like through a spectator's eyes. I don't like the word crash particularly, but that's what Derek Minter did while holding fourth place on his third lap. As Derek suddenly appeared from behind a cottage at speed he lost it going into the S-bend. The bike hit the outside kerb and bounced off it, shedding bits and pieces as it spun across the road. The engine was screaming with a deafening roar. Third gear was still engaged so each time the rear wheel came in contact with the tarmac the bike took on a life of its own. It lunged forward, shot up in the air and spun around. Eventually, it wobbled onto its side in the middle of the road. Two marshals ran towards it, trying to corral the beast as it kicked up and turned around a few more times.

By now following riders had appeared, all hastily trying to find a way through, adding to the confusion. To everyone's relief, and I expect the owner's grief, some part in the tortured engine broke, bringing silence and sanity to a dangerous situation. As it was wheeled away it wobbled about like half-set jelly. The rebuild would be long and expensive.

The press described the incident as 'a 110mph crash' and Derek as having suffered 'severe bruising'. All through the history of the Isle of Man TT, if a fallen rider could walk and talk the report would read 'rider okay'.

Derek appeared to be relatively unhurt and began walking towards the Sulby pub, a kilometre or so up the road, so I joined him. Under the circumstances he was quite calm, definitely a 'tough bastard'. Once at the pub, he phoned his wife to come and collect us. She was able to take the back roads, avoiding the track. When she arrived, she had a pet cat on a leash, which seemed rather novel under the circumstances.

As in previous years it was with relief that I boarded the ferry and shrugged off the weight of the island's demands. During the relaxing four-hour journey to Liverpool, I thought about the two meetings ahead of us.

These next challenges, on the 12th and 13th of June, while being substantial, were much easier to get my head around. Success or failure relied solely on my riding ability. On the island the problems were complex, there were many potentially fatal objective dangers on the circuit, mechanical trouble was never-ending and I seemed to be beset by so many issues beyond my control.

Practice went well at the Post TT International meeting at Mallory Park near Birmingham. I was using the AJS 7R that I had ridden to sixth place on the island and Tom's 500cc G50 Matchless. Both bikes seemed to be competitive, especially Tom's Matchless. During the first 500 practice it had been over-revving. Tom raised the gearing. During the second practice it was still going over the 'safe' limit of 7200rpm. When I told Tom, he said, "Let the f---er rev." My head was clear, without doubt or confusion and comfortable with the decision I had made on that seat in Douglas Bay. For the first time, I wasn't daunted by the pace shown by the best of the short-circuit stars. This meeting would be the first test of this new approach. Perhaps having accepted death removed the fear of it.

I had good reason to feel little more than an apprentice at Mallory. All I had learned during my first ride on this track in 1960 was how you should not fall off. The circuit is just 2.13km long. It contains a 180-degree, never-ending, third-gear sweeper at Gerrards, one of the most daunting corners of any English track. The right and left bends, known as the Esses, lead into the tightest of hairpins. Then it's flat-out around Devil's Elbow to the start. The record lap was just 53 seconds at an incredible average speed of 91.7mph, 148kph.

Bob McIntyre, on the new 285cc Honda four, the sister bike to the one Tom was killed on, led from Hailwood on the Italian MV Agusta for the first seven of the 20-lap race. Behind him a wheel-to-wheel, shoulder-to-shoulder battle developed between Scotland's Alistair King AJS, me, Phil Read and Paddy Driver on Nortons with Lewis Young mounted on an AJS. Bob stopped and we were now fighting for second. With two laps to go my usually powerful front brake cried enough, causing me to go wide at the hairpin, and allowing Driver to slip through. The ever forceful Phil passed me at the same spot on the last lap.

Tom was disappointed that I hadn't finished second. I explained how the front brake had faded badly. With that typical trace of a smile and a glint in his eyes that eased the harshness of his tone, he pointed out that I had been losing a little at Gerrards and making it up under braking, causing the drum to overheat. The crafty bugger did not miss a trick. I could only agree.

From the second row of the 500cc grid, I again made an excellent start and immediately tagged onto Bob McIntyre's rear wheel. He was often described as the greatest rider not to have won a world championship. He was many times a winner here and, let's not forget, the first man to lap the Isle of Man at 100mph.

My Matchless engine was running really well and the suspension setup coped better with the surface irregularities at Gerrards. While a ride that gains you 4th place in such company at an international meeting in England could hardly be described as comfortable, this was less demanding than expected. Hailwood and Hocking fought for first place on their MVs. They were two superbly gifted riders, each one unwilling to accept defeat in a highly charged amphitheatre setting occupied by 30,000 enthralled fans.

After 25 laps Hailwood won by two-fifths of a second. McIntyre and I finished 20 seconds behind them, with a further gap back to a stream of followers. Tom was as happy as I was.

The downside was that during the latter part of the race the engine had developed a slight vibration and a noticeable loss of power. Tom felt that perhaps the drive-side main bearing had moved, a regular problem. With another international at Brands the next day, urgent action was required.

After spending some time in a phone booth and visiting a colleague in Birmingham, whose engine wasn't available, it was decided that with the help of the race shop foreman, Jimmy Boughen, we would repair the existing motor. We arrived at my London lodgings at midnight. Tom shared my double bed, got up at 5am and by 7am we had the G50 engine out of the frame on the footpath outside the AMC race shop just as Jim arrived.

With the 7R in my van, I drove to the circuit, completed the necessary formalities and retired to the cafe for a well-earned, large, late breakfast.

Tom arrived at 1pm with the rebuilt G50.

Hailwood was riding an MV and all the hard-charging regulars were entered. From the start Mike gradually opened up a gap while Read and I led a trail of closely matched riders. On lap 17 Mike, rather carelessly, slid off his MV at Druids hairpin. He hastily remounted. Phil and I were now leading him. On the last lap I passed Phil and led into Clearways, the last corner, only to be once again pipped at the post by Phil. Later we found that the inlet tappet had loosened, causing sufficient loss of power to allow Phil to squeeze by at the flag.

Not having practised on the 500, as Tom and Jim Boughen had been rebuilding the engine, was something of a handicap. Luckily, the organisers, who I knew well and could have put me at the back of the grid, moved me up to midfield. Once again a good start put me into the top eight. As I adjusted to the bike, I steadily moved towards the front and almost snatched second from Phil. Mike won easily on his MV. These two meetings were proof to me that lifting my performance, reducing lap times and going quicker did not necessarily compromise safety.

Next test was the Thruxton 500-mile race, Britain's round of the FIM International Endurance Championship for 'standard production' machines. Only the spectators laboured under the illusion that the various factory-prepared models, entered by their major dealers, were standard. However, as all teams involved carried out major, go-faster internal modifications, no one protested.

Mike Duff and I were entered through Tom Arter on the AMC factory AJS CSR 650cc sports model. We were of similar height so quickly arranged a riding position that suited both of us. Our testing at Brands Hatch revealed the engine had little vibration and was powerful. The brakes were excellent and apart from some minor suspension adjustment, Mike and I were very pleased.

It was a measure of the importance of 'production machine' racing for commercial sales that had chief engineer Jack Williams spend several weeks building the engine. In general, AJS and Matchless motorcycles were not recognised as high-performance machines, but they had won this event by a whopping three laps in 1960.

Our strategy was simple. We had a race-winning machine, our responsibility was not to use maximum engine revolutions, save the brakes and not to fall off. Our intention was to keep the leaders in sight then go racing seriously during the last hour. Soon after half distance, we moved into second place but it wasn't to last. A few laps later Mike pushed in with ignition trouble.

Tom Arter eventually found the problem. The advance-retard cable nipple had slipped out of the points-activating cam plate. The factory mechanic who was helping us said he had been told that this had occurred during early testing and quite obviously had not been rectified. Tom was furious. He told me later, "I could have broken the f-----'s legs."

We rode on to finish well out of contention but lapping effortlessly at a similar speed to the winners. This little gem was included in the extensive two-page report in *The Motor Cycle* magazine: 'Hugh Anderson and Mike Duff, a partnership whose superb riding and composed bearing lent the marathon a veritable aura.'

Finishing positions in the open class were: first Norton, second AJS, third Norton, fourth Matchless, fifth Triumph, sixth BSA. During the race, our speedometer was reading 125mph on the fastest part of the course. Factory testers claimed to have seen

The works AJS CSR at Thruxton. A very special bike. The Nick Nicholls collection at Mortons Archive.

135mph on the open roads. The race-winning 650 SS Norton of Phil Read and Brian Setchell was ridden by a journalist at Thruxton a few days after the race. In his opinion the bike was capable of a genuine 125mph. This was proof that these machines were in a totally different performance category to standard production models.

The Dutch TT on the 30th of June was the first of a series of Continental Grand Prix events. When I arrived at the garage of the Suzuki team I was pleased to learn that they had been testing their bikes at Zandvoort, an international circuit in the west of Holland. They felt they had found more speed and improved reliability.

Late in the day I took out my 500cc Manx Norton. It was always a treat to get on it. After putting in some rather useful laps I caught friend Sid Mizen, who had travelled with me occasionally; Sid was not finding the fabulous rider's track easy to learn. After breezing past, I slowed. While cruising around a hairpin, aptly named Knee Bocht (Corner), the Dunlop experimental triangular rear tyre suddenly slid away. Surprised, I over-corrected. It savagely regained grip and tossed me over the high side. I landed heavily on my right knee.

Australian racer Jack Findlay and I had finished our evening meal and I had almost completed repairing the crash-damaged Manx when I heard a voice that I thought had been forever lost to me: "Hello", spoken with a strong Dutch accent.

It could only be one person — Janny Oeseburg. I turned and there she stood by her father. The mental picture I had retained of her was but a faded image of this beautiful young woman who radiated a disarming brightness that was breathtaking. Without speaking, I dropped my tools, walked to her and held her in an intense embrace. Janny responded in kind. I shook Gerrit's hand and we all stood laughing and smiling, but were lost for words.

Their pleasure in seeing me again was obvious, so say something.

"Thank you for coming, you look so well."

"It's good to see you again."

Another long silence.

"Oh, I fell off my bike; I will have it finished soon."

"Why did you fall off?"

"The rear tyre slid at the Knee Bocht."

"Are you hurt?"

"No, I'm okay."

Very slowly the semblance of a conversation was established.

Jack had put the kettle on. Gerrit had to leave. Janny went with him to get her jacket from the car. The first words Jack said were: "If you don't marry that girl, you are a bloody fool." Janny returned and we had a coffee and slowly thawed. As our parting had not been one of animosity, there was no reason not to pick up where we had left off. Quite soon we had.

My love life may have been back on track but I was destined to miss the Assen TT. The heavy landing from the low-speed spill had caused a blood vessel to burst in my knee. It quickly swelled up and there was no option other than go to the hospital with Janny. A long-needled syringe was inserted at various angles in different places to suck the blood out. No painkiller, of course.

"Total rest and come back on Monday" were the instructions as they handed me a pair of crutches. Janny took me back to 31 Schaperstraat. Tinie was pleased to see me. Without question or doubt I was back where I belonged.

On Monday morning, with a knee that was improving and being confident of riding at the Belgium Grand Prix the following weekend, I drove back to the hospital. Again a long-needled syringe was inserted several times, even up under the kneecap. Ever larger needles were used. They had larger holes, you see. All to no avail as the blood had thickened. Within hours an infection entered the lower half of my leg and a course of antibiotics was required to kill it. Missing the Belgium Grand Prix caused me no grief.

However, the Assen race results showed the benefits of their testing. Ernst Degner won the 50cc class with Jan Huberts second on a Kreidler, just 0.9sec in front of his team-mate Hans Georg Anscheidt. The world championship placings and points were Degner 16, Anscheidt 15, Huberts 14, and Taveri 14.

Ernst gained a very close fourth on his 125, only 0.8sec behind Tommy Robb on a Honda. This was easily our best performance so far. Frank Perris was fifth in the 250 class. Even though he was almost lapped, the bike did finish. Jim Redman gave Honda their first win in the 350 class, trouncing Hailwood on the venerable MV.

Later I put my crash down to the new triangular rear racing tyre Dunlop was developing. As they gave no major bother in the Isle of Man and, as they were paying me to use them, I had one fitted to my Manx Norton in Assen. But obviously something was wrong. I had reduced my speed by 50 per cent and even though the bike had been at a very conservative lean angle it had abruptly slid away. At the time it was all kept quiet but I wasn't the only one who fell. Dunlop redesigned the shape of the tyre and the following year it was introduced for all classes.

Having missed the Belgium Grand Prix I was keen to compete at the West German

GP at the Solitudering near Stuttgart the following weekend. Slowly the antibiotics did their job. The pain and swelling in my leg subsided enough to make me fairly confident of being able to ride. Jan Schuurman, a local friend, offered to drive me to the track in his Mercedes.

On arrival we had dinner with the Suzuki team. Jimmy Matsumiya, the team's go-to man in Europe, offered to take Jan and me on a sighting lap of the 12km road-based circuit. The moment we turned right and the tyres of Jimmy's 3.8-litre Jaguar rolled onto what tomorrow would be part of the racetrack, he changed. No longer was he a laidback raconteur. He had morphed into a racer with the stony-faced countenance and pushed-back-in-the-seat, straight-armed stance of a Grand Prix driver. This hybrid version of Stirling Moss and Juan Fangio took a deep breath then floored the accelerator. Apprehension hit me like a brick. We arrived at a 90-degree corner, braked way too late and then, with tyre-screeching savagery, Jimmy swung the big Jag around. Just as quickly he corrected a non-existent rear-wheel drift and continued sawing away at the steering wheel. The Jaguar's long engine bonnet swung to and fro and the tyres continued to squeal. Jimmy drove with increasing aggression. I glanced back to see how Jan was coping.

He was suspended over the back seat, his arms braced against each side of the car. All colour had drained from his face and his staring, unblinking eyes bulged grotesquely. His was the face of true fear.

Jimmy increased his tyre-screeching urgency and began encroaching on the wrong side of the road on blind corners. Something had to be done. Luckily, as we roared past the circuit's control tower, there was a hotel. "Pub, pub, stop at the pub!" I shouted. Jimmy got the message. He enjoyed a drink, especially in the company of a top rider, and appreciated the social benefits it afforded. As we turned into the car park a strange, rhythmic sound came from the back seat. I turned to find Jan exhaling each breath through clenched teeth. This puffed out his cheeks, making the sound of a small air compressor. He staggered out of the car and was so unsteady on his feet I felt compelled to take his arm. This appeared to activate his speech, which wasn't necessarily a good thing. Luckily, he spoke in Dutch. Not many people understand the language, which has been described as 'a disease of the throat'.

All of this was lost on Jimmy. He had heard none of it as he was already inside the bar ordering the first round. It took three beers for the colour to return to Jan's face, an indication that he was ready for further travel. I mounted a strong case with Jimmy along the lines that I would learn the sequence of corners and the layout much quicker if I was driving. Much to Jan's relief Jimmy agreed and we left the pub to cover a few quiet laps of the undulating tortuous course.

Friday dawned fine and clear and in practice our 125s gave no trouble, but suffered from significant and mysterious vibration. My 250 was noticeably faster, but still tended to seize. As I had done all season, I completed a few steady laps on it and qualified somewhere in the middle of the pack. The well-ridden, fast and reliable Hondas dominated the front row of the 125cc grid. Only Mike Hailwood, on an EMC, had pushed himself among them, qualifying fourth ahead of Bob McIntyre. Three Suzukis, Two EMCs and two fast Bultacos filled the next two rows of the large field.

Early in the race Ernst passed McIntyre and was closing on Hailwood, who was in third place, when he slid off, unhurt. My 125 was running well and there was good reason to believe I could finish a race for the first time. So from the start, for the first two laps, I carefully used the choke lever to gain the correct fuel mixture, and then started to push on. At mid-race my pit signals indicated I was closing on sixth-placed Paddy Driver on his EMC.

Vibration in the footrests became so acute that I had to lift one foot off at a time to be able to cope with the pain of the burning sensation it was causing. Meanwhile vibration on Frank's bike was so bad he retired with a broken engine mount. I passed Paddy on the run to the flag. Considering he had finished third at the previous weekend's Belgium Grand Prix, it was a good result. I now had an engine that responded to change in an understandable way and a mechanic in Nagata-san I could rely on. The vibration problems were solved before the Ulster held three weeks later.

Having qualified midfield in the 250cc class on a bike that was difficult to start, yet potentially the fastest machine in the race, promised to cause some pretty exciting moments. Even though I knew the engine would seize before it completed the first lap, I felt duty bound to go as hard as possible. Once the engine cleared, it went like a rocket. For the first 2km, keeping up with how fast it screamed to maximum revs through the gears, then diving to the left and right side of the road avoiding much slower riders and decelerating sufficiently for corners that were hidden by clusters of competitors was, at times, hair-raising stuff. The absolute busiest times I ever had. Yes, you could go slowly and carefully, but a flag had been dropped and the race was on. Who could resist? Midway around the first lap, I was clear of the slower riders and on the fast back straight closing quickly on the leaders, Redman and McIntyre on their Hondas, when I felt that subtle, difficult to detect, softening of power a split second before it seized at more than 220kph. I whipped in the clutch and with a mixture of relief and frustration coasted to yet another stop. Why, oh why, don't we carry out properly organised test sessions that involved me? I thought. I was sure we could improve the reliability, they were so fast and steered and stopped well. Perhaps now that we had better-quality pistons, the team might see the merit in thorough lead-up testing. Again the 50s were performing very well, with Ernst winning and Suzukis taking four of the first six places. My wish for proper team testing was granted 10 days later at Zandvoort. After covering several laps on the 125 I left it with the mechanics to remove the barrel and piston so I could rub down the high spots. The 250 was next. After several laps running it in I went flat-out down the main straight hitting over 200kph, sat up and braked hard for a hairpin bend. The front wheel seemed to just fold up under me and I hit the deck. As I slid along the track beside the grinding, scraping, flame, sparks and bits streaming out from under the rather pitiful-looking thing, I wondered what the hell I had done wrong. We finally came to rest just before the corner, an indication, I suppose, that travelling individually we could stop sooner than using the orthodox method.

I picked up the bike to find the front tyre was totally deflated. The valve cap was missing. When you reach speeds exceeding 170kph centrifugal force opens the valve, air escapes and you have a problem. The rather nervous team manager called a halt to proceedings before more bikes and, I like to think, riders were damaged.

When I could, I spent time with the team at their hotel near Amsterdam airport. They asked if I were interested in riding a 50cc. As it had an engine and two wheels I didn't see why not. A few days later an unofficial race for 50cc machines was included in a festival at St-Truiden, in Belgium. The parents of Jacky Ickx, who went on to become one of the top Formula One and sports car drivers of the late 1960s–early 1970s, were involved with the distribution of Suzukis.

Jacky was competing in trials riding and became Belgium champion. His experience on tarmac was limited but to impress the locals it was agreed that he should win. The circuit was short, using narrow roads in a park. What I would call a 'picnic meeting'. We duly buzzed about on the miniature motorcycles with Mitsuo Itoh and me following young Ickx over the finish line.

The Suzuki team management were impressed and asked me to continue riding it. I happily agreed and put it in my van, along with a few spare spark plugs and main jets. Then I made contact with Mr Foster, the organiser of the British Championships, to be held the following weekend at Oulton Park, to gain a late entry. I had not ridden here before but found the fast-flowing nature of the track easy to learn. The main challenge was just beyond the crest of Clay Hill, which curved slightly left, was a blind double left, all taken as one that then merged into a sweeping right. But at all British circuits, every corner was taken on the limit, each one demanding your best effort.

New challenges always energised me. I was quite happy riding a small, low-powered bike. I reasoned that if you fell off, the slower you were going, the better. There were secrets to be unlocked regarding how to get the best out of them with their eight gears and maximum power available in a 500rpm window.

After two practice sessions I felt comfortable riding the high-revving toy-like machines. The Suzuki being the fastest bike in the race allowed me to become a British Champion. What I had not expected was that Edna Graham, my hero Les's widow, was presenting the trophies. Obviously, it was an emotional moment for me, and Edna, being a warm, charming person, left me feeling very fortunate to have met her.

On the start line of the 350cc race the carburettor on Tom's 7R flooded and petrol ran freely from it. A clout on the float bowl housing cured the sticking float but a bad start would be the result. I had qualified third on a track I didn't know and had ambitions of finishing higher. So much for that. I got away well down the order and rode with passion to pass my fellow factory-sponsored rider, Alan Shepherd, on the last corner for a rather disappointing fourth place behind Hailwood, Minter and Read.

Light rain fell as we wheeled the bikes out to start the 500cc race. These were the conditions that suited my skills, starting from the front row, and after passing Phil Read, I led for three laps until my goggles began to fog up. I took them off and struggled on. This is the British Championship, you don't stop. The rain was painful and blinding, I was being passed and had to stop at my pit for a spare pair. Angered that such a simple thing, which had never happened before, had denied me the chance of pulling off my biggest win so far, I set off in midfield riding hard. There was a wooded area on top of Clay Hill rise where late in the race the rain had become heavier. As it intensified, water began running across the track. Bob McIntyre had battled from the middle of the grid to fourth and was about to challenge Read for third place when he slid off in that stream of water. I arrived at the same spot seconds later. Even though the caution flags were out and I slowed, both my wheels slid

Above: The pleasure of meeting Mrs Graham, the wife of my hero, shows. The Nick Nicholls collection at Mortons Archive.

Left: On Tom's 7R closing on Alan Shepherd for fourth place. T.C. Marsh.

Leading the 500cc on Tom's G50. Luck is ffff---fickle. T.C. Marsh.

savagely. I pressed on, gaining places with every lap, encouraging journalist Mick Woollett to write: 'The race drew to a close with Anderson providing the excitement, passing Mike Duff and Paddy Driver to snatch fifth position.'

As was fairly typical of the British short-circuit scene, Bob slid off the track onto a smooth grassed area that would normally have seen him up on his feet again in seconds and attempting to restart his bike. But in this case his head came in contact with an unprotected large hoarding support pole — something which just would not happen these days. He was taken to hospital with serious head injuries, from which he succumbed nine days later. Another legend lost. 'Bob Mac', aged 33, five Grand Prix wins including three on the TT course, the first man to break the 100mph barrier at the Isle of Man. Ten years of racing by a man who personified dignity and quiet determination.

Northern Ireland's Ulster Grand Prix on August 11 gave a chance to build on the progress Suzuki had made following the Isle of Man races. Every year, it seemed to rain on race day. Some years heavily, which did not put off the large crowd who faithfully supported the meeting each year.

The 125 was going so well during practice that I passed Ernst with speed and confidence. He was moved to comment that if I wasn't careful, disaster might strike. It was so wet during practice that no less than 18 riders failed to qualify. But this was Ireland and a way was found to allow most of them to take part. The 350 race turned into a battle for fifth place. I led a group that consisted of Franta Stastny on the Jawa, Mike Duff, Peter Middleton, Alan Shepherd, Ron Langston and more.

On a works AJS leading team-mate Mike Duff and Phil Read. The Nick Nicholls collection at Mortons Archive.

From the last corner before the finish, team-mate Mike Duff managed to get a run out of my slipstream and beat me to the flag by the smallest margin. We were given the same race time of 1 hour 23 minutes 50.4 seconds. Mike was delighted to have, for the first time, beaten me. "Beat you that time, you bastard," he exclaimed with a broad smile. These long demanding races could leave you mentally a little drained but a cup of tea and a sandwich prepared you for your next outing.

The 125 race was a Honda benefit, with Luigi Taveri leading a small freight train of four to the finishing flag. I was fifth, the first non-Honda rider, which is all we could hope for really. Honda's high-revving twin-cylinder four-strokes, at that time, were in a class of their own. In comparison our bikes were still in the prototype development stage. The important thing was that my bike seemed fine and I buzzed around close behind the last Honda and well ahead of the rest. At the end of the hour-long race I had beaten Paddy Driver EMC by 1min 14secs, and Frank Perris, also on a Suzuki, by 3min 20secs. Not such a bad ride. Unfortunately, Degner fell, fracturing a knee cap.

At this time the Suzukis were at an early development stage, and we the riders were learning how to ride them. I felt the main objective was to make every effort to have the engine performing reliably. The 250 proved a much more difficult customer than the 125. Minimal piston bore clearance was important as was carburettor settings. I concentrated on these. I worked with Nagata-san, my mechanic, very closely and rubbed the high spots off my pistons and studied intently the relationship between atmospheric conditions and the effect they had on carburation and engine performance. In the long term it paid off. However, I always rested my left hand on the clutch lever and remained very much aware of the engine's performance, ready to release it immediately at the first sign of hesitation, a new important skill.

The 250 race was next. Practice had been run under wet conditions, which had allowed the engine to run cooler and made it less prone to seizure allowing me to qualify on the front row. For once I gained an excellent start and tore off close behind Jim Redman. The Suzuki was fast and I could stay with him. I was hoping to sweep through the start challenging Jim for the lead, but the engine locked solid before completing a lap. As Jim said, "I was hoping it would last at least one lap to give the Suzuki team some much needed encouragement."

Travelling to the East German Grand Prix held on the 8th of August at the Sachsenring near Chemnitz was an experience to remember. The border of the German Democratic Republic had high electrified fences and heavily armed sentries, one of whom demanded to see my race acceptance papers and passport. He then

Chasing World Champion Jim Redman. Spectators give a softer landing than a fence, and they pay to get in. The Nick Nicholls collection at Mortons Archive.

148

instructed me to "Stay in your vehicle until reaching the office grounds." I drove across a 100m-wide strip of bare earth, cut through the surrounding forest between two high electric fences, disappearing into the distance on either side, with heavy-machine-gun posts every 500m.

The next obstruction was a massive piece of iron in the shape of the letter 'H' blocking my way. Eventually, it rolled back, allowing me to drive through and join a group of riders that included Jack Ahearn, Paddy Driver and Willie van Leeuwen sitting around a table enjoying a traditional Continental Circus meal of bread, jam and coffee; healthy stuff!

It seemed that every year the officials insisted each rider complete a comprehensive list of every spare part and tool that he carried, down to the last nut, bolt and screw. When we left the country the van could be searched to verify that all those parts and tools listed were still in stock. This was to stop us selling anything while in their country. Each year this occurred and each year the riders refused. They carried sufficient food to last for two or three weeks and enough stories describing their much travelled, far from ordinary lives to last even longer. It was a question of calling the officials' bluff.

Soon after I drew up a chair at the table, a group of young soldiers walked out of the trees armed with submachine guns and holding large Alsatian dogs on leashes. Having come from a free country it was a jolt to realise that these teenagers would shoot to kill and the dogs would tear you to bits. The standoff lasted several hours, probably to intimidate us, before humourless officials slowly processed our documentation. We were given a map of the country with the roads that we were to follow highlighted. "Don't go off these roads" was the final emphatic instruction. During the journey I needed to relieve myself and drove off the designated road. Before I had completed the job, I could hear sirens in the distance. Two police cars arrived, armed men approached. They wanted to know what I had been doing. I pointed to the evidence and was let off with a warning.

The Sachsenring circuit, like the great Nürburgring, was built in 1927. Both are magnificent circuits that stand proud in motor-racing history. Here the circuit had become part of the public road system. One lap in the van was quite sufficient to get me excited by the challenge it presented. Fast sweeping corners, a challenging high-speed S-bend and medium-fast corners through the town of Hohenstein-Ernstthal; very much my kind of circuit.

The championship points standing for the 50cc class was: Degner 32, Anscheidt 27, Taveri 22, Huberts 17, Itoh 11, Robb 11. This was the first time I was competing at a 50cc Grand Prix. My biggest disadvantage on the 50cc was my size and weight. Jim Redman, Frank Perris and I were probably the tallest riders competing in Grand Prix. I weighed well over the 60kg minimum weight allowed in all classes. All the other competitors were under the limit, some less than 50kg. The factories favoured these lightweight jockeys so nobody protested about it. On the rare occasion we were weighed, they put chains down their boots and wrapped them around their waists, drank a litre or two of milk, then managed to pass. Luckily, my flexibility was such that it had allowed me, in my youth, to put one foot, though try as I might, not both feet, behind my head. This suppleness allowed me to tuck in around the small bike, get inside the fairing and with my chin on the tank gain forward vision through a slot at the base of the screen, just. The following is how the Suzuki team reported my introduction to this ultra-lightweight category: 'Suzuki did not expect good results as Anderson, at 175cm and 75kg [actually I was just 70kg] was not suitable for a tiny 50cc racer. But Anderson was able to fold his "king-sized body" around the machine and gained excellent results.'

During practice the little bike gave no trouble at all and I became accustomed to braking very late and squeezing through corners while keeping the throttle wide open. Due to the 500rpm power band it was necessary to constantly slip the clutch to keep the rev counter within the power revs. I quickly learned to keep it flat-out when changing gear by just lifting the clutch sufficiently to allow the next gear to engage as I had on the Gold Star and 7R when needs be dictated that I should. This created something approaching a constantly variable drive system. It was a busy ride as I tried to extract every fraction of the small amount of power it produced. At the end of practice it was encouraging to find that I was lapping at the same speed as the leaders. I had learned a lot but there is always more to know.

The race was a buzz. Jan Huberts on a Kreidler won, Mitsuo Itoh, Suzuki, a close second. Luigi Taveri, Honda, and I passed and re-passed the whole race. At the end I managed to arrive at the flag just 0.02sec before the current leader of the world championship standings. Seven seconds covered the first four home in a 50km race at an average speed of 121.5kph. A podium position seemed like a good start. British champion one week, on the podium at a Grand Prix the next. The team were very pleased with the results.

As the 1962 season was coming to an end the Cadwell Park International in North Lincolnshire on September 16 would be my last ride for Tom Arter. It was a little unfortunate that I had been asked by the owner of the circuit to ride the 50cc and 125cc Suzukis too. Without a mechanic, preparing the Suzukis took most of my time and, up to a point, my concentration. The full 3.6km winding, demanding, complicated mountain circuit was definitely challenging for anyone competing here for the first time.

After a short practice session for each class, the seven-hour race programme began. After finishing second in both the 350 and 500 qualifying heats, I went out on the 50 and won with a new lap record. After leading for a lap, the plug lead came off the 125. I stopped and replaced it on two occasions, then retired. I led the 350 race from the start and held on until midway through the third lap when I very nearly lost it on a long, third-gear, flat-out corner. The bike went down onto the footrest and megaphone. I was fortunate to get it all back together again courtesy of a wide grassed run-off area, but was promptly demoted to fourth.

So close was the racing that Tony Godfrey, who beat me by a few metres for third place, set a new lap record. Phil Read won. Phil was parked close by and came over laughing, as we did, about our near get-offs. He said, "If you are able to control such a long full-lock slide, you should try your hand at speedway!"

The 500 race didn't start until 6.45pm. After an average start, I became involved in a battle for third with up-and-coming Chris Conn and John Cooper, who were fast making names for themselves, and knew their way around Cadwell. Phil led Godfrey and we closed on them, with Conn making a new record lap. At the finish it was that man Read again, Godfrey second and I was third.

Our season together had come to an end. My only regret was that I had not won a race for Tom and, of course, the factory. We had come close on three occasions and were never far from the front, fifth on two occasions being our lowest position, both occasions due to minor machine problems. Considering that I was taking on the best riders in the world at that time, on their home tracks on which I had little or no experience, it wasn't so bad. Tom was never critical of me, provided I didn't criticise his bikes. Altogether it had been a congenial time. Tom appreciated that I was quite happy to do more, transporting the bikes, helping in preparation, than what we had agreed to. Above all, we had become close friends.

Next there was a mad rush to get to the Grand Prix in Finland. That country's first world championship meeting was to be held at Tampere, 160km north of Helsinki. Jim Redman needed a lift to Finland and then intended to fly to Italy. When we got to Germany, I began to doubt that a full-scale Grand Prix event would have just one practice day, as the instructions that came with the entry forms stated. If as normal they ran two, we would not arrive in time. Was this a mistake in translation? I broached the subject with Jim, who said, "I was thinking the same thing, Hugh."

We laughed. "Okay, what can we do?"

"Hamburg is not far," he said. "We could take a plane from there. I've got a friend in Helsinki who will take us to the circuit."

I needed to take the 50cc Suzuki with me.

"Well, it's not very big, maybe we can put it on the plane too," Jim said.

Soon we were at the counter of Finn Air explaining our situation. Being a quiet time of the day we soon had the attention of most of the staff, who all wanted to help. Decisions were quickly made. I had a return ticket to Hamburg, Jim had one going to Italy, and they would take the Suzuki free of charge so long as we got it up the steps into the plane. With the bike weighing in at 60kg, it wasn't a difficult task.

Tampere's narrow, bumpy, 3.62km circuit wound its way through a forest, with trees growing within two or three metres of the tarmac. Track conditions were so bad that after practice Alan Shepherd, the well-performed English rider, had intentions of leaving for home. However, the MZ factory had entered him in both the 125cc and 250cc races, so he stayed.

On the night we arrived, Frank Perris and I visited Ernst in his hotel room. He was pale and stressed, although he felt fit enough following his knee injury to return to racing. The problem was Finland bordered Russia and the possibility of him being kidnapped and taken back to East Germany was of great concern. As protection he had brought two personal bodyguards armed with .44 calibre handguns. Frank asked to have a closer look at one. He waved it about a little carelessly. When Ernst told him to be careful as it was fully loaded, he almost dropped it in his haste to give it back to the guard. During the event, the only time Ernst left his room was for meals and to attend the activities at the circuit.

Practice produced several incidents. Mike Hailwood fell heavily when his MZ seized at 160kph. He missed the trees but slid 30m into a wooden picnic seat, badly bruising his chest and legs. Any slippery, dodgy, narrow circuit suited me and I qualified second fastest in the 50cc class, splitting Anscheidt and Taveri.

Race day dawned cold and wet, creating conditions that caused the circuit to be described by one observer as 'forbiddingly dangerous'. After a slow start in the 50cc class, I gained and held third position until a misfire near the end caused me to lose three places and finish a disappointing sixth. The riders' world championship points positions were now: Anscheidt 36, Degner 35, Taveri 29. Manufacturers' championship points were: Kreidler 44, Suzuki 44, Honda 31. The final round was in Buenos Aires, so it looked like Ernst and I would be flying to Argentina.

By midday the weather had improved and the track was drying out. Again I had qualified well with the 125 but a poor start left me lying in seventh place. As I entered a slow right-hand corner, I got hit very hard from behind and was sent spinning into the straw bales. Isao Morishita, my Suzuki team-mate, had lost control under braking and fallen awkwardly. His bike launched itself off a large roadside rock and landed on the rear of my seat, completely flattening the curved hump and bending the supporting subframe down onto the rear tyre locking the wheel. I was dead lucky, or lucky not to be dead. A few centimetres farther forward and my back would have been broken. From there a wheelchair would have played a prominent part in my life. I escaped with no more than a surprisingly large hole in what little flesh there was on the front of my right hip bone. There were times, after a spill, when your leathers might show little more than scuff marks. But on occasions when you peeled them off you might find some bloody surprises.

On my return journey I called in at Assen. That hole on my right hip, which really needed a few stitches, was annoying me. I showed the family my 'war wound'. They were impressed. To help the healing process, they felt some wonder fluid called what sounded like 'yodium' should be applied. Being eager to have it heal, I agreed. Using a cotton wool ball liberally coated with the stuff, Janny dabbed it on. Yow and ow! It was iodine.

The absence of contact between us from April to June had increased our understanding and respect for each other. I now knew that when Janny made a decision, she meant it. And Janny now understood how serious I was about my emerging race career. There was no question or doubt about our love for each other. This lack of time we had together created a sense of urgency. It was decision time.

Next year I intended to ride for Suzuki only. Back at the factory they were making major improvements and were already testing new 125cc twin-cylinder machines with a four-cylinder 250cc in the planning stage. It was time to concentrate on the Grand Prix events, do a few internationals for pocket money and enjoy a less-demanding life. There was now time and a place in my life for another person.

We spoke at length about our future. I felt it was for Janny to decide. She was the one who would be uprooted and taken away. As Janny was their only surviving child, Gerrit and Tinie also had to be consulted. They, like many people in Holland at that time, were contributing to a fund that would eventually provide them with a unit in a retirement village. I explained that in New Zealand at that time, children took care of their parents. To push them off to an old folks' home was the last resort of the uncaring. And so was born the idea that they too, upon retirement, would come to New Zealand. We would, as a family, be separated for a few years, but in due course we would be reunited.

It was decided that we would become engaged immediately and be married next year on April 19, Janny's 20th birthday. Next day we bought two identical plain gold rings. We wore them on the third finger of our right hand. On our wedding day they would be transferred to the third finger of our left hand and become our wedding rings. All very economical and convenient. Mine is inscribed '6th October 1962 Janny'.

There were no candlelight dinners, or bended knees, however with our rings in place, we walked together through Assen Park, sat on the same seat that we had used after I'd hobbled, nearly blind, out of hospital 18 months ago. This, admiring our rings and what they represented, was sufficient for us. Life would continue, sort of the same really, just a whole lot better. As always, time was short. I needed to get back to England, pack my bikes, all manner of parts and car to be sent on two different boats, to Auckland and Wellington (to have sent it all on one boat would have raised a few red customs flags), and get organised to fly to Argentina.

My red Ford Thames van and blue Mk I 3.4 Jaguar, on a murky late-autumn day, outside the home of my hosts, Rose and Geoff Maynard. Archives.

The De Havilland Comet jet refuelled in north-east Brazil. During our stop, a commuter plane crashed on the tarmac and burst into flames. There were no survivors. After a long delay we re-boarded. Going by the amount of empty seats, the sight of a plane crashing had encouraged a large number to seek alternative forms of transport. By this time I had become quite fatalistic: what will be, will be.

Arriving late at night, I joined the Suzuki team for breakfast. The acting team manager, Osamu Suzuki, was the son-in-law of Mr Shunzo Suzuki, the factory president. Osamu had been given the job to broaden his horizons. As always, Ishikawa-san was the race team's go-to man. I was quickly brought up to date. They had been practising for two days. Honda were not competing, as their points total was insufficient for them to win the championship. Anscheidt and Huberts were faster than Itoh and Ernst, so they were worried. The circuit was short with three interesting features. The first corner was a long right-hander with a medium-fast entry tightening to a slower exit. A fast S-bend followed, tight enough to have to brake a little. Both corners created exactly the kind of challenge I enjoyed. A few nondescript turns brought us to a 90-degree left, a short straight, a 180-degree corner into another straight running parallel in the opposite direction and around a left sweeper back to the finish. Advantage could be gained on the first corner and at the S-bends. When the track ran parallel and in the opposite direction, you could clearly see riders travelling in the opposite direction, allowing me to monitor the position of the following riders.

I was riding well and it didn't take long to tune my two bikes making typical carburettor and gearing alterations. Within 30 minutes I was lapping 1.8 seconds faster than the Kreidlers, with more to come. The 50cc race followed our practice

positions. Even though Ernst had my best bike, he was unable to lower his lap times. To win the championship he had to finish ahead of Anscheidt. I led from the start and watched Anscheidt as he settled in behind me. Then came Huberts with Ernst lying fourth. As we had decided, on my initiative in our pre-race plans, at the 15- to 18-lap point of the 25-lap race, I slowly drifted back to Anscheidt and Huberts. I didn't obstruct them in any way but for some reason they both seemed to lose their concentration. Huberts ran off the track and slid down on the grass without injury. Anscheidt overshot a corner, allowing Ernst to pass him. I followed Ernst as a rear gunner. For the last few laps he kept a steady three-second advantage on Anscheidt, so I slipped past and won.

The Suzuki team were over the moon with the results, especially team manager Mr Osamu Suzuki, who is the current president of the Suzuki Motor Company. In effect, I had delivered to Ernst and Suzuki the 1962

Top: On the first of 25 occasions. Standing before our flag while our national anthem is played. Archives.

Bottom: A reception at the factory for Ernst and me on our return from Argentina. Archives.

50cc world championship. I then won the 125cc race.

A non-world-championship event in Japan, the first race to be run at the new Honda-owned circuit at Suzuka, signalled the season's end. Suzuki racing department's new twin-cylinder 125 was ready to be run. It was not as fast as the improved rear-exhaust 125 single-cylinder, but it was obviously a machine of the future. Suzuki did not have a test track; Mr Okano wanted it ridden over the full race distance. As the race was not particularly important, I was the guinea pig. It was very smooth, compared to the single, and less temperamental to prepare.

During a wet practice session on the freshly finished circuit, using Yokohama tyres — Avons had yet to be fitted — and wanting to impress the top factory staff who were attending, I overdid it and slid off into thick, soggy, yellow trackside clay. At least it was soft. By the time I had come to rest, I was covered in the stuff. The mechanics thought it was really funny while they cleaned me up with a hose and scrubbing brush.

Meanwhile the stakes were being raised in the 50cc class. Honda had built a new eight-valve twin-cylinder 50cc that ran to a staggering 22,000rpm and used a bicycle-like rim-clamping front brake. During the 50cc race Irishman Tommy Robb and I had a race-long 'squabble' over first place. The new Honda was fast with an extremely loud exhaust note. It was hard to believe that something so small could be so noisy. Tommy never tires of describing our race-long skirmish. He claims that at one point even our handlebars became entangled as we bumped and pushed and leaned on each other. Whatever we did, he was better at it on the day and won by half a bike length.

In contrast the 125cc race was something of an anticlimax for me. My job was to test the endurance of the new bike. It ran perfectly sweetly, proving its reliability, and we gained eighth place, which was okay.

The Suzuki Motor Company was a generous host. At the best restaurants we were introduced to the various Japanese specialities. I enjoyed them all and quickly learned how to order, in Japanese, 10 lightly cooked oysters and two fried eggs — a handy snack. As in so many areas of our lives, Frank Perris and I differed greatly in our food preference. My eating large raw oysters tended to put him off his beef sandwiches!

We were dressed in the same clothes as all the employees, regardless of rank, and were encouraged to walk through the factory's many assembly lines. The workers were very serious, conscientious and highly skilled. Every bike was started, warmed up, put on rollers and its performance monitored through all its gears.

Discussions concerning machine changes and planning of the 1963 season were carried out on a daily basis. Management was quite clear in what they hoped to achieve. As riders we were respected for our knowledge and involved in brainstorming sessions on how we thought the expected results could be achieved. With our wealth of collective experience, we were able to make a substantial contribution. Contracts for the new season were discussed. Ernst wasn't prepared to tell us what he was being paid, but that was okay. Frank and I decided that 2,500 pounds was a reasonable figure. This was readily accepted by them and simple two-page contracts were drawn up. When an oil company contract with Shell and start and prize money, paid at every meeting, was added, the season produced a net non-taxable amount of 6,363 pounds, an amount that would have purchased a reasonable home at that time.

I flew down to Wellington, as I had some of Colin Meehan's personal effects. I intended to visit his parents and explain a little about how he had conducted himself, how well he had ridden, what he had achieved and that the fatal crash was not his fault. Another responsibility of the captaincy of the New Zealand TT team, willingly carried out. After booking into a hotel, I phoned Colin's dad to tell him I'd be around about 10am next day, then phoned Mum. I was amused to hear her long, drawn-out "Yeeeees" in a heavy Kiwi drawl. It had been a busy eight months since I had last heard her voice.

I was woken early by a dawn chorus of New Zealand birds. Wellington is a beautiful city on a fine, late-spring day. I took a taxi to Fox Street, on the wooded slopes of Ngaio, walked up to the open door of a classic Kiwi weatherboard bungalow and knocked. No one came. I waited a while and knocked again. Still no one came. The house was immaculate and it seemed obvious that someone was in there. What to do? For reasons of his own, Mr Meehan was not able to meet me, so I placed the satchel containing Colin's personal papers on the kitchen table and left.

Above: In the Suzuki foundry, explaining an experience I had at the small foundry in Huntly. Archives.

Below: During one of many brain-storming sessions. Archives.

156

CHAPTER 11

Marrying my Janny, and winning two World Championships

FACING DOWN AN ANGRY BELGIAN COPPER WITH A PISTOL POINTING AT MY HEAD

The New Zealand domestic summer racing season of 1962–63 was one to remember. With Dave Kenah conscientiously looking after my two Nortons, we were beaten just once when Peter Pawson was sufficiently inspired to ride to his full potential and pipped me at an event in Tauranga.

As well as many race wins, there was the landing of two shipments of bike parts. So I was feeling great when I left New Zealand early in February 1963. Having sold all my surplus equipment, I had money in the bank, a secure future with Suzuki and a wedding to my first and only love on April 19.

The second shipment included a 3.4-litre Mk I Jaguar I'd bought in the UK for Gordon. I drove that Jag home from Wellington feeling like a young laird of the manor. It was a revelation. I had no idea that the Brits made such good cars. Out on the open road it was superb, cruising effortlessly in overdrive at 150kph. It had been bred on a racetrack, not designed and produced to a tight budget. Then there was the smell of the leather upholstery, the large speedo and tacho, set in a wall of polished walnut veneer. Life that day felt complete, especially when munching on a hamburger with one hand while the Jag was eating up the road at 130kph on the Desert Road north of Waiouru.

When I arrived home at 11pm Mum came out in her dressing gown, took the keys and after an explanation of the dashboard toggle switch operations, took it for a spin. She was gone for an abnormally long time. Deep down I feel sure she had a sense of suppressed rebellion and adventure that on rare occasions she allowed herself to indulge.

My final race meeting for the New Zealand summer season was back near Wellington at Levin. After an extremely wet but successful day's racing, I left setting a cracking pace on the 450km drive home with my bikes on a trailer. As I whistled along the Sanson straights north of Levin, I noticed a car some distance behind. I kept travelling at 130kph and checked at the end of the next straight. The car was still there about the same distance behind, so I slowed. Sure enough the traffic officer finally caught up in his Ford Mark II Zephyr and I pulled over. He was completely without humour, due perhaps to his claiming to have been flat-out for 20km and not being able to gain on me. My inference that his vehicle was probably more unsafe at that speed than mine, even with the trailer, may not have helped.

Each time I came home I amassed a long list of tickets for speeding. Three in one day was the record. Being only a short time in New Zealand had some advantages, as the processing of traffic offences was slow. In due course a policeman would arrive at the farm to serve the first summons to appear in court. As I had left the country, it could not be served and was returned to the sender. From then on a policeman would call at my sister's, who lived in Huntly, and had her sign a declaration that I had left the country, so saving himself a 17km drive. They were more amused than annoyed.

My first ride for Suzuki in 1963 was at the Daytona Speedway on February 10. It was an international event run by United States Motorcycles. This was an organisation set up by the FIM (Fédération Internationale de Motocyclisme) in an attempt to gain a foothold in the American Motorcycle Association (Harley-Davidson influenced) controlled area of North American motorcycle sport.

An American Suzuki representative met me at Los Angeles airport. He took me for a tour of this ultra-modern city in a Pontiac Firebird. During our conversation he mentioned that he recently had a top engine tune, i.e. spark plugs, ignition points, oil change, etc. It had cost him the equivalent of 55 pounds. Really? I had had a new motor fitted to my Ford Thames van for the same price in the UK.

We drove up Sunset Strip, of television fame, and on to Hollywood where the houses were huge, typically with four-car garaging. Welcome to the world of real wealth. A few days later I was equally impressed when I hit Daytona in Florida. You enter Daytona Raceway via a long tunnel and drive out into this huge stadium.

Qualifying for the Daytona 500 was taking place. Big Chevrolets, Pontiacs, Fords and more were thundering around the oval. Along the back straight you could hear the engine revs building in that unique V8 growl. One car would closely slipstream another and drive into the rear of it, bunting it along to increase both their speeds, at the time they were averaging around 260kph. Perhaps the most impressive thing was seeing these large vehicles, with a huge exhaust pipe protruding out each side, hurtling around the steep banking in a drift. They sure knew how to drive. The PR man for the circuit showed us films of some of the most dramatic multi-car crashes. At the time it was hardly believable. The rest of the world was unaware of how the Yanks went racing.

After practice we were asked to take part in a publicity stunt riding two laps of the banked circuit flat-out. We were surprised and pleased to find that our 125s were as fast as most of the 500s that were taking part. Honda did not arrive, leaving Suzuki and Yamaha to win every event. Mitsuo Itoh won the 50cc race with Ernst Degner and me side by side in second place. Ernst won the 125cc class while I retired with gearbox problems. The very capable Fumio Ito won the 250cc race on a Yamaha and American Don Vesco rode another 250cc Yamaha to victory in the 500cc race.

The downside was that during the 250cc race the clutch mechanism on my bike failed, but I continued, only to have the engine seize in a corner. The high-side that followed left me with my right hand trapped under the handlebar. The bone was exposed on three knuckles, the rest severely lacerated. With my arm in a sling, and pumped full of antibiotics, I flew back to Holland to find Janny and Mrs Oeseburg well advanced with our wedding plans for the 19th of April. Yet another step up to a new and exciting stage of my life.

In March, Janny and I flew to Stuttgart and collected a new Mercedes that we had bought, duty free, in Janny's name. North-eastern Europe was covered in deep snow, prompting the factory to give us a set of chains to help us on our way. We called on Ernst Degner and enjoyed a pleasant evening in his good company. Then went to England to collect my van, which had been garaged at Vinson's farm, found a suitable caravan and proceeded to complete the myriad of pre-season tasks associated with the planning of participating in a world championship series. Vehicle documentation, oil company contracts, insurances, catching up with friends and so much more.

We arranged to meet Ginger and his friend Clair at the site of the Cutty Sark, an historic sailing ship at Greenwich, South London. It seems they had suffered severely from the cold and much later claimed to have spent most of the first three weeks in bed. In New Zealand, Ginger and I had spoken at length regards all the details a first-timer needed to attend to. I had given him addresses and phone numbers and how the system worked regards travel documents for his race bikes, and how to obtain them, and advice on every conceivable subject. There is little more that others can do for you, and of course each person has their own take on things and different priorities.

When Janny and I became engaged, and committed to each other for life, on the 6th of October last year, that was to me the most special day we had shared.

April the 19th was a confirmation, among family and friends, of that. We first attended the official ceremony held in the Assen Council Chambers. As Janny's parents were active members of the local Presbyterian Church, we also had a church service. Our guests attended both. We then moved on to a reception where friends and acquaintances came to congratulate us and wish us all the best for the future. The wedding breakfast followed and we were delighted to have representatives from the Suzuki Motor Company, friends from England and the racing world join us.

No greater response to the ringing of a doorbell could a young man hope for. Archives.

Love, pride and happiness. Archives.

Jan Meierdres, my best man, signing the register. Archives.

Packed and ready to leave. Archives.

It was late when we left. Our first night was not in the bridal suite of a posh hotel, but in a caravan in a lay-by beside a motorway. The next day I took a school for potential road racers at the Zandvoort Grand Prix circuit. We then took in the world-renowned Keukenhof, a vast area of tulips arranged in blocks of brilliant colour. However, due to an exceptionally cold winter and late spring, we were denied the beauty of it.

Then we visited the war museum at Arnhem, which commemorates events that occurred there during World War II, including the heroic battle for a local bridge depicted in the renowned film A Bridge Too Far. Janny's introduction to my world was probably rather abrupt. Museums, especially those depicting a war the locals wanted to forget, was understandably of little interest to her. But the ever patient Janny didn't complain.

There are few things a rider looks forward to more than the first

160

Top: Taking our vows. Archives.

Above: As we leave the Council Chambers, Janny greets a former patient. Archives.

Grand Prix of the new season. What improvements have been made to the bikes and what effect will those changes have? Equally important is the question of what improvements have the opposition made? These questions would be answered on May 5th at the Spanish Grand Prix, the venue being Montjuich Park in the centre of Barcelona, the tightest, toughest, most tortuous circuit in the Grand Prix series.

We were kicking off the season from a much better base than in 1962. The Japanese staff had a greater understanding of European systems. The new twin, now with rear-facing exhaust expansion chambers, had not been track tested but looked to have potential. How long would it take to sort out the ever present teething problems before serious racing could begin? This was the first time the complete team had been assembled. We were all in good spirits, enjoying being together again with the collective optimism that flows through all teams at this time. As the bikes were quite different from last year, our data from 1962 was only a rough guide. I started on the safe side, with an over-rich mixture, lowish gearing and suspension settings on the soft side.

Typically of most Grand Prix events, practice was held on Friday and Saturday, consisting of two sessions a day, with the races run on Sunday. As the Spanish enjoy an afternoon siesta and like to have all their racing over early, the 50cc race began at 9.15am.

Unlike the previous year, the team had no serious mechanical dramas. Having two bikes for each class meant running them in and sorting out the one showing the most potential. There are always differences between them even though, to all intents and purposes, they are identical.

We made competitive lap times all through practice. Hans Georg Anscheidt set the fastest 50cc lap. His 12-speed Kreidler suited the steep uphill section and Hans had always performed well here. Then to everyone's delight Frank Perris was the fastest on the 125. Honda had made only minor changes to their never-beaten, all-conquering 1962 models.

At the end of the first lap of the 50cc race I lay second, 50m behind Hans, with Ernst on my back wheel. My engine was a little rich so if I were to run on full throttle the spark plug would foul. It took several laps to set up a rhythm using just three-quarters of the throttle available. It is not in the nature of a full- blooded racer to use less power than what is available. Another discipline to learn.

Once that was set, I gained on Hans. At half distance Mitsuo Itoh and Ernst retired with fouled plugs, euphemistically labelled 'ignition trouble'. I took over the lead but a third of the circuit was uphill and not being able to use full throttle was a handicap. With two laps to go Hans slipped passed and won by 1.4 seconds. I was happy enough. The engine settings that I had chosen were the most suitable for the hot conditions. The only other Suzuki to finish was in fourth position some 53 seconds behind.

There were no less than eight potential winners in the 125cc race. Reliability was the deciding factor. Jim Redman, Honda, led a tight bunch at the end of the first lap with Englishman Peter Inchley, EMC, second, Luigi Taveri, Honda, third, me in fourth place all in a tight bunch. Perris was out on the first lap. Ignition trouble was the given cause. By the end of the fourth lap I had passed Taveri and Inchley and began to work out how to attack Redman when a serious misfire set in. Within

a lap I was out. Sure enough, ignition trouble. Austrian Berti Schneider, newly introduced to the team, was the only Suzuki to finish, way back in seventh.

The meeting had been a test session, and from that point of view it was a success. We had formed a sound basis from which to approach the West German Grand Prix at Hockenheim, the fastest circuit in the world championship series.

After a leisurely 10 days of camping in the warmth of Spain, Janny and I drove up to the West German Grand Prix. Hockenheim is set in a pine forest. The trees provide marginally more oxygen than at any other circuit. Our two-strokes thrived under these conditions; having the oil mixed with the petrol and able to use larger jets allowed more fuel and consequently more oil into the engine.

During practice I set the fastest lap in the 50cc class and Ernst topped the 125cc field. In the smaller-capacity class Anscheidt and I led a pack of

Top: Winning the West German 50cc Grand Prix by a small margin. Photo by Wolfgang Gruber.

Middle: Sharing the joy of our first European win with a journalist. Archives.

Left: The original caption from Motor Cycling *magazine was 'One of the instigators of the modern aggressive riding techniques'. Archives.*

50cc riders from the drop of the flag. But at the end of the first lap Degner led and I held third place in a line of five Suzukis with Anscheidt holding sixth. After three laps, the three leading riders of Ernst, Isao Morishita and I were swapping positions constantly and drew away from the rest. Ernst's bike slowed but Morishita and I kept at it until the finish, when I crossed the line just 0.6sec in the lead. The new lap record stood at an amazing 143.3kph.

More than 120,000 enthusiasts surrounded the circuit and many had gained access to the paddock area. Following the podium ceremony I crossed the track and went through a heavily guarded gate into the paddock. Immediately, I was surrounded by autograph-seeking enthusiasts. Over the preceding years, there had been times when a group of supporters would ask me for my signature, but this was quite different. As I signed my name over and over again, mainly in genuine autograph books, I edged slowly towards our caravan. Janny had lunch ready and was a little impatient about my signing autographs when I should be sitting at the table. I had won a Grand Prix, so what. I finally made it and, with apologies, slipped in and locked the door. We weren't expecting the faces of as many as eight fans to be pressed against the windows watching our every move.

I joined Ernst on the front row of the 125cc event with Hungarian Lazlo Szabo, MZ, Taveri and Redman, Hondas, and Berti and Frank filling the first two rows. I got a good start but Ernst took over the lead on the first lap and steadily pulled away. Szabo lay third ahead of Berti and Taveri. Ernst had a handy lead at half race distance, leaving me in a safe second with Frank on his Suzuki having moved up to third with Szabo and Taveri in his slipstream. Ernst won comfortably. I was second with Szabo gaining a well-earned third ahead of Taveri. Frank and Berti both retired.

The organisers of the post-race dinner and prize giving had little idea that their intended rather formal evening would become the party of the 1963 Grand Prix season. The Suzuki team were in high spirits following the most successful meeting in their competition history. Food and as much alcohol as you thought you needed was free. People began dancing as a brass band played. A cry went up: "Who can do the Charleston?" Jim Redman suggested his wife Marlene might but she wasn't so sure. To my utter surprise Janny stood up, strode confidently onto the stage and gave an impeccable demonstration for which she received cheers, whistles and clapping hands. What else don't I know about this young woman I have married?

The evening progressed with snake dances, neckties tied around heads and pot plants placed in some unexpected places.

On the following Wednesday, England's *Motor Cycling* had the front-page headline 'Suzuki steal the show at Hockenheim', followed by: 'What a magnificent meeting with each of the four solo classes providing needle-sharp competition between widely differing types of works machinery. Enthusiasts can really look forward to one of the most exciting years in the history of the sport.'

The French Grand Prix at Clermont-Ferrand was run on June 2, the day after practice had begun for the all-important Isle of Man TT. This created travel problems for the Grand Prix contenders and their teams.

Suzuki decided to charter a plane and fly their equipment and key personnel directly to the island with their vans to follow. My Ford Thames was often used to help move the race bikes and the plan was that following the 125cc and 50cc races

Janny and I would drive the 650km to Dieppe, take the 11pm ferry that landed at Dover at 5am Monday, go to Brands Hatch, ride in the 50cc and 125cc classes, then carry on to Liverpool and the Isle of Man.

NATURAL TALENT IS THE BASE ON WHICH YOU BUILD; HOW YOU DEVELOP THAT BASE IS YOUR TRUE ABILITY

We arrived at Clermont-Ferrand on Wednesday night. I woke quite early on Thursday morning and thought about the upcoming race. This magnificent purpose-built track was my favourite. The satisfying results in Spain and then a first and a second at Hockenheim, the fastest track in the series, was proof that this year's Suzukis were the goods and I was fast gaining the necessary knowledge to successfully carry out the required engine preparation. Two-strokes, with their impossibly narrow power bands of just 500 revs and never-ending carburettor, piston-seizing and plug-oiling problems, had not suited a slow, twisting track such as this. But if I could overcome these disadvantages and win here, on the slowest, least favourable circuit, I would have a very good chance of becoming the 1963 125cc world champion.

Until this moment I had never considered, dreamt or thought that I could reach such heights. My strongest and most persistent thoughts had always been how much I had to learn and that had been my focus. But this was a new beginning and the slate was clean. The opportunity of joining the heroes of a 13-year-old on the world champion stage was beckoning. I had served a searching and demanding three-year apprenticeship in Europe. I was good enough. No one, but no one, was going to take this from me. History was now my driver and a cold, calm resolve enveloped me. I knew full well that if I rose to the occasion, my life would be changed forever.

I spent Thursday morning with my mechanics and machines, deciding on gear ratios, approximate carburettor settings and so on. After leaving the garage I drove up the Auvergne mountains to the track. While the French traffic laws and the arm-waving mannerisms of the drivers were all foreign to me, this circuit was not. As I drove the van onto the track I sensed an unusual feeling of warmth, pleasure and, to a degree, security.

This was the venue where all those personal doors and barriers that were impeding me from disregarding the inhibition, lack of confidence and self-esteem could be flung open. With a strong feeling that destiny was waiting, I scoured the track for every form of advantage that might be available to me.

During practice I became acutely pedantic regarding every detail of my bikes, especially carburettor settings and gear ratios. Barcelona was by the sea, Hockenheim in a pine forest; here we were in central France, 1,500 metres up in the mountains. Under these varied air pressure situations, our ultra-sensitive prototype engines required quite different carburettor settings. Having learned to 'feel' what the engine required, not what you think it should have, during practice I was quite bold and confident when changing these.

The mechanics saw humour in my critical approach. When I asked them to have the carburettor float chambers lowered 0.8mm, they extravagantly went into great detail to gain perfect accuracy. Even though we had eight gears it was necessary, after changing up, to slip the clutch until the bike and engine speed matched before you could release the clutch. Then you hit peak revs, changed gear and went through the clutch-slipping routine again, allowing the engine to be kept in the 500rpm power range. Frequently, the choice of gear ratios could be the difference between winning and losing. In this regard, Clermont-Ferrand was the most demanding.

I had learned the importance of gearing during the second half of 1962. I had found that by isolating myself and mentally once more circulating the track and noting on which corners the gearing suited and those it didn't, I could advise on changing the sprockets for the next practice session.

The gear used for a particular corner, due to the very narrow power band, could, and often did, regulate your speed through it. Some corners you would sort of waft in a little fast, hold your breath and gain the best exit speed. Others you might approach on the slow side and begin pouring on the gas and driving out from the moment of entry.

I am speaking of quite small increments but on a track with 55 corners, the difference is shown in your lap times and proves or disproves your accuracy of thought. The stopwatch is your absolute master. Everything else is a variable.

Without disclosing this new-found form and urgency to my team or opposition, I qualified fourth fastest for the 125 race. Six-time world champion Jim Redman, riding a Honda, was on pole.

Having read through my notes, made after the last practice session as was my way, I hugged Janny and with a "See you later, kid", and approached the start totally focused.

Urgency in every line. A moment captured during a race that changed my life. Archives.

Someone made a move on the start line before the drop of the starter's flag. I didn't wait, gained a cracking start and was gone. Riding with concentrated intent, I broke the lap record by eight seconds and won by 38 seconds from Jim Redman.

While standing on the podium, a disappointed Jim protested that I had jumped the start. My reply was: "Jim, I won by thirty-eight seconds, this is just the first time you have been beaten. There will be many more, so you will need to get used to it."

Jim realised that Honda had lost the world championship, while I felt that, provided I sustained the work ethic and routine established here, and with a little luck, Suzuki and Hugh Anderson would win it.

In his race report the assistant editor of *Motor Cycling*, Norman Sharpe, wrote: 'At the end of the first lap, Anderson, with his right knee well out, fairly streaked around the corner into the start-finish straight.' He continued: 'At half distance, Degner and Schneider were suffering from carburettor problems, but there was nothing wrong with Anderson's twin, which handled and performed like a dream. Hardly letting up despite his terrific lead, Anderson continued to pull away from Redman at about five seconds a lap to win by a cool 38 seconds.'

The 125cc race had been run in the morning. A thunderstorm hit during the three-and-a-half-hour lunch break, covering the track in hailstones. When the storm abated, the starters lined up for the 50cc race. I was on pole with Anscheidt on his Kreidler beside me. Hans made a good start and at the end of the first lap I was 100m behind him, but I slid off on a winding downhill section. In the wet, on a 50cc, there is but a blink between being on the bike or on your butt. A few seconds later I was joined by team-mate Mitsuo Itoh. He too was unhurt and we enjoyed the humorous side of it, as did the team. Anscheidt went on to have a well-deserved win.

When interviewed some time after the French Grand Prix, Ernst Degner made the comment that "Hugh has learned surprisingly quickly the relationship between carburettor settings, piston clearance, reliability and the importance of gear ratio selection relative to lap times."

Perhaps this needs further explanation. On a British racing four-stroke single, typically the correct gearing for a given track was to reach peak revs in top just before your braking point at the end of the fastest straight. However, Suzuki's high-revving machines, with exceedingly narrow power bands and eight or nine gears, meant I would have to choose the overall gearing that suited the majority of corners on the track and gave me the best lap time. I would tend towards using the lowest gearing to benefit from the advantages it gave when accelerating and avoid over-revving on the fastest parts of the track by using the ignition cut-out button to hold the engine back keeping it just below the revs when the big ends failed.

After a mad race across France to Dieppe, we caught the ferry with minutes to spare. Our early-morning arrival meant we had plenty of time to get to Brands Hatch, just 100km up the road. A dual carriageway, bypassing Maidstone, was the ideal place to give the 125 a pre-practice run. I unloaded it and screamed off up the road. Janny didn't have a licence but as she intended to get one, it was obviously okay for her to follow driving the van. With an unmuffled screech that carried a long way, I covered a few very quick kilometres, reloaded the bike and pressed on to Brands leaving the locals to wonder what had made that ungodly noise. At the circuit I changed the main jets and rode off around the lanes on another test session.

The day went well. I won, breaking lap and race records.

It was Tuesday when we arrived on the Isle of Man. Official practice had started four days earlier. Time was limited; could I get the bikes running as well as they needed to on this the most difficult of tracks? Yet another meeting loaded with pressure.

This year I was approaching the TT in quite a different way. My situation had changed. I was married now and had the perfect partner to accompany me — and one who believed in me. Janny's presence had lifted my self-confidence to a level not experienced before and replaced the self-esteem problems with a calm, secure feeling of wellbeing. There was little need to associate with others. Together we were complete.

I had a contract with Suzuki, the second-largest manufacturer of motorcycles in the world. My relationship with the engineers with whom I worked, Nagata-san, who prepared my 125, and Matsui-san, who was responsible for my 50cc machine, had reached common ground. We were, with the assistance of Ishikawa-san, cutting through the frustrations of language barriers and formulating our own communication. We had respect for each other; we listened, discussed and had steadily built a partnership that was allowing us to produce success on the racetrack. We had become a team within a team.

At most Grand Prix, after the field of riders had been assembled in their starting order and engines stopped, a call was made to clear the start area. It was at this time that Nagata-san would take me by the arm or shoulder, we would make eye contact and he would leave. This to me was a confirmation of unity between mechanic, rider and the race. Nagata-san wasn't always with the team, as he got rather homesick. But normally he was there for the first half of the season.

Ernst Degner and I had an excellent professional working relationship. From Ernst's point of view it was not important if he won, although if he could he certainly would. His condition of employment was to help and advise his team-mates in the understanding and preparation of their machines.

I was in a position to learn a considerable amount as I worked alongside him in the garage. He answered my questions honestly and was prepared to discuss in detail any particular problem that arose. Even though I had gained sufficient knowledge to have my engines performing reliably and was now finishing ahead of him on the track, our relationship had not changed. Suzuki was winning and that was our combined goal.

We were working with prototype, two-stroke engines. The horsepower rating for the size of engines we were using was the highest in racing history. This put us in the unenviable position of having to deal with totally new problems, some of which had never been experienced before. My main focus lay in this area. The results gained so far indicated the technical skills I was gaining and the sympathy towards, and understanding of, these demanding and at times exasperating engines was giving me an advantage. It was a matter of unlocking their potential.

I felt confident that I could prepare my engine to the point of being reliable and fast enough to win. Although this was my fourth year at the TT there was still more for me to learn. Not all of it was associated with the course itself, but in the way I needed to ride it and how my Suzukis needed to be set up. Understandably, both the 125cc and the tiny 50cc models needed to be prepared and used in quite a different way to the larger British machines I had ridden here before. That would be my focus this year.

Janny did not restrict or restrain my need to spend time gaining an ever better understanding of this tortuous 37.7-mile track. Nor the hours spent in the garage, or the time I sat in silence mulling over an engine problem or racing lines on a particular series of corners.

I was now free of the workloads of a private rider and the responsibilities that I had been proud to accept as captain of the New Zealand team. Every rider is, or should be, aware that the next race may be his last. My experiences had hardened me. All of those who have lived through a few years of this sport are emotionally damaged; some for life. More than most, it would seem, I needed a quiet environment where only the race was considered. All other thoughts, subjects, activities, conversations or associations were avoided.

At times people were offended by my extreme focus on the task in hand and solitary approach. I was only answerable to my ever present need, not only to ride to my full potential but to keep raising the bar of excellence. I was well aware too of my responsibilities to the members of the Hamilton and other motorcycle clubs where my skills and attitude had been moulded, to my young country of which I was immensely proud and the place in history that I had the opportunity to forge.

The excitement of carrying out the detailed planning required to win a TT had now come to me; a level I never thought I could rise to. However, arriving late and missing vital practice sessions was just about the worst way to begin a campaign here.

A refresher lap of the track in the van showed me there had not been any significant changes. It was surprising how covering just one slow lap brought back 90 per cent of it. The sequence of corners fell into place, the many braking and peel-off markers came immediately to eye. Circuit knowledge wouldn't be a problem, but in the limited time available adjusting those various markers, especially for the 50cc machine, and gaining the correct carburettor settings and gearing would be.

Wednesday morning's practice catered for 50, 125 and 250cc classes. Barring mechanical failure, I should manage two laps on the 125 and one on the 50.

Just before midnight I slipped between the sheets and set that damned alarm clock for 4am.

My bikes ran well, too rich as always, but it was only our first practice and by using reduced throttle openings, I didn't have any plug-oiling problems.

Although I had covered a total of just six laps before Saturday morning, the last session available to us, I was able to break the 125cc lap record. At the end of 50cc practice, the fastest five riders had all broken the lap record, with Ernst being the fastest and me a few seconds back in third.

Wednesday dawned wet with the mountain buried in fog. The 11am start of the 125cc race was delayed one hour. At noon a signal was given to warm our engines. Then a further delay of 30 minutes was announced. Finally, we were called to our starting positions in pairs along Glencrutchery Road.

Number 1, Alan Shepherd, MZ, was a non-starter, leaving Tommy Robb, Honda, on his own. Mike Hailwood, MV, was another non-starter, so at Number 4 I also sat on my own. Tommy was preparing to push off when a further delay was announced due to fog returning on the mountain. Eventually, he was flagged away and I followed 10 seconds later. The overnight rain had washed the roads clean, although a slide on the double right at Greeba Castle and another on Greeba Bridge was a strong reminder that this race is not won in the first 10km.

I caught Tommy before Ballacraine, just 11km from the start. I knew where the road surfaces would be at their worst and felt confident from the feedback I was getting from the tyres that my pace, while being very quick under the conditions, was not foolhardy; though being first on the roads had its disadvantages — I would be the one that hit any greasy sections first and cleared the seagulls off the road. This could be my first TT victory but caution wasn't going to win it for me.

I began the mountain climb into an umbrella of clouds. Eventually, at the Black Hut, visibility dropped to perhaps 25m. At 140kph it may as well be nil, but I knew my markers and lines, braked heavily and peeled off for the left-hand corner at the Black Hut that I couldn't clearly see. I missed the apex by half a metre and got thrown wide, ending up on a narrow strip of grass between the road and a drain. With considerable luck I got back on the track and continued on into the three rights of the Verandah, where the fog began to clear. Well, if that is the worst thing that happens today, I will be okay.

My pit board read 1+8 Degner; I was leading the race by eight seconds from Ernst. These were our positions halfway through that first lap. I knew the track conditions now so the second lap should be faster. The signal board at Sulby Straight showed 1+19 Degner. This was the gap at the pits. I had pulled out 11 seconds over the mountain. That blast through the fog would have put a gap on anyone.

The bike was running perfectly. As expected it was a little rich up on the mountain — 500m above sea level makes a difference — but three-quarter throttle was sufficient. In fact it was reassuring, as it told me that at sea level it was correct. This time round the mountain was still quite foggy but I didn't ease off anywhere. Through the pits at the end of my second lap, my pit board showed 1+31 Degner.

I love this place: my challenge is the track, make it your friend and be rewarded, here you only race against the watch, that suits me. No dramas now. The drying track allowed me to increase my corner speed, the gearing I was using began to suit the situation, and the ride became more fluid and faster. Our Sulby signalling station gave me 1+50 Degner. With just 22km to the finish, surely nothing can stop me now.

The finish flag dropped, I lifted the clutch and the engine became silent. I can hear the traditional polite applause from the packed grandstand. Nagata-san ran out to the pit entry lane and pushed me into where Janny was waiting. I'm pleased to have won and enjoy her cuddle.

The team was ecstatic. All our bikes had finished. The results: Anderson first by 1min 20secs, Perris second, 6.6secs ahead of third-placed Degner. Taveri fourth on the first Honda to finish, then Schneider and Redman. The cream on the cake for me, even when the roads were still damp, was taking 20 seconds off the existing lap record.

Few experiences would be more emotional, in my racing life, than standing on the winner's rostrum, before the New Zealand flag, with the national anthem playing in my honour, here in the Isle of Man. With a large lump in my throat, with Janny, I hurried to leave the paddock.

Ernst and I being interviewed by Murray Walker and Gordon Pitt for Schofield records. The Nick Nicholls collection at Mortons Archive.

A reward richly deserved. Archives.

A possible win in the Isle of Man tends to focus the mind. Archives.

Mr Suzuki joined us at the prize giving and with Ernst, Frank and me standing behind him he accepted the Manufacturers' Team Prize. There was also the Bob Holliday Trophy for the fastest lap and no less than five Silver Replicas awarded. What better result could he have hoped for? It was a clean sweep.

Friday's 50cc event gave Mr Suzuki another reason to congratulate his race team.

Motor Cycling's headline trumpeted: 'All Japanese win, 50cc TT history'. The report read: 'History was made in the 50cc class on Friday when Mitsuo Itoh became the first Japanese rider ever to win one of the mountain classics. This is the second year since the class was introduced; that the fastest five riders in practice have all broken last year's lap record is a good indication of the improvements that have been made during the past 12 months.'

Above: Being interviewed on the TT podium with Frank and Ernst. Richard Garrett Services Ltd.

Left: Mr Suzuki receives the Manufacturers' Team Prize. Ernst, Frank and I stand with him. Archives.

The weather was fine when we lined up for the start of the 50cc race on Friday. There were 36 entries. Berti Schneider was having an outing on a Suzuki production racer. Being Number 1, he started with Number 2, Hans Anscheidt, Kreidler. Being Number 4, I started 10 seconds later with Italian Alberto Pagani, Kreidler. Ernst at Number 5 was 10 seconds after me and Mitsuo Itoh a further 10 seconds back on start Number 8. My little 50cc buzz box started immediately and I pedalled it through the gears towards Bray Hill. Berti retired soon after the start when his engine seized. I was surprised to catch and pass Hans as soon as Ballacraine and once again I led on the roads.

Above: The team assembled behind a fine, hard-earned array of trophies. Archives.

Left: A photograph to send home. Archives.

Below: Mitsuo Itoh #8, the first Japanese rider to win a race in the Isle of Man. Anscheidt #2 and me. Archives.

With my engine running slightly rich and his 12-speed gearbox arrangement, a system of four gears and three overdrives working well for him, Hans passed me on the Mountain Mile. At the end of the first lap Ernst led by 0.6sec from Itoh, who was 7.6secs in front of me with Anscheidt 9.8secs farther back in fourth place. Hans actually led me on the road by just 0.2sec and Ernst was 1.8secs behind me. Just two seconds separated the three of us as we raced past the pits. This was a good example of the vagaries that pairs of riders starting at 10-second intervals creates. The first-, second- and third-placed riders had passed through the start in exactly the opposite order with just two seconds covering all three. Don't try to work it out; that's just how it is and part of what makes the Isle of Man TT unique.

The second lap was a further indication of how closely we were matched; there were just 10.3 seconds covering Ernst, Itoh and me, with Anscheidt just 10.2 seconds farther back.

Ernst passed me but soon after his engine slowed I re-passed him and pressed on. Perhaps 'squeeze on' is a better description as you squeeze everything you can out of the bike and squeeze through corners, cutting every line to a kerb-brushing, wall-touching experience.

Itoh came slowly by me soon after the jump over Ballaugh Bridge. I moved directly into his slipstream, gaining more revs. Like my 125, the 50 had a safely rich fuel mixture but appeared to be more affected each lap. Anscheidt rode past me again. To hold my third place I would have to stay within 10 seconds of him.

As we climbed the mountain, he gained on me. As we dropped back to sea level the power slowly returned. I bullied the little bike, hitting Hillberry corner flat-out and hammering it through the bumpy left and rights down to Governors Bridge. I have gained on Hans, I must be within 10 seconds of him, surely. Yes, I finished just 5.4 seconds after him, giving me second place. Itoh had won by 26.2 seconds, Ernst retired but gained the satisfaction of a new lap record of just on 130kph. That speed would have given him 11th in the 125cc and 250cc races and 21st in the 350cc class. Remarkable, isn't it?

The TT results were a huge fillip for Suzuki. It proved the company had the engineering skill and knowledge to produce reliable, race-winning motorcycles. The following week, the front-page headlines of *Motor Cycling* were 'Anglo-Japanese tie-up. New AMC company to market Suzuki two-stroke motorcycles'. The report read: 'Associated Motorcycles intend setting up a new sales organisation to market Suzuki motorcycles throughout Britain and Eire (Southern Ireland).'

On the way to Holland, Janny and I stopped off at the popular International Post TT meeting at Mallory Park. I won the 125cc race, setting new lap and race records.

Back in Assen, it seemed hard to believe that we had packed the French Grand Prix, Brands Hatch, Isle of Man and Mallory Park into just 18 days. Not to mention gathering on the way four wins, four lap and four race records, one second place, and a spill.

Janny was aware, now that she was experiencing it, that my commitment to my sport, although extreme, had not lessened my commitment to her. They were quite separate issues. Janny embraced my sporting ambitions as she embraced me.

My 'home Grand Prix' was here in Assen on June 29th. In the lead-up to the event

New Zealand flags were fluttering from many of the windows in the square where we lived. Race fans were pouring in from all over Europe. The Dutch TT was established in the late 1920s, and the annual meeting now brought 150,000 people to this small market town in north-east Holland.

To avoid the well-intentioned fuss of our neighbours in Schaperstraat, where we lived, we chose to stay in our caravan in the race paddock. Thursday evening's practice alone attracted 30,000 spectators.

Assen is a rider's circuit that allows a high average speed and incorporates pretty well every conceivable corner within its near-8km length. It is safe, provided you keep out of the drains! On each of the two previous occasions here I had ended up in hospital. This time was different. I broke the existing 125cc lap record during practice to set pole.

I led the 50cc race from the start but on the fifth lap Ernst passed me and went on to win by a narrow margin, setting new lap and race records in the process. I managed to hold second, just 1.4 seconds ahead of Ichino. I also led from the start of the 125cc race ahead of Ernst, Taveri, Perris and Schneider. Setting a speed that continuously broke the lap record, I steadily increased this lead. With just three laps to go, Ernst retired when his engine crankshaft broke, allowing Perris into second place, ahead of Taveri. Berti was forced to call at the pits to change spark plugs and then, to everyone's surprise, he set a new lap record to finish fourth.

Marrying an Assen girl did not a Dutch man of me make, but winning the 125 race did, if only for that day. Few of these races had been won by a local. With noisy enthusiasm the huge crowd welcomed Janny and me to the winner's rostrum.

Nine race and lap records were broken at the meeting. In his first year, fellow New Zealander Ginger Molloy finished seventh in the 250cc class on a Spanish Bultaco, and Morrie Lowe seventh on his 500cc Matchless. I now led both the 50cc and 125cc world championships, as did Suzuki in the manufacturers' titles.

To understand and gain the best from these small quirky and temperamental engines, it was necessary to become a virtual integral part of it. The main jet controlled the fuel flow only during wide throttle openings. I could control the fuel flow by the twist grip position creating a virtual variable main jet. There was very little difference in performance between three-quarter and full throttle. Done with skill this was the most important function, relative to reliability and the key to winning, an advantage that gave me by far the most reliable machines. It would have been pointless to tell my team-mates. Not having the throttle wide open in a race would have been foreign to them.

At the Knee Bocht and gaining second place. Archives.

Top: The end of the first lap of a typical 50cc race. #1 Ernst Degner won. Archives.

Left: Passing under the chequered flag, waved vigorously by 'The Major', as he was known. Archives.

Below left: Just nine weeks after our wedding, Janny and I are sharing the podium at her hometown Grand Prix. Archives.

Below right: Matsui-san and others enjoying their down time. Archives.

Another point that seemed to escape others was that after three or four laps of a typical 7km circuit, the two-stroke engines would tend to lean out and need more fuel. Later in the race they would become rich again and oil the plugs. This is why Grand Prix race results showed a lot of engine seizures early on and oiled plugs in the latter part of the race.

I was aware of these issues and my ability to control the fuel flow with the throttle opening worked a treat. Next stop was the Belgium Grand Prix, at Spa-Francorchamps on July 7. This was the first time I had raced at this world-renowned circuit in the picturesque Ardennes in Belgium's French-speaking south-east corner.

The 14km track contained the fastest corners I had experienced. For example, on a 50cc I only closed the throttle and braked twice each lap. Considering that my engine was not running quite as well as I would have liked, fifth place on the grid was okay.

As we knew from our experience at the Isle of Man TT, the Kreidlers were very fast. Anscheidt led until the last lap when his clutch failed at the La Source hairpin, and Morishita and Degner passed him. Morishita became the second Japanese rider to win a Grand Prix. Back in fourth place I missed out on the fun by 3.5 seconds. Just 0.6sec covered the first three riders.

My 125cc did not perform well at all and, to be perfectly honest, this was not my kind of track. There was so little to do. With just La Source hairpin and the very fast uphill left, right, left swoop of Eau Rouge followed by a slowish left-hander at the highest part of the course, the rest was top gear except for Stavelot, at the end of the very long Masta straight, where you changed down one gear. Then it was flat-out up a steady incline back to La Source hairpin and the finish. Not a place that excited me at all, reflected in my rather average lap times.

However, to be first, first you must finish, so I tootled about with Berti, at first disputing third place, then when Frank's engine stopped it was for second. Then Ernst broke a crankshaft and so it was on for first place, but at the flag Berti had the speed and won. As his lap record in Assen proved, on occasion he could display his latent ability and turn in surprisingly fast laps.

During the Grand Prix mid-season break I joined other world championship riders at three of England's top short circuits. I won the 125cc races at Brands Hatch and Mallory Park. Then it was on to the important British championship event at Oulton Park. My convincing win in the 50cc race included a new lap record, 13.2 seconds faster than when I first rode a 50cc there, a huge difference. Benefiting from Saturday's two generous practice and tuning sessions, I cleared off in the 125cc race.

Motor Cycling magazine had this to say: 'Hugh notched new records in a 50cc and 125cc double, shattering lap and race records. In the 125cc race, Hugh shot into an immediate lead. Adding yet another lap record to his long list, he streaked away to an easy win.'

As we waited for the van to be unloaded on the Belfast docks, just breathing the Irish air was sufficient to trip the switch, initiating the enthusiasm, excitement and anticipation I now had for world championship events. The early-morning predictions that I had formed in our Clermont-Ferrand Hotel back in May were coming true.

Lashed by westerly winds from the Atlantic Ocean, Ulster has few GPs run in dry, sunny weather. So Saturday's 125cc race was run in a typical Ulster drizzle. As mentioned here often, wet slippery conditions were my strength. The easier it is to get the tyres moving, i.e. drifting, the happier and more competitive I was. From pole position, I took the lead from the start, Ernst stayed with me, and we gained a healthy lead on the rest of the field.

Just when I was getting a little concerned that he might slip by for a win, his crankshaft broke, leaving me with a huge 82-second lead over Frank, who was only 10 seconds in front of Taveri, Honda, and Schneider. They closed on Frank, passing him on the last lap. Schneider just beat Taveri to the line gaining second, Frank finished fourth.

Reporters had begun to comment on my phenomenally fast machines. Rumours began that I was being given the best engines; perhaps initiated by disappointed team-mates. When we received them, all our bikes were identical. My reliability and speed were due entirely to mechanic Nagata-san, and my obsessively detailed preparation both with regard to the track and the bike. Unlike my team-mates, I was teetotal, and avoided the distraction of posh restaurants. I also worked with my bikes regularly until 1 and 2am.

While no one admired the political situation that existed in the Communist-controlled German Democratic Republic, we all admired the enthusiasm shown by East Germans and enjoyed their brilliant circuit.

The Sachsenring was one of those places where, with study, advantage could be found on every corner. I had been taking the season race by race and not looked further ahead. It was still just do your best and see what happens and now my best was very good. I didn't dwell on the thought of losing a championship or winning it; just follow the same routine that was giving me such superb results. There was no reason to change. There were fast and slow corners on this undulating circuit, along with very challenging S-bends. Though each was quite different, they melded together in a superb flow. With 200,000 incredibly enthusiastic spectators starved of international motor sport, this created an inspirational situation that brought out the best in riders.

After practice and during Saturday evening's meal, for no apparent reason Janny had seemed a little irritable. She had never shown this tendency before. It had been a long, hot day and perhaps she was tired, I thought.

Practice went well. Both my 125s were good but, as I often did, I cannibalised the two using the best of each to create the bike I thought I could win on. With the other lying dismantled in a corner, I looked forward to the race with great anticipation.

Although sitting on pole, a poor start put me way back in the field. Not everyone had taken into account that there would be a stiff headwind along the flat-out straight at the back of the circuit. I had changed my gearing to suit. It surprised me how comfortable I felt while passing riders on the inside, outside and under brakes. I guess form, excellent bikes, success and confidence puts you, for a limited time, into something of a special category.

At the start of lap two I led by 100m and riding consistently at the lap times I had planned, broke the lap record by 7.1 seconds. Increasing the average speed by 6kph, I rode away from the field. Immediately after the start line there was a right-left S-bend. It was neat to get through flat on the tank, always a buzz, and then, after climbing a steep hill, rush down the other side challenging yourself to push the bike at a risk-taking speed into an over-160kph S-bend leading on to that fast back straight.

I enjoyed it all, I was on a high. The bike ran perfectly and I won by 1min 51secs from Alan Shepherd on an MZ. Frank's bike broke on the first lap and Berti's again oiled its plugs finishing third. It was further confirmation that Nagata-san and I had most of the answers, as far as speed and reliability were concerned, than any other group in the team.

I was well aware as I stood on the podium that the world championship was mine. I felt pretty good about it, of course, but there was no elation or element of surprise. The challenge and the excitement felt at every Grand Prix, as I carefully constructed my points tally, was over. As is often the case, it is when you wake next morning that the true value of the moment hits you. I had joined my boyhood heroes, those wonderful riders Les Graham and Freddie Frith, on the stage that world champions tread. My heart swelled; what had been seen for so many years as an impossibility had become a reality.

Winning the East German Grand Prix and the 125 World Championship. This was the culmination of a long season and cold, calculating commitment. Archives.

After leaving the podium and rejoining the team, I learned that during the race, Janny, in full view of thousands of people, had collapsed in the pits. After receiving medical attention, she had needed assistance to return to the caravan where, by evening, she had made a full recovery.

Ishikawa-san asked the question: "Was Janny's fainting due to the sun or a son?" Being a little naive, we had little idea. No wonder she had been off colour the previous evening. Caroline would be born nine months later.

The Finnish Grand Prix, on September 1, 1963, was the final 50cc round of the European season. Practice, though wet, went well and I gained pole position in both the 50cc and 125cc classes.

All went according to plan at the beginning of the 50cc race. I gradually built a small lead on Anscheidt until the seventh lap, when I was caught out on a wet patch on a tight corner at the bottom of a steep rise. The rear wheel snapped out from under me. When it made contact with the dry surface, it flicked me off.

Incredibly, almost like a cartoon, I landed on my feet and running at 30kph, but it didn't last long and I fell flat on my face. I managed to get back to the undamaged bike and attempt to start it up the steep hill. The engine was flooded with fuel. I pushed and pushed. Finally, as I crested the rise, the damn thing started.

There was no chance of catching Anscheidt, but I rode on with purpose and on the last lap claimed third place after having once again set a new lap record. The 50cc championship hung by a thread. Anscheidt had a total of 32 points and I had 30.

As the 125cc race unfolded, I found myself the only Suzuki still running. With a handy lead, I reeled off the 28 laps in 52 minutes, which was a new race record. That went well with a new lap record. Luigi was 87 seconds behind in second place with Alan Shepherd on an MZ third.

Janny and I intended to return to New Zealand after the Japanese Grand Prix. I bought an airline ticket that zigzagged around the world from Amsterdam to Buenos Aires for the Argentinian GP, then to Honolulu, Tokyo (for the Japanese GP), and on to Amsterdam. A few days later we would take a flight via Canada, Honolulu and Fiji to Auckland. Then back to Holland in February 1964.

There was also the need to compete at the US Grand Prix on February 1 the following year. I intended to fly there, do the meeting and return to New Zealand. At that time flying was expensive and incredibly the cost of those flights in today's money would probably be over $NZ50,000. I booked and paid for the tickets and Suzuki reimbursed me.

The first glitch came at Holland's international airport check-in. I didn't have a visa for Argentina.

"But I was there last year and didn't need one," I said.

"But now you do," was the reply. "There has been a political coup and regulations have changed. You can't go."

Too late to do anything today, so all the way back to Assen.

At 6am next day, I left for the Argentinian embassy to get a visa. I returned to the airport with the visa but all flights were fully booked. A world championship was at stake here. As more airlines flew to South America via Zurich, I was advised to go there and try my luck. On arrival I found the opportunities were no better, but was told to return next day as there might be an empty seat on flights going out. No such luck and the last plane out that day was leaving in 45 minutes. My options were down to one. Did I have sufficient money on me to buy an upgrade to first class? The cost was 87 pounds.

I added up the cash and travellers' cheques I was carrying but fell well short. Bugger. I had my Bank of New Zealand London chequebook with me. That might do the trick. I approached the counter, emptied my pockets, counted out the cash and added the travellers' cheques. Now what does all that come to? We need another 42 pounds. Would they take a cheque drawn on the Bank of New Zealand in London? A deep discussion took place. One of the staff hurried out to consult a senior member and returned with a smile. Before she said yes, I had begun making out the cheque. I was hurried through the barriers, personally guided to the boarding gates and shown to my seat to enjoy, for the one and only time, first-class airline travel.

When we landed at Buenos Aires I took a taxi directly to the racetrack to find Ishikawa-san, who was delighted to see me at last and paid the taxi driver. My bikes were fully prepared. So I signed on, got kitted up and, like last year, in a short time was lapping faster than those who had already been practising for two days. Unfortunately for Anscheidt and the Kreidler team, Hans had fallen quite heavily and, with a suspected broken collarbone, was out of the race. Without Hans as opposition, I won the 30-lap race by 62 seconds from Ernst, and lapped all the other competitors.

People would say why go so fast when it isn't necessary? My routine involving machine performance, rhythm and concentration levels were intertwined. I felt perfectly safe and seldom, if ever, suffered from mechanical failure. Anyway, riding near the limit is one of life's pleasures!

Frank and Berti had been in Japan testing the new four-cylinder 250 before Ernst and I arrived from Argentina. This extract from an aerogramme I posted to Janny sets the scene: 'The 250 does look good. The engine is something really new and next year, when it comes to England, will create a lot of interest. We spent most of the day working on engines. That evening Mr Suzuki came to our hotel. He stayed with us for some time discussing the season, what had taken place, how pleased he was with the progress the team had made and how much he appreciated our efforts in gaining such outstanding success. Mr Suzuki has a happy, bubbly personality, an open and forthright man without airs or graces or any display of superiority. The staff holds him in enormous respect bordering on deference.'

In our first test session at Suzuka, riding my 125 I followed Berti and Frank on the new 250s. After three laps they increased their speed, but on a fast corner just a few hundred metres before the end of the lap, Berti came off, Frank hit his bike and came down too. Berti's gearbox had locked up.

I stopped to help. They didn't appear to be badly hurt, although each time Frank stood up he fainted. I got them both sitting comfortably then I rode down to the pits to let them know what had happened. An ambulance was sent and I followed it out and helped them. Berti had a cut hand and thought he had a broken collarbone. Frank had a sore shoulder but nothing too serious. He must have suffered from shock, as his helmet wasn't marked yet he fainted several times and needed to lie down.

The race team was deeply disappointed. Nothing had been achieved. They had two badly damaged bikes and Berti was no more than a passenger for the rest of our stay. Testing can be more difficult and, let's face it, more dangerous than racing. The word 'testing' describes the situation well. Major modifications, alterations, and in this case totally new machines were being used. Problems had to be expected.

Before the Japanese Grand Prix on November 10, Hans Anscheidt had 32 points and I had 34. I needed to finish in front or behind him to claim the 50cc championship.

The race department gave me the engine that performed best on the dyno test bench, while Matsui-san did all he could to help me, during practice, to have it running reliably. Above all we had to finish. Even with so much hanging on the results, it made little difference to how I approached the preparations. The same routine and as usual I felt no pressure. The aim was to shadow Hans and see what happened.

Hans' crankshaft failed on the third lap, leaving me in second place in the race and a second world championship won. Luigi's well-ridden, very fast Honda twin won the race.

The new Honda fours were very competitive in the 125cc class and six of us had similar lap times in practice. During the first five laps of the race, Jim Redman and I swapped the lead several times. Not surprisingly, I felt that being the world champion, it was my race and I was committed to win it.

Top: If I finished behind Anscheidt #7, the championship was mine. But you win if you can. Archives.

Above: Holding fourth place while leading Hasegawa, Yamaha, and Provini Morini. Archives.

While the problem hadn't arisen during practice, from the first lap of the race when I was cranked over to the limit the rear tyre let go, putting me into a dramatic slide. It happened two or three times a lap; slowly the will to win was eroded and I drifted back to fifth place at the finish.

After the race, Jim asked me what was wrong as he gave exaggerated displays of the odd and difficult angles and situations I had been in. Finishing his action replays, he said, "How the hell you stayed on it, I'll never know." A rear suspension unit had failed.

Frank rode to his potential and won, giving Suzuki at least one race at their home Grand Prix, run on the Honda-owned track.

The last act in the process of race preparation. Polishing your goggles takes on an almost spiritual significance. Archives.

Ernst and I walk out to the start. Archives.

Ernst is lying unconscious on the left of the fiercely burning machine. Archives.

During practice for the 250cc race I had overcome most of the problems that come with a totally new design. The 250 was made up of two 125cc engines in tandem, one behind the other. While the engine developed sufficient power, it was difficult to have it running properly on all four cylinders. Carburation problems were a huge headache. Like the 125, each cylinder needed different settings and tuning it was a nightmare.

The bike steered well enough but handled badly. Flex in the steering head area and rear section of the frame caused the bike to weave when accelerating under full power around a right-hand sweeper; as my speed increased, it became a case of shut off or be tossed off. Being a right-hand corner, the first movement was for the rear wheel to move out to the left. It then would correct itself and swing back to the right. I found that if I concentrated really hard and pushed against the right bar just as the rear swung left then pushed on the left to catch it as the rear swung back to the right, I could keep it reasonably straight and hold it on full noise. It wasn't easy but it was possible and surprising how that big heavy machine could be balanced by the short racing handlebars.

From the start, the Yamahas of Fumio Ito and Phil Read took over the lead from Jim Redman's Honda. After a poor start, I had made contact with the main group by the end of the first lap. As we came out of the first corner on the start of the second lap, we were confronted with frantically waved yellow flags and a great cloud of smoke and flames.

Japanese Grand Prix, 50cc podium. Second in the race but first in the world championship. Me, Taveri and Masuda. Archives.

Being congratulated on my success by Mr Suzuki. Archives.

Mr Suzuki presenting me with a laurel wreath for second place. Archives.

Ernst had crashed heavily and was lying unconscious. Frank had stopped and marshals, after having dragged Ernst from the flames, were busy with their fire extinguishers trying to control the inferno, fuelled by 25 litres of petrol.

The race carried on. By the sixth lap I had cut through the field from last to disputing fourth with Italian Tarquinio Provini, Morini, and Hasegawa, Yamaha. Provini had won the 250cc race at the Spanish Grand Prix, the slowest circuit in the series, won again at Hockenheim on the fastest circuit, an indication he had an excellent bike and could ride it, but inconsistent results allowed hard-riding, consistent Jim Redman to win the championship by just two points. Back to the race. Provini came by me and with his left hand behind his back, attempted to give me signals. He obviously wanted me to finish behind him in a futile attempt to finish high enough to gain sufficient points to beat Jim Redman. In my view, and that of many others, he was riding the best motorcycle but it was one of those days when he hadn't come to race. Hasegawa came past, his Yamaha handling nicely. They left gaps and I took them. So long as I stayed in absolute tune with the bike, I could ride with them, but occasionally I got out of phase with its eccentric handling behaviour and they would re-pass.

My brakes had overheated and been quite poor for several laps, I was surprised I hadn't been passed much earlier. As we entered the fast first corner on the last lap, Hasegawa came under me and fell off right under my front wheel! I was left with the options of running over him, hitting his bike or laying my bike down.

I chose the latter and suffered no more than abrasions but the Suzuki was a bit of a mess with broken handlebars, both right-hand carburettors ripped off, a footrest gone and the fairing destroyed. There was no chance of completing that last lap. As I got up I saw red, and gave Hasegawa two good clouts on his helmet before walking off to find the first-aid department.

At 24 laps the race had been long and the ride the most difficult I had experienced. Yet a beckoning fourth place in this company, first time out, on a complicated, poor-handling prototype 250cc machine was tremendous. Perhaps it had been a mistake to try to race it so early in its development cycle. But when the flag drops you are in race mode or not. I believe that during the two years of development that followed, the best lap time I achieved that day was never improved on. How hard was I riding? The front brake had generated so much heat the spokes were discoloured.

The last few days of our stay were taken up with long discussions about next season and how the team would function, what could be improved and, most importantly, machine development. The 50cc and 125cc were basically fine racing machines. While a little more power was required, I felt strongly we should not sacrifice reliability to gain it.

However, I made a long list of improvements that I felt needed to be made to the 250cc. I felt it was far from being a true racing device, but my main interest still lay in the 50cc and 125cc classes.

After a respectable amount of haggling and with the knowledge that Shell would double their contribution for 1964, I signed a contract for 6,000 pounds. I have no idea what other members of the Suzuki or any other team member was paid; the opportunity to win more world championships was the most important factor, as far as I was concerned.

Walking out of the arrival hall at Schiphol Airport in Amsterdam on November 15 and seeing Janny waiting for me was something else. We had been separated for six weeks. It had seemed more like six months. I had written to her every day and we had missed each other terribly. Our letters show an outpouring of love and loneliness. Janny was no longer a memory. Her perfume was as subtle as she was beautiful and she was most definitely real. Once again I was reminded just how lucky I was to have her. Six days later we left for New Zealand.

We flew to Honolulu, had a 24-hour stopover, then boarded a turbo-prop Lockheed Electra for home. I assured Janny: "It won't be long now. Straight down to New Zealand. The worst is over."

The plane laboured into the air and, with its surprisingly flexible wings flapping in protest at the slightest turbulence, we were on our way. The sound system crackled and we got the usual: "This is your pilot speaking; our estimated flight time to Fiji will be fourteen hours." What? Surely planes can't stay up for that long? And foolish me thought we were nearly home. We made it to Fiji to refuel and then it was another six hours or more to Auckland.

Above: With pride, confidence and a radiant Janny. New Zealand Herald.

Below: The morning after our return. Janny is washing the Jaguar. Archives.

If not before, Janny now realised that New Zealand was indeed on the other side of the world. Finally, we touched down at Whenuapai, passed through Customs and walked out to a large welcoming party of family and friends. I went to Mum first. Her eyes were sparkling, her face glowing with pride. While I may have become a double world champion, I think the main attraction for many was my radiant Dutch wife.

Back home at the farm in Ohinewai south of Auckland, I took Janny for a walk along the bank of the Waikato River, the favourite place of my childhood. We sat on a fallen tree that had always been there and looked out over New Zealand's longest river and the island headland that had been one of my havens. I wanted to allow her fully into my life and this place had been a big part of it. With her, at that moment, I rejoiced in that the boy had become a man, and now here with his wife, one more of the many circles within a life felt complete.

The 1963 Wanganui Boxing Day street races had a special attraction. Jim Redman had negotiated terms with the Castrol Oil Company and Honda that enabled him to compete in Australia and New Zealand during the southern hemisphere summer. Wanganui was his first ride in New Zealand.

Due to local issues, the Wanganui Motorcycle Club was unable to use the fabled Cemetery Circuit. Instead they used a 1km-long pocket-handkerchief alternative based near Moutoa Gardens. It consisted of five 90-degree corners. Four turned right and one left. This was a popular meeting and, typical of the times, there was no limit on entries. With more than 30 in the 350 race, I found the track was still manageable and finished second to Jim on his very useful 305cc twin-cylinder Honda production racer.

However, there were 43 starters in the 500cc race; foolishly, every rider who had entered the meeting, regardless of experience, performance or class of motorcycle, was allowed to start on this pocket-handkerchief course. A bizarre decision.

On the fifth lap, after already having lapped 11 riders and now hard on Jim's heels, another rider suddenly appeared on my left riding at almost right angles to Jim and me. He rode between us and I hit him hard. After being thrown clear and going through the usual assortment of rolls and flips, I hit the back of my head on the road painfully hard.

When I came around a marshal was sitting on me. I asked him what he was doing. He explained that I had been trying to get back on my bike. I had been knocked out before, and more than once since, but that was the only time I felt the pain of impact. I was taken to hospital for observation. Janny and Dave Kenah joined me soon after. I felt okay, just a sore head. Later a sidecar passenger, who had been involved in a serious accident, was placed in a cubicle next to me. There was only a fabric curtain separating us and he was in a bad way. It was disturbing to hear him moaning and his laboured, gurgling breath. Janny, with her nursing experience, recognised his noisy symptoms and was aware that he was dying. Later in the evening he was moved and died during the night. As I was feeling fine next morning, they allowed me out and Dave drove most of the way home. I kept it to myself but for six weeks a low-key niggle persisted at the back of my head.

Although a week later I went on to win the Rotorua Grand Prix and finish behind Jim at the New Zealand TT, the usual sharpness of judgement and confidence didn't return for months.

CHAPTER 12

From being entranced by the wonders of parenthood to the depression of failure

'To last another day, week or month. That was our target.'
— Tommy Robb

As I was double world champion, the 1964 season would be demanding. Could I retain those 50cc and 125cc titles? We knew Honda, whose corporate pride had been badly bruised by my twin victories, would fight back with some very special motorcycles.

A 45-hour flight that included long hours in airport lounges took me from New Zealand to the Daytona Speedway and the US Grand Prix on February 2. With Honda and Yamaha absent, the 125 class was a race among my team-mates, which I won with a record lap of 144kph. The two-man Kreidler factory team should have made the 50cc race more competitive. But while they had good acceleration, aided by their 12-speed gearbox, and at times an excellent turn of speed, the Kreidlers were a little off the pace that day. I won with another record lap of 128kph.

When I returned home, Janny and I rented a house at Mount Maunganui, New Zealand's equivalent to Australia's Bondi Beach. It was time to be together, enjoy the surf and chill out. Janny had progressed through her pregnancy with little discomfort or sickness and being the person she is, never complained.

The easiest way I knew of how to improve my riding was to gain a high level of fitness. After you have been through the pain of long, exhausting runs and a demanding series of exercises, you are not going to settle for less than your best. The beneficial side effect was better health and in the case of injury, faster recovery. I began a programme of running, sit-ups, press-ups and working with various gym-type equipment. I conscientiously continued this routine for the next six years, reaching a point where I could cover 7 kilometres at a good clip, and doubled the number of press-ups, sit-ups and so on. At that time this was not the norm among my contemporaries.

The imposing 250cc four with Mr Pirelli checking the Dunlop tyres. Archives.

I approached the Spanish Grand Prix at Montjuich Park in Barcelona with a mixture of confidence and caution. As in previous years we hadn't done any testing or even seen the updated bikes, so it was a test session as much as a Grand Prix for us.

Our team was working in a period of the most rapid advance in the history of racing motorcycle engine technology. This year Honda had entered their twin-cylinder 50cc and four-cylinder 125cc machines revving to 18,000rpm. How well would these miracles of mechanical engineering perform? More importantly, had our development engineers made enough changes to keep us competitive?

We were struggling to have the new engines running anywhere near their best. In a search for more power, the stroke of the piston had been shortened on the 125, with revs increased to 14,000rpm and different exhaust expansion chambers, but finding the correct settings was difficult.

Preparing the 250cc four was also a challenge and took up much of the little time we had. It did not suit the tight, twisting, low-speed circuit at all so I set it up for a steady ride, feeling a finish was the best we could achieve.

My 50 was running okay and again, provided I could finish, it should be in the top four placings. The performance of the 125 was the most promising. During the last practice session I broke the lap record and gained pole ahead of Taveri and Redman on their Honda fours.

But the sensation of the 50cc class was the speed of the Spanish Derbi. José Busquets had taken two seconds off last year's lap record. Hans Georg Anscheidt was fast too. At the end of the first lap of the race, Morishita, Suzuki, led from Anscheidt, Itoh, Suzuki, and Busquets. After a poor start I was holding fifth. On the second lap Busquets swept into the lead, closely followed by Anscheidt. By the sixth lap I had moved up to third but was unable to close on the two leaders. As the race progressed, the three Hondas retired with mechanical trouble and Anscheidt and Busquets led the race in close company, making new lap records as they pushed for a win.

The always animated Spanish crowd was loving it and the usual waving of handkerchiefs followed their determined progress. Perhaps for the first time a Spanish rider on a Spanish machine would win a Grand Prix. It was not to be. A rear suspension unit broke on the Derbi with just two laps to go. After being so close it must have been an absolute heartbreaker. With the drama removed, Anscheidt won followed by me, Itoh and Morishita.

From the start of the 125 race Taveri led from me, Redman and Takahashi, on Hondas. I closed on Taveri. We continually broke the lap record, but on the sixth lap I fell victim to the slow-circuit syndrome of oiled plugs. Finally, I pulled into the pits to have them changed and continued to finish a disappointing fifth.

Seventeen special works machines faced the starter of the 250 race. Tarquinio Provini, who had ridden the very good Italian Morini last year, was entered on a new four-cylinder Benelli and had been fastest in practice. Phil Read was second fastest riding the only special works Yamaha entered. Redman led a team of Honda fours and then there were Aermacchis, Patons and Montesas along with three Suzuki fours.

Redman led from the start but Provini, riding at his brilliant best, soon caught and passed him to win. Evidently, during the closing laps he was waving to the animated Spanish crowd. Kasuya, Honda, took fourth and I followed him in fifth place, the first 250cc Suzuki to finish a Grand Prix, more or less accomplishing what I had set out to do.

Having flown to the Spanish GP, I returned on the Monday evening to find that Janny had been in labour for some hours. At 10am on Tuesday the 12th of May, Caroline was born.

After a long labour, Janny was remarkably well and determined to accompany me to the Isle of Man TT. Caroline would be only 13 days old, but my ever well-organised Janny didn't see a problem with that. However, Caroline needed a passport. With a photo and the completed forms, I hurried off to The Hague and the New Zealand Embassy.

Early on Thursday morning I began a 1,000km road trip to Clermont-Ferrand and the French Grand Prix. What with the anxiety of seeing Janny suffer during Caroline's arrival and sleep deprivation I was in something of a manic state. Being so conscious of saving time when on a race bike, I had long ago brought a similar haste to my driving style. Every second counted. I had the van balancing between under and over steer, ignoring speed limits, squeezing past slower traffic and constantly checking my watch, the kilometres travelled and the average speed achieved. Of course, this had the effect of building stress levels ever higher. No matter how fast I travelled, it wasn't fast enough. A competition against no one, just another version, bordering on obsession, of beating the clock. It was so strong that I was at times reluctant to stop for petrol.

At the track, Alan Shepherd, who had just bought a Mark II Jaguar, was boasting about the average speed he had maintained from Calais to Clermont. Over a greater distance, on more congested roads, I had averaged a higher speed in the van.

Staying in a hotel, mixing with other riders, not sleeping well and feeling stressed out, nervous and uptight was not the way to go racing. Having been present at the birth of your child is surely one of the greatest moments of a man's life. For me it had reduced the status of a Grand Prix to 'not so very important'. For the first time in many years, I was not waking up thinking about racing motorcycles!

During practice, my favourite circuit was not falling into place as I had expected. My 50 was performing well but I was finding it difficult to get my 125 lap times down to my lap record of last year. The engines appeared more difficult than ever to set up and, apart from the supposed benefits of higher revs, I doubted that they were as fast as last year's versions.

The 250 was still a real challenge for mechanics, tuners and riders. While I was able to have the carburettor settings of my choice on the two smaller machines, the mechanics handling the 250 were loathe to reduce the main jets sufficiently to ride it at any real speed without oiling the plugs.

Not having the tranquil little world of Janny and our caravan to escape to, and relax in, and carefully plan the strategy needed to be competitive in three classes only worsened my situation. Tension and stress levels seemed to be enveloping me. The climax came on Saturday when after a light lunch and cup of tea with Frank Perris and Berti Schneider, I found it difficult to hold the food down. As soon as I could, I left and walked to the back of the paddock. In a secluded spot, I lost the lunch, breakfast and remnants of the previous day's dinner.

Knowing that my only chance of success that day was the 50cc race, I put all of my effort into that class. I made pole and there was more to come. The Honda twins were fast. Kreidler had won here from the time the 50cc class was introduced and Anscheidt had made the second-fastest lap.

My bike started immediately and from the very first series of corners I fell into a near-perfect rhythm. Suddenly, my head was in the right space. It wasn't difficult, only a matter of using the first lap to settle in and then begin to intensely scavenge every fraction of a second that can be found on this 55-corner masterpiece of race-track design.

We were so in tune even my breathing became part of a near-perfect rhythm. The rev counter was the key. I had one eye on it as I prepared to make every upward gear change. The fingers of my left hand were rapidly twitching on the clutch lever, like a barber and his scissors, maintaining his rhythm between clippings. When the needle hit 14,000rpm I lifted the clutch for an instant and slid the gear lever into the next gear with perfect timing. It was done so rapidly that even though the throttle was still held wide open, the engine revolutions hardly rose. At every point of the track I was centimetre perfect. The 10 gears meant there were hundreds of changes during the race. It was essential to gain from each one and I did.

After experiments with the rear tyre pressure during practice, I settled on what allowed the tyre to roll and flex with the added pressure of cornering. This and the flex of the frame carefully controlled by the judicious use of the rear brake allowed a tightening of the line. More room and a marginal increase of speed on most of the 55 corners. Total concentration was imperative as there was absolutely no margin for error. Quite a different technique to riding a Manx Norton that in comparison was like driving the family car.

After a satisfying near-perfect race, I won comfortably from Anscheidt, setting new race and lap records, and had developed new techniques on how to find advantage. Advantage is a very special word in a Grand Prix winner's vocabulary. The only other Suzuki to finish was Morishita in fifth place.

Despite qualifying second fastest, I formed up on the starting grid for the 125cc race more with hope than confidence. Having seized pistons twice and broken a crankshaft in practice, I doubted if things would be any better in the race. Boosted by the 50cc ride, I felt less tense than earlier but I wasn't in anything like my usual race mode. After having lost my lunch the day before, I hadn't bothered having any today.

I gained a good start and with Taveri smartly pulled away from the field. Under the circumstances it was best to follow him and be as kind to my engine as possible. A wise enough decision but, on the second lap, the crankshaft failed yet again. Luigi went on to win easily enough and, after Jim Redman retired, Berti and Frank gained second and third places.

After qualifying sixth on the 250, I found myself in fourth position on the second lap of the race behind Redman, Read and Taveri. Soon after, as I knew it would, the Suzuki started missing badly on two cylinders. I called at the pits and changed all four spark plugs, but five laps later it happened again and I was out. Frank had pulled in a few laps earlier with the same problem but Berti boxed on to gain third place. Under the circumstances it was no mean feat, but he was a massive 2mins 52secs behind the winner, Phil Read.

Above: Quite unbeatable on the day. Archives.

Below: With Hans Georg Anscheidt, Jean-Pierre Beltoise and our national anthem. Archives.

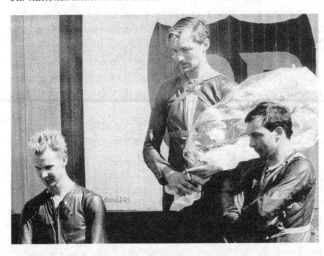

I left the track after the final race and hurried back to Assen, arriving at 5am. To my surprise Janny was home already, just three nights after the birth of Caroline. Against everyone's advice, she had discharged herself from hospital. Janny had no intention of lying about for 10 days; not my girl!

Now the three of us were off to the Isle of Man TT. The huge build-up was best described in *The Motor Cycle* magazine:

'It had to be the greatest last year, with a staggering 406 entries. So what can you call this year's TT, with a colossal total of 450? Stupendous!' screamed the headlines. 'All the reigning world champions are here, with riders drawn from as far afield as Argentina to Japan, Sweden to South Africa, Australia and New Zealand to Canada, 20 different nationalities. Interest by manufacturers has never been greater. No fewer than 18 have nominated official, or semi-official, entries. Four-cylinder jobs in 500, 350, 250 and 125cc capacities, parallel twins, two strokes, horizontally opposed overhead-cam twins, vertical singles, horizontal singles, three speeds, 12 speeds, cylinder sizes ranging from 50cc to 499cc. Every conceivable design, water cooled or air cooled.'

The magazine's description of me read: 'To see Hugh cornering with his inside knee stuck out and the bike cranked over so far his shin is parallel to the road — and precious close — you'd never dream his first sight of British racing scared him stiff. That was four years ago when the shy, serious Kiwi was 24. Long before that he had turned his hand to every form of racing New Zealand offered — grass track, scrambles and road — and topped the lot. What he didn't know by then, the European rounds soon taught him. Suzuki's 50cc and 125cc world champion, he could easily retain the titles this year.'

Honda was obviously determined to regain the domination they had enjoyed during the 1962 season. Last year Suzuki had not only retained the 50cc title but taken the 125cc as well and now Yamaha was pushing them in the 250cc class. This was of such concern that Honda chartered a plane to fly in six new machines, 50, 125 and 250s, along with a number of engines. They were more aware than most of the importance of winning. Cost was of little concern.

Caroline had been crying within two hours of being fed. Janny had been using a Dutch milk formula, and we felt that a change to an English full-cream brand might help. It made a remarkable change and we were able to sleep again. From that time on Caroline became a model child and never cried again. I was still a little uptight. What with the responsibility of this fragile little baby and ongoing lack of sleep, I was denied my normal controlled, relaxed planning routine.

The 125 was a challenge for me. I managed only a few trouble-free laps, due to crankshaft and carburettor problems. My best lap time, made on damp roads, left me fifth fastest. Frank had also not practised well and was out of the top six. Berti rose to the occasion and was second fastest to Taveri's Honda.

Our Achilles heel was poor lubrication of the crankshaft big-end bearing. Go only 50–100rpm over the recommended maximum and the bearing cage would fail. Last year I found total reliability with maximum revs set at 13,500rpm but this season a new improved bearing cage was being used. Now 14,000rpm was the limit but causing constant problems. As the power band was from 13,500rpm to 14,000rpm it wasn't possible to reduce the maximum revs used. Piston seizures too were a regular occurrence. The team's chief engineer during 1963 was Shimizu-san. He was now working on the development of the highly successful new 250cc, six-speed road bike. Nakano-san had replaced him. It would seem that the search for more power and higher revs had come at a cost to reliability.

Luigi Taveri and I pushed off together in the 125 race. The Honda started before my Suzuki but I closed up on him surprisingly easily. I had intended to follow him, be very careful with my engine and hope to finish. Unusually, he was riding conservatively. I had, as always, committed to memory how many gears to change down for every corner. With our engines creating power across such a narrow span of revs, this was critical.

I passed him entering a slightly downhill right-hand corner changing down the usual two gears but over-revved the engine. Due to riding at a slightly slower pace, I was one gear lower than usual. My heart sank, my race was over. I carried on up a steady climb towards Glen Vine, waiting for the slight tremble of the engine that always occurred a fraction of a second before the rear-wheel-locking, engine crankshaft seizure. It happened before I reached the crest of the hill. I lifted the clutch and coasted to a stop. It was of little consolation that Berti's engine also seized on the first lap and Frank retired at the pits. The reality was that I had made one of the biggest on-track mistakes of my life.

The results show that Luigi had been travelling steadily. He was down in third place at the end of the first lap, with Jim Redman leading. Luigi sped up on the following laps to win by just three seconds from Jim, with Ralph Bryans third. Not a good day, which I filled with self-criticism and many if onlys.

There was still the 50cc event on Friday and this time I was determined there would be no mistakes. Handling was of vital importance, but front and rear suspension adjustment was limited. At times I chose to use English Girling rear suspension units, at others I found the Japanese-made units were fine. With the demands, serious bumps and seldom a smooth surface and the fact that on these bikes we would take tighter and wider lines than riders in the larger-capacity, faster classes left us with our own unique set of problems. I approached Girlings, who made up a pair of units that were ideal.

The front fork seals were located by screw-in retainers that caused the seal to 'pinch' the fork stanchions and caused friction that interfered with the action of the forks. I found that by loosening these locating rings and taping them in position allowed the forks to function much more efficiently.

Suzuki used very thin fork oil leaving little room for adjustment. The forks tended to be over-damped. To gain a softer movement, I mixed a carefully measured amount of kerosene with the oil —10, 15 or 20 per cent depending on conditions. These subtle changes and an engine that performed well allowed me to win. Afterwards, *Motor Cycling*'s front-page headline read: 'Hailwood wins one TT, Redman two, Honda three, but ton-up tiddlers steal show'.

It continued: 'The tiddlers have topped the ton. Headed by winner Hugh Anderson's Suzuki, no fewer than six machines did 100mph or more through the speed trap in Friday's 50cc TT. Only 18.2 seconds separated second and sixth men after a frantic last lap leader board scramble.' Another headline read: 'Heaviest rider wins tiddler TT'. The report explained: 'With a lap record at 81.13mph and an average speed faster than the old lap figure, Hugh Anderson, the heaviest man in the race, won Friday's 50cc TT for Suzuki. Taking the lead on the first round, the tall New Zealand double world champion was never pushed. But behind him, a fantastic six-sided dice developed for second place. Going into the third and final lap only 15.8 seconds covered Hans Georg Anscheidt, Kreidler, Haruo Koshino, last year's winner Itoh and Morishita, Suzukis, and Ralph Bryans and Naomi Taniguchi, Hondas. In the most hectic scramble for places ever seen in the Isle of Man, Bryans came out on top moving up from sixth to second place to finish half a second ahead of Morishita. In fact, the finish was so close and confused that at one time there were five men in the enclosure reserved for the first three riders home.'

The alterations I had made to the suspension worked perfectly, allowing me to get through most of the really bumpy corners faster and several more nailed.

The speed trap had: Hugh Anderson, Suzuki, 103.2mph; Anscheidt, Kreidler, 102.0mph; Ralph Bryans, Honda, 101.1mph; and Isao Morishita, Suzuki, 100.6mph.

Speeds for the other classes obtained through *The Motor Cycle* magazine's speed trap make interesting reading when compared to the performance of today's highly developed classic racers: 500cc: Mike Hailwood, MV, 144.6mph; Stuart Graham, Matchless, 138.5mph; Derek Minter, Norton, 136.9mph; Jack Ahearn, Norton, 136.4mph; Jack Findlay, Matchless, 136.4mph; Phil Read, Matchless, 135.3mph. 350cc: Jim Redman, Honda, 143.4mph; Franta Stastny, Jawa, 134.8mph; Derek Minter, Norton, 126.3mph; Mike Duff, AJS, 126.3mph; Jack Findlay, AJS, 123.3mph; Jack Ahearn, Norton, 121.2mph. 250cc: Berti Schneider, Suzuki, 141.1mph; Jack

Getting the best out of a 50cc can be a difficult, awkward exercise. Archives.

Receiving the ultimate trophy for the second time. Archives.

Ahearn, Suzuki, 139.0mph; Tarquinio Provini, Benelli, 139.0mph; Jim Redman, Honda, 136.9mph; Phil Read, Yamaha, 132.8mph; Alan Shepherd, MZ, 132.4mph. 125cc: Jim Redman, Honda, 121.6mph; Luigi Taveri, Honda, 121.6mph; Frank Perris, Suzuki, 120.8mph; Bert Schneider, Suzuki, 116.9mph.

Janny's mum was delighted with the progress that Caroline had made, as was our doctor. Janny didn't tell them about the change of food. There seemed to be a constant coming and going of friends and neighbours, all wanting to see Caroline. There are times when the smallest human being, who had done nothing but breathe, eat, cry and fill her nappies, was much more important than a Grand Prix-winning double world champion. So get used to it and go and unload the van.

Having a full six quiet days before we began preparing for the Dutch TT gave us the opportunity to relax, be together as a family and get back to normal. We took our baby in the pram to the lake and the park, fed the ducks and swans and sat cuddling on the bench. A short interlude of normality.

As my TT-winning 50cc had run so well, I had insisted that it should not be touched in any way before the Dutch TT. (The team had an almost obsessive compulsion to strip an engine regardless of how little work it had done.) This would give me the opportunity of running it here and using its performance as a standard. As good as it had proved to be, strangely here at the Dutch TT it was not as fast as my spare bike.

Practice went well enough. The situation with the 125 had not changed and the best I could do was seek reliability. I was quickest on the 50 in practice, so there was hope there.

Houses in the square where we lived, as last year, had New Zealand flags flying. Having won here they were hoping for more, however I'm not sold on the theory of home advantage. It may work if the game is physical and more energy makes a difference. But as I see it, Grand Prix racing is a vastly different animal and to find that winning edge for me comes at a social cost, as only when I am fully engaged in every aspect of my routine am I able to find that elusive focus, rhythm and edge.

We arranged tickets for several of Janny's family, including her grandparents. With extra seating under the awning, our caravan was a busy, vibrant place. However, the imperatives of racing meant I spent most of the day with the mechanics.

I led the 50cc race with Ralph Bryans and Mitsuo Itoh in my slipstream. Not being able to make a break, I allowed Ralph to go by and sat on his tail. Just when I felt optimistic about winning, my bike slowed and I retired at the pits. Being a little annoyed with that result, I went to the start of the 125 race with the idea of having a bit of a go. I knew I couldn't win it but I hoped to get among the leaders for a few laps at least.

A good start allowed me to mix it with Phil Read on the new Yamaha and Jim Redman on the Honda four. Read's Yamaha went surprisingly well and the Honda, as they had been at the previous rounds, was fast. By the third lap Jim and Phil had found their feet and pulled away from me but I was happy in third with Ralph, Berti and Frank following.

Soon after half distance a misfire set in, Ralph passed me and then Berti. Fifth was the best I could do with Frank sixth. This was a major turnaround from our team's last year's finish of first, second and fourth and disappointing in front of my 'home' crowd.

Above: Irishman Ralph Bryans and I hard at it during the Dutch 50cc TT. Archives.

Left: A post-race discussion with Janny, Berti and Frank. Karl Schleuter.

Luigi was not competing in the 50cc event at the Belgium Grand Prix on July 5. He had suffered concussion in a spill in Assen and was ordered to take complete rest. Twenty riders entered and just three seconds separated the fastest five qualifiers on the long, fast, 14km circuit. Anscheidt made the fastest lap on the Kreidler and the race was shaping up to be a repeat of last year's slipstreaming exercise.

After an excellent start I led at the end of the first lap with four riders in my slipstream. Then, as reporter Mick Woollett described it, 'Bryans took over the lead as they screamed into Eau Rouge sweep at almost suicidal speed'. With the lead changing several times each lap, the effects of slipstreaming on the long Masta straight could allow the last in the group to slingshot past the leaders. This would enable each passed rider to pull out into the other rider's slipstream, relegating the leader to the rear. Here more than any other track, the commentators got very excited about it all. There was nothing boring about the 50cc class.

The Kreidler team had improved their machines and were marginally the fastest with Ralph's Honda next, then me. On the last lap, I sat on Ralph's rear wheel while climbing the long, slightly uphill drag to the right-hand La Source hairpin just above the finish line. He in turn was slowly reeling in Anscheidt. Four hundred metres before the braking point we rounded a gentle left-hander and, as I expected Ralph to do, he moved to make a pass on the right of Anscheidt. I went with him, then

How fast is the opposition? Karl Schleuter.

quick as a flash, he flicked his Honda to Anscheidt's left and I lost the tow. Only an Irishman would think of that! It cost me precious metres, too many, I thought, but I'll out-brake them anyway and who knows what will come out of that.

I was by far the last to sit up and hit the brakes hard, really hard. The little bike bounced about when the front wheel locked up. It had done it before, so it didn't matter too much. I took the lead but ran a little wide. The engine ran rough due to excess fuel and I was pipped at the post. So third it was that day, with 0.6sec covering all three of us, and Ralph taking his second win. New lap and race records were also made. The tiny 50s managed the amazing average speed of 147kph and a lap record of 149kph. I now led the championship with 34 points from Anscheidt 29, Morishita 25 and Bryans 22.

After running in first or second place during three of the previous five 125cc Grand Prix before mechanical problems arose, any thoughts of retaining my world championship were fast slipping away.

The West German Grand Prix at the Solitudering near Stuttgart, where in 1962 Jimmy Matsumiya had frightened the life out of Jan Schuurman, was next. After setting up the caravan in the paddock behind a large hotel, a short distance from the pits and race control, I left to call at the Suzuki team's hotel. To my pleasant surprise Shimizu-san had arrived with a new engine.

Practice went well. The new engine responded to the alterations I made and my lap times were similar to Jim, Phil Read, Yamaha, and Taveri. I gained pole position without too much effort.

For the first time since the birth of Caroline, the racer in me had returned. The presence of Shimizu-san and his responsive, reliable engine seemed to coincide with a moving on from the good fortune of Caroline's arrival. As there is from a crisis, perhaps there is a similar slow process of recovery from a period of joy. Confidence came flooding back, anxiety and tentative decision-making had gone, and I felt strong and without self-doubt.

After an extremely hot practice session on Sunday morning, surly black clouds began gathering as we lined up for the 125 race.

I made a poor start but recovered to take over third place from Luigi and began closing up on leaders Jim and Phil. At the beginning of the third lap I made my move on a medium-fast double left-hander, visible from the pits. I will let a journalist of the time describe what followed:

'For the opening laps, every eye was focused on Redman and Read, battling fiercely up front, but a storm was threatening and so was Hugh Anderson. If Hugh

198

had a safety margin in hand, you couldn't notice it. Knocking the lap record silly, he effortlessly rode around Read and Redman and immediately drew away.'

Back in my element I pushed on to make a break. Light rain started as I approached a fast corner at the highest point of the circuit. I managed to lose a little speed, change down an extra gear and get through it okay. Continuing down a long straight that included an S-bend in a dip, I noticed the light rain had stopped. At a following 90-degree corner it was perfectly dry. Then I rode around a 180-degree left and downhill towards a long left followed by a right. I sat up and hit the brakes hard. Instantly both wheels locked. A very light sprinkle of rain had fallen but there was no unusual shine or wheel marks to warn me.

Most of the 250,000 spectators had crossed this section, along with food and drink delivery trucks, leaving a coating of dirt and dust. It was as greasy as it gets. I found myself travelling at 130kph towards a heavy wire netting fence with my options fast running out. I locked and released, locked and released, locked and released the wheels, managing to scrub off enough speed to enter the left-hander. Now I was hard on the right-hand side almost against a high netting fence. To avoid slamming into the stone wall on the outside of the corner, high above a ravine where a river flowed, I coaxed the bike around the following right-hander sufficiently to be aimed at the relative safety of the beginning of a line of straw bales. I laid the bike down and crashed into them.

Still straddling the bike, I hit the bales at a good 80kph. The impact was impressive. My goggles flew off my helmet into the rock-strewn ravine below. Burst hay bales flew in the air. Straw filled my tight-fitting leathers and boots. Caution flags were waved. As Jim rode slowly by I managed to thrust my hand in the air, giving him a thumbs-up signal that he in turn would give Janny as he passed the Suzuki pit.

Eventually, I was carried across the track to a medical centre. Luckily, my only injury was a severely twisted right knee. At the end of the race I was taken by ambulance to our caravan and handed a pair of crutches and a cheery "better luck in the future". Keeping the knee iced helped contain the substantial swelling.

Jim and others called later in the day. He was impressed with my quick reactions. All he saw of me was suddenly an arm thrust out of a mound of hay with a thumbs-up signal. He was in high spirits having won the 125 and 350cc classes and gained second in the 250cc class.

There had been a multitude of crashes during the weekend. My friend Karl Recktenwald, who had joined us for a meal the previous evening, had fallen from the Norton that I had been instrumental in arranging for him. I was relieved to learn he wasn't seriously hurt.

The next morning, after struggling out of bed due to all the bruises and stiffness associated with spills and using my crutches, I revisited the scene of my spill. I thought I had covered 150m before crashing into the bales. Actually, it was only half that. An impressive example of how your mind speeds up in awkward situations, allowing time to call on your experience to overcome the problems presented. There was no buzz up the spine, just a cold, emotionless call on your survival skills and experience. I sat for some time observing the scene, reliving the lucky escape and feeling very satisfied with what I had done. The thought came to mind that I had looked death in the face but hadn't flinched.

*My mate Karl Recktenwald with the Manx Norton
I helped procure for him. Archives.*

Soon after, Janny and I had a luncheon appointment with a Mercedes sales representative in nearby Stuttgart to finalise payment and delivery details of a new car. We had ordered a 220S on 'tourist delivery', free of all taxes at half of the New Zealand price, one of the perks of our international lifestyle. We were ushered into an upmarket restaurant. Not being particularly comfortable in such surroundings I was careful not to put a crutch wrong and was most surprised and pleased to see a large New Zealand flag on our table.

Our host was a motoring enthusiast who had attended the Grand Prix. Understandably, an interesting conversation followed. The meal was great and the business side of the meeting soon completed. But on returning to our caravan we were told the tragic news that Karl had died.

The boy who had survived the discipline and dangers of the Hitler youth programme, had known the hardship and privations of post-war Germany, who had steadfastly forged a career in the police force and progressed to achieving his greatest ambition of all, lining up yesterday at the start of his country's world championship points-scoring Grand Prix, was now no longer with us.

Needing to be on my own I drove around the track to the scene of Karl's accident. It seems he lost control on a not very difficult part of the circuit but, like so many others before him, suffered head injuries that proved fatal. Sitting down I leaned against a tree and went back three years to our first meeting and the trip to the Norton factory, the great times that followed, the nights when I had stayed with him, the beers, the heart-to-heart, let-it-all-out chat sessions that are shared by few. How many friends and associates have been killed or suffered permanent injuries? Perhaps 15, 20 or more.

Four decades have passed since I was sitting by that tree. As I write this, bringing Karl back into my life, the feelings of loss and sadness remain strong. Perhaps these emotions are for all those I knew who died or suffered debilitating injuries, never able to ride again or, in some cases, even communicate.

The feeling of hollowness that I felt when returning to our caravan was eased and slowly left me after I took Janny and our small baby in my arms. In an effort to avoid further emotional damage I became ever more reluctant to allow new friendships to flourish and withdrew into and gained solace within my own small loving family. Baby Caroline will never know how much strength she gave me. Nor will Janny understand how important to me the stable platform her inner strength and cool-headed, down-to-earth common sense provided then and throughout our lives together.

We packed up and drove off to the East German Grand Prix.

After having looked death in the face and not flinched the previous weekend, I now felt in an elevated mood where I could cope with any challenge that might arise in a race situation. This had triggered a return of self-confidence. The despondency, depression and anxiety that had weighed so heavily during the previous three months were cast off.

The race season had a new beginning. Shimizu-san was back with us, we shared an excellent working relationship with trust in and respect for each other's ideas and opinions. We were here to win races.

On arrival at the Sachsenring, I began my usual pre-practice routine of driving around the circuit several times, before the roads were closed to the public. For me, winning is in the detailed planning; it does not happen by chance.

I made a note of the wind direction at various points, particularly on the long back straight relative to the start where large flags clearly indicated its direction and velocity. Choosing the correct gearing for wind conditions is critical on lightweight, small-capacity machines.

Having used notes from the previous year and taking into consideration any improved machine performance characteristics, I would normally be able to approach the first practice session with excitement and confidence. As always during the first session, I would establish a base lap time, one where I was totally conversant with braking markers, lines on corners, engine revolutions at any given point, suspension, steering, gearing, carburettor setting and the lap times these produced.

Visualisation is a powerful weapon in any elite athlete's armoury, but back then I sometimes seemed like the odd man out.

I would sit in a quiet corner mentally lapping the track at precisely the speed of that 'base' lap time. I would then mentally make small changes to the gearing, suspension and carburation, and again lap the track at the maximum speed the new setup allowed. I could clearly register the benefits and drawbacks, mainly shown on the rev counter, relative to the base lap time. During these intense sessions I would lap the circuit using different setups, checking their benefits and drawbacks on every part of the circuit and mentally establish the lap times they would produce. Today this mental exercise is named visualisation; I benefited from it enormously.

At this meeting, after a five-lap practice session I went to the team timekeeper and told him what my times had been on each of the three fastest laps I had completed.

This chap had a wonderfully expressive face. On checking his time sheets and realising the lap times I had given him were within one or two tenths of a second of those he had recorded, he demonstrated his whole repertoire of facial contortions. Then, with disbelief, he confirmed that I was correct.

Lowering lap times is the objective, not going faster. It may sound odd, but the former, mainly done in the garage late at night, will help you to a win, the latter could send you up the road on your backside. I learned the value of time gained from having a higher corner exit speed on entering a straight with, say, 200rpm at points all along the following straight, than on the base lap, or any other lap that I was working with. From this I could gauge quite accurately the split seconds gained. This process was carried out on all sections of the track and remembered with total accuracy.

Your team-mates could be your main opposition. After all, they had the same equipment as you. Frequently during practice, as my lap times came down and theirs didn't, there were questions such as, "What jets are you using?" "What gearing are you using?" "What gear are you using in specific corners?" and so on. I have to admit I was often evasive. There were two reasons. First, I was always in the garage from the time we returned from the track, having dined on sandwiches with the mechanics until 1am or 2am. They, after a night out in a high-class restaurant, would breeze through the garage at 11pm in a state of wine-induced ebullience. Then, in a haze of cigarette smoke and the smell of alcohol, they would depart to continue socialising. Second, as I'd often said, each cylinder was different, regarding gearing, what I had fitted was tailored to my very precise needs and was of no use to them either as each rider has different racing styles and demands.

I don't think Frank and Berti ever understood the gains that could be made by quite small gearing changes. I rarely used the gearing that gave me the highest speed on the fastest section of the track. I geared it to gain the lowest lap times. Frequently, this meant being, at times, in an over-rev situation but by using the cut-out button and holding it flat-out limited the revs and cooled the engine.

Spectators had been building over two days from the beginning of practice and by race day there were 220,000 packing the circuit. These enthusiasts were very knowledgeable about the history of our sport and were fully conversant with the skills required and regarded the top riders as true artists. The atmosphere on race day was absolutely electric. As always I rose early to beat the queues to the local bakery and soak up the energy from the developing atmosphere. As early as 5.30am spectators were moving to their favourite vantage points; many had been there all night. Anticipation and excitement was mounting. In this highly charged environment, it was very much he who feels the moment the most intensely takes the win.

Time hung heavily. We ate our breakfast quietly without fuss. As always I mixed with the Suzuki team attending to last-minute decisions regarding carburettor settings, gear ratios and other issues that had arisen, carefully avoiding all conversation regarding topics not associated with the bike or the race.

Thirty minutes before the start, I returned to our caravan to review the notes I had made, slip into my leathers and boots and go through that lengthy, thorough ritual of goggle polishing, as I mentally moved into race mode. Janny, being very much part of that ritual, as always was sitting silently close by waiting for the farewell hug and whispered "See you later, kid".

Mechanics and riders were taking their positions on the starting grid and Nagata-san had our Suzuki waiting on pole position. I walked out to join him, oblivious to any distractions, even well-wishers. I slid into the Suzuki's seat. As so often happened, our eyes met without speaking. I tightly gripped his shoulder and he moved away. With a pleasant feeling of anticipation I thought, How good is my homework this week? Without nerves or anxiety I awaited the starter's orders. Later, Mick Woollett of *Motor Cycling* wrote: 'The big upset of the meeting was the way in which New Zealander Hugh Anderson thrashed the previously invincible 125cc Honda fours. Taking the lead at the end of the first lap, Hugh shattered lap and race records to humble the Hondas for the first time since they made their debut in Spain. From the start Anderson and Taveri shot away but then Anderson's Suzuki faltered and he was passed by several riders before the first corner. Even so, Hugh led again at the end of the opening lap. And on the second he shattered the lap record to gain a 200m lead on Taveri and Redman. Riding with the style that won so many races last year, the New Zealander pulled away from the Hondas.'

At these levels of concentration it seems that part of your mental activity is in race mode, paying attention to the feedback of the frame, suspension, brakes and engine. How close to the limit you might be; where you are able to brake a little later, enter corners later, open the throttle sooner, all minute fine-tuning that gives smoothness, rhythm and the sense of perfection that you always seek. You move into your own world, the confidence in self and bike setup lifts you into this mentally detached state that allows your true skill and experience a free hand. At the same time you are observing, recording and enjoying the experience. A kind of freedom without being inhibited or controlled in any way, avoiding pit signals or anything that might affect this perfect rhythm.

Totally in the zone or place of peace, perfection and silence, yet the unmuffled two-stroke is constantly screaming between 13,500 and 14,000 rpm. The tyres are on the edge of adhesion as the machine drifts and weaves, coming within millimetres of roadside kerbs and brushing the roadside hay bales. Mistakes do not occur. This perfect form is the justification of the work, the hardships and the search for advantage and the endless preparation and overcoming self-doubt and occasional bouts of apprehension. Money cannot buy it. Trophies don't reward it. This, to me, is the true and only reward.

At race end I was unable to walk, stand or talk. It took a few minutes 'to come back' into the real world. Nagata-san knew it well. He patiently stood beside me, a bottle of water in his hand. I slowly removed my gloves and helmet, being careful not to swallow as my mouth was so dry I could choke on my tongue. We shook hands and I managed a sincere, though mumbled, thank you before carefully dismounting. Nagata-san held the Suzuki with one hand and steadied me with the other. I turned to the massive grandstand rising behind me and 60,000 fans roared their approval in recognition of another great race. The lap record had been reduced by seven seconds and the winning margin was 17 seconds. Another very special day.

From East Germany we travelled to the Ulster Grand Prix. Practice did not go well: one of my 125s had crankshaft failure and the other was mysteriously down on power. As a last resort I decided to use the engine Frank had run so successfully at Oulton Park the previous weekend. I took it out onto country roads for limited testing.

Come race day it was slow to start and I was last away. Towards the end of the first lap, on a tight downhill 180-degree hairpin bend that turns on to a steep uphill climb, my front wheel hit a patch of sand and down I went. Few things can be more disheartening than attempting to push-start a reluctant engine up a steep incline with bike after bike roaring past. Finally, the engine fired and again I tore off, passing a host of riders in my effort to regain lost ground.

As I braked heavily for the same slow corner on the following lap, the engine died again. Riders roared past, one after the other. Finally, after another long uphill push, it reluctantly came to life and again I set off on what now seemed like a hopeless chase. But I had to win this to keep alive any chance of retaining the world championship. I fought to establish a rhythm. The gear lever was awkward to use and under heavy braking the engine was dying due to fuel starvation, so I had to keep it screaming

Left: The intensity of record-breaking form. Archives.

Below: Great to be back on top of the podium again. Archives.

with the clutch disengaged. By the fourth lap I had finally settled, and controlled anger took over.

As I tried ever harder through the 160kph Rushey Hill section of S-bends and forced the bike from left to right then left, the forks twisted so much the front wheel lagged behind the movement of the handlebars. The rear was swaying as the frame flexed. I could feel a faint sense of harshness through the bars and seat. I knew the tyres had sufficient grip and I could ride faster until that faint harshness was replaced with a softer, more vague response. This was the crucial warning that the tyres were beginning to lose adhesion and the limit had been reached.

As I rushed through every corner I mentally noted what changes I could make on the following lap. The desperation of the moment and my mood had me decisively making these changes. As every lap had perhaps 20 corners, these continual adjustments reflected in my constantly lowered lap times. I passed the Hondas and had only Berti and Frank to catch. At the beginning of the second-to-last lap, I could see them. I swept past them and continued without easing the pace.

I was in that special place. How can money and trophies reward you for this? Once again the 'intensity of form' was taking me and my machine to the extreme edge of our joint abilities. Yet again, I was enjoying 'that other world' where man and machine become one indivisible unit, and as in the previous week's German Grand Prix, enjoyed the reward I always sort.

I had lowered the existing lap record by 15 seconds; this now stood just 5.4 seconds slower than Jim Redman, around this 11.3km lap, on the unbeatable 350 Honda four. Even after falling and stalling I made a faster average speed than the second-placed 350. *The Motor Cycle* wrote: 'Nothing if not taciturn, Anderson described his winning ride as hard work. To everyone else it was a sheer masterpiece of dogged persistence and skill.'

Ray Battersby, author of that very good book *Team Suzuki*, wrote: 'With sheer guts, determination and brilliant riding, Anderson lowered the lap record by 15 seconds as he strove to make up his lost time.'

Noted journalist and author Vic Willoughby wrote: 'Hugh's bad start, crash and engine stalling problems during the first two laps of the race prompted him to produce a typically dashing display of utter invincibility.'

If I can continue riding like this, I thought, and gain more consistent engine reliability, that championship could be retained.

The Finnish Grand Prix on August the 30th was where I could retain the 50cc championship and lose the 125. The meeting had been moved from the dangerous tree-lined circuit in Tampere to a more open street race at Imatra, a small town a few kilometres from the Russian border.

Practice times showed there was virtually no difference between Ralph Bryans, on the little Honda 50cc twin that seemed to improve at each meeting, Anscheidt and me. Ralph had not accumulated sufficient points to be a title contender. It was down to Anscheidt and me.

Ralph gained a good start and led while I sat behind Anscheidt. There was so little between us that I wouldn't have been able to get away from them, so it seemed best to follow and learn. Ralph's Honda clattered to a stop halfway through the 10-lap event.

This is how Bengt Bjorkland, of *The Motor Cycle* magazine, described the rest of the race: 'For the next three laps, Anderson and Anscheidt fought tooth and nail, passing one another time and again as the Kiwi fought to clinch his second title. And he just made it, pulling away in the last two laps to win by less than a second.' Championships are not given; they are earned with hard graft on and off the track.

With their 125 fours having been beaten at the East German and Ulster Grand Prix, Honda flew over improved engines from Japan. Practice times showed Taveri, Bryans and Redman on Hondas and Frank doing similar lap times as me. Knowing I had a little more to give, I was determined to gain a good start, then make a break and head off alone. This would allow me to listen and feel how my bike was running. If required, I could then adjust the handlebar-mounted carburettor mixture control lever. It seemed to be a better option than when juggling positions with four other very competent riders.

My start was excellent. I pushed hard on that first lap. The carburettor settings seemed fine so I set about creating a decent cushion between myself and the rest. After five laps I had settled into a comfortable rhythm, each lap adding a second to my lead. I felt a slight hesitation, then another and another. Soon it began to occasionally misfire. Gradually, it got worse as one cylinder started closing down.

I stopped in my pit, Nagata-san changed the plugs, we still had hope. I pushed off again, Nagata-san running beside me. It fired, stuttered then revved up. I was about to get on it but it died again, revved again then cut out, only to give an occasional pop. After 100m we gave up. The slight chance of retaining the title was gone.

As we returned to the pits, Nagata-san's efforts to hide his tears were not entirely successful. Taveri won and went on to be champion that year. Strangely, perhaps you don't feel real bad about losing a world championship. I couldn't have done much better, as a rider, with the bikes I was given and there was no guarantee, in this highly competitive situation, of even winning one Grand Prix. Having Janny, enjoying Europe and my position in the Grand Prix scene, softened any disappointment.

I wasn't a great fan of the Monza circuit the scene of the last European round of the world championship. Even on a 500 you only closed the throttle on five occasions and braked at four corners. On a 125 it was a case of closing the throttle on four occasions. Not much meat to get your teeth into.

This would be Ernst Degner's comeback ride following his horrific accident at Suzuka last year when he had been trapped unconscious in that fierce petrol fire. Although he had undergone extensive facial surgery he still had several more reconstructive procedures to endure. He was a gutsy bloke and even though he hadn't been on a bike for almost a year, he was still able to qualify well.

The world 125 championship had been lost for me, but there was still a race to win. Due to the simplicity of the track and the similarity of all the machines' performance, Monza always produced a group of riders with similar qualifying times. This year was no different with less than two seconds between Taveri, Bryans and Redman on Hondas and Ernst, Frank and me on Suzukis.

Above: How Taveri and I finished at Monza. Another lap? Archives.

Left: Traditionally, I supplied the watermelons at Monza. From left: Suzuki-san, designer of the GT 750cc, Toshio Fuji, Ishikawa-san and Nagata-san. Sadly, in 1966 Toshio Fuji was killed on the Isle of Man. Archives.

From the start of the race I rode in Luigi's slipstream with Ralph, Frank and Jim close behind. After five laps I was braking for the Parabolica corner that turned us on to the start-finish straight. As always I had the rear wheel semi-locked, but then it became almost locked. I quickly eased off the brake but there was still 'drag'. I whipped in the clutch. A piston had tightened. Not wanting to give up, I quickly released the clutch, kept the throttle open and pushed the cut-out button. The sudden rush of cold air cooled the piston. I changed down a few gears and, without losing a place, pressed on.

Ralph had caught me and Luigi was 400 metres ahead. As the piston and rings slowly 'bedded' in, the engine's performance improved. As always in this type of situation, when your feathers have been ruffled a little, you try even harder. Over the following 12 laps I dropped off Ralph and inched ever closer to Luigi, but when the flag dropped there was still a gap of 0.6 of a second.

Back in the garage Ishikawa-san asked why I had slowed on the fifth lap. "It seized," I said. He gave me a doubtful look. Nagata-san quickly removed the barrels to reveal a badly scored left-hand piston. I had managed to save a full-on lock-up, gained second and set a new lap record. They were impressed.

The importance of the Japanese Grand Prix could not be overestimated. Obviously, the manufacturers gained huge advertising material to use at home and throughout their Asian markets. Being the season's last Grand Prix meant a rider's performance could affect the value of his contract fee for the following year.

The Suzuki Motor Company had completed their test track. It was of such a high standard that some countries would be pleased to have it as their Grand Prix circuit. Extensive use was made of it. Competition among the riders, especially the Japanese on their 50s, was fierce, even more so than at a full-on GP. For the first time, during the four seasons I had been with Suzuki, on arrival at a track my bikes would be in race-ready condition. Now only the fine-tuning of the suspension and gearing were required during practice beginning on Thursday, October 29, 1964, through Friday with a short run for each class on Saturday morning. I did just enough laps to sort out the bikes and kept a close eye on my rivals' lap times. This to me was the opportunity to put right the wrongs of the season. After the last session on Friday I was a comfortable 1.6 seconds faster than any other rider in the 125 field.

Due to our hotel being a long drive from our garage near the track, I was unable to stay with my bikes until very late, as was my custom. Arriving at the track on Saturday morning, I was told that Mr Okano had felt that the piston-bore clearance on my 125 was excessive so new barrels and pistons had been fitted to my ever so patiently prepared bike. This arbitrary decision left me totally bewildered. That I had for two seasons been their most successful rider, influencing the preparation of my machines that had proved the most reliable and just yesterday on that bike set the fastest lap by a substantial margin, well below the existing lap record, seemed of no account.

Riders thrive on confidence, not only in their own ability but that of those around them. As if the on-track competition wasn't enough to contend with, I had to cope with workshop obstruction as well. There were a lot of questions that needed answers about this change. It normally took at least two half-hour practice sessions to run in the engine, strip and rub the high spots off the pistons and set the carburettors and gearing to suit that particular engine. I had one 20-minute run available to get the settings right and avoid having the pistons seize. No chance. It seized on the third lap while running at only half throttle and I disappointedly rode it slowly back to the pits, handed it to Nagata-san, changed out of my leathers and left the pit area.

Late in the afternoon we returned to our workshop. I worked with Matsui-san on the 50 and ignored the 125. A very uneasy Ishikawa-san and Mr Okano finally came to me and asked what I wanted done with my bike. My first words were an angry, "Now you ask me?" Many of the words that followed do not grace the pages of any book offering English-Japanese translations. Of course, I had no idea what Mike was telling his boss, but Mr Okano frequently said "Hai" (yes), so he must have been in agreement with my assessment of the decision that had been made. The original barrels and pistons were refitted and Nagata-san and I were left in peace to finish the preparation as we saw fit.

Honda, Suzuki and Yamaha all fielded strong teams. Four four-cylinder Hondas, five Suzukis and five Yamahas confirmed that frequently, during 1964, the 125 class was the most competitive race of the meeting: we had world champion Phil Read, who went on to win another seven; Jim Redman, a four-time champion with two more to come; Luigi Taveri, a double and current world champion with another to add; Ernst Degner with one; me with three world titles and one more to claim; and Ralph Bryans, who would join the elite the following year. This group won a total of 23 world championships. Impressive in anyone's eyes.

The previous day's hassles were put to one side. I was sufficiently relaxed to gain a perfect start and, as I had planned, put in three very serious laps. At the hairpin during the fourth, I looked across at the rest. Ralph was leading a tight group of eight riders. I put my head down for five laps, dropping my times to below those made in practice. Ralph crashed out spectacularly on the fifth lap and Taveri took over second place. Again I looked behind at the hairpin. The gap on the chasing group had increased to eight seconds. Now Degner had taken over second place from Luigi in the tight group. All I had to do was ride on to the finish.

At the halfway stage I was leading a field of the world's best riders by an enormous 12 seconds. Then a misfire set in that got worse. I called into the pits and changed the plugs but it made no difference. The ignition condenser had broken free of its mounting, which had never happened before. Ernst saved Suzuki's pride by winning from Luigi with Katayama, Suzuki, third. As had so often been the case, I had set a new lap record of 2min 35.1secs, taking exactly two seconds off the existing time; the 350cc lap record was only 1.6 seconds faster than mine. Confirmation surely that Nagata-san and I were on to it.

Left: The Suzuki pit at Suzuka with Ishikawa, Moroshita and TT winner Mitsuo Itoh. Archives.

Left: Members of the team carried out action dances. This chap depicts catching fish in the shallows. My contribution was a barefoot, stripped-to-the-waist, well-rehearsed (in the toilet) haka. They were impressed. Archives.

Below: Enjoying a social evening in the company of Mr Okano. Archives.

I was smothered in apologies for the bracket failure, but there was no need. It was no more than what occurs on any race bike.

As in previous years, contract discussion for the next year took place after the Grand Prix. I'd had a disappointing year on the 125 using a machine I felt was much less than the factory could provide. The engines that Shimizu-san had brought to the West German Grand Prix were proof of that. When as a rider you have the capability of winning Grand Prix and world championships, it is frustrating not to be supplied with engines to the standard the factory is capable of. After all, it is in their interest too, so why not make the extra effort?

Naturally, I gave the contract situation considerable thought; money wasn't the reason I was doing this. My ambitions were to be the best I could be, and join the historic list of champions I admired so much. I decided that better bikes were much more important to me than an increase in my contract fee.

In previous years, contracts had been discussed and agreed to, in an informal way, with senior members of the factory race team. This year, for some reason that was never explained, negotiations took place in a boardroom. There were perhaps as many as 20 men sitting at the table; some were Americans. I took the offered seat and sat there rather nervously.

The conversation opened with general small talk about the past season and the bad luck we had suffered. When the question of what my expectations were, as far as the content of my contract for next year was concerned, I said very clearly, surprising myself a little, that I was prepared to accept the same amount of money as I had for this year but I wanted much better bikes for 1965.

A long fidgeting, embarrassed silence followed. Mike Ishikawa, showing signs of nervousness, said: "Hugh, you will have better bikes next year. We intend to water cool the 125 and have our water-cooled 50cc twin completed. Shimizu-san will be in charge of the team and we feel sure you will be satisfied. But what else can we do for you?"

Hmmm, hadn't thought of that.

"Could Janny come to Daytona with me?"

"Yes."

"A ten-day stay in Honolulu on the way would be a nice break."

"Yes."

"We will be returning to New Zealand at the end of next year."

"Yes."

"Perhaps my petrol and travel expenses in Europe could be paid."

"Yes." (Suzuki organised for Shell Oil Company to pay for those.)

I had run out of ideas, so I said thank you.

Mike, Okano-san, Shimizu-san and others shook my hand. The room's atmosphere had changed from dead silence to one of general conversation and light-heartedness. Well, they now knew where I came from, even if they hadn't before. After adding up the obvious benefits and bonuses of the contract that I signed, it came to much more than I would have had the gall to ask for.

As I flew back to the start of an English winter I pondered the results of a strange season. I was 50cc world champion, having gained four wins and setting four lap and race records, competing in nine Grand Prix. I'd picked up a British championship on the way with new race and lap records. Third place in the 125cc world championship came about through finishing first or second in all but one of the points-carrying events that I finished. I had been in first or second place at the time of retirement or enforced pit stops in all the other events, but still set five new lap records and new records in each of the three races I won.

Back in the UK we rented a pleasant, furnished, semi-detached home with a back yard and garage in Orpington, Kent. This was close to all our friends in the south-east London area and would be the staging ground for my new off-season activity of scrambling, or what is now called motocross.

My first job was to attend the Suzuki stand at the huge motorcycle show at London's Earls Court, opening on November 14. Suzuki Great Britain had all the current models imported into England on display. The changes to the machines to meet the demands of the English market were quite noticeable. Also on display was the bike on which I had won the 50cc race on the Isle of Man, along with my Ulster Grand Prix 125 winner. Pieces of wood had been tied to the seats with the sharp end of nails protruding through: sitters not wanted! The cylinder heads had been removed and the pistons melted so the aluminium flowed into the transfer ports. No one was going to learn the secrets of our success.

I took the opportunity to meet the Rickman brothers on their stand and ordered a Matchless Métisse kit. Through Tom Arter I was able to buy a new 500 Matchless G80CS scrambles engine, gearbox and Norton forks. The lounge at Orpington seemed the ideal place to build the Métisse. Covering the carpet with strong canvas-based sheeting and an old blanket, I began the assembly with enthusiasm.

Ten days after I began building the Métisse I was riding it at Gordon Jackson's farm. Gordon was a brilliant trials rider, supported by AJS, and had won the hugely demanding 1961 Scottish six-day event with the loss of just one mark.

My first scramble was in the Midlands at the Bolsover club's open meeting. The track conditions suited my limited ability, allowing me to gain second in a qualifying race and finish eighth in the final, which I was happy with. In the South London area entry levels were so high that newcomers like me had to compete as a Junior. The first 10 Juniors would qualify to take part in an all-comers race at the end of the meeting. To gain Expert status you needed to display an ability to compete with them. It wasn't easy. Typically there were 25–30 Expert entries compared to as many as 400 Juniors.

Motocross had spread across Europe from France and Belgium, where 120 and 30 meetings respectively were held each season. Now the Brands Hatch organisation had built an impressive 2.2km circuit near their famous road racetrack. On December 26, instead of racing at Wanganui's Cemetery Circuit summer street meeting, I was preparing, as the snow gently fell, to compete next day in the 500cc Junior motocross class on the other side of the world As it was just down the road, Janny and Caroline came too. I frequently met up with world speedway champion Barry Briggs, and he and his wife June joined us.

There was 30mm of snow coating the countryside and during practice the track surface became muddy and tyre grooves soon developed. I won the first of the two heats. Then at midday the temperature dropped from plus one to minus several degrees. The ground had frozen over by the time of my second race. Being rutted, uneven and icy, it became quite an achievement just to make headway, while closing the throttle was sufficient to lock up the back wheel and stall the engine. Parts of the track took in the sunken walkways used by spectators at the road race meetings, which were dished and covered in ice. It was here that I slid off the Métisse and quickly set about picking it up.

Just as I nearly had it upright, my feet would slide out from under me and leave me sprawled over it. After several attempts I eventually got it upright and was the overall winner from the two heats. The conditions were so bad that a competitor riding a trials bike won the second heat!

Every solo rider, Junior and Expert, went on his ear at least once. It was so cold that at race end the snow that had become packed around the engine didn't melt. Whilst I was sweating, my hands were frozen and Janny and June had spent the day in the van with the engine running and heater on.

For the first race Barry gave me his advice on how to get a good start. His brief but sage advice was: "In muddy conditions, start in third gear, rev it to near valve bounce and dump the clutch." With a wildly spinning rear wheel cutting a groove through the mud, I arrived at the first corner leading the pack. Speedway riders know.

Above: My first ride on the Métisse was sort of okay. Archives.

Left: A sport for the hardy. Archives.

CHAPTER 13

The report of a radiologist: Your foot is fine, but your leg is broken

HONOLULU AND THE DANGERS OF SUNBATHING AND WATER SPORTS

A relaxed winter competing in motocross to such effect that I had gained expert status in the UK, punctuated by a brief visit to Japan to test the new water-cooled versions of the 50cc and 125cc Suzukis, had me feeling confident and fully prepared for the 1965 season. Janny and I, having left Caroline in Tinie's care, looked forward to our stay at the Hilton Hotel in Honolulu. I spent time in the water with an early version of a surf ski, enjoying the ride that the two-metre waves gave. On the third day when I hired one, the owner said take care as there will be an occasional big one coming in today.

No worries, mate, I thought, I have surfed at Mount Maunganui since I was a boy. Within 15 minutes, as I picked up yet another nicely sized wave and prepared to ride it with a double-ended paddle to the shore, I noticed the rear of the ski lifting more than usual, then more and more. I looked behind and there curling four metres above and over my head was a massive wave. Naturally, there was little water below it and my only thought as I was being bashed onto the coral reef was keep your head up. I fought hard, shredding skin and flesh from hands, knees and feet. With bursting lungs I finally surfaced and began swimming with real purpose, but it took time to realise I was going the wrong way. Janny suffered from a severe rash from lying on the sand. We recovered in time to fly on to the North American mainland.

Support for the 1965 USA Grand Prix at Daytona was poor. Honda didn't bother going, leaving only 10 riders in the 50cc class, 19 in the 125 and 38 in the 250. Race day dawned fine, except for it being so windy that some riders were almost blown off the track. With no opposition the team decided that as Ernst probably had the best chance of winning the 50cc world championship and me the 125 title, it made sense we should win those classes. Yamaha made a similar decision in the 250cc class. Of course, Mike Hailwood cleared off on the MV in the 500cc race.

This is America. Janny can sit on my tank any time. Due to the tightness of my leathers, I lowered the zip to gain some freedom. Archives.

Before we had left for Honolulu and Daytona, I had decided that to make progress in developing my motocross riding ability I needed a lighter bike, giving me the confidence to try new things without, as the Métisse tended to do, getting tossed off. The best available was the new 250cc Husqvarna. Torsten Hallman had won the 1963 250cc motocross world championship on a special factory prototype but a production model had been slow to follow. In the heavy sand in Holland and Belgium, where the British bikes had been found wanting, the few Husqvarnas in private hands were winning and mechanically trouble free. I phoned the Dutch importer the day after we returned and arranged to meet him. Not having seen one close up, I found it to be very light and well made. Then I realised why so few were in private hands. The price was 400 pounds! My new Ford Thames van had only been 515 pounds, with a heater and side-loading door.

If I had a future in motocross, this was my last chance. Taking a deep breath, I paid the man. That evening I was back at Makkinga where international meetings were held. Only a few laps of this difficult track confirmed I had made the right decision. It was light, fast, responsive and manoeuvrable. Its relatively high-rise, narrow handlebars and overall riding position suited me perfectly. Motocross is riding a bike in its rawest sense. Mistakes were not treated as harshly at these lower speeds. Sure I was not going to be a top rider, but I was going to enjoy whatever level I reached.

Following my complaints while negotiating my contract at the end of 1964, the Suzuki race team had agreed to make a 125 available for testing. My Easter schedule was going to be a busy one. Brands Hatch on Friday, a motocross in Cheshire on Sunday, then compete at nearby Oulton Park on Monday. The Suzuki had to be returned to the team on Tuesday and we needed to leave for the first round of the world championship at the Nürburgring on Thursday. Soon after the sun was up on Friday morning, Alan Jones drove the van

A form of pleasant recreation squeezed in when possible. Archives.

while I gave the bike a test run, yet again, up the Maidstone bypass on the way to Brands Hatch.

After dialling in the carburettors, the bike ran very well. Young up-and-coming Bill Ivy rode the wheels off a production Honda, at his home track, to gain a surprisingly close second in the main race. Bill had been steadily improving and now had become a very competent competitor. Just 5ft 3in, he was ideally suited to ride small-capacity machines. I mentioned this to Ishikawa-san but after some thought he felt that our team was settled and bringing in a new rider at this point may alter its harmony. The Runthorne Club's motocross event was an open meeting with around 150 competitors; many were Expert. I won my qualifying heat and came fifth in the main race. While being well aware that I had not cracked it, I felt well pleased with my progress. Having been hassled by Bill at Brands, I got myself focused at Oulton Park and scorched off to an easy win, leaving him to dice with Tommy Robb, who was riding a very competitive 125cc Bultaco. I arrived back home late to find Janny busy packing our belongings. Early on Tuesday we were on our way to Holland.

The snow and ice of winter had not long thawed at the Nürburgring. During practice we had to contend with bitter winds, thick fog, drizzle and sleet. The short, southern loop circuit wound its undulating way through thick pine forests. A rider's track for sure, but with a reputation of being treacherous in the wet.

On Saturday the weather began to clear and when we prepared for the 125 race, the first on the programme, a bleak sun broke through. The conditions may not have been pleasant but by keeping the engine temperature low, they suited our bikes. At the end of the first lap the two four-cylinder Hondas retired with ignition problems. I led Ernst by a narrow margin at a fast enough pace to set a new lap record before he slid off unhurt on the eighth lap. I went on to win at record speed. At first Luigi then Ralph Bryans led the 50cc race then to the surprise of all, Nieto, Derbi, passed them both and took over the lead. Unfortunately, the Derbi began to slow and he fell back to finish fifth ahead of Hans Georg Anscheidt, the lead rider of the three-man Kreidler factory team. We had over-jetted my 50cc twin but I adjusted to the situation and slowly gained on the leaders, passing Luigi with two laps to go. He fought back and beat me to the line by 0.6sec, setting a new lap record in the process.

After-race celebrations at a freezing German Grand Prix. No man hugs today. P.3 Motorsport *photos.*

The organisers of the Austrian Grand Prix had offered me a large sum to take part at their annual event. Wet conditions during practice made the cobblestone areas lively and I always enjoyed being there. The circuit, atmosphere and helpful organisers, topped off with a knees-up prize giving, made for a fine Continental Circus event. Having the best bike in the class allowed me to win with record lap and race times. It was rewarding to find that my new record lap, without being under any pressure, was just 1.6 seconds slower than the best factory MZ 250cc rider. Interestingly, Endel Kiisa led the 350cc race on a four-cylinder Russian 350cc Vostok and nearly created history. He would have become the first Russian rider on a Russian bike to win a race in the West. A mile before the finish it expired. Success is never guaranteed in racing.

We arrived at our favourite camping ground north of Barcelona, and as we had each year Janny, Caroline and I enjoyed the lovely warm weather. A place where for a couple of days you have the opportunity to regain your breath after the rushed start to a season. The tight, twisting, bumpy, track made Montjuich Park one of my favourites, however the area acting as the race paddock was an entirely different matter. There was a water tap, but no formal facilities whatsoever. The toilets were in the open air anywhere, necessitating an early-morning walk, and you had to be very careful where you put your feet when stepping over and around the best efforts of others.

Soon after arriving I learned that Percy Coleman had died on April 24 while visiting his daughter Audrey in Zimbabwe. Life would have been tough without Percy's generous sponsorship at the Isle of Man in 1960. His interest and help gave me the motivation to find the resolve required to search for the limits of my ability. Our association had borne fruit, not only in a close personal friendship. The coincidence that Percy Coleman Ltd was the importer of Suzuki motorcycles and cars added to that fruitful meeting at Silverstone in 1960.

For the first time when competing at Montjuich my bikes had been run and thoroughly tested. From the start of practice they ran pretty well perfectly and it wasn't difficult to gain pole position in both classes. However, in the race a locally made Derbi challenged. José Busquets shot into the lead at the start of the 50cc race chased by Bryans on his Honda. My bike was reluctant to fire up cleanly and I was one of the last to leave the start. On the fourth lap I took over the lead with Busquets second, Bryans third, Taveri fourth, Salvadore Conallas, Derbi, and Australian Barry Smith, Derbi, fifth. For various reasons Degner and Itoh were well down the list on Suzukis. Even Kreidler's Anscheidt, who was always hard to beat here, was struggling in sixth place. Bryans finally got the better of Busquets and took second, with Taveri fourth. Anscheidt took over fifth place when Smith's Derbi blew up near the end of the last lap. The Honda team had not been able to overcome the ignition-mechanical problems that had put them out of the 125cc German Grand Prix but, like my 50cc, the 125 was running like a dream. After a good start I settled into that sweet spot of rhythm where each of the eight gears, when selected, give you the exact engine revolutions required to enter a corner at the precise speed that gives you that perfect on-the-limit tyre-scuffing, kerb-brushing exit. Once again during practice I had cut the key to open the door to that room containing perfection, a place that pre-race I always sought to enter. I led the race, steadily pulling away from Degner who, surprisingly, was followed by Derek Minter, MZ, with Frank back in fourth. Ernst ran into gearbox trouble and retired while Frank moved into second place. Ramon Torras, who had ridden very well at the Nürburgring, lost fourth place with a broken primary chain. Ginger Molloy had a rear brake anchor arm break when holding sixth place.

Señor Francisco Bultó, head of the Bultaco factory located near Barcelona, approached me at the prize giving and offered his hand in congratulations. Each year he had a timing device set up to check times taken from the end of the start-finish straight to the bottom of a fairly steep and winding downhill section. I had made the fastest time of the meeting. It was a surprise as Phil Read, Yamaha, and Tarquinio Provini, four-cylinder Benelli, had fought a great battle during the 250 race before Read finally gained the ascendancy.

This year the French Grand Prix was held at the Les Essarts track, a simple four-mile circuit in a wooded area south of Rouen. It was fast, wide and, apart from two cobblestone corners, smooth with an emphasis on speed. From the start of practice Ernst was fast on his 125 taking pole ahead of me and Frank. The Hondas had overcome their problems, discovering it was carburettor trouble, not ignition failure, and were lapping at a similar speed to us. Honda had added considerable spice to the 50cc race by flying in new engines the day before practice. They were obviously much-improved versions and Luigi and Ralph made the fastest practice times with me in third.

Luigi led from the start of the 125cc race but a swarm of two-strokes were all around him. At the end of the first lap an inspired Ernst led from me, Luigi, Perris, Bryans and a bunch of East German MZs. Ernst was slowly increasing his lead on me. He was a very determined person who, after his rather too many serious falls, always made impressive comebacks. Most of my time and effort had been focused on the 50s during practice as we couldn't get either of them running well. This had left me a little rusty as far as riding the 125 was concerned, so it was time I made a real effort. After a series of record laps I closed the gap and passed him on the last lap. The 50cc race was anybody's. Ernst had been fastest in practice followed by the two Hondas and me. After a good start Ralph made a break on the field with Taveri, Degner, Anscheidt and Itoh ahead of me. A journalist wrote: 'Anderson lay in sixth. His engine sounded very sick.' Ralph won, Luigi managed to just pip Ernst. Hondas first and second.

The Dutch Moto-Cross World Championship 250cc round at Makkinga in north-east Holland was my first opportunity to observe the world's best 250cc motocross riders who came from 15 countries.

The new purpose-built, two-stroke CZ motocross machines had caught the Western manufacturers napping. They were light, mechanically rugged and reliable. Being produced in Czechoslovakia, they were bought by government-funded clubs and made widely available to riders from behind the Iron Curtain. This was an opportunity for them to compete at the highest level and they were revelling in it. Russian Victor Arbekov dominated the 250cc class followed by Dave Bickers, on a British Greeves, past champion Torsten Hallman and Belgium star Joel Robert. I watched from every part of the track, which included at least 12 significant jumps and continuous undulations. I knew it well.

The 35 riders left the start in a shower of dust with the ground shaking as they thundered past me. Abecov led both 45-minute races from start to finish. Greeves riders fell by the wayside; a broken piston, seized gearbox, a whiskered plug.

Robert withdrew from the second race with stomach cramps. Fritz Selling, a brilliant Dutch rider who had worked at the Greeves factory, finished second overall to Abecov. Another Russian, Gunnor Draugs, was third and Czech Victor Valek, Jawa, was fourth. Young up-and-coming Dutch rider Ton van Heugten was sixth on his Husqvarna. These guys were talented and very experienced, physically fit and tough. They gave their bikes no mercy and hammered them to an extreme that made finishing very much a lottery for riders of British bikes.

As in all sports there is a substantial step up from national to international level and yet another to join the world championship elite. I realised that this level of motocross was perhaps something a 50cc road race world champion should not be aspiring to.

THE DAY A 125 WAS THE FASTEST BIKE ON THE TRACK

The 1965 TT was hit by constant rain, and fog clinging low over the mountains. The first practice that was designated for all solos except 50cc took place in foul weather on the evening of June 3. Perhaps I was inspired by having seen the top riders in motocross, who were paid little but gave their all to achieve. In comparison I had the tools, the backing, the experience, the skills and was well paid. Go and use them to the max and revel in the doing of it, I told myself.

My Suzuki had been fitted with lower gearing, carburettor settings that suited the conditions and was fuelled for two laps. Wearing good-quality wet-weather riding gear and having always excelled in adverse conditions, I enjoyed my first lap and began the second with enthusiasm. I didn't find the surface particularly slippery, but with pools of water having formed, the bike tended to aquaplane frequently. Using the speed, angle of lean and throttle openings that suited the prevailing conditions allowed me to slide relatively gently on the puddles and hook up, with similar ease on the tarmac surface. I made good progress, thoroughly enjoying the movement of the bike, nicely clipping kerbs and being excited by that risk we seek from an on-the-edge experience. I made good time riding through the fog up on the mountain. Having pre-determined markers all over the mountain that allowed me to know exactly where on the road I needed to be and clear brake and corner entry markers meant lower visibility wasn't a huge problem, but the black blobs of slower riders were. When approaching one at much higher speed you had to make a quick decision of do I pass him on his right or left? This was to allow me to line up the next corner or curve to best effect. To stay on line at times I actually brushed them. More than once, when back in the pits, I was subject to some quite exotic language! I must say it was exciting to brake for a corner you couldn't see, but as you peeled off to enter it realise you were almost inch perfect. Yet another challenging aspect of this place.

That lap was the most pleasant, exciting, satisfying and rewarding I ever completed there. Most of the top riders took part with over 100 out on the circuit. On my 125 I made the fastest lap beating all the 250, 350 and 500s. This had never happened before in the history of the TT races. The riders taking part included Giacomo Agostini, Phil Read, John Cooper, Jack Ahearn, Ernst Degner, Dave Croxford and many more capable of finishing in the top six in any class at any event. Conditions became a little better during the following morning's session and Jack Ahearn made the fastest 250 time on the new Suzuki four-cylinder eight-speed. Phil Read and Jim Redman were close behind. I was still going strong and again on my 125 achieved the sixth-fastest lap regardless of capacity. As well as speed and confidence you also need some luck at the TT. When preparing to leave the pits to start my second lap of practice in a later session, an observant marshal pulled me to one side. He had noticed the silver head of a nail in my front tyre.

During practice I had broken Taveri's existing lap record and was as confident as I dared of winning the race. The weather was fine, I was on form and the bike the best Suzuki had produced. After it was warmed up a discussion took place regarding jet size and the heat range of spark plug that would be most suitable in the existing conditions. My mechanic gave his opinion. I felt what he suggested would not be suitable and that we should use a size-smaller jet or hotter plugs to cope with the rich mixture he had suggested, as there was a real risk of the plugs becoming fouled with excessive oil. The mechanic was being extremely cautious. Had Nagata-san been with me, what I suggested, after checking our rather primitive weather station and reviewing what had worked in practice, would have been used without question. The discussion began to move to the point of a full-on argument. After my heated outburst in Japan regarding the change of pistons and cylinders last year, I was not going there again. The few minutes before the start of the race of the year is not the time for an emotional eruption. I quietly put the hotter plugs I wanted, along with a plug spanner, in the pouch attached to the inside of the fibreglass fairing, then prepared mentally for the start. It fired up instantly and the race was on. At full throttle the engine misfired, it was too rich, as I knew it would be. Although Mike Duff, on a factory Yamaha, had started 10 seconds before me, I caught him at the 13th Milestone, much sooner than expected. But passing him was difficult. Mike's Yamaha had good acceleration and a slightly higher top speed. I could only gain under brakes and in cornering, but he was able to accelerate away again, giving me no opportunity to pass. Having to be careful how much throttle I could use hindered my efforts. I led the race at the halfway point of that first lap by 10 seconds from Read and Duff. As I gained height on the mountain climb, the slightly thinning air worsened the excessive fuel problems. Using less and less throttle didn't help. The plugs oiled and I was forced to stop on the Mountain Mile and change them.

You know how it is, lean the bike against a fence, loosen the extremely hot plugs, try to unscrew them with your gloved fingers, constantly changing hands as the pain becomes unbearable. After what seems like an age, with very painful fingers, you restart and continue. At the end of the first lap the order was: Read, Duff, Katayama, Taveri and Degner. After 37.7 miles just 12 seconds covered them. My engine responded immediately to the change of plugs so I rode on with purpose. Of course there was absolutely no chance of winning or gaining a very high placing, but I had an opportunity to enjoy two laps riding at my pace without pressure. I was in the zone, just me, the bike and the track, much like that day in 1960 on Percy Coleman's AJS. *Motor Cycling*'s Mick Woollett wrote: 'Hugh Anderson was forced to change plugs on the first lap. After that he twice shattered the lap record and finally pushed it to a staggering 96.02mph.' By the third lap I was getting my eye in and was near my safe limit. *The Motor Cycle* described my last lap: 'Hugh Anderson's progress was almost frightening on that last desperate dash. A record and how! Small wonder he jumped from ninth to fifth.' Another commentator wrote: 'Anderson had no chance of winning, yet he still put in those fantastic laps. What could he have done had he contested the lead?' I would have thought that 97mph would not have been out of reach.

The choice of jet and spark plug had cost Suzuki and me a certain TT win, yet at race end no word was mentioned of our pre-race discussion. At the prize giving that evening I was presented with the Bob Holliday Trophy for the record lap and a silver replica for finishing fifth. The trophies, as per my contract, were handed to the team management.

Meanwhile, Jack Ahearn was struggling with the new 250cc Suzuki. During practice he crashed on the climb out of Glen Helen. The bike was badly damaged and Jack split his helmet, causing concussion and three days' observation in hospital. Being a tough old-timer, Jack had every intention of competing in the Senior TT eight days later. He did, pushing on through wind, rain and even sleet on the mountain to finish ninth. It was a credit to his commitment in a race where the conditions caught out Agostini at the same spot as Jack had fallen and then Hailwood, although he restarted downhill in the opposite direction of the other riders. This is an offence that carries automatic disqualification but, amazingly, there were no witnesses. Jack was taken seriously ill on his way to the Ulster Grand Prix on August 2. He was rushed to hospital, a blood clot was removed from his brain and he was out for the season. It was after this nasty fright that Jack nicknamed the bike 'Whispering Death'.

The 50cc race was on the same day as the Senior TT. The little Hondas had been going well from the first practice session and Luigi dominated. Ralph demonstrated their real worth during Wednesday morning's second session when he lapped at a remarkable 82.46mph. Drifting mist on the mountain, rain squalls and high winds delayed the race twice.

The two Hondas didn't run well from the start. Ralph actually left the circuit at Quarter Bridge, only a mile from the start, and returned to the pits. Once there the fault, a continuous misfire, improved so he rejoined the race. Luigi's also was playing up and it took some 15km before a persistent misfire cleared. The road surface was difficult to read. Showers then sunshine, negotiating wet and dry tarmac, and being hit by high winds when passing a gap in a hedge or similar meant we were constantly dealing with the unexpected.

The climb up the mountain was the worst. Galeforce winds blew up from the valleys. Attempting to avoid the worst, I kept hard to the left of the tarseal, hoping the wind would go over me. Mostly it was to no avail, as on several occasions each lap I had to sit up on the tank to put more weight on the front wheel to stop it being blown out from under me. Riders were blown into banks, others suffered nasty incidents. Our positions at the end of the first lap were Mitsuo Itoh, Luigi and me, with only a few seconds covering us. At the end of the second lap, Itoh stopped for a plug change. Now Luigi led me by 20 seconds with Ernst two minutes farther back. He had also been a victim of the treacherous winds and blown into a bank but was able to carry on. Luigi won comfortably, I was second and Ernst third. Due to the conditions, no records were broken. I now led the world championship with 25 points, Taveri was on 23 and Bryans 22.

The benefits of the much-improved and reliable 125 became very obvious at the Dutch TT in Assen: I repeatedly broke the lap record during practice setting times that few of the 500cc riders could better. All I intended doing on Friday morning's practice was to test two minor chassis changes that we had made and shake down the engine that had been completely stripped, checked and rebuilt overnight. During the fourth lap the engine unexpectedly locked solid on a medium-fast corner and I hit the deck hard. This left me sliding some distance up the track before cartwheeling along the grass verge wondering what the hell had gone wrong.

On returning to the pits it was discovered that the slow-running jet, situated on the intake side of the carburettor, had vibrated lose and been sucked into the engine. This had caused the engine to lock solid within 1mm of rotation from over 13,500rpm. Under those circumstances, when in a corner a rider has no chance to free the clutch. Naturally, I suffered bruises and friction burns and was given an anti-tetanus injection. During the evening I began to feel unwell with hot flushes and sweating. Our doctor was called and thought my symptoms were a reaction to the anti-tetanus serum. During the night I sweated profusely and suffering from low-level delirium had little sleep as I whistled and sang the night away. Understandably, next morning I had little enthusiasm for racing.

The 50cc race was second on the programme and, typically, the six fastest had all qualified within little more than a second of each other, so it was going to be another 'stuck up each other's exhaust pipe' event. After a poorish start I found myself at the back of a group of five with Ralph and Luigi leading on their high-revving Hondas. Riding much better than expected, I took just three laps to fight through the pack, slip past Luigi and chase after Ralph, who by this time had made a break. Setting new lap records I closed on him. A typically close finish was on the cards when suddenly, and on a 50cc with narrow knife-edge-like tires it is very, very sudden, the rear tyre let go on a fast sweeper.

With lightning-fast reactions honed by a couple of seasons racing these ever-evolving prototypes I corrected the slide. The rear tyre regained grip as savagely as it had lost it. I tucked in again to keep hard on the heels of Ralph only to be startled by a rhythmic thump-thump-thump from the rear wheel. What is it? The tyre must be damaged. Will it blow out? If so, when? How long have I got? Do I stop or carry on? The thoughts rushed through my head. While I was playing the role of a worrywart, Ralph was easing away. Either I stop or I forget about it, simply press on and whatever happens, so be it. I held second place to the finish. The problem was a badly buckled rear wheel. When I corrected that slide three spokes had been ripped out of the rim; the mechanics were impressed, they had never seen that before.

After the podium ceremony I had a light lunch with Janny and Caroline. Feeling even worse than before I lay down beside my bikes and this time drifted off to sleep as the mechanics worked. When Nagata-san woke me to prepare for the 125cc event I felt weak and depressed. There had been the odd occasion when I had not been enthusiastic about a particular race, but not like this. Negative thoughts took over my normal pre-race routine with a premonition entering my mind that 'this may be it and I won't be coming back'. Janny had no idea how I felt or what I was thinking and she never would. It was imperative for Janny's health and wellbeing that she should retain confidence in me, so this was a load for me alone to carry. As I struggled into my leathers I began my usual preamble of 'donning my suit of armour and going forth to do battle'. Then I polished my perfectly clean goggles yet again, held Caroline close and said goodbye, gave Janny a traditional hug and with a whispered "See you later, kid", slowly walked away. As I walked, for some unknown reason an old schoolboy poem came to mind. I found myself involuntarily reciting from Tennyson's 'The Charge of The Light Brigade', which took place at the Battle of Balaclava, in the Crimean War, in 1854:

> *Theirs not to reason why,*
> *Theirs but to do and die:*
> *Into the valley of Death*
> *Rode the six hundred.*

Slowly, a steely resolve pushed all doubt aside, my concentration took on its normal intensity and I moved into that silent, beyond-communication state. That there were 150,000 spectators present was completely lost on me.

Having qualified fastest I slid into the seat of my Suzuki Nagata-san had readied for me on pole position. He wished me luck.

The starter's flag dropped but my bike refused to start. I kept pushing but it was not until long after the last man had passed me and the leaders were 1km ahead that it finally screamed into life. Frustration flared and barely controlled anger took over; not a good start. Setting new lap records on most laps I passed rider after rider. On the fourth lap I overtook Luigi on his four-cylinder Honda. At half race distance I brushed past Bill Ivy on his Yamaha and closed on the two riders contesting first place, Yamaha-riding Mike Duff and my team-mate Yoshima Katayama. I out-braked Katayama at the end of the long start-finish straight. Half a lap later and closely following Mike around a fast right-hand corner, Katayama made a suicidal inside pass on me.

There was no room and on the inside at the apex of the corner he caught the edge of the grass verge, lost control and veered back out in front of me. He missed my wheel by millimetres and careered on almost taking out Mike. All this at 190kph. He could have caused a real mess. So much for team-mates! Suddenly, feeling exhausted from my illness and the hard ride, I thought, Katayama-san, if you think you can beat Mike, go for it, but I knew he couldn't. His riding was really ragged, and he had been following Mike for most of the race and was stuck there. Sure enough Mike made a gap on him and won by 2.6 seconds. Keeping close but out of harm's way, I finished third, two-tenths of a second behind Katayama.

After suffering from those sobering pre-race premonitions, seeing Janny and holding Caroline once more released a great sense of relief and wellbeing. I made no comment to the team regarding Katayama's irrational behaviour.

Riding small-capacity machines to the limit is not a stroll in the park and this event produced some remarkable comparisons. My new lap record on the 125 stood at 3mins 19secs, giving an average speed of 86.60mph. This was faster than Agostini's 350cc third-placed race average, faster than the race average of Jim Redman on Honda's 250cc six-cylinder when he rode to second place in that class, and even faster than the third-placed finisher in the 500cc event. During the bad blood and battles

Above: Lying on the grass feeling as sick as a parrot. Matsui-san and my 50cc in the foreground. A scanned magazine copy of the original photo by Wolfgang Gruber.

Left: I did come back. Jan Heese.

between Bill Ivy and Phil Read on their four-cylinder 125cc Yamahas, producing about 15 per cent more power than the bike I was riding, it was two years later, in 1967, that Ivy took just 1.3 seconds off my time. Once again my race speed on a 125 was faster than that of Katayama on the 250cc four-cylinder Suzuki. You would have thought that sometime soon Suzuki management would accept that the 'Whispering Death' 250 could not, with the expertise available within the racing department at the time, be developed into anything resembling a race winner.

As last year, the 125 race was not included in the programme at the Belgium Grand Prix. The 50cc race had become a straight clash between Suzuki and Honda as the Kreidler team, disappointed by their practice lap times, left before the race. The Hondas had been fastest in most of the previous races, but here Ernst set the best lap in practice, some three seconds below last year's lap record. So another close race beckoned. As photographs of the time show, space was at a premium when squashed into a 50cc. At Spa-Francorchamps, we used the brakes on only two occasions. This left us 'tucked in' 99 per cent of the time. As my elbows were adjacent to the cylinder heads and the calves of my legs tight against exhaust pipe shields, the heat penetrated my leathers. I suffered large water blisters on my elbows and legs. I wrapped asbestos sheeting around the exhaust pipes but Shimizu-san was adamant it would affect the resonance of the very special exhaust expansion chambers so it couldn't be used. In jest I pointed out that it was me being burned, not him. Their in-house sheet-metal worker fashioned new exhaust pipe guards and we spaced the fairing out a little so I could keep my elbows away from the engine. Problem solved.

At the end of the first lap Ernst and I led with Ralph and Luige just metres behind us. On the second lap Ernst passed Ralph, who stayed in Ernst's slipstream. It was a four-cornered dice for the lead. I led by the narrowest of margins at the beginning of the final lap. Ernst and Ralph were side by side with Luigi tucked in behind. We constantly swapped places riding within centimetres of each other and using each other's slipstream. At the end of the long, slightly downhill Masta straight, the Hondas led. I felt confident that provided I could place myself within a few metres of the leaders I could out-brake them into La Source hairpin, make a rapid exit and rush down the hill to the finish.

For once everything went according to plan. A few hundred metres before La Source I popped out of Luigi's slipstream, tagged onto Ernst and out-braked him into the hairpin. Pedalling my bike to the max, I headed to the finish. I could see the flag. The race and points were mine. Suddenly, the engine screamed free. There was no drive. Change gear. Nothing. There must be. Change gear again. Still nothing. Ernst swept past. The rear chain had broken. Bloody hell, so near, yet so far. I was coasting, going ever slower. Where was Luigi? Don't look, stay on the tank and hope. In total silence I reached the flag 0.9sec before Luigi as his 22,000rpm screamer flew past. Mitsuo Itoh gained fourth and Ralph dropped to fifth. Luigi had set a new lap record of 153.866kph. My bike had been geared for a maximum speed, in 14th gear, of 186kph, and 181kph in 13th. I had set up my bike to gain maximum speed in 13th when on my own and use 14th when slipstreaming. The four-stroke twin-cylinder Hondas had an over-rev capability. They could gear for a maximum of 21,000rpm, but if a faster bike came by they could run on up to 22,000rpm. Our two-stroke Suzukis did not. When we hit 17,500rpm there was a total power drop-off. Because of this I saved 14th gear for the race to make sure I could stay with the lighter riders and/or faster machines. There is considerable skill and trust required to sit within a metre of your adversary's rear wheel. The question of whether he will suffer a possible engine seizure has to be completely deleted from your mind.

At La Source, Francorchamps: me, Ernst, Bryans and Taveri. Archives.

A free weekend between the Belgium and East German Grand Prix gave me an opportunity to compete at England's Essex Grand National, on July the 11th, in a bid to get my international motocross licence. A fifth-place finish would do it for me. The event was headlined by *The Motor Cycle* as 'The bumpy battle in Essex'. Its report read: 'Dramatic spills were frequent at the bumpy little Loveney Hall Circuit, which was in prime condition for catching the unwary during Sunday's National Essex Motocross. The most serious prang was when 50cc road racing champion Hugh Anderson was tossed off his Métisse while lying seventh in the 500cc motocross. He badly bruised an ankle.' There is a little to add. I lost it over an awkward series of jumps and the rear of the Métisse landed heavily on my right foot. The ambulance staff said no bones were broken, just severe bruising. I was given crutches, my van was loaded and off I went to catch the ferry home.

On the drive up to Assen, my foot was badly swollen and too painful even to use

How can you get hurt when going so slow? Archives.

225

it on the accelerator. The next morning it was X-rayed and I was pleased to be told that no bones were broken. I certainly wasn't expecting to be told "but your leg is broken". My foot was so painful I hadn't noticed. A plaster cast was fitted. Being just the tibia it wasn't too serious but hardly an ideal situation. One thing was certain: I wouldn't be riding next weekend at the East German Grand Prix. I had a huge points lead in the 125 championship and Honda had withdrawn their unreliable 125 fours, so my championship chances were not in jeopardy. I notified the team, put my foot up and relaxed.

The next round was the Czechoslovakian Grand Prix, on July 25 at the Brno road circuit. On the evening of Tuesday, July 17, I decided to cut off the plaster and see how the foot and leg felt. Janny's dad helped me. He had been a bit of a larrikin in his youth, I'm told, and, while being highly disciplined after 29 years in the Army, still enjoyed nudging the system. The foot was far from pain free. I couldn't walk on it. Understandably, my leg didn't hurt at all. My initial reception from the team was on the frosty side. Acting manager Nakamura-san said, "At the end of the season I will be handling the contracts and there will be a clause stating no motocross." Putting my hand on his shoulder, I said, "Let's wait until then before making any decisions." He wasn't aware that behind the scenes Suzuki management had committed to a programme that would have them enter international motocross in 1967. He also wasn't aware that I was part of it. During the 1962 season I'd spoken about competing in off-road events. They had sent a modified 250cc twin-cylinder road bike to New Zealand for me to test.

Part of the team's concern was probably due to Frank having difficulty beating the much slower MZ riders at the previous weekend's East German Grand Prix. For the first few laps, in wet conditions, he was led by Heinz Rosner, MZ, who had set a joint fastest lap in practice with Frank. When Rosner retired, Deiter Krumpholz, on another MZ, caught and passed Frank, leading him until his engine began misfiring. This allowed Frank to win. No wonder they were just a little annoyed at my absence.

My broken leg was never mentioned as I only admitted to a sprained ankle. With the help of painkillers I was able to walk slowly for short distances without crutches. When preparing my bike I sat on it and found it far too painful to lift the gear lever to change down through the gears. The only option was to make up an aluminium shield fashioned to my foot and taped in place. It worked great. During practice, I lapped a full five seconds faster than Frank, around the undulating public-roads 14km course that snaked through forest and villages and out onto fast, open farmland. My bike went well apart from the front brake's steel liner coming loose and rattling around the hub, almost tossing me off.

I had not attempted a push start before Sunday's race, as I'd had the mechanics to push me off. We lined up, the starter dropped his flag, and I pushed off with my left foot then my right. Before reaching full stretch the too-long gear-change aluminium shield jammed into my instep, causing excruciating pain.

I rose up on my toes, dropped the clutch and fell on the seat side-saddle. Luckily it started and I was just behind the leaders. It hurt so much I couldn't feel the footrest. Partway around the lap on a right-hand corner, my foot was off the rest and dragging on the road. Fortunately, within three laps it was fine and I knuckled down, passing riders and putting five seconds a lap between Frank and me. On the last lap the engine

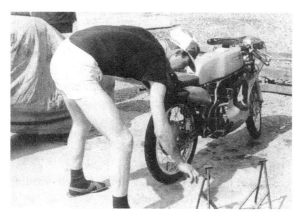

Top: Early in practice an astonished Frank is informed by team manager Nakamura-san that he is five seconds slower than my new lap record. Archives.

Middle and bottom: I was asked to lose weight, but from where? Archives.

abruptly went on to one cylinder as I entered a straight. This had never happened before. I felt under the tank to confirm both plug leads were secure. I then looked for any loose wires. Silly really, as I was doing 140kph. The straight was perhaps half a kilometre long but short at race speed. I looked up too late and realised I was not going to get around the following 90-degree bend. I braked heavily to the inside apex of the corner, slammed on the rear brake and laid the bike down, pulling my feet clear and using them to kick it away from me. That sped up the bike and slowed me down as I followed it on my back. The Suzuki shifted the hay bales and some shrubbery, leaving me with a relatively smooth passage.

When you can, it pays to lie still until the dust clears, then take stock of what hurts and what still works. Three marshals helped me to a safe place where a doctor was in attendance. There were numerous bumps and bruises and I recuperated with a terrible Czech cigarette, and tried to drink what, for them, was coffee while I gathered what German I had together. I'd fallen initially on my right side and my leg hurt. How to tell them that I had broken my right leg two weeks ago, perhaps it has been re-broken and could I have it X-rayed, please? Having pretty well got the sentence memorised I began, "Fourteen days ago I broke my leg ..."

As soon as they heard the words 'broke my leg' out came a knife to cut open my leathers — normal practice to gain access to it. I had to push them away. It took time but finally they understood. They put me in an ambulance and trundled me off to hospital. Luckily, it had not re-broken, was healing very well, but along with my foot was painful enough and I was back on crutches again.

The Ulster Grand Prix was two weeks after Czechoslovakia so there was ample healing time. After making the fastest lap in practice, I felt everything was under control. From a good start, I built up a handy lead in less than two laps only to have the crankshaft seize. Frank's had done the same thing on the first lap. Out on his own, Ernst quietly went about winning it.

I took advantage of having a free week in England to visit the ACU in London to discuss the possibility of gaining an international motocross licence. As always, Mr Cornwell received me with a smile, took me into his office and over a cup of tea chatted about things generally. I brought up the subject of motocross, what I had been doing in an effort to qualify for an international licence, and the reasons for wanting one. I had finished fifth at the Runthorne Club's event and was lying seventh at the Essex Grand National before falling and breaking my leg. "Goodness gracious, Hugh," he exclaimed. "You didn't need to go to such extremes. It is not only ability that we judge a rider on but also how they conduct themselves." I walked out of his office with that all-important addition to my international licence: all motocross, all classes. Life was good.

Going into the Finnish Grand Prix, I had a total of 45 points in the 125cc world championship tally with Frank Perris on 42. Having been outclassed by both Suzuki and Honda, Yamaha had withdrawn from the series. Both teams were working on improving their bikes for the all-important Japanese Grand Prix in October.

With three more events to go I needed to win two of them to beat team-mate Frank. Engine reliability could lose or win the championship for either of us. By nature, being something of a 'press on regardless' sort of rider, after two consecutive retirements I had become concerned about actually finishing races. As insurance,

in Finland I intended to follow Frank, conserving the engine until the last few laps, then challenge for the lead.

After my missing the East German event then having spark plug problems and laying the bike down in Czechoslovakia, Frank was aware that he had a sniff of the championship and was riding to his potential.

From the start we were together. The race length was 126 kilometres taking nearly 59 minutes at an average speed of 129kph. An hour is a long time to hold back, staying calm, riding at someone else's pace, watching your engine revs, being super careful in everything you do, but not letting nerves take hold.

On the second-to-last lap as we approached an S-bend leading onto the start-finish straight we caught a group of four lapped riders. Frank hesitated; I didn't, slotted through into the lead and stayed there to win by 0.7sec. Now if I won the Italian Grand Prix on September 5th, the title was mine.

When the conditions are at their worst, the risk factor at its highest and the challenge the greatest, that is when the reward of skill and effort has its highest value.

Monza conditions were typically hot and dry during practice with the top riders achieving almost identical lap times. However, steady rain, which was to continue all day, began five laps from the end of the 350 race causing havoc. Riders slid off on every corner, including Mike Hailwood, giving Agostini an easy win.

Top: The pressures a must-win situation creates are obvious. Archives.

Left: Winners are grinners. Archives.

Left: Thursday is spent socialising in the pits. Archives.

Below left: And the rains came. You beauty. Archives.

Below right: With my family, loaded with the rewards of a winner but mentally still somewhere else. Archives.

Leaving instructions with Nagata-san to lower the gearing and alter other settings to better suit the conditions, I returned to our caravan to prepare for the race.

Due to constant testing and a recent Formula One car Grand Prix, the surface was liberally coated with rubber and oil. To assess the surface conditions I felt it prudent to allow Frank and Ernst to lead and to observe how their bikes, and my own, reacted to the conditions. I made a good start then slowed a little to allow them to lead. During the second lap Ernst started to create a gap on Frank. Not wanting him getting too far in front, I passed Frank and closed on Ernst. Without warning he crashed heavily at the first of the two Lesmo curves. He hit the straw bales very hard. They burst and scattered over the track. The impact was such that the petrol tank and part of the fairing flew off and spun across the track with Ernst and the bike. My main concern was to miss Ernst and by chance I avoided his bike and the wreckage flying about and pressed on.

Journalist Vic Willoughby in *The Motor Cycle* magazine wrote: 'In heavy rain, the 125s were wheeled out onto a flooded track. If only Hugh Anderson, never guilty of excessive restraint, could keep his Suzuki upright to win, the world title was his. The pace was fearsome, it just couldn't last. With only a lap and a half behind him, Degner crashed at the Lesmo right handers and sustained a fractured thigh. That left Anderson way out ahead of Woodman, MZ, and Anscheidt, who managed to keep his MZ special in Perris's company. Next Woodman spun out, Anscheidt slowed, leaving Perris second. So much had happened it was difficult to believe that the race was only three laps old.

'For the rest it was Anderson with a capital A. In his time he has ridden some blinders but nothing surpassed this. It was championship stuff and then some. By lap 13 he had lapped Perris as well as the rest of the field. The chequered finishing flag was waved but Anderson screamed on oblivious.'

Having once again entered that state of perfection, I was only aware of what was relative to my riding. Pit signals, my huge lead, finishing flags were not part of it and not seen. I was told later that I had won by one and a half laps from Frank and lapped all the riders up to and including sixth-placed Ginger Molloy twice.

On that day my race speed would have given me a close second to Provini on a four-cylinder Benelli in the 250cc race and third in the 500 behind Hailwood and Agostini on their MV Agustas. The Monza circuit has no camber, allowing water to form in large shallow pools. It was a real buzz to be chin on the tank, flat-out around a left-hand curve, using all the track as the bike drifted on the water, then hooked up again quite gently on the slippery seal (quite the same as on the Isle of Man) giving a surprisingly smooth passage. Being confident and relaxed was an essential ingredient. I lapped an MZ rider here. He was on a much slower bike but sat up and closed the throttle. He would have been impressed when I rushed around him on the outside under the screen absolutely nailed. Apart from Ernst falling, it was a wonderful, unforgettable experience.

Each year Cleaver-Hume International presented the Turbo Visor Trophy, as advertising for one of their large companies' products, to the rider judged by a panel of journalists to have made the best wet-weather performances at Grand Prix during the season. For that rather special Monza effort, I was awarded the impressive trophy at a large reception in London.

As well as the trophies, I was accumulating some healthy earnings and decided to open a Swiss bank account. I had taken our savings from our English bank to Holland. Due to the strict control on the amount of money a person was allowed to take out of England, I hid a substantial amount of it in the air filter box of the Métisse scrambler and the rest behind the van's heater. Combined with what I had accumulated in a security box at my bank in Assen it all came to a tidy sum. On our way to Monza, we had pulled into the Zurich camping grounds. With the contents of the bank's safety deposit box with each currency now arranged into neat rubber-band-secured bundles and packed in a slightly crumpled shoe box, I set off downtown. The first bank I entered didn't feel right. It was very cold and remote. I entered another and was greeted with a smile. I asked to see an investment manager, was invited to wait a few minutes and given a coffee.

Paul Nagell of the Swiss Bank Corporation introduced himself and led me to his office. After the essential preliminary small talk, he asked how he could help me.

"I have ten thousand pounds [$NZ300,000 now] and I would like to discuss what secure forms of interest-bearing investments you have available."

His interest increased: "Where is the money at present?

"In a shoe box in my van," I replied.

His demeanour became questioning: "Where did it come from? How did you come by it?"

"I race motorcycles, successfully, all over the world," I replied.

Now I had his full attention. I guess meeting a person like me was a rarity in a banking executive's life and he seemed to be enjoying the novelty. When I retrieved the money from the van, the bulging box looked a trifle incongruous on his immaculate desk.

We settled on what seemed the best thing to do and he took me to lunch. I was now the owner of bonds issued by various European cities. Drawn together by our differences, over time Paul and I became good friends. He was multi-lingual and during the following years helped in negotiating appearance money with motocross promoters all over Europe. Although unpaid he thoroughly enjoyed playing a part, however small, in the robust, devil-may-care domain of motorcycle racing.

With a seven-week break between the European Grand Prix season and the Japanese Grand Prix, I applied to motocross organisers holding events on the three weekends following Monza. This would still leave plenty of time to take the van, bikes and gear to the London docks ready to ship to New Zealand, fly to Japan and prepare for the Grand Prix. I didn't care where I rode or how much I would be paid. Becoming involved for the first time at international level was sufficient motivation. An event was being run on September 12 at Zabok, Yugoslavia, just over the border from Italy. By chance the Austrian Motor Racing Club was running an international on the 19th at Murau and on the 26th at Wimpassing. My entries were accepted and good start money offered. The stage was set. Having broken my leg back in July, I had fallen behind in my state of fitness; it was not going to be easy.

As it had been when entering East Germany and Czechoslovakia, driving through Yugoslavia was something of a time warp back to the 1920s. We found the village where the event was being held and the house where the organisers had an office. In a boisterous welcome they insisted I join them in drinking a glass of plum brandy.

The glass wasn't small and it was a powerful brew. Before I could move them on to documentation we had to have another drink. Once the forms were signed, all in a language I knew nothing of, yet another glass had to be drunk. Luckily, more riders arrived and I could leave while I was still standing. Considering where my fitness levels were at, I was relieved to find the circuit was not too demanding. Having agreed to ride in both the 250 and 500 classes wasn't very wise. On the first lap of the 250 there was a pile-up on a hill among the first group of riders. Being in the centre of the track I couldn't avoid them. Those on each side could. After returning to the bottom I restarted and rode flat-out from near last without a thought about fitness or length of the race and managed 11th from 35 starters. Naturally, I was a little tired after a 30-minute race, but okay.

The 500 started soon after. I got a reasonable start but these guys were really aggressive in the way they pushed and shoved their way into the first corner. You would have thought there was a large pot of gold at stake. I had experienced this in England, of course, but these riders didn't have the same finesse. On the first lap of each race several riders fell; most were helped to restart. I gained places every lap, and at about two-thirds distance a new friend signalled that I had reached sixth place. That was when I hit the wall. I was shot. On the last few laps of a long race, I could manage little more than stay on and fell back to ninth. At the finish I rode back to our caravan, gave Janny the bike — she claimed I threw it at her — and fell on the ground exhausted. I was surprised how painful it was. During the second 250 race I was hit by a bike that had lost its rider. The spill was more spectacular than damaging but was sufficient justification for me to retire. The Métisse handled the conditions well and, after several retirements during the second race, I was awarded fifth place overall.

The next weekend's race was just over the border in south-east Austria. Murau had an immaculate camping ground in a picturesque setting. For me it was an idyllic situation, living in the comfort of a caravan, two bikes to prepare, a lively 18-month-old daughter helping me and both of us being cared for by a lovely, loving young wife. On Friday, with toddler Caroline I checked out the circuit, which wound through pine trees.

Saturday morning was overcast, by midday it was raining, became heavier and continued all night. Parts of the track become a quagmire. It was a 500cc event but as the 250cc Husky was by far the easiest to pick up I wisely decided to use that. While the conditions were bad, the track was rideable. Four very good Swedish riders on their superb 500cc Monarks and Husqvarnas showed the rest how to do it. Some of us were badly in need of the example. As expected I occasionally fell off, mainly using the frontal exit over the bars. There could be a rock, tree stump, rut or similar in the liquid mud but the landings were soft. The advantage of these misadventures was that when I was lapped by the top guys I was fast enough to keep up with them and able to observe and learn, that is until the next misadventure delayed me.

I learned a lot during the first two long races, allowing me to finish a very creditable sixth in the third. The pleasing thing was that while upright I was as fast as the best. Now to learn how to stay on the thing; it is much easier to slow a rider down than it is to speed them up. Next day, with Caroline's assistance, I happily laboured away cleaning the gear.

The Wimpassing meeting was near Vienna, on a circuit in a valley with the track on one side, the crowd opposite and the start-straight along the valley floor. Again I had entered both 250 and 500 classes. My best result was second in one of the 250cc races and I gained fourth overall in both classes, a great effort. Burly John Burton, an ex-works BSA rider, only just beat me for third in the 500 class. The motocross atmosphere was friendly, open and social.

Yep, three or four years of this, after I've had my fill of road racing, will do just fine, I thought; I don't have to fit anyone else's agenda. I can retire from road racing when I please. Return home when it suits me and my family. There, that has taken care of the next few years. Now it's a two-day drive up to Assen.

Before flying to Japan on October 9 I needed to prepare parts, tools, spares, my two motocross bikes and get all our belongings packed in the van and shipped home. It would land in New Zealand within days of our arrival and allow us the option of staying in New Zealand, if that was our decision.

Then it was once more on a flight over the North Pole, a stop at frozen Anchorage, Alaska, and on to Haneda Airport, Tokyo, to be met by a guide and taken via the bullet train to Hamamatsu. A well-travelled, familiar route to the Japanese Grand Prix. Word had just got out that Honda had completed a five-cylinder 125 and had been lapping Suzuka at record-breaking speeds. Duplicating the technology used in their 50cc twin-cylinder racers had created yet another brilliant race bike. First a six-cylinder 250, now a five-cylinder 125. Amazing, and I am employed to beat them? Having our own test track helped our preparation. My 125 went well, but we were unable to find why one of the cylinders on the 50 started blowing back through the carburettor at particular revs. It might misfire at 17,300rpm but was okay at 17,200 or 17,400.

Practice went well enough on the 125 and I lapped just under the record I had set the previous year. The sensational Honda five-cylinder 125s were fast and reliable. Their 22,000rpm engines produced a strange, piercingly deafening exhaust note that drowned the circuit in noise. Even when riding your own bike you could never pinpoint where they were. With this being a Honda-owned track, they had the advantage of testing daily long before the event. Even though the 50cc engine problem continued to mystify, we had managed to break Ralph Bryans' lap record from last year by a significant 6.2 seconds. There was much hope that atmospheric conditions on race day would be in our favour: cold and wet. Mike Duff fell heavily during 250cc practice, badly fracturing his hip, yet another victim of the pressure always present here. Yamaha flew in Bill Ivy as his replacement. Luigi and Ralph were fastest in 125 practice. I was third, Jim Redman fourth, then Phil Read, Bill Ivy, Frank Perris and various Japanese riders on factory bikes followed.

All three Hondas made an excellent start in the 125 race. Just my luck to have mine refusing to fire until the rest had gone. The race was well advanced before I managed to get past Perris, Ivy, Read and Bryans into second place. By this time Luigi had a 10-second lead. All I could do was press on. Lowering my times by fractions of a second each lap, I gained a little but not enough. Trying even harder had me in an out-of-the-seat, feet-off-the-foot-pegs moment at Spoon corner, a long right-hander. Second was all I could do today. Then, at three-quarter distance, the gap seemed to close. Another lap and, yes, it was definitely closing. With two laps to go I swept past Luigi and on to the chequered flag.

Top: Congratulations from Luigi Taveri and Ralph Bryans after winning the 125cc race. Archives.

Above: Nagata-san and I drink a toast to our success and hopes of a fast-healing process. Archives.

It had taken three years and last year's disappointment, but I had at last won a Japanese Grand Prix and with a new race record. Luigi nursed his Honda home in second, with Ralph and Bill a whopping 42 seconds behind. I had lapped Frank, while Phil and Jim had retired. This event was recognised as probably the toughest and most important race of the year. Last year I had scorched off to a big lead only to have the race taken from me by a minor mechanical problem. This time it was Luigi's turn. That is Grand Prix racing.

The 50cc championship was close on paper. Ralph and I were equal on 32 points and Luigi third on 27. But due to the championship rules I had to win the race and Ralph finish no higher than fourth. Yet again I made a poor start. The bike ran fine for five laps allowing me, while setting a new lap record, to catch and pass Ralph and Luigi, only for the feared misfire to begin. It cleared, I put two great laps together and took over the lead again only for the problem to return. I was far from pleased. As we rode around a fast right-hand downhill corner into the main straight I heard Luigi coming around the outside. I took a very wide line, almost to the grass, hoping to deter him, but he persisted. The track narrowed abruptly, so I moved over and he rode past on the left, while Ralph passed me on the right.

After working so hard making several new lap records, I wasn't ready to give in. Through a series of right, left, right, left, right corners, with the engine blop, blop, blopping back through one carburettor I closed right up on them. A long flat-out, tucked-in-under-the-screen, on-the-limit left-hand corner followed. The rear tyre let go and in a blink I went down.

At these times so much happens so fast your reactions in trying to protect yourself are far too slow. First it was my left foot trapped under the bike, the boot being torn off and the flesh of my foot being ground away. Then a hand, an elbow and the other hand. As quick as you might be in moving them and your body, you are always too late. Marshals lifted the bike and, as I began to limp away, an official rushed over and handed me a sheet of paper and pen to sign it. I'm afraid it was a case of very bad timing. I tore it up and gave it back to him. The medical team did a good job cleaning up the cuts and bruises, but my left foot was quite bad. A distinctive 'flat' had been worn on it. That night the winners and their bikes were to be on display on a national television show in Tokyo. Both hands and elbow were bandaged. My foot, although being well covered, was freely seeping blood from my open sandal wherever I stood. The Suzuki officials pleaded with me to take the bullet train to Tokyo and appear on the show as Honda had won the other three races. Reluctantly, I agreed. We were filmed sitting on our bikes where I did my best to keep my battered hands in my pockets and my bloodied foot out of sight.

'Hugh Anderson, when his Suzuki went well, was quite unbeatable. A prolific maker of lap records. No one wins world titles unless they possess that fine edge that allows a rider to go from being really good to brilliant. Hugh had it in bucketfuls and used his skills wisely.'

— *Ralph Bryans, World Champion*

CHAPTER 14

To experience a mother's glowing pride and calling on a strange old bugger in Invercargill

One of my first thoughts after winning two world championships during 1963 was to retire. My original reason and ambition had never risen to such heights. This is special, I am so fortunate and I'm out of here, I'd thought. But I stayed on.

At the end of each season the same thoughts occurred but another reason to continue had too easily been justified. The thought persisted that after demonstrating one of my factory bikes in New Zealand, I should quit. It seemed a common sense thing to do. Feeling I'd be in a better position to decide when back in the relaxed comfort of home, I flew back to Holland after agreeing to but not signing a contract for 1966.

The screech of tyres as they hit the concrete landing strip at Auckland's new Mangere Airport signified the possible end of a demanding racing career and my much loved European lifestyle. It would be replaced by a permanent return to the pleasantly laidback and slightly predictable Kiwi way.

We exited passport control and met again the familiar faces that had greeted us two years ago. Caroline had coped with the 40-hour trip better than we had and was delighted with the attention she was given. Having always had caring people around her applauding literally each new step in her development, her attention-seeking special was going down on her hands and feet and lifting one foot high in the air. Some of the faces of the welcoming party wore questioning looks. Others followed

October 1965 arriving home tired but happy. New Zealand Herald.

our lead and laughed and applauded. She regained her feet and with hands on hips looked around her with the confidence of an experienced circus performer. Enjoying the fuss, she smiled and did it again. Sure is good to be back.

I had harboured the ambition to bring a 125 to New Zealand since that double-championship year. I spoke to Mr Okano about it but it went no farther. The bikes had been rather poor during 1964 and having an ongoing desire to further my motocross skills, we had wintered over in England during 1964–65.

Due to my doubts about my future in road racing, the New Zealand 1965–66 season had to be the one. The timing was right, the bikes reliable and performing brilliantly. After my having won so many races and set even more records, the New Zealand public deserved to have the chance of seeing one of the bikes in action.

Generally, the team leadership would agree to reasonable requests. The procedure was that you would float an idea and wait for a reply. If there wasn't one, it wasn't going to happen. This occurred after my initial request. So I asked again. Still no response. Mitsuo Itoh, who had won the 1963 50cc race on the Isle of Man, held considerable respect within the team, spoke English and was being groomed for leadership. He was aware of my request and the lack of response. He took me to one side and said, "Speak to Mr Suzuki." I saw him quite frequently so the next time we met, after explaining the reasons why, I asked him if it could be arranged. Without hesitation he said yes.

A complete bike with a spare engine was prepared. I tested the bike before leaving Japan after the final Grand Prix. It gave 32hp with a top speed of 209kph. To simplify the shipping and importing arrangements, the crate was sent to Percy Coleman Ltd, the Suzuki importers in Wanganui.

We settled back home in Ohinewai and the van and its contents were cleared through Customs with the minimum of fuss and cost. Having my racing gear at hand gave me direction. For so long these basic possessions had been my job security, enjoyment and profession.

On December 15 I attended the first round of Tim Gibbes' seven-race International Gold Leaf Series motocross at Woodville, near Palmerston North. Tim, a vastly experienced international motocross and International Six Day Trials gold medal-winning rider, had contracted a group of internationals including American Paul Hunt, Triumph Métisse, Englishman Frank Underwood, Triumph-engined Wasp, and Swede Burt Lundin, brother of world champion Sten Lundin, on a Lito. All the top Kiwis took part, including Ken Cleghorn, Cheney Matchless, who had enjoyed two successful years overseas, Tim Gibbes, national champion Alan Collison and many more. I won the 250 class and came third in the main race. With such a large crowd swelling the gate, Tim would have slept well that night.

At the Christchurch event the following weekend, I won the 250, was second in the 500cc classic event and was again third in the Gold Leaf race (Gold Leaf tobacco was the series sponsor). Seven days later in Timaru I finished in the same three positions. Next it was time to debut the 125cc Suzuki at the Wanganui road race on Boxing Day. As in 1963 the traditional Cemetery Circuit was unavailable so the organising club had to use a part-seal, part-shingle circuit out in the countryside at Matarawa. The Suzuki was put on display at Coleman Suzuki where its sleek, purposeful lines were a drawcard for motorcycle fans.

We couldn't race it on the full circuit as the carburettors, sitting low on each side of the engine, would suck in sand and grit thrown up by the front wheel on the unsealed section. But I would demonstrate it at lunch time, making a few passes using just the start-finish straight and the winding, downhill, sealed section.

A large silent crowd gathered as we prepared to start the Suzuki for the first time. Unlike four-strokes, these engines need very little warming up. I let it burble away quietly for 30 seconds, then gave it a 12,000rpm burst that had people literally recoiling from the unexpected and shattering noise of it. All the previous small-capacity racing two-strokes they had seen were smoky, feeble things. I rode up the start-finish straight in the opposite direction taken by the competitors and as far as possible beyond where they entered it from a side road. To impress, I wanted to arrive at the start-finish and sweeping left-hand corner faster than any of the racers had and sweep as close as I dared to the spectators as they leaned forward in anticipation then tore up and down the hill as fast as possible. In the silence of the moment the speed, noise and the business of constant gear-changing was totally unexpected. That very special 14,000rpm motorcycle could be seen and heard perfectly at all times. The impact on those present could not have been greater.

During the Christmas period, the Tauranga Motorcycle Club also ran a short-circuit road race in their port city. These meetings, where speeds were not high and the competition laid-back, made for a low-key occasion. But with two very slow and one medium fast corners and the circuit just one-kilometre long, it was not the place where a 125cc Grand Prix bike would normally be expected to be used, let alone excel. However, by gearing it right during practice and with an indestructible clutch, I was able to keep the engine screaming. By changing gears up to 32 times per lap, I managed to be competitive. At the time, Mum lived nearby at a beach resort, so for just the second time she attended a race meeting. She was waiting by my van when I returned to the pits after winning the first race. Her eyes sparkled, her face was radiant and years seemed to have fallen from her countenance. I removed my helmet and hugged her.

For the first time, she had seen me in my element, understood the reason for my years of commitment and was immensely proud of me, who I had become and the standing I had within New Zealand motorcycle sport. With Mum having held a very responsible position, her family depending on her and frequently being barely above survival most of her life, she would have had difficulty coming to terms with my apparent carefree attitude to life. She had no way of knowing how deeply I had considered my situation and future back on the Isle of Man in 1962. Our values had been miles apart; perhaps they still were but an understanding had been realised.

In what was shaping up to be a busy summer, I prepared for the New Zealand Grand Prix, to be held at Pukekohe on January 8. It was also the first round of the Tasman Cup series for cars, with such famous names as Jackie Stewart, Graham Hill, Phil Hill, Jim Clark and New Zealander Bruce McLaren taking part. This was New Zealand's motorsport event of the year and the first test of how the 125 would compete head-on with the country's best riders on 350cc and 500cc British bikes. The motorcycle races that were run carried New Zealand TT status. Dave Kenah was with me and for the sake of reliability, we ran the engine marginally on the rich side. With the gearing sorted, in practice the little bike was buzzing effortlessly past many of the bigger machines. The 350 race was our first and I was able to clear off and win it easily. The 500cc event was a much greater challenge, as several well-developed Manx Nortons and the G50 of Dunedin's Neville Landrebe were all capable of winning.

The Suzuki started well and at the end of the long back straight I was still close to Neville. I braked quite late but just could not scrub off speed as fast as he did. As we approached the hairpin, my front wheel was on the inside of his rear. He peeled off into the corner a little earlier than I expected, clipping my wheel, and down I went. Luckily it was a gentle affair and little damage was done. The real problem with falling so early in the race was trying to get back on the track. I had to wait impatiently as 35 bikes droned by. Once clear, I restarted and began what appeared to be a hopeless chase. The bike was okay and I was sufficiently annoyed by my witless mistake to make a spirited effort. I was able to scythe through the slower riders during the first three laps. The banshee scream of the Suzuki's exhausts and the constant gear-changing that eight speeds demanded added heightened drama to the spectacle. At the beginning of the last lap I lay third, quickly moving into second 150 metres behind leader Neville. A bike length separated us at the chequered flag.

Top: On Mangere Mountain leading Frank Underwood, the star guest from the UK. Archives.
Above: Gaining a reasonable amount of air on a bike that was twice my weight. Archives.

The chase had roused the crowd. The ingredients were volatile: small bike and world champion against a larger bike and national champion. A journalist described it as 'the race of the decade'.

The day after Pukekohe, the fifth round of Tim Gibbes' Gold Leaf motocross series was run at Mangere Mountain in Auckland. Again I won the 250cc race, and took my Métisse to second in the 500cc Classic and third in the main Gold Leaf event.

Levin was New Zealand's first purpose-built racetrack and had a relatively tight layout that tested brakes. During practice I slid off on the slowest corner. My first thoughts were whether motocross had caused me to become optimistic regarding braking points. I had taken for granted that I could out-brake virtually anyone, as I had done over the years, but I was now finding my brakes to be inadequate. They had been okay when competing against other 125s, but the British bikes stopped better. During the races I was using the hand adjuster to take up the excess slack in the cable as the drum expanded with the heat it generated, but back in the pits when the brake cooled, the wheel would be locked solid. The efforts of the day produced two second places.

The race team management expected regular reports on the results gained and the performance of the bike. In one of these, I asked for an improved version of the front brake, advising that simply converting the present double-sided single-leading shoe to a double-sided twin-leading shoe arrangement would increase its power considerably.

The busy season continued the next day with the Hamilton Motorcycle Club's major motocross meeting back up north at Gees Farm, Whatawhata, where it had all begun, with five wins, when I was just 17 years old. There I was presented with a life membership by the Hamilton Motorcycle Club and won most of the races.

Bob Coleman, his wife Chic and their two boys enjoyed a holiday in the South Island transporting the Suzuki to the last two major events of the season. Janny, Caroline and I flew to the South Island where Tom McLeary, a major Suzuki dealer, loaned us a car. The Lady Wigram Trophy event in Christchurch was held at the airfield used by the Royal New Zealand Air Force. Like Ardmore and Ohakea, this event had illustrious traditions. The main straights were two landing strips connected by taxiways, fast left- and right-hand curves that swept around the control tower into a slow left-hander leading into a long back straight, a left turn onto a taxiway followed by another into the start-finish straight. It provided width, space and challenge for all the competitors. A bonus was ample parking and spectator space for the huge crowd, and ease of control and low cost for the organisers.

The four top New Zealand racers were competing. I was facing Ginger Molloy, with a freshly rebuilt 250cc Bultaco engine after major problems at Levin, Christchurch's international rider Tommy McCLeary, and Neville Landrebe. By the end of the second lap of the first race Ginger, Neville and I were in close formation. My 125 was a little slower in acceleration and I was being cautious under brakes, but the few metres lost could be regained through the fast swerves past the control tower. As the race progressed, Neville and Ginger became involved in a contest of wills. Their fairings clashed more than once under brakes and when entering corners. Under the circumstances I was content to be an entertained observer. The closeness of the contest was such that even the international car drivers were taking a very keen interest. Later

I spoke to Jackie Stewart. He had been a close friend of fellow Scot the late Bob McIntyre. Due to that friendship he had attended motorcycle events in Scotland and had a keen understanding and respect for the motorcycle racing fraternity.

I had been told that when in Invercargill, competing at the last round of the international car series, we should visit an interesting old bloke. It seemed that he

Working from the back of the Percy Coleman Ltd van. Fred Williams, a friend from our teenage years, looks on. Archives.

Burt Munro during the 1950s with his absolutely remarkable 1920 Indian, which morphed into this 300kph record-breaking streamliner that spawned a highly successful film, The World's Fastest Indian, *directed by Roger Donaldson. Neville Hayes.*

had, for many years, been modifying an old English motorcycle and, of all things, an even older American bike, for beach racing and flying quarter-mile speed events. One well-intentioned chap claimed his British bike had been timed at over 210kph and the American one at something like 240kph. In my position, from time to time, you meet people who want to impress and you hear this sort of thing. As it happened, we did have an afternoon spare and Janny, Bob Coleman and I carefully followed the directions given and pulled up outside a concrete block shed surrounded by long grass. We walked along car wheel tracks to a large open door and there in an untidy workshop was a scruffy old bloke operating a small lathe.

I knocked on the wall, no response, I called to him, still no response, so I shouted but all to no avail. Obviously he was deaf. I stepped carefully over all sorts of motorcycle bits and pieces and got into a position to catch his eye. He stopped the lathe and looked at me quizzically. Speaking loudly, I said: "I'm Hugh Anderson, I've been told to come and see you."

"Oh, I've heard of you," he said. "You ride those little Japanese things. I like these old bikes," he said, pointing at his two rustic speed machines. "They really make a bang, especially when something breaks."

He liked an audience and was soon in full flight regard the speeds he had achieved and the parts that had broken. This included almost everything in an engine and, as evidence, they were lined up on long shelves — pistons, con rods, cylinders, crankshafts and valves. Broken pistons seemed to be his speciality; 20, perhaps 30 were on display. He wanted me to sit on the bike that he had cut and welded, lowered, lengthened and added to, with a tiny fuel tank and a huge carburettor that he had made, poking out behind.

"Lie down on it," he instructed. The handlebars were way down around the level of the front wheel rim. The footrests were somewhere near the rear wheel axle. "Oh, you look good," he said. "It would go faster with you on it. You're so light and much slimmer than me."

Well, we will never know. I would be reluctant to do 100kph on it, let alone 200kph.

He showed us how he made his own aluminium pistons in a homemade mould and machined his con rods from Caterpillar tractor axles. Evidence of food preparation was invisible and apart from bike bits and some machine tools and spanners, there seemed to be little else in the shed other than an unmade single bed.

It had all been very interesting, most of it unbelievable, but the speed certificates pinned to the wall were proof enough not only of his engineering ability, knowledge of mixing exotic fuels (the main ingredient being nitromethane), but his apparent fearless approach to riding the crude-looking things. Soon after the compulsory cup of tea (we missed out on the fruit cake as it had gone mouldy) we left. Well, our advisers were not wrong. A strange old bugger is that Burt Munro.

Some years after our visit an award-winning documentary, based on a live interview with Burt, was made for television by Roger Donaldson. This in time led to a highly successful feature film, *The World's Fastest Indian*, with Anthony Hopkins in the main role. This too was directed by Roger Donaldson.

At Teretonga in Invercargill, New Zealand's second-oldest purpose-built circuit, the main races were again a duel between Neville Landrebe and me. Ginger had crashed in practice and was unable to take any further part. Neville and I were close throughout the first race. As always, the 500cc G50 had better acceleration and brakes but the Suzuki was more nimble through the corners. We finished the first race 20m apart. Having full knowledge of the track I felt that if I could pass Neville through the corners on the back part during the second race, it could be possible to create a large enough gap to beat him to the finish line. The idea was great but as was to be expected the G50 had superior acceleration compared to the 125, and he beat me to the line by a bike length.

Once again the noisy little 125, with its multitude of gears and 14,000 revs, really impressed the spectators. Of course, that was why the bike was here: a speedy, noisy PR exercise.

Having enjoyed every facet of our stay, my enthusiasm for racing had been rekindled. I had only just had my 30th birthday, time was on my side. I signed and returned my contract with Suzuki, ordered a new van and a pair of CZ motocross machines.

Kitty litter of the 60s. Maurice Bula.

CHAPTER 15

Suddenly a scream of sirens and being surrounded by heavily armed military police; I had no idea that we were so important

RETIREMENT AND REFLECTIONS DURING MY LAST VISIT TO THE ISLE OF MAN

The 1966 season saw the most exotic line-up of Grand Prix motorcycles ever. It was a time when factories were enjoying rapidly increasing exports to a hungry, ever-expanding world market. These sales were also reinvigorating the motorcycle ethos throughout the traditional markets of the wealthy Western world. This was a time when machine development had never been so creative, expansive and dramatic. A time when one Grand Prix season did not just roll on into another.

Yamaha had 125cc twins and 250cc fours. Suzuki had dropped their 250cc four and we were campaigning the same 50cc and 125cc twins as last season. Honda were using their 50cc twins, 125cc fives, 250cc and 350cc sixes and a new 500cc four. MV had 350cc and 500cc three-cylinder machines. Benelli had 250cc and 350cc fours. The exhaust notes of these multi-cylinder machines were quite amazing and a very important part of the show. Bultaco and Aermacchi had improved their bikes considerably and now Mondial and Montesa had entered the 125 class and Husqvarna the 250. Every class of competition had a new level of technical excellence.

Kreidler had withdrawn from Grand Prix to concentrate successfully on taking the 50cc world speed record and Hans Georg Anscheidt had joined the Suzuki team. Superstar Mike Hailwood was now with Honda. New attendance records were set at every motorcycle race meeting throughout Europe. But first I had to deal with the news of the death of another friend and fellow racer. My English mate Sid Mizen was killed at Le Mans on April 2. Aged 37, he had said he was planning to retire at the end of the season. Sid was slipstreaming another rider during the first lap on the 7km Mulsanne straight when the bike ahead seized. He crashed into it, was thrown against a tree and killed instantly.

Ever cheerful Sid, who had said the pit area was pretty dull when I wasn't around. Sid, the friend I had passed in practice at Assen in 1962, slowing to show him the lines before crashing and damaging a knee, an injury that helped get Janny and I back together. A good bloke who loved racing and tended to ride within his limits. He had finished fourth in the 350 and 13th in the 500cc class at the 1963 Isle of Man TT, earning the trophy for the best aggregate performance for a rider of a British machine. But he had been caught out in France. The loss of yet another, but it had little effect. If you go off racing a motorcycle you could be killed. Any fool knows that. It's like joining the Army — you are playing with deadly weapons and when the time comes to use them, someone is going to get hurt. I had seen too much of it and it had little effect now.

As they had last year, Suzuki made bikes available for Frank, Hans and me to take part in two pre-Grand Prix international meetings for all-important practice. I decided to ride at the Nürburgring on April 24, the Austrian Grand Prix on May 1 and then meet up with the team at the Spanish Grand Prix on May 8. To improve reliability, experimental separate oil pumps had replaced pre-mixed oil and petrol to help extend the life of the crankshaft bearings. Testing and time were needed to adjust the pump output and gain the reliability advantage without oiling the plugs. In the time available and without the assistance of mechanics, I erred on the safe side, going for conservative settings to avoid engine seizures.

At Nürburgring the 50cc race was between Hans and me. Being on his home circuit he was highly motivated. We rode together for five of the seven laps, but when I tried to increase my pace, a persistent misfire allowed Hans to go on to a comfortable win.

I had made the fastest lap in the 125cc practice and looked forward to having a dice with Luigi, on a Honda four. Soon after the start, my bike suffered from yet another oiled spark plug. The new pump had dumped a lot of oil in the engine when it was being warmed up. This took time to clear and, being rather impatient, I'd used full throttle too soon. At the end of the lap I changed both plugs and set off in last position, intending to have an enjoyable ride if nothing else. The track was wet in places but safe enough. At the end of the 80km race I found myself in third place having set the fastest lap.

Then it was a pleasant return to Salzburg, home of the Austrian Grand Prix, one of my favourite meetings. Having won last year, even though Luigi was here again on the four-cylinder Honda, I knew there was a good chance of a repeat. Practice went well, with Janny and Caroline 'manning' my pit. The Suzuki was running better than at the Nürburgring. I gained pole position, breaking the lap record I had set last year in the process. Twenty minutes before the race, I began warming the engine, but just when I was about to switch it off it gave a pop, bang and stopped. What the hell was that all about? Having no option I carried on as normal, changed the plugs and lined up at the start. The flag dropped and I kept pushing and pushing. It fired often enough to keep me pushing in the hope it might run well enough, or long enough, to qualify for the substantial start money at stake. But no, the crankshaft had broken.

The organisers too were disappointed; having Luigi and I there they had hoped for a close race. That evening we had an interesting discussion regarding the percentage of start money they would pay. My view was that, like myself, the spectators had arrived not knowing I wouldn't be able to start the race, so I should be paid the full amount. Their view was that all riders were expected to complete at least 10 to 20 per cent of the race to warrant full payment. I replied that I had run a kilometre with the thing and had almost collapsed from exhaustion (which wasn't far from the truth) so I had done my best to comply. The ace in their pack was that someone had told them my engine had failed before the race. The discussion was good humoured and I asked them what they thought was fair. They offered 75 per cent of our agreed amount. I was happy with that and we parted, as we always had, on very good terms.

As in previous years, the long drive from the cold of northern Europe into the welcoming warmth of a Spanish spring released me from the depression I invariably felt when surrounded by stark, skeletal trees and a cold, colourless countryside. This was the true beginning of the new season and optimism became my friend. As in most years, this was the first occasion when the performance of the new season's bikes, and the riders, would be truly tested. There was no place to hide at Montjuich Park right in the centre of the beautiful Catalan city of Barcelona.

The worst part of the track had been resurfaced and all lap records were smashed during practice. In the 50cc class Luigi, Ralph, Hans and I had lapped in similar times. From the start of the race the locally manufactured Derbis of José Busquets and Salvadore Conallas whipped into the lead but at the end of the lap Luigi led with Ralph and me disputing second place. Hans had made a poor start but was gaining on us. On the seventh of the 10 laps Hans got by Ralph and me to take second place as all three of us crossed the line in close formation. Ralph was third with me fourth.

As was expected in the 125cc class, the seven high-tech works bikes, in practice, dominated the field of 30. Read, Taveri, Ivy and I were the fastest but there wasn't much in it. In the race, five riders arrived at the hairpin after the start in close formation. Having so little flywheel effect, the engines of Bryans' and Taveri's Hondas stalled and they had to restart. In the general melee that followed I took some chances, and at the end of the first lap led from Ivy, Read, Anscheidt and Perris. Unfortunately, my lead was short-lived. On the second lap both my and Anscheidt's bike seized, leaving Ivy out in front and no one could catch him.

The 250cc race had all the ingredients for an epic battle between the Honda sixes of Redman and Hailwood, the Yamahas of Read and Ivy, and the mercurial Provini on the four-cylinder Benelli. Redman led from the start but a spectacular 130kph crash on the first lap turned his Honda into a fireball. Hailwood got past and in the confusion gained a 10-second lead over Provini, eventually cruising to a win.

As the organisers of the French Grand Prix had not included the 50cc or 125cc racers in their 1966 programme, I entered the San Remo International in Italy. The enlightened organisers were the first to pay the amount of start money I requested, 450,000 lire, today roughly $NZ8,000. We enjoyed a long drive around the Mediterranean coast through exotic Nice, Cannes and the city state of Monte Carlo to this resort town on the Italian Riviera close to the French border. The circuit had a long straight that curved gently to the right before a tight uphill left-hander and through an assortment of corners, then down onto the straight again. This ran behind a long row of hotels that fronted the main road and the sea beyond. On just the fourth lap of the first practice the Suzuki began holding back towards the end of the straight. I lifted the clutch to find the motor was free so I did another lap with the same result, so I pulled out.

I fitted larger jets for the second practice but the same thing occurred. Then, as I accelerated uphill from the first left-hand corner, the gearbox locked solid, dumping me heavily on the road. What the hell caused that, I wondered, as I impatiently dragged it to one side. A broken crankshaft at Salzburg, an engine seizure at Barcelona and now a gearbox lock-up. When on full gas at 200kph on a curved straight the gearbox had been at the point of seizure due to a collapsed bearing. That fast section had unprotected concrete walls, gates and pillars. There is nothing more to add. Once more the wrangle over start money had to be endured. Surprisingly, officials who had spoken English very well on my arrival seemed to have become hard of hearing and lost their fluency. Finally, they gave me half the agreed amount.

There was no need to hurry up to Hockenheim so we had three lazy days in this internationally recognised, upmarket holiday resort. I was not thinking of the next race or how to improve my performance. Caroline had become our focus. At two years she was speaking English and Dutch fluently and was a born entertainer.

Cause for thought. Oiled plugs at the Nürburgring.
Broken crankshaft at Salzburg. Piston seized at the
Spanish Grand Prix. Now the gearbox has locked solid
at San Remo. Archives.

Janny and I were completely smitten. We set aside the time to enjoy this luxury of sharing the world, as seen through the eyes of our unspoilt child. Caroline could have quite strong views on things and with hands on hips she would nod her head in agreement with herself. As with most young parents, during times like this, our union grew ever stronger. The feeling of fulfilment and completeness bound us closer.

Arriving at Hockenheim for the West German Grand Prix, we received the totally unexpected news that the Isle of Man TT would be postponed or even cancelled due to a shipping strike. When the dust had settled, a decision was made to run it in late August after the Ulster Grand Prix.

As a motorway had been built on part of the old original circuit, the Hockenheim owners had constructed a new, state-of-the-art 'motordrome'. There were massive grandstands and a line of roomy, immaculate pits near the start-finish area. From the start a right-hand bend took us on to a long straight that was a section of the old course, and into a fast tightening right that led us into a chicane and back onto a long straight to the beginning of the arena section. This consisted of a right, left and a double right into the start-finish straight. Laid out in the oxygen-producing pine forest, which had given our two-strokes a slight advantage in 1963, this circuit gave me high hopes of a favourable result.

Ansheidt made the fastest lap in the 50cc class practice with Luigi, me and Ralph all within a second or so. A good start and the required skills to hold the slipstream of anyone on a faster bike would be essential on such a high-speed circuit. Hans and I got away well, but Luigi and Ralph's very special Hondas did not. I led for two laps but on the third the engine tightened momentarily. Keeping the throttle wide open and using the cut-out button to kill the engine allowed cold air to cool the pistons. Opening the choke lever a little more gave the engine more fuel and oil so I was able to continue. Understandably, the engine had lost some power and Hans slowly pulled away. Ralph, now steaming along on his Honda, also caught me. We got involved in some cut-and-thrust friendly rivalry, but he had the edge and pinched second from me with Luigi fourth. Hans enjoyed the top step of the podium; after three years of effort and close finishes on his Kreidler he was finally celebrating his first home Grand Prix win in front of 130,000 fans.

The 125cc class promised to provide the closest racing of the day. Honda, Suzuki and Yamaha had entered; all the works riders qualified in a tight group with Read, Yamaha, being marginally the fastest. Phil led from the start, but by the end of the first lap Taveri had taken over and Phil was lurking in his slipstream. Behind were Ivy, Yamaha, me, Ralph and Hans Georg Anscheidt. Seconds earlier I had been slipstreaming Hans as we approached the right-hand corner that led us into the grandstand-lined infield. Long before I expected him to, he sat up and hit the brakes. I avoided him, and what could have been my nastiest, highest speed crash ever, by millimetres.

It's the near miss that gives you the biggest fright, the spine tingle was more like a rattle! Luigi and his five-cylinder Honda had too much steam for Phil's Yamaha and he inched ahead. I passed Bill and closed on Phil, only to have Ralph ride past. I sat in Ralph's slipstream and we caught Phil and rode past him entering the infield. Phil hit back but Ralph re-passed on the long straight after the start and, like Luigi, slowly pulled ahead, leaving Phil and me to do battle. We swapped places for several laps as we fought over third place; then my Suzuki cut out on one cylinder and that was that. Frank finished fourth, a long way back, and Hans, after changing plugs, gained fifth, a lap behind. Bill had problems all race and finally finished ninth.

Hailwood comfortably won the 250cc and 350cc races on 'the screeching' six-cylinder Hondas, and Redman, on the new Honda 500cc four, had an easy win over

Phil Read and I actively engaged yet again. Archives.

MV-mounted Agostini. Winning four of the five solo classes was a very convincing display of Honda's technical superiority. The name Stuart Graham was appearing ever more frequently among the first six race finishers. Now in his second Grand Prix season, the son of English legend Les Graham gained a very creditable fourth place on a 500cc Matchless G50 single.

Back home in Assen preparing for the Dutch TT, I noticed more and more New Zealand flags hanging from the apartments in the square facing ours in Schaperstraat. Having so much overt support was well intentioned but, as mentioned earlier, created tension, expectation and a diversion that was not compatible with my well-planned routine. Having unpredictable machines that year didn't help the situation. As in all the preceding years, Assen did not close on the night before the TT. The floodlit streets were packed with noisy crowds celebrating the country's biggest sporting event. At dawn they slowly emptied as the revellers made their way to the nearby circuit. Let the battle begin.

As in 1964, all season we had been having difficulty finding workable carburettor settings for both the 50s and 125s. It was no different here in practice. After my best 50cc engine seized during Thursday afternoon's practice, I was left trying to get my second bike up to speed during Friday morning's short session. Time was running out as final adjustments were made. I needed to cover two laps to allow the spark plugs and piston to gain the carbon colour from which we could read the heat of the combustion chamber and decide what further carburettor adjustments might be required.

The flag marshal, a man known as 'The Major' (pronounced 'Mayor' in English) played a very public role, and was aware of it. When he waved the finishing flag, indicating the end of practice, all the riders were expected to stop immediately and return to the paddock. I passed him flat on the tank looking the other way and continued for another lap. I came out of the last corner, close to the finish line, to be confronted with a rather agitated Major dancing about in the middle of the road furiously waving his flag. I went to ride to his right. He moved to block me. I turned to his left. He ran that way. I couldn't stop so feinted to the right and accelerated to his left, passed him, cut the engine and returned to the pits. The plugs looked good; one jet size smaller on the left was the only change required.

But the Major was furious. A rider had ignored his instructions and that thousands of spectators had witnessed this heinous action must have really got up his nose. Perhaps I was the first to have done it; all unintentional of course. The organisation was well aware of the publicity value of such an indiscretion and, like the previous year when the Suzuki team had been threatened with disqualification for not conforming to a minor technical rule, I was going to be banned for not obeying the flag marshal. No doubt this minor episode would add a little packing to next morning's multi-page newspaper report. It didn't bother me. Henry Burik, president of the FIM (Fédération Internationale de Motocyclisme) Commission Sportive, was a tall dignified man whom I had spent time with, the previous year, at the Japanese Grand Prix. There was an unmistakable twinkle in his eye when he came to our caravan. A man of few words, he said: "You didn't see that flag indicating the end of practice, did you?" I said "No" and was reinstated. The Japanese, who always get decidedly twitchy over such things, were relieved.

For the first three laps of the 50cc race I mixed it with the two Hondas but after almost coming off on four occasions I ceded to the superior, extremely well-ridden little red screamers of Luigi and Ralph, and settled for third. Anscheidt and Katayama were some 23 seconds further back. Bridgestone had entered 50cc twin-cylinder machines for the first time. Ridden by ex-Suzuki teamster Isao Morishita and Australian big-bike specialist Jack Findlay, they finished sixth and eighth. With seven Japanese factory machines entered and ridden by no less than five current or future world champions, journalists were quick to promote the 125 class as the race of the meeting. As with the 50s, we had difficulty finding optimum settings. The engines were slower than the previous year and more temperamental than ever. During practice no one got near the lap record I made the previous year. I finally qualified fifth after using up most of the practice periods making adjustments in the pits.

For once I led from the start only to have the engine bog down badly, costing me several places before it cleared. From then on I could not get on even terms with the leaders and had to settle for fourth place. Bill Ivy won from Luigi and Phil, my lap record from last year had not been broken, Katayama retired with mechanical problems and Frank had to change plugs and finished

Above: Henry Burik, President of the FIM Commission Sportive, was obviously amused at my indiscretion. Photo by Wolfgang Gruber.

Left: With Bill Ivy at the Dutch TT. Yes, team-mate Phil Read can be a problem. Archives.

12th. I was attempting to fly the Suzuki flag, but for now it was hanging a bit limp around the pole. On a personal note, Mike Duff had finally recovered from the badly broken hip he had received at Suzuka almost eight months before. He was entered on a 125cc Yamaha but naturally his riding was tentative. I had caught Mike in practice, slowed and encouraged him to follow me in the hope that he would benefit from my guidance. He needed to rediscover form quickly as Bill Ivy had taken his place in the team and his future with Yamaha was far from secure. Mike finished sixth in the race.

The following Belgium Grand Prix only ran 250cc, 500cc and sidecars races. I didn't attend; being a spectator wasn't me. But it was interesting to learn that during the rainswept 500cc event, Stuart Graham finished second to Ago after Hailwood retired and Redman crashed out. Being fourth 500 home at Hockenheim, then fourth and fifth at Assen indicated that Stuart had the skills required to compete at the top level. He seemed to be even better in the wet than the dry and, having served an engineering apprenticeship with Rolls-Royce, he obviously had the engineering skills required to prepare his bikes.

A 'riders' union' was formed after the meeting. The top six from each class were invited to become members of a group that intended to create a grading system of international riders based on their finishing positions in international and world championship events from the previous season. This list would be made available to organisers who would accept entries in the order given. This would stop Grand Prix organisers filling their fields at minimum cost with no-hopers on small start money. In due course the group intended to become involved with negotiating a minimum start-money figure. Henry Burik, the well-respected influential member of the FIM, was sympathetic to the riders' initiative. The outcome would be interesting.

Nanou Insermini and Australian Jack Findlay prepare for the start at the Belgium Grand Prix. Maurice Bula.

I was struggling in the lead-up to the East German Grand Prix on July 17. Throughout 1963, part of 1964 and all of 1965 my very important pre-race routine

252

had been based on a reasonably consistent, manageable machine performance. Without this, the results do not and cannot come. Walking out on the start line without a plan, having little idea of how the bike will perform and how many laps you might manage before the spark plugs oil up, a piston seizes or the crankshaft fails is a depressing situation. Gone now was the clear-headed, steely commitment to a winning formula and the confidence to push hard enough to enter that zone where you become unbeatable. For me, this was the reason, the challenge and the reward of Grand Prix racing. As at every round this season, the journalists were again focused on the 125cc class. It was seen as being the most competitive, having the most interest and providing the best racing. Once again all nine of the Japanese factory riders qualified in tight formation with Luigi on pole.

Plagued throughout practice with an inability to find settings to give consistent speed, the final hit came towards the end of practice when a piston seized. Left with no choices we were forced to fit new barrels and pistons but needed to cover up to 20km to run it in and make final adjustments. There was only one option: the autobahn. With 200,000 fans attending, this meeting was the biggest sporting event behind the Iron Curtain and for a few days the racers were above the law. The Japanese respected all local laws, but when the need arose I didn't. Brushing aside their protests, mechanic Matsumoto-san and I loaded the bike and required tools into the van, drove out onto the nearby motorway, warmed it up and I whistled off up the almost deserted, wide concrete strip. Eventually there was a gap in the dividing barrier where I turned and raced back. I continued for a further lap, passing an occasional Trabant or Wartburg car rattling along at 60kph. I've often wondered if the drivers thought, for at least a split second, that perhaps they had taken a wrong turning.

A buzz of activity in the Suzuki pit. Note the stance of the policeman in front of the vast grandstand. Archives.

When I arrived back at the van, two police cars and four coppers were waiting, Matsumoto-san was sitting in the van looking decidedly uneasy. I cut the motor and, with what German I possessed, explained the terrible luck we had suffered during practice and the absolute necessity of running in the new parts fitted to the engine. They asked how long it would take to carry out the task. Thirty minutes should be enough. Okay, we will close the road they replied. One car sped off, a few minutes later I followed, covering the necessary mileage and twice changing the carburettor settings, thanked our highly amused guardians and returned to the paddock.

At the end of the first lap of the 125 race all seven of us, in a crescendo of sound, streamed nose-to-tail through the start. Already my engine was hesitating, the first indication of oiling plugs. Using less and less throttle I tried to clear them but to no avail. At the end of the second lap they had to be replaced. I restarted only to have an ignition problem, but carried on to finish 17th, the lowest position ever in my racing career. Taveri won, followed by Katayama, Ivy, Read, Perris and Bryans. Katayama was in luck. His bike was running as it should and his second place gave the team a much-needed boost.

Janny returns to the caravan after yet another retirement. Jar Sajk.

CZECHOSLOVAKIA, JULY 18, 1966

Having crossed the border from East Germany into Czechoslovakia we decided to spend the night on the edge of a hay field. We were on the western side of a vast shallow valley. Perhaps 7km in the distance I could make out an airfield; that it was not a civilian one was quite obvious but I thought, She'll be right, and ignored it. Before Janny had peeled the potatoes the wail of sirens could be heard, four large cars then roared up the incline and skidded to a halt. A dozen military police armed with submachine guns leapt out and surrounded us.

There was every reason to believe that the next few hours were going to be quite interesting. We were well aware that behind the Iron Curtain the authorities were still operating on a war footing and Janny had reason to be concerned.

Their first demand was to see our cameras; we said we had four and a telephoto lens, then before we could add that three were for friends they demanded to see them. When they found that three of them including the large telephoto lens were still in their display boxes they were disappointed, but took my camera and removed the half-used film.

With shouted commands, we were told to follow them and with two cars ahead and two behind we were escorted to the local police station.

Janny and Caroline were sufficiently dangerous to warrant two armed guards and while the caravan and van were searched, I was taken up several flights of stairs and questioned, in German, as to what I was doing in Czechoslovakia, where I was going and why I was parked near a military aerodrome ad nauseum.

I felt only amusement at all these silly buggers, dressed immaculately and full of the importance that only a dictatorial police state could provide, all huffing and puffing about the threat of an imaginary case of espionage. Janny meanwhile saw other riders driving past on their way to Brno — none stopped. She felt abandoned and feared the isolation.

My bag of documents was brought to us. I showed them my licences, entry forms and so on. They wanted to know if I knew Comrade Stastny and Comrade Havell — of course I did, and added comrades Rossner, Bischoff and Krumholz of East Germany.

Phone calls were made, the film was taken to be developed and coffee and cigarettes were produced, both as awful as the other. I offered them some of my du Maurier from an expensive-looking 25-pack tin, their mood lightened, more phone calls were made and received. After three hours they finally tired of their task and we were escorted, in the dark, to a suitable spot to stay the night.

Janny had not enjoyed the experience but being resolute and strong as always, it wasn't long before she saw the lighter side.

The next test was the Czechoslovakian Grand Prix on July 24. Here the challenging 14km Brno circuit took us from undulating farmland through cobblestoned village streets, stone walls, lampposts, all with hardly a protective straw bale in sight. Taveri and Bryans were fastest in practice followed by Read, Ivy and me. On this, one of the fastest circuits, the gear ratios and engine revolutions showed convincingly that these extremely temperamental 1966 engines were not as fast as the previous year. But to be fair, the Suzuki team wasn't the only one suffering from this heightened period of technological development. Ivy led from the start with Taveri and me close behind. We passed Ivy and I was able to stay in Taveri's slipstream well ahead of Bryans. Already the factory bikes were failing. Katayama and Perris stopped at the pits to change plugs. Read's Yamaha had refused to start and Ivy had stopped to change a plug out on the track. All this happened on the first lap. My bike seemed to be performing really well so I passed Taveri and pressed on. Then, as had happened the previous week, a persistent misfire began on the sixth lap. Slowly, I fell farther back and finished a distant fourth.

As there were ample spares I asked that during the total engine overhaul that followed every Grand Prix the complete ignition system should be changed for the Finnish GP in two weeks. Meanwhile Mike Hailwood was showing his true brilliance in the other classes. By winning the 250cc class he took the world championship title from Read. Then he went on to win the 350 and 500cc classes by comfortable margins from Agostini.

Top: The start of the Czechoslovakian Grand Prix. Bill Ivy, Luigi Taveri and me. Jar Sejk.

Above: Leading Taveri on a damp road until the misfire began. Note the spectators standing in front of the fence. Jar Sajk.

On arrival at Imatra for the Finnish Grand Prix my mechanic, whom I had asked to replace the total ignition system, told me that the problem had been caused by a faulty condenser. I had my doubts and as complete ignition systems were part of the comprehensive stocks carried there seemed little reason not to fit one. The bikes went well enough during practice. As always it was a question of covering four or five laps then stopping to check spark plugs and, from the information these gave, make what adjustments required.

Read and Ivy, on their very good Yamahas, qualified fastest ahead of Taveri and me. From the start Read, Katayama and I led from Taveri and Ivy. Little Bill fought with Luigi and during the ensuing battle they caught and passed Katayama, only for Bill's Yamaha to expire on the fifth lap. I was managing to hang on to Read and my confidence of perhaps a first podium of the season rose. But, as usual, halfway through the 20-lap race the misfire began and I slipped down the order to finish fourth again. Katayama must have had his problems too as he was well over a minute behind me. The Suzuki team had little to celebrate.

I took stock of this dire situation. I knew I had the ability, and that the bike was good enough. The missing link was that it had to be prepared in the traditional manner, where nothing was left to chance. Detail, as always, was the key, but confrontation had become ever more prevalent between rider and support crew. A change in responsibilities seemed to have arisen. There appeared to be a conscious effort by the mechanic to get between me and my bike, which was never the case with Nagata-san. Perhaps it came about due to the race team no longer wanting to have Degner or Anderson bikes. With Degner at the end of his career and doubt regarding me, perhaps the Suzuki personnel needed to gain the knowledge, that we had, in setting up the engine. But at what cost for the company and us?

Confirmation of the potential I felt I still had came at the Hutchinson 100 Trophy event, the oldest in England's mainland motorcycle competition history. The basis of the competition is simple and unique. The trophy winner is the rider whose race average speed is nearest to or faster than the existing record. All solo classes and sidecars are catered for. For many years this much-publicised event had taken place at Silverstone; this year it was at Brands Hatch. To avoid the local scratchers having an advantage, it was decided to run it in the reverse direction. With virtually all the works riders and the big guns of the British short-circuit brigade competing, it had the makings of a meeting with intrigue, witnessed by a vast crowd. A minimum of practice time meant it was a case of who would master the 'new course' in the short time

The oldest award in England's motorcycle racing history. The huge Mellano Trophy. Archives.

available. With my Suzuki running well, I won the race at an average speed that, coincidentally, equalled the current record when run in the normal direction. This was quite an achievement and I was awarded the huge Mellano Trophy.

When we arrived at the Ulster Grand Prix I felt rejuvenated and competitive again. I had every reason to believe that, on one of my favourite circuits and with the promise of having a new ignition assembly installed, I would do well. Two laps into the first practice session, a carburettor jet nut came loose and dropped off, stranding me out on the circuit. Frank was good enough to stop and pillion me back to the pits. On the third lap my spare bike seized. At a reduced pace I returned to the pits, carried the required tools in my boots back to my first bike, exchanged the parts and made the best of what little practice time was left. Having become involved in stripping the engines, it was 1am before I returned to my hotel, mentally flat and physically tired. The only consistency we had now was frustration.

During Thursday's practice we had reduced the jet size to avoid oiling the plugs, only to have a piston seize. We despondently left the circuit that evening being no closer to an answer. On Friday, which was a lay day, Frank and I called into the garage to find the assembled bikes lined up but the place deserted. I'd gone to bed early in the belief that preparation would be carried out as usual on the Friday. It all seemed rather strange. When we phoned the hotel, we were told that the team would be at the track tomorrow morning and meet us there. At the track no one would speak about the situation, apart from saying they had worked through Thursday night and had a free day on Friday when they had gone fishing. We learned later that 'gone fishing' was a euphemism for withdrawing their labour. There had been some discord between the mechanics and managers, about which we were never informed. No doubt this was a contributing factor to our mechanical problems.

This unacceptable level meant my performances were bordering on humiliation. The risk-to-reward ratio was way out of kilter. The weather on race day was not unexpected. As reporter Mick Woollett wrote: 'A near record 70,000 crowd braved the dismal weather.' Rain and glistening wet roads greeted us as we assembled on the starting grid for the 125 race. With Ivy a non-starter due to injuries received at Brands Hatch the previous weekend, Irishman Tommy Robb had taken his place. Read got away to a good start followed by Taveri, Robb, me, Bryans and Perris. Running with a very rich mixture to avoid seizures, I did the best I could, but after just three laps the telltale hesitation and misfire began. Ralph passed me at the top of Deer's Leap as he pressed on. A quick change of plugs allowed me to continue for another four laps before the oiling problem arose again. Another call to the pits. New plugs, and a fifth-place finish was the best I could muster with Frank even farther back.

Our reliability problems and the weather conditions had me operating in survival mode. Any professional sportsman has an obligation to his entrant and sponsors to give his best performance, but there are times in motorcycle racing when the risks become too great. It takes as much courage to back off the throttle and give up an unequal struggle as it does to continue on the ragged edge. The decision I made that day in the rain on a misfiring bike took me out of the darkness and into the refreshing light of relief.

The reasons for competing in Grand Prix no longer existed. I had no hesitation in deciding that this would be my last season of road racing. As the sixth most successful Grand Prix rider in the history of the series, the driving lifelong need to succeed had been satisfied. The residue of ambition had been left in the workshops and the frustrating winding miles of the Ulster Grand Prix. Finally, the fire had been extinguished. There was nothing more for me to gain except a large contract fee but that could never be sufficient justification to continue. I felt okay about it. The decision had been made for me really. I didn't owe anyone anything any more. I had paid my dues and given good value. I felt a strong tension-relieving sense of release. I woke the next day with a clear head and a tingle of optimism, as you do after making a major decision, telling myself, Hugh, you only need to survive another two meetings, concentrate on them and find satisfaction and contentment in what you have achieved.

Later that day a special ferry sailing took riders and their equipment from Belfast to the Isle of Man. That year a record total of nearly 500 entries had been received. Janny and I sat with Stuart and Margaret Graham and Ralph and Sally Bryans who provided pleasant, uplifting company. Having decided that this would be my last TT, I was determined to make the most of it. Forget about the problems we had experienced; it was time to put a smile on my face and make a fresh start.

It might seem hard to believe that on the longest, most demanding and notoriously dangerous track, a rider can, after very few practice laps, circulate as fast or even faster than he had the previous year. First a lap in the van; occasionally I might stop and make a closer detailed study of a complicated section. I would then read my race notes and the recommended improvements from the previous year. Such is the memory, commitment and affinity you must have and feel for this place.

Practice began at 4.30am on Monday, September 2. As soon as the garage had been set up, I began doing what I could on my bikes to try to gain greater reliability. We worked until late. Ralph Bryans made the second-fastest 125cc time on his first lap but on the next his five-cylinder Honda caught fire. Evidently he was lucky to have sufficient time to brake to a halt, get off it and run before it literally exploded and was destroyed. During that first session I concentrated on running in the overhauled engines of both bikes. All went well. During the day the engines were dismantled. I worked on the pistons and made decisions regarding carburettor settings, the spark plugs to be used, suspension settings and gear ratios.

My bike felt good on the first lap of the Monday evening session. After stopping at the pits and changing the jets and spark plugs, I set off on again. I intended to lift my pace, be fast but sufficiently conservative to allow me time to cope with a sudden engine failure. It ran well and I felt exceptionally comfortable and relaxed. The circuit came to me surprisingly effortlessly and I found a flow through the many and varied sequences of corners. I had never expected it to be this easy; it was a great base to build on.

Back at the pits I swapped to my second bike and left on another lap. The engine seemed fine so I lifted my pace. Braking late for the slightly uphill, right-hand turn at the Ballacraine Hotel, I peeled off and dived into the shaded tunnel under the trees. As I opened the throttle again a slight telltale shudder through the footrests jolted me out of my short-lived, uplifted state. The crankshaft had gone. With relief I missed the wall and freewheeled to yet another heart-beating stop. On returning to the garage I was pleased to learn that on that free-flowing second lap I had broken my own record from the previous year. It was reassuring to know that under the circumstances my form was holding.

The first practice for the 50cc class was Tuesday morning. My bike went quite well on the first lap and after I stopped at the pits and changed the carburettor jets and spark plugs, it went even better. This encouraged me to make a real effort and enjoy a fast, crisp, using-all-the-road lap. When the times were announced I was pleasantly surprised to learn that I had broken my existing lap record by no less than 38 seconds. That I was slower through the maximum-speed trap (100mph compared with my winning bike's 103mph in 1964) seemed odd but of course conditions on the island are continuously changing. Sadly, the 125cc I took out for a lap wasn't as obliging, this time seizing before I even got to Ballacraine.

Light drizzle greeted the riders on Wednesday morning. Disappointingly, I had piston-seizing problems on my best 125. After riding it back to the pits, I took out my second bike but it was running too rich and oiled the plugs. That evening Shimizu-san flew in direct from Japan with a new modified engine for me. It was a desperate attempt by Suzuki to get on even terms with the superior Honda and Yamaha machines. Shimizu-san played a key role in the development of not only the Grand Prix engines but also the standard production models.

WHEN A 125 BECAME THE SIXTH-FASTEST SOLO DURING PRACTICE WEEK

During our discussions Shimizu-san said: "This engine is very good, not seize or break crankshaft." Very good news indeed. So far I'd only competed two laps in each class without stopping. Conditions were perfect for Thursday afternoon's lightweight practice. Mike Hailwood broke Jim Redman's 250cc lap record and Bryans demolished my 50cc lap record with an average speed of 141kph. Very impressive for such a small engine. I carefully ran in the rather special 125cc engine. When the cylinders were removed to check the pistons, for once there was no indication of tightening or excess heat. But these engines are capable of only a limited mileage and I was able to do just one more lap at speed before the race. After sitting in the van mentally covering several laps I set off. The personal relationship, good or bad, that every rider has with this circuit is his own domain. I could absorb, and much later when alone in a contemplative mood, still be fascinated with the sensation gained from faultless and fluent riding on the world's most demanding circuit, with over 250 corners in its 37.75-mile (61km) length. That I was capable of this always left me surprised and grateful.

On that lap I averaged 96.77mph, setting a new 125cc lap record. This was the sixth-fastest lap made during all of practice regardless of capacity. And I was only on a 125cc machine.

Yet again, the 125cc class was seen by journalists as promising to be the fiercest-fought race of the week. With eight riders, entered on the most exotic motorcycles ever built with all but two having won, or who were destined to win a world championship, their assessment could not be contradicted. Even Mike Hailwood saw fit to join the fray. Honda and Yamaha's reliability made them favourites, but it was noted in *Motor Cycling* that the biggest surprise in practice was that the fastest

For the last time, embracing the speed and fluency of the legendary 37³/₄-mile circuit. Archives.

time and new lap record had been set by Hugh Anderson. In his race preview Mick Woollett wrote: 'Recently the fabulous little five-cylinder Hondas have gained the upper hand and I predict a Honda victory. But selecting the rider is the problem. Hailwood will be riding to win, otherwise he wouldn't be competing. Taveri, leader of the 125 world championship to date, is a hard man to beat. Last year's winner Phil Read will certainly press the Hondas hard and may well upset my predictions, as could Anderson if Suzuki provides him with a reliable bike.'

Due to thick fog all over the mountain, the start of the race was delayed for three hours, finally getting under way at 2pm. I set off at a speed that was fast but manageable, leaving me able to cope with a sudden engine failure should it occur. So as not to be swayed by any outside influences, I decided not to read my pit signals and ride my own race, taking the opportunity to, for the last time, enjoy the rider and circuit relationship that exists here, without the pressure of having to win. At the end I was surprised to be ushered into the winners' enclosure to find I'd finished third behind Bill and Phil on their Yamahas. The Suzuki team seemed happy about it, which was important.

When Bill, Phil and I climbed the stairs to the podium, I looked across the road to the scoreboard. Phil had finished just six seconds ahead of me. Bloody hell, I could so easily have finished second. The disappointment wasn't due to not having beaten Phil but not having gained second place for Shimizu-san and the team. That is one of the few regrets that I have from my racing career and half a century later it still grates. My lap times were 23min 40sec (the first lap from a push start), 23.14 and 23.15. The consistency of the times was an indication perhaps of the control I was exercising. Duff (Yamaha) was fourth and Perris fifth.

It had not been Honda's day. Hailwood finished sixth and declared that technically the 125s were much more difficult to ride than bigger bikes. He had also learned that the class had become exceptionally competitive and specialised. Taking part as a 'drop-in rider' was just no longer an option. The win hadn't been easy for Bill Ivy either. On his first lap, at the Waterworks series of corners, he struck the wall with sufficient force to create a gaping hole in the side of his Yamaha's fibreglass fairing. He hit the bank at Windy Corner during his second lap but was able to continue without any slowing of pace. Such is the urgency and the good fortune of a 'new boy'.

The end-of-race machine condition report in *Motor Cycling* stated: 'Hugh Anderson's third placed Suzuki finished in clean condition but the tyres showed more evidence, compared to Ivy's and Read's Yamahas, of scrubbing. The rear Dunlop was chopped much more than those of the Yamahas. Being near or on the limit is where the pleasure lies.'

It was obvious that the Suzuki factory race organisation was in a state of change. After three serious accidents and more than one minor 'get-off' during the past three years, Ernst had lost his enthusiasm for racing. Naturally, a drop-off in form followed and this led to his contract not being renewed for the 1967 season. Frank Perris was told that his contract was not going to be renewed either. The original team was breaking up. Suzuki Motor Company appeared to be putting less into the race team with more of an emphasis on their new road machines which, it must be said, were excellent. The race mechanics continued to seek ever more control over engine preparation. There was no reason for any second thoughts regarding the retirement decision, but naturally I told no one. Suzuki had to be the first to know, but not until after the last race of the season.

On the last free evening we would have on the island, and without thoughts of ever returning, on Thursday evening we drove up to the Bungalow and turned left onto a narrow lane that would take us to Ballaskella, high above Sulby Glen. Mount Karrin was on our left and the high rolling lands of Slieau Managh to our right. Way below crops spreading into the distance formed a patchwork of greens, greys, yellows and the browns of fallow land. I had first come here with Janny one evening in 1963. We had sat holding hands in silence, hidden away from the suffocating madness of it all. We had come again in 1964 and last year with Caroline as a baby. Now she was more than two years old, very active and wondering what all the solemnity was about.

My thoughts go beyond individual occurrences and attempt to encompass the island as a symbol of the art of motorcycling and the effect it has had on so many lives, including my own. From a boyhood dream of adventure to the hardship and difficulties of that first year, when Percy Coleman generously found a bike for me. Then each step by difficult step to now, where I am a very happy, wiser, vastly more experienced person sharing the last chapter of a life's dream, well lived, with his young family. Caroline was impatient for her customary walk but there were no flowers for Mum here, just a vast panoramic scene of the island, and memories. Not of the deaths, injuries and screaming nightmares, but of the success of overcoming fear and confidence issues that have been shared with no one, balanced by the personal success of coming to terms with, and succeeding at, what to so many has been, is and will continue to be, the ultimate challenge of life, the Isle of Man TT.

To increase spectator interest, the organisers decided to use a mass start for the 50cc race on Friday, September 2. Ralph and Luigi made excellent starts, my engine was running well and by moving from one rider's slipstream to another I was ramping up my speed to gain on them. I felt good, using every inch of the road while flowing through the corners better than I ever had. The head-to-head competition of a mass start had beefed up my competitive spirit. The Hondas had been faster than me in practice but our late nights in the garage might have bridged the gap. Having made extremely good time through Union Mills and Greeba Castle, my favourite 'swervery', I was now on the tail of the two leaders. At Ballacraine, just before a demanding, winding, high-speed section begins, I braked past Luigi and Ralph hoping to be able to make a gap on them. But then the engine died soon after as I left a tight uphill corner and I was soon back to third. Three miles later I managed to catch Luigi, only to have the engine seize momentarily, however I was able to carry on but the bike was slower now.

Ralph led at the end of the first lap from Taveri, Katayama, Anscheidt and me, with Degner sixth. At the end of the second lap Ralph had increased his lead, Katayama retired at the pits with a holed piston and Anscheidt stopped on Bray Hill when his engine locked solid, leaving me a distant third. Ralph's engine stopped when he was coming down the mountain on his last lap. He coasted for a kilometre and it restarted when he let the clutch out. The luck of the Irish. At the finish it was Ralph, Luigi, me and Ernst, with a host of private riders on much slower machines way behind.

The only time the first three riders have finished in their race-numbered order. Archives.

So after winning 12 silver replicas, one bronze, won a team prize, set three lap and two race records and having walked up onto the stage at the presentation 14 times, that was my 16th and last race on the Isle of Man. It was with a mixture of relief and nostalgia that I rode the ferry from Douglas to Liverpool on Saturday, September 3, for the seventh and final time.

There was little time to dwell on the past, however. As frequently happened, I was in a hurry. To keep my budding motocross hand in, I had entered a major event near Winchester, in the south of England, on the Sunday. Race day was windy, wet and greasy, just like the Waikato in New Zealand. While the conditions may have been unpleasant for the large crowd that attended, it suited me. Choosing my 250 I finished fourth in both the 500cc and Open classes, managing to head off competitors who had gained success at national and international level on a track that traditionally suited 500cc machines.

All aspirations of gaining a respectable placing in the 125cc class had long gone by the time we arrived at Monza in Italy. Suzuki had entered only the 50cc class in the Italian Grand Prix on September 11th. My two machines weren't running very well and Monza, being such a fast track, the best I could manage was fourth place. Anscheidt won, ahead of Taveri and Bryans. The race of the weekend, not for the first time, was the 500cc class. A win for either Mike Hailwood or Giacomo Agostini would secure them the world championship. It was a promoter's dream and the circuit was packed.

The field lined up in total silence, the air shimmered with tension. Hailwood made a good start. Ago didn't. At the end of the first lap Hailwood led by 100m, at the end of the second by 50m and Ago took the lead on the third. Hailwood stayed glued to his rear wheel but on the seventh lap the Honda suffered valve failure and he retired. Ago was the 500cc world champion, the first time an Italian had won the title since 1957. He was carried shoulder high to the podium as the passionate crowd streamed onto the circuit in their tens of thousands. Hailwood's response was: "Good luck to him, he's been trying hard enough for it."

I saw Ago at a most unlikely venue a week later. I had entered the Malpesa Motocross, organised by the MV Agusta Motorcycle Club and run near the famous factory. Agostini was in attendance as the race starter and was astonished to see me competing. He spent some time with us during the day. The track was fairly basic and not too demanding; I was quite happy to finish fifth overall. We enjoyed the 'ambience' of Italy as we lounged about in our swimsuits enjoying the perfect weather; I looked forward to the relaxed life of a motocrosser next year. Meanwhile we had been invited back to Wimpassing in Austria where I had ridden last year. From the lakes in the lowlands to the forest-clad foothills and up to the snow-covered Alps of northern Italy then winding down into Austria, which at this time of year has you passing through places of great scenic beauty. Now we would have time to appreciate it.

With a third overall in the 500 at Wimpassing and while attempting to move into second in the 250 race, two of us went off over a low bank; I got back on the track and finished fourth. Riding in two classes is demanding and enjoyable until you try to get out of bed the next morning. I hoped that the fitter I got, the less it would hurt.

For the first time since 1962, when the Japanese Grand Prix was introduced, the Honda-owned Suzuka track was not being used. The Yamaha and Suzuki factories, undoubtedly backed by Kawasaki and Bridgestone, had finally convinced the Japanese federation that a neutral venue should be used and the new Fisco circuit had been chosen. Honda declined to compete as they felt that the 6km circuit was dangerous — it had originally been built to cater for American NASCAR-style car racing.

When I arrived in Japan I received some bad news about Ernst Degner. When his Suzuki contract was not renewed, Ernst had been approached by Kawasaki to carry on the development work started by Toshio Fuji before he was killed on the Isle of Man. During tests at the Fisco circuit, the rear chain had broken, locking the rear wheel. The reports were not detailed but it seemed there was concern about the head injuries he had received. The past three years had not been kind to Ernst: during that time he had been in hospital or in rehab for more than 12 months.

On arrival at the Hamamatsu factory I received more bad news. Mr Suzuki was quite ill. He had seemed so well when I last saw him in Europe. Our association had been such that he had encouraged me, if I felt it necessary, to contact him directly and had given me his personal factory address. Race preparation at our test track did not go particularly well. We were still having problems with the 125, although the 50 seemed okay. I tested their 250cc motocross bike again, but development had been slow. It was fast and light but still at the prototype stage. After the Grand Prix a full-on test was to be carried out at a purpose-built motocross track.

Fisco was a fairly straightforward affair apart from a steeply banked speed bowl-type right-hand corner at the end of the long start-finish straight. There were no markers to position yourself and with the near-vertical banking being decidedly bumpy I found it difficult to find the best line. At Daytona a less tight but similar corner had been lined to guide you. The Fisco version had such a tight radius that, when lying on the tank going flat out, you were looking into the track just 30m or so ahead. The 50cc practice went well but my number one 125 seized as I approached the second corner. Unbelievably, the second bike did exactly the same thing. During later practice sessions we had better luck but on race day neither the bikes nor I were in a seriously competitive situation. I didn't find the circuit much fun and agreed with Honda's view of it.

The Bridgestone factory had been using Suzuki 50cc technology, supplied by Isao Morishita who had been a Suzuki team member. Unfortunately, soon after he was married his wife died in tragic circumstances, leading him to start afresh with an alternative employer. Having reached a competitive stage the factory invited Jack Findlay and Tommy Robb to join Morishita in a three-man team. During practice Katayama Itoh and I were in line astern, lapping near the limit, and caught Jack on the third corner. The radius of this gradually eased and while accelerating hard we were able to hold an inside line over its full length. Aussie Jack, accustomed to riding larger, more powerful and faster-accelerating bikes, entered the same corner on a much wider line so we rode under him at speed with our chins on the tank. He was a little taken aback and after practice his comment was: "I'll never get the hang of riding these things."

To win the 50cc world championship, Anscheidt needed to finish first or second to exceed Luigi Taveri's points total. Having little competition, Suzuki team management, for publicity purposes, wanted a Japanese rider to win. Katayama was to lead with Anscheidt second and myself third and that is what we did. Not a race to remember.

The 125cc field left the start almost in one group. I was lying fourth and as we entered its steeply banked, tight, poorly surfaced first corner the stench of hot rubber wafted over us. The tyres were stressed to the max due to the poor surface and the added stress of rider and machine being pressed into the surface by the tightness of the curve. Bill Ivy began pulling away from the leading group and just when I was beginning to relax, feeling that I could compete and even enjoy the proceedings, the plugs oiled up. I called in at the pits and changed them, then cruised on to the finish.

As I have stated several times, I would not ride for money alone. My reward has always been riding to my full potential. The Suzuki race team gave me that opportunity, recognised in the many wins, records and awards received. They too have gained from my efforts. These may be difficult to ascertain but by any form of measurement they would be more than substantial. However, 1966 had seen us become under-achievers with little motivation or drive. Being unable to compete at my best had left me disillusioned, joyless, depressed even. During all but one of the season's 125cc races, I had held first or second positions before mechanical problems caused me to slip down the finishing order or retire. The results from nine races amounted to a third, two fourths and a fifth place.

Road racing had no further place in my life. For nostalgic reasons I had a pair of very good Manx Nortons back in New Zealand, which I had intended to keep for life. They now seemed to be little more than a waste of space and money. Dave Kenah had enjoyed a few rides on the 350, coming second in the New Zealand TT. This satisfied his desire to race and he retired, so I wrote asking him to sell them.

When I first broached the subject of retirement to Suzuki a hush descended on the discussion group and a look of disbelief shadowed the faces around me. Reasons were not requested or given. The question of who to suggest to replace me then arose; Stuart Graham, Ginger Molloy and Peter Williams were three riders who possessed the sought-after skills. The most important category for the team was the 50cc class where the size and weight of the rider were major factors. It cost the race department a fortune to remove as little as 1kg on these super-lightweight machines, built using the most exotic materials available. Understandably, they were very reluctant to employ a rider over the minimum weight limit of 60kg.

Of the riders discussed, Stuart Graham was a standout, light in weight and making exceptional progress through the ranks of Grand Prix privateers. He had already ridden for Honda and finished second in the Isle of Man 250cc TT on the famed 250cc Honda six. Had Mike Duff not recovered from the serious hip injury he had suffered at the Japanese Grand Prix, Phil Read would have advised Yamaha to take Stuart on. However, I was asked to give my retirement serious thought and convey to them my final decision before the end of the year.

After the Japanese Grand Prix, Ishikawa-san and I, with two motocross bikes and technicians, travelled by car and a light truck to a track in the highlands about four hours from the factory. We arrived to find the circuit under a metre of snow so we made our tests on waste ground at the site of our test track. Improvements had been made but it certainly wasn't a CZ or a Husqvarna. At this point it was low priority and not a lot of money had been spent. However, they were very serious about competing in selected European Grand Prix events the following year. New frames were being built, improved forks were being developed and major engine modifications were planned.

Back in the UK in early November I called on good friend Keith Arney, and we went out into his tidy workshop. Pinned up on the walls were blown-up action photographs of the top riders of the day. There was an excellent on-the-limit action shot taken of Hugh Anderson riding a 125cc Suzuki when winning the French Grand Prix in 1963. For a long time I silently took in every detail of that enlarged photo. I searched for me, but I wasn't there. The rider shown was a complete stranger. At first I didn't understand why but eventually I realised that it represented that 'other me'.

That person on the wall was who I had become during those record-breaking rides across the globe, where heightened concentration levels had lifted me into that 'perfect place'. He was the reason I had willingly continued on that dangerous but rewarding path; that other persona who first presented himself in 1958 at the Marton Road Race in small-town New Zealand, where Maurice MacDonald had been killed, and carefully refined over the passing years. Now he had gone forever; that rider of the bike pinned up on the wall no longer existed.

Those seven European seasons had produced a lifetime of experiences, from the depressing situation in 1962 when I felt my life had little value, to the undreamt success of 'being there', when Team Suzuki had played its part in allowing me to stand on the podium at every Grand Prix circuit in the world.

But I now had Janny and Caroline and belonged to a loving extended family. More than once luck had been on my side; fortunately there were no serious injuries to impede my future life. There were also the financial rewards: a substantial bank balance and investments. But above all, I had experienced the opportunity of becoming, from time to time, that other person, in whose guise I had gained the greatest rewards of all.

In December I confirmed by letter that in 1967 I would be riding motocross only. Ishikawa-san asked me to contact Stuart Graham with the good news and suggested we fly to Japan in February where I could introduce him to the team and give technical advice, should it be needed, on how to get the best out of the temperamental little flyers. I phoned Stuart on Christmas Eve. Understandably, he was delighted to receive my call.

Above left: The 32.5mm-diameter one-ring piston of the 1966 twin-cylinder 50cc Suzuki.

Above right: Built like a watch! The 14-speed transmission of the 1966 50cc model. The gearbox is only 203mm wide.

CHAPTER 16

A satisfyingly successful international motocross experience
AND HOW SUZUKI CAME TO DOMINATE THE MOTOCROSS WORLD

We decided to spend the winter in England and prepare my CZs for a full 1967 motocross season, and rented a three-storey townhouse in Tonbridge, Kent. As always, Janny soon made herself at home and Caroline, now two-and-a-half years old, became friends with the neighbour's young children. Caroline was a bilingual chatterbox, but never having played with English children, she didn't know the words used or their games. It was priceless watching them during their first meetings. Being outgoing, Caroline told them all about her doll, in Dutch of course. They looked at her as though she were rather strange then told her about a particular game they wished to play; with the local accent thrown in, Caroline was bewildered. They began a game of alternately skipping and hopping in a large circle while reciting a nursery rhyme. Caroline followed, working on a three-second delay, attempting to imitate them, but within no time she had learned the language and the rules.

Alan Kimber of Suzuki GB loaned me a 120cc Suzuki that had been converted for trial use. Every weekend I was able to ride in a trial or motocross, sometimes both. Mike Bashford included in his weekly piece 'Cross Chat' in on December 17, 1966: 'Hugh Anderson, the ex-world champion road racer, has improved his motocross ability with every outing this winter. Part of the improvement, Hugh says, is due to frequent trials riding.' Perhaps, but my memories now are that my trials-riding ability improved little, however hauling the bike out of bogs, holes and gullies, where I frequently got stuck, were great strength and fitness training.

I accompanied Stuart Graham to Japan in February 1967. To the very obvious surprise and disappointment of the race shop staff, I arrived in Japan without my leathers. Now the spotlight turned to Stuart. Having been employed by Honda, he had experience of working with Japanese engineers and mechanics, which helped him fit in immediately. Quiet and pleasant by nature and an intelligent engineer, he readily understood and absorbed all the information presented. By the end of his first day at the test track he had gained the basic skills to cope with the 14 gears, the extremely narrow power band of the temperamental 50cc machines, and the less-demanding nine-speed 125s. By the third day he was putting in times that were close to the existing lap record. Team Suzuki was impressed and Stuart was offered a comprehensive contract.

While I spent most of my time with Stuart, I also tested a much-improved version of their RH66 250cc motocross model. A new frame had been built and the engine's power increased at higher revolutions. However, more power at low revs, a basic requirement for a motocross engine, was needed. Nevertheless it was a good enough basis to allow the team to learn from. Hopefully, enabling them to move to the next stage.

I dismantled my CZs, had the frames nickel-plated, engine side covers polished, exhausts chrome-plated and the bodywork painted in a pleasant maroon. Every detail was checked and rebuilt with care. They were completely reliable during the following two seasons that I used them. Throughout the English winter I rode as often as possible. Being an Expert, and an International Licence holder at that, I gained entries wherever I wanted. On one occasion when closely following Freddie Mayes, the British 250cc champion, I came off and my little finger on my right hand was under the end of the handlebar when it crunched against a large rock. I rode on.

After a few laps it began to feel odd so I stopped and removed my glove to find that a large piece of flesh from the end, under the nail back to the first joint, was almost severed. The sight of it left me feeling a little faint so there was no option other than returning to the van, wrapping it in a handkerchief and finding a doctor's surgery

Above: Chasing 250cc British champion Freddie Mayes. Archives.

Below left: Alan Jones, Caroline and my immaculate 360cc CZ at Lydden motocross. Archives.

Below right: With our équipe outside our house in Tonbridge Kent. Caroline advises. Archives.

269

that was open on a Sunday. It took some time to clean it up and stitch it back on.

During December, January and February I kept up a rigorous, daily, physical training programme. More than once, soon after the start of an intended a long run, I had to give up and walk home, a case of 'hitting the wall', and have a few days off. I typed out individual entry applications to 138 motocross promoters, all in the language of the country involved. The popularity of motocross in Europe at the time was shown by the fact that France alone ran over 120 international meetings, compared to England's five or six, with further events in Switzerland, Germany, Belgium, Holland, Italy and Spain, and more behind the Iron Curtain. Replies trickled back offering a fair amount of money and containing an entry form. I was pleased and relieved to gain sufficient starts to have a ride most weekends.

Typically, all international events were run as three heats of 30 minutes plus two laps. The winner was the rider with the lowest aggregate of points awarded during the day's three-heat event; one point for first down to the last rider to finish. Payment was an agreed amount of start money or a minimum guarantee plus prize money, or prize money only, in each of the three heats. An overall fifth place would normally earn you about 70 pounds (over NZ$2,000 in 2014 money). The two CZs and spares, purchased directly from the factory, cost just 200 pounds each, half the retail price in England. If ridden with respect, maintenance costs were minimal.

The French had a real passion for the sport, with many events being used as fundraisers to subsidise local council expenditure and various charities. Often the international competitors were invited to ride into town, behind the local copper, and join the mayor and his staff in the council chambers for an official reception. Riders were expected to carry an attractive female on the pillion, so they would line up at the paddock exit wanting to be involved. I would have Janny on the back and Caroline on the tank. Some riders would drop back then race forward, pulling massive wheelies with the terrified girls clinging on for dear life. No protective clothing was ever worn.

The noise was deafening as we travelled through a town's narrow streets. All the inhabitants were made well aware that a race meeting was taking place just up the road in a few hours. When we assembled in the invariably impressive council buildings, and the official speeches had been completed, we were invited to enjoy finger food and a variety of aperitifs, all immaculately presented on white cloth-draped tables. After an hour or so, riders began returning to the track, some at high speed. A breathalyser on the starting grid would have given some interesting readings! In contrast, silence would be called before the race at some of the meetings held in the northern regions of France, and a prayer read over the sound system.

I was invited to take part in the Assen round of the Dutch grass track championships on July 1, 1967, a well-supported, high-profile series. The venue was the local sports park with the athletic oval used as the track. A wooden fence was assembled in sections along the start-finish straight to contain and protect the crowd. The race programme was made up of events for 250cc and 500cc motocross-based bikes, termed the 'petrol class', and a full-on methanol-burning speedway-engined long-track racer class. Each category was run in three six-lap races. Large crowds attended and speeds were quite high and I won my events on the 250cc CZ; a pleasant diversion from the sweat and toil of motocross.

Enjoying a lap of honour at Assen.
Lee van Dam.

Attempting to improve my skills. Training
hard in Holland. Archives.

The following weekend was the 250cc British Motocross Grand Prix. I knew the organisers quite well and they accepted my entry in the National 250cc Support Class. This was run over two heats and I gained a first and a second place, making me the winner overall. This was my first motocross win of any importance, but the ego tends to become a little bruised when you observe the skills of the world's best.

The Grand Prix was won by Joel Robert (Belgium) from Victor Arbekov (Russia) and Olle Pettersson (Sweden). I had met Olle earlier in the season, and he impressed as a well-organised, pleasant young man.

On July 30 I rode at Lavaur in France. Unusually for a motocross track, it was dry, smooth, grippy and fast, so as a road racer I was in my element. However, at the very moment that I felt this was going to be my day, all hell broke loose. On a flat-out third-gear corner the bike, for no apparent reason, went end-over-end with me still attached. It was the only time that I had no idea what had caused a spill. When we came to rest I was still locked to the bike. The footrest and brake lever had to be removed as the lever foot plate had penetrated my boot and was embedded in my foot.

For the first time in my life I suffered from shock. Janny wrapped the bleeding foot and, feeling faint and sweating profusely, I lay on a lounger for some time with a very concerned Caroline sitting by me. Eventually, I regained sufficient composure to face the journey to the local doctor and with some amusement, the organisers sat me at the front of their town's ancient fire engine. Vigorously ringing the hand-operated bell, we inched our way through the vast crowd. I asked the doctor not to stitch it as I was riding the following weekend. He cleaned the gash and applied a very effective healing agent that came in powder form. Consequently, I was able to ride at Toulouse the following weekend, and finished fourth. There was some opening up of the wound and a blood-soaked sock, but I was able to continue my busy schedule by competing at Lacapelle, where a collapsed rear wheel put me out. Two days later I finished sixth at Laguepie, then third at Remalard and third again at Saland, Switzerland.

The highlight of that first season was being selected by team manager Harold Taylor as reserve rider for the British Motocross des Nations team on September 2, in Markelo, Holland. The team was made up of Jeff Smith, Vic Eastwood, Arthur Lampkin, on factory BSAs, Keith Hickman on a Cheney BSA and Dave Bickers and me on CZs. I spent a lot of time walking and mapping the difficult, winding 2km track. If any of my fellow team members had struck problems during practice, it would have been great to have faced the starter's flag at this, the major international event of the year. However, they didn't. The finishing order was Britain, Sweden, Belgium, Holland, East Germany, Denmark, Finland, France and Switzerland. A press headline read: 'Britain again, but only just. Winners for the fifth successive year.'

My last meeting in France was on October 1 at Vaulx-Milieu, near Lyon. I had entered the 250cc and 500cc classes. The programme's timing could be tight at these events so at the end of the first 250cc race Janny would be waiting at the paddock entrance with the 360 and dry gloves and goggles. This allowed me to be one of the first onto the start line with the hope of gaining a favourable position. She would then refuel the 250 and have it ready for the next event. The 250cc races went well. I swapped places several times with Jacques Porte, the French champion and Montesa works rider, to gain a strong second place. The first two 500cc events were okay, with me lying third overall, but towards the end of the third and last heat the bike began to handle badly. I was sure the rear axle, swing arm pivot or frame had broken as it seemed to constantly flop about. I struggled on and still managed fifth overall and afterwards I was surprised to find nothing wrong with the bike. It was then I realised I had run out of energy, understandable perhaps after four and a half hours, including practice, of intense physical effort.

The results of my first season were better than I could have imagined. From 22 meetings, not counting the outings on the Suzuki, I gained 21 top-six positions made up of two wins, one second, eight thirds, four fourths, three fifths and three sixth places.

As with Caroline, Janny's second pregnancy was also trouble free. The day I returned from a business trip to London, Janny went into labour. Births are never easy, however Janny managed well and 3.5kg Hugh Gerrit Anderson, complete with a full head of hair, arrived on the 8th of December 1968. He gained a very warm welcome into our large extended family, with Tinie and Gerrit playing the part of ever helpful, loving grandparents to the full. The new baby was efficiently absorbed into the family with big sister Caroline enjoying and playing her part in holding and entertaining him.

For the 1968 season I applied for and was granted what was probably a unique International Licence by the Auto Cycle Union of England. It allowed me to compete

Top: A podium at Balkbrug.
Lee van Dam.

Middle: Caroline thinks I am the
greatest. Lee van Dam.

Left: Assen, and again the customary
lap of honour. Lee van Dam.

at international level in all classes of road racing, motocross, speedway, and 1,000m long-track. Between motocross commitments in France, I rode in Holland at two international and one national 1000m grass track meetings at Balkbrug, Stadskanaal and Assen. I won all of them riding a modified 400cc Husqvarna motocross engine in a purpose-built long-track Hagon frame. As the Assen event did not have sidecars competing, with sidecar wheels digging trenches around the corners, the track was left with a smooth grass surface, just like my old grass tracking days back in New Zealand. I won my class and made the fastest race time of the day, beating all the national-class riders, who used methanol-burning J.A.P. engines, on my petrol-burning two-stroke.

During the season I got another taste of the big time when the organisers invited me to enter the French 250cc Motocross Grand Prix on May 12. It seemed worthwhile to take up the challenge and enjoy the experience and see how good I was. No harm done. On April 28 I had ridden my 360 into third place at Rouen. Then on May 1, I had finished third and fourth in the 250 and 500cc classes at Grasse and a few days later had finished third in the 500 class at Vannes.

Naturally, after such a condensed schedule, I was more than a little 'motocrossed out' by the time I arrived at the GP. But my fitness and skill levels had improved considerably. I met up with the Suzuki motocross team and their new bike looked great. I took it for a short ride and found it to be a much-improved version of what we had used the previous year. I congratulated them on just how good it was and they thanked me for the contribution I had made. A full history regards the development of the Suzuki Motocross machine comes later in this chapter.

I didn't take part in Friday's practice session but instead walked the course. I was learning as much as I could about how the top riders attacked, with engine screaming, wheel spinning, dirt flying, skill and aggression, the difficult sections of a typically French open and fast hillside circuit. They appeared to give their bikes no mercy; as they weren't paying the maintenance bills, it didn't matter.

A day of instructive observation gave me a much-needed lift, mentally and physically. Tiredness gave way to the enthusiasm of the challenge; the instant I woke the next day a wave of excitement hit me. Today and tomorrow would define how far I had come and what my standing in the motocross world was. Not that it mattered a lot, but what an opportunity! The fast hillside circuit suited me, although being on an older, standard machine, against factory teams and many dealer-sponsored riders was a handicap. However, during practice I found I could match most riders for speed while feeling safe and relaxed.

In the first race I made an okay start and kept out of trouble. During the 45-minute plus two-laps race I passed four riders and finished 12th. A great start in the second leg put me in ninth place. As in all events, I rode as hard as possible for five or six laps, took stock of my position relative to those around me, how well I was coping, and managed my effort according to my energy levels.

At half distance I was feeling good and closely following a Russian rider up one of the steep climbs when a large stone was thrown up from by his rear tyre. It hit the plastic body of my throttle twist grip, smashing it. A ninth-placed position added to the first-race 12th would have given me 10th overall. The 1965 world champion, Victor Arbekov of Russia, was sixth, and then there would have been just three riders between us, including Olle Pettersson on the Suzuki. But there you go, it was denied me.

Still it was a good effort and that performance, and consistently being the top CZ rider competing in France at that time, meant the factory took an interest. At first they supplied the works-type, under-engine exhaust pipes and had the chief mechanic, a Czech stationed with the French CZ importers in Paris, to 'spanner' my bike at the major events. This led to my being invited to the factory for complete machine overhauls.

The next weekend I finished third at a well-supported event at Blargies. A week later I got second at Montfort, then a win at Orléans. Close friend American Bryan Kenney, who went on to captain the first American team to compete in the Motocross des Nations, his partner Laurie, and Janny and I went out to a café for a low-key celebration. For the first time since February 1963, partly because of the effects of a duodenal ulcer, but also the need to be at my best at all times, I broke my self-imposed teetotal drought. Not excessively mind, but we had an enjoyable evening and felt very much at peace with the world.

It all came undone at Mezieres in central France on August 4. Again, on paper, it was my kind of circuit with a fast surface baked hard as concrete by the fierce French summer sun with temperatures exceeding 30 degrees. I soon mastered the simple track and being conscious of practising far more than necessary slowed down, moved off the racing line and cruised slowly back to the pits. As I crested one of the high man-made mounds the front wheel dropped into a deep hole hidden in long grass.

I was thrown high over the handlebars, fell a good 4m rolled in a ball and landed very heavily on the concrete-hard surface. Taking the brunt of the impact across my shoulder blades, I heard the cracking and crunching of broken bones and was left gasping for air. This was much worse than a typical winding and I lay there in a rather pathetic state. A Czechoslovakian rider I had got to know took off my helmet. An ambulance arrived; I was loaded aboard and taken away. I kept trying to tell them to take me to Janny in the pits, so I could tell her I was okay, well sort of, but I couldn't talk due to the severe winding. The ambulance staff drove straight to the hospital, ignoring my wheezing, barking and hand waving. The Czech rider took my helmet to Janny and made a slicing motion across his throat with a finger. Poor Janny was trapped with two young children in the parking crush of vehicles in the pits. She was unable to get the van out and had no idea where I had been taken. Going by the Czech's demonstration it could have been a morgue.

As Janny had done before, she relied on her natural stoicism and waited until the meeting and prize giving were over. With our English friend Dennis Smith, she finally found her way through the busy streets of Orléans to the hospital. X-rays had revealed no broken bones but I didn't believe them; I well knew the sound from past experience, got up and walked out. Next morning I loaded the van and drove back to Assen in Holland. There, two days after the spill, an X-ray revealed two broken vertebrae and one cracked.

Another long stay in a plaster body cast crossed my mind. Surprising to me at least, I was told to go home and rest, with no lifting and instructions to be patient for eight weeks. Well, it's only a broken back, I thought, what the hell. The first time I broke it in a car accident in New Zealand, it hadn't caused much bother, so I thought I'd see this out okay too.

Results gained at the 17 meetings before my 'crash' were four wins, 14 first-four places and two fifth finishes. To add to that I'd won two international and a national championship 1,000m grass track events in Holland. All in all, this was a step in the right direction that would lead, hopefully, to greater recognition by the promoters and more starts during 1969.

As a family, we decided to return to New Zealand permanently at the end of 1969. I was almost 34 and my troublesome left knee was steadily deteriorating and, as much as I loved my sport, Europe and the lifestyle, I had to accept reality. The time to retire was near. Janny, Tinie and Gerrit were quite neutral about it as it had been a reality for them from the time we became engaged. Tinie and Gerrit had every intention of flying out and visiting us from time to time.

My back injuries were slow to heal, but I took the opportunity to drive to the CZ factory and take delivery of a pair of the latest single-port models. I had started with walking, running and other light exercises and finally in January I joined a local motocross training club that gathered each Sunday morning. Slowly, strength and fitness returned. By the end of March I was on the pace. A physiotherapist who incidently owned a Jawa and was employed by the hospital helped me. I maintained his bike and he looked after me. During the winter, Gerrit Rump, a close friend, and I built a fully covered trailer for my bikes. Gerrit would use this to transport his grasstrack

Méru, north of Paris. A win is a win. You enjoy each one. Archives.

European champion Dave Bickers and I in deep discussion about something that I do not recall. Archives.

Clearing the snow and ice off the new Mercedes and trailer. Archives.

BMW outfit during the 1970 season. We worked in an unheated shed at minus 12 degrees, but you get used to it. I intended to hook it up behind our large caravan using a powerful new Mercedes as our tow car.

The gypsies in France used a large van and caravan and had a trailer containing their hens, ducks etc. attached behind. If they could, so could I. One thing I ignored was the round disc, which had to be attached to the trailer displaying the maximum speed allowed: a miserable 50kph.

On April 4th, the day before we were to leave for our first meeting, I caught chickenpox courtesy of Caroline. After missing two events, I finished seventh at the first and won the second; we were on song again. Our towing ensemble performed well; a steady 100ks could be maintained on good roads and as the French tend to ignore foreigners with German registration plates, we had no problems.

One of the highlights was riding with European champion and UK legend Dave Bickers midway through the season at a major event in the mid-west of France. The circuit was unusual in that soon after the start a long top-gear straight ended in a fast right turn that led to a stream. The track ended abruptly about 4m above the water. Of course speed carried you over, but less able riders had a much slower choice of riding to one side of the jump and through the stream. The track continued to a left turn that took you up a steep incline around a hairpin bend that had been cut into the bank, and back down towards the stream again. There were four of these loops making

On the road, with Laurie and Jan parked behind us. Archives.

for an unusually slow technical section that was at variance with the typically open, fast French tracks. But as we found, the French could be quite creative. The only thing each circuit had in common was speed and something difficult or spectacular. In general they were less demanding than the rough tough tracks in England, or the deep sand of Belgium and Holland.

Late in the afternoon, after many of us had completed a short practice session, European champion Dave Bickers arrived and parked beside us, saw my motorcycle trailer hooked up to our caravan and came over for a closer look.

"Great idea," he said. "Just the thing I would do." After admiring our setup Dave walked around the course. When he returned he started unloading his bike. "I won't be able to sleep tonight if I don't try that jump over the stream first," he said. An indication of how daunting these tracks could be.

After a good start I was holding fifth place in the first race. A rider fell and I was fourth. Towards the end of the 30-minute heat Dave rushed past using a near-vertical bank in a 'wall of death'-style pass. After the race he came and apologised when there was no need, saying, "Sorry about that but I had to pass you. I couldn't let you beat me." Then he had another cup of Janny's tea. He finished third overall and I was fourth.

With Janny's kettle constantly on the boil and cups of tea and sandwiches freely available, our table and chairs under the caravan awning were always a magnet for British riders. In the main they travelled light. For them it was a quick weekend trip and back to work on Monday morning.

In August Laurie Shephard and his English wife Jan joined us for three weeks. Laurie and I had moved on from those carefree successful days of 1961, having achieved a great deal during the intervening eight years. He was now deputy principal at an English private school. Laurie and Jan had married in 1962 and returned to New Zealand to take up a principal's position at a primary school near Taumarunui in the King Country, before returning to the UK.

At that time it was a thriving rugby community, and he played for King Country, home of the legendary All Black Colin 'Pinetree' Meads. Now he was back in the UK for good, saying the freedom of the independent schools beat working for the New Zealand Government. Within hours of their arrival, Laurie, in school teacher fashion, said: "Jeez, Anderson, you've got a terrible accent."

Having been based in north-east Holland for seven years and having lived in a Dutch and French environment for the past three obviously had an effect. Our next meeting was at Blargies. As usual competitors were free to practise on the day before the meeting. This wasn't official and marshals were not present. Laurie joined us on my spare bike wearing one of my helmets and his street clothes and shoes. He was rapt to be part of it.

During the races I shadowed the 'king of French motocross', Englishman Andy Lee. He usually competed in as many as 30 meetings a season, winning most of them on his highly developed Matchless Métisse frame special. Second place and a great day was followed by a very pleasant evening. I had taken to doing what the French did, drinking water with a little wine added, but as the evening progressed the ratio tended to change. A stimulating form of rehydration, a pleasant meal with Laurie, Jan and friends outside on a warm evening was finished off with a traditional light cigar or two. Motorcycling at its very best!

Top: Janny as always in her bikini, does the chores while we play. Archives.

Bottom left: Child labour is exploited, especially if they are enjoying it. Archives.

Bottom right: A world-class musician no less. Enjoying France, our country of choice. Archives.

Knowing that within a matter of weeks my chosen career would be finished heightened my appreciation of it. The mainspring of my life was being wound down and the centre of all ambition was fast coming to an end. Of course the future was a new challenge, but what part would motorcycling play in it?

279

Personally, my 1969 season was a definite step up from the previous year. During August there had been four second places gained on consecutive weekends. Wins had been elusive but three were okay, with a rare mechanical failure denying me a fourth. Overall there were 17 first-four finishes, two spills, a collapsed rear wheel and a broken piston ring. Having a factory mechanic looking after the CZ always lifted my performance and took the pressure off. On one occasion I had led ex-world champion Sten Lundin for over half a race finishing second with Andy Lee third. As important as the finishing position was, I still gained the most satisfaction from the fluency of the extra speed and the satisfaction of exercising new skills as they were learned.

Early in November I swapped our caravan for a new 400 Husqvarna sourced through factory development rider Gunnar Nilsson. This involved a 2000km drive to the factory in Sweden, and returning to Assen with the dismantled bike in the boot. Now I was confronted with the formidable task of packing a mountain of gear, which included seven CZs, the Husqvarna, Janny's Fiat and our Mercedes tow car. The whole Anderson touring circus. There were also the tasks of finalising shipping, air fares and carefully assembling all the paperwork relating to our possessions. New Zealand Customs pulled no punches and had become ever stricter.

Lack of sleep and mental tiredness began to set in. The sense of adventure involved in racing and motocross throughout Europe and the world, the whole scenario of emotion and the energy this provided was now about to be reversed. I was dismantling what had taken not only the 10 years I had been in Europe but, as I saw it, all my life to build. The boyhood dream that had become a reality was over. The source of my values, ambitions, pride, all based on my motorcycle success and virtually my reason for living, was gone. My mind was dull, limbs heavy, without the will or resourcefulness to complete the job and I slumped into a deep depression.

Confused emotions, thoughts and doubts racked my consciousness as I battled to get to grips with the major changes I had initiated in our lives. I can't pack the large wooden crate. Should this go first, or that? Maybe take that out and replace it with something smaller, heavier, lighter? For God's sake, I don't know. It was all quite obvious to Janny, and later she confided that she had been waiting for it to happen, but with the aid of modern medication, I managed to get it together and pack everything in time.

Finally, on the morning of December 7, 1969 we closed the door on 31 Schaperstraat and on a fine frosty morning drove down the street and out of, what to me, had been a perfect way of life; a life which had introduced me to a huge range of cultures, people and experiences that would never have happened if I had stayed in New Zealand. Fundamentally, my motorcycling career had expanded my personal horizons, introduced me to new ideas and outlooks, and raised my awareness of life a hundred-fold; something I am ever grateful for. Janny too had more than one moment of heartache. As we were led across the tarmac from the departure gates to the plane, she looked back to see her mother and father waving goodbye to their only child and their grandchildren walking out of their lives to make another life on the other side of the world.

With changes of planes and long waits, the flight was tiring and tedious but, as in the past, we received a warm welcome at Auckland's Mangere Airport. Gordon had organised a welcome home barbecue, with friends and family, at his place. It was a very pleasant evening for me and Caroline, who was always up for fun and adventure. Janny and little Hugh found it hard going, but managed. Early on the first morning after our return, I said to Janny: "I wonder if we have done the right thing?"

Faced with a different lifestyle, returning to my country after years away in Europe and the challenges of the so called 'real world', one I knew little about, raised all the old feelings of doubt.

THE EVOLUTION OF THE SUZUKI MOTOCROSS

I tested a much-improved version of the RH66 model when I was at the factory introducing Stuart in February 1967. However, more power at low revs, a basic requirement for a motocross engine, was needed. Nevertheless it was a good enough basis to allow the team to learn from, enabling them to move to the next stage.

The Suzuki Motor Company's interest in motocross began in late 1962 when I first visited the factory. Being interested in the sport myself, I spent some time with Mr Okano and his management group discussing the future of that form of the sport. They were sufficiently taken with my enthusiasm to ship a 250cc twin with off-road tyres for me to try when I was in New Zealand during the 1962–63 season.

Development began in late 1963 and in 1965 Mr Mansuri Nishi entered a two-rider team using experimental twin- and single-cylinder machines in the Swedish Grand Prix on July 25, and the Finnish Grand Prix a week later.

Unfortunately, the machines were found to be non-competitive at the Swedish event, so the Finnish Grand Prix was abandoned. Nevertheless, Mr Nishi had talked with several top riders, including young Belgium world champion Joel Robert and Swedish ex-champion Torsten Hallman. Suzuki's stated objective was to have competitive machinery competing in the 1967 season.

Following the Japanese Grand Prix on October 12, 1965, I carried out a basic test at our test track. While the engine was quite powerful at high revs, when pulling out of slow corners it lacked that all-important initial grunt. The suspension was okay but the main problem was severe engine vibration.

The Suzuki team returned to Europe early in 1966 to compete at the Belgium Grand Prix on April 30, and the five following world champion rounds. Kazuo Kubo was teamed with Matsuhisa Kejimu riding upgraded machines called the RH66. In a pre-meeting test ride, Hallman felt the Suzuki was as fast as his works Husqvarna but the handling needed to be improved.

Torrential rain turned the Belgium circuit into a sea of mud, allowing only a small percentage of the entry to get round the circuit. In the first leg, Kejimu pressed on doggedly to finish 20th, three laps behind the winner Hallman. Unfortunately, he was unable to finish the second leg due to the conditions. Kubo retired in both races. At the German Grand Prix on May 15 only Kubo qualified, but then retired after just five laps of the first heat.

Realising more development was required, the team returned to Japan to rethink the project. When they realised that I had most definitely retired from road racing and was going to compete full time in motocross, Mike Ishikawa, previously the road race team accountant, secretary and interpreter and close friend, invited me to join their team. My job was to quietly go about assisting them in this still early stage of the project. As a rider of little standing, I wasn't expected to do well anyway, so we could work away under the radar avoiding the media.

It became apparent that the factory would be carrying out all development in-house. Although it had not been obvious to me earlier, some of the Suzuki race team engineers had not agreed with the decision to introduce, in late 1961, Ernst Degner with his MZ knowledge, into the road race team.

Perhaps it was due to instructions from Mr Suzuki himself that the motocross development was done in-house. It would not be a Degner bike or, more to the point, a copy of the CZ or Husqvarna, a Joel Robert- or Torsten Hallman-inspired machine. It would be a Suzuki.

Alan Kimber, sales manager for Suzuki GB and a good friend, followed with close interest the development of the factory prototype scramblers. Alan believed strongly in demonstrating the quality of the product he sold through open, tough events. He had standard machines suitably modified and entered them in long-distance competitions. Don Barrett won the 1965 Welsh Three Day Trial outright on basically a standard unbreakable 80cc road bike, beating all the larger-capacity factory specials. This was the beginning of a long run of impressive successes in British off-road competition. Alan's sales-orientated activities were effective and must have helped open the floodgates for Suzuki, which sold 40,000 motorcycles in the UK between 1964 and 1966.

I missed the first round of the 1967 world championship in Spain on April 2 due to having a contract with an alternative promoter. I first rode the much-modified RH67 at the Swiss Grand Prix on April 9.

Team-mate Matsuhisa Kejimu and I finished the first heat towards the rear of the field. Severe engine vibration caused frame fractures and we both retired in the second heat. We had the frames strengthened for the French Grand Prix on April 16 and I finished in the first race in 19th position. During the second race, the frame broke at the steering head.

We missed the Belgium Grand Prix as we were carrying out modifications and testing. At the German round on May 14, Kejimu crashed heavily in the first race, breaking a collarbone. I retired in both races. A collision with another rider during the first race locked the rear brake on. In the second, the frame broke yet again at the steering head, when landing off a high jump.

After extensive repairs had been carried out, we arrived at the Dutch Grand Prix on May 28. This meeting was run at Norg, a small town near Assen.

All motocross circuits in the area were laid out among stunted pine trees in sandy wasteland. I had ridden on sand tracks before, but none had been as deep or as loose as there. One area was called the 'Sahara Section' where the sand was so deep it swept your feet off the footrests. Ever tried riding a motorcycle through loose sandy areas above high tide at the beach in third gear?

There was a spectacular jump into a pristine athletic park amphitheatre complete with a large grandstand. There were fast left-hand corners taking us around the sports ground then a right turn back into the trees and sand. I finished 13th in the first race, but the forks had been bent when landing from that dramatic jump.

The mechanics set to work to fit some from a spare bike, but they were found to be of an earlier design. As a last resort, they fitted the originals in the opposite direction, hoping they might straighten after one or two more heavy landings!

The race started before the bike was re-assembled and I got away almost a lap after the field had left. On my fourth lap the race leader, ex-world champion Russian Victor Arbekov, passed me. We flew high over the jump into the grassed sports arena; when I rode around him, a cheer rose from the partisan crowd and I led him back into the Sahara Section. The Europeans seldom rode on grass and they didn't trust it but my experience of it was a definite advantage. I finished the second 45-minute plus two-lap leg again with badly swollen fingers and hands from the vibration and burst, bleeding blisters from the effort. However, we had managed 18th overall and the forks lasted more or less.

That was the first time a Suzuki had finished a Motocross Grand Prix. The team was well aware of the limitations of their bike and returned to Japan once again to reconsider the project.

Guy Mallet, a journalist employed by , whom I had met at the Earl's Court Show the previous November, was helping me gain entries to French international events. It appears that I would have a full season riding at the premier meetings.

My knowledge of how to set up a world championship-winning motocross machine was minimal and due to my worn left knee I would not be able to gain the fitness levels required and I had insufficient ability to compete consistently at the top level. I had nothing more to add to their development. I was not in the business of letting people down, riding just for the money or being seen as a bit of a plonker. The friendly, no-pressure enjoyment of taking part in the international events and the regular high placings I gained suited me just fine. My ambition went no further.

Suzuki thought my reasoning was not soundly based and project manager Mike Ishikawa was very disappointed with my decision. I thought the right man for the job was Olle Pettersson, who had finished third in the 250cc world championship for Husqvarna. I had found him to be without conceit or any sign of intolerance, which is an important trait when developing a new machine.

I finally convinced Mike of this and he contacted the Swedish importer. He made the required connection with Olle, who flew out to Japan on January 17, 1968. Timing is everything as Olle was about to sign for Husqvarna. Olle rode consistently well for Suzuki in the early rounds of the 250cc Motocross World Championship in 1968, finishing as high as second overall at the Belgium Grand Prix.

Unfortunately, his season ended when he crashed heavily at a round of the Swedish championships in early June. He broke a leg in three places and suffered facial cuts and concussion. At the time, he was lying fourth in the world championship.

A letter to the editor of magazine from a Roger Welch of London summed up the new era of motocross. Mr Welch had laughed in 1959 when Honda first entered the Isle of Man TT races. He admitted the smile had been wiped off his face 'when they led a Japanese invasion which all but monopolised the record books. Now it's all happening again but this time with motocross', he wrote. He went on to write: 'The Japs milked road racing for all the publicity they could get. Now they are out to do the same in motocross.' How right he was.

Throughout the 1969 season, the new Suzuki proved completely reliable and Olle consistently finished in the first six. The end of the season results were: Joel Robert,

The twin-cylinder machine.
Archives.

An RH67, the second
prototype. This was the
version I rode in 1967.
Suzuki website.

The TM68, the first standard
production model.
Suzuki website.

An RH68, the much improved
works model. A result of our
development work during the
previous year.
Suzuki website.

world champion with 102 points, Sylvain Geboers 96 and Olle third with 71. Suzuki was now a serious world championship contender, but who would be riding them in 1970?

On September 24 the headlines of every European magazine carried the historically significant announcement that Robert and Geboers had both signed three-year contracts with Suzuki. They finished first and second in the 1970 250cc world championship. Suzuki machines went on to dominate the sport with Belgian Roger DeCoster going on to win the 500cc class too.

After five years of steady development, Suzuki was the first Japanese factory to dominate world motocross. I have good reason to believe that my interest in the sport, stemming back to our original discussions in 1962, coupled with my active participation and advice over the intervening years, had played no small part in their overwhelming success.

Sylvain Geboers demonstrating his typical dashing style on the unbeatable 250cc works Suzuki. Suzuki website.

CHAPTER 17

Challenging two of the world's most successful motocross riders before returning once more to where it all began

MOTORCYCLING THROUGH THE EYES OF MY YOUTH

The road unfolds in front of me: 60km of one of the most scenic seaside routes in New Zealand. The day is perfect. Children are swimming at the many small beaches while their fathers fish from the rocks. I ride this winding route under a canopy of flame-red pohutukawa trees in full flower.

I'm not in a hurry. As each mile passes, I seem to be moving back in my life. I am again the same 16-year-old; seeing, sensing and living everything through his eyes. I am riding a 1947 Triumph Speed Twin I have just finished restoring. It is the same model Roy Foster and I had ridden as 14-year-olds, often with my dog Pippy on the tank. As a 16-year-old I bought it from brother Gordon, and odd as it may now seem, I seldom if ever exceeded 110kph.

The Triumph runs exactly as the one back in the early '50s. The subdued burble of its twin exhausts mingles with the rustle of tappet noise from the top of the engine. Its low, relaxed, riding position and modest performance acts as a kind of tranquiliser for an ageing ex-racer. A totally unexpected transformation.

The bottle of wine Janny and I will share this evening will be the finishing touch to a life-changing day. My love of motorcycling is stronger than ever. I am now a classic enthusiast through and through. The die is cast.

I started my 'retirement' pretty much as I'd finished my European scrambling career, by competing at the first round of Tim Gibbes' International Gold Leaf Series on January 1st. Tim had contracted twice 500cc world champion and nine-time British champion Jeff Smith, and double 250cc European and five-time British champion Dave Bickers, two of the greatest ever British motocross riders.

Not having ridden for three months and having suffered yet again debilitating stomach problems, third and fourth positions at the first round in New Plymouth had me feeling confident for the next round on January 11. The Woodville track in the Wairarapa was a Tim Gibbes creation, built along the lines of a typical open, fast French motocross circuit. Tim made the best use of the natural terrain and used his machine operator skills to add spectacular jumps. It was a crowd favourite.

Having had my engines overhauled by the CZ factory before leaving Europe, they were performing well. Speed would be more of an advantage here. The only thing that worried me was a blind, near-vertical drop-off from a hillside into the floodplain of a large stream. Few local riders had experience of this type of challenge and, understandably, rode steadily down it. We, on the other hand, descended it in the air at speed. Before practice I approached the marshal at the top asking him to warn us, with his flag, if any other riders were in the area. I had almost landed on a rider in France once and didn't want to repeat the experience.

Within a few laps I was 'in the groove'. On another section I was flying ever faster over a substantial hill, floating down the other side for a longer distance at an increasing height each lap. During the second practice session, I found myself drifting to the left caught in a strong gust of wind. This phenomenon was well known by the locals. Being well off the ground, I had no control and finally landed in an extremely rough patch 10m off the track. I had no option but to lay the bike down and my right knee came into painful contact with the footrest.

I moved out to the start of the first leg of the Rothmans Trophy race with a heavy elastic bandage supporting my swollen knee. After an excellent start I stayed as close to Jeff as possible. Physically it wasn't a demanding circuit and the race was just 12 laps long, so I thought I could stay the distance, even though I was in considerable pain. When we began lapping riders, I saw a gap, took it and shot into the lead. Well, what about this, I thought, as my exuberance returned now carrying a touch of fearlessness. The effects of the wind completely forgotten, I became determined not to let the chance to beat a legend go begging.

Corner after corner I could hear the throb of Jeff's 500cc four-stroke BSA single and, occasionally, the wail of Dave's two-stroke CZ. I braked ever later, gassed up sooner, flew off the jumps harder and higher, and floated high and long over that hill and down the steep drop-off.

These were New Zealand conditions, grassy and relatively smooth, with a touch of the French dash and daring added. I was in my element and had never ridden better. I could sense a win and with it the defeat of the craft and guile of arguably the best rider in the world on perhaps the most exotic motocross bike in existence, the latest 500cc factory BSA. On a slow, tight corner entering the straight in sight of the unfurling finishing flag, I made my one and only error, missing the deep berm and sliding wide. Jeff was through to the flag just a bike length ahead of me. Was I disappointed? Not at all.

An indication of the popularity of the European International Motocross events during the 1950s and 1960s.

Above: An action I later regretted. Archives.

Below: I am going to win this. Archives.

I actually bathed for days in the warmth of the risk, exuberance, excitement and the knowledge of having experienced my ultimate form.

Early in 1971 I was invited to become a commission salesman for a major Yamaha retail outlet in Hamilton. This coincided with the booming farm motorcycle market for which the Yamaha range of Trail models were well suited. Later in the year we received new 250 and 360cc models. These handled the local coditions well and were competitive with my CZs and Husqvarna. In due course, I became fully sponsored by the importer.

Farmers would get together during summer evenings organising their own grass track events with many enthusiastically entering the sport. I met a group from the Thames area who had, for a few years, been clearing historic kauri logging tracks and goldmine access roads in the Coromandel Ranges. Within six months a trail-riding club was formed and well-supported trail rides were organised. I would take Janny on the pillion of my 175 Yamaha and Hugh on the tank. Caroline rode pillion with a friend.

Top: Doug McLaren on my right and multi national champion Alan Collison. Archives.

Above: A winner is duty bound to wheelie over the line. Archives.

Some of the Saturday evenings, post-barbie and beers, very unofficial grass track events were absolutely hilarious. One chap, who had been practising wheelies all day, after a few drinks finally got the hang of it. He approached an old gate and, not wishing to stop a good thing, with his front wheel high in the air, he rode straight through it. Great stuff. As well as providing a new use for motorcycles, it helped Yamaha trail bike sales soar in our area.

Having always admired the history surrounding the superb Brough Superior motorcycles, the first true superbike, I had intended to bring one home at the end of 1969. In 1972 I began making enquiries about old bikes and was given the address of a farmer, near Tokoroa, who had a Douglas. I arrived at his place after dark. The shed housing the Douglas was pitch black, with no lighting. I felt the bike all over and confidently declared that it was a 1927 EW 350, the same model I had enjoyed so much as a 12-year-old and learned skills from that helped me through the years that followed. Soon after, a 1947 Triumph Speed Twin, identical to Gordon's, that I had started riding as a 14-year-old, joined the Douglas.

Working for Yamaha, building apartments to rent, riding motocross and trials most weekends slowed any plans to restore the pair and I went through the 'I'll never get them finished' stage. At the time when my enthusiasm was at its lowest, a major vintage car and motorcycle rally took place just an hour's drive away. I met people I'd known and raced with before going to Europe, enjoyed their company and soon got inspired to persevere with the restorations.

First was the Douglas. As humble as it might be, few bikes before or since have given me so much pleasure. Early in the morning before work it was off up the road for a test run. In the evening I would have another short ride, tinkering with it to obtain a perfect, ridiculously slow idle. I was totally gripped by the magnetism of another form of motorcycling. Soon the classic-vintage addiction took full grip in the form of a Vincent Touring Rapide, one of the most admired post-war motorcycles. I found it lying in a rotting shed when I was up in Northland attending a national motocross championship. Luckily, the amount of oil it had leaked, now turned green by the elements, had weatherproofed the engine and it looked much worse than it was. I also found an Army Indian that had covered only 3,700 miles. I swapped a good pushbike for a 1931 600cc Douglas in poor condition. And that was only the beginning.

Good post-war motorcycles had little value, were unwanted and so my collection grew. Many were passed on to friends as I busily made my contribution to the fledgling classic motorcycle movement.

For many there was time and money to allow for a new direction in their lives. Mortgages well in hand, children looking after themselves. My friends and associates from the Hamilton Motor Cycle Club became involved. It was a good reason to reconnect with people I had associated with in the past. Within two years, the Classic section had some 80 members.

The hardest-working, most-committed members of the Hamilton Motorcycle Club were the trials riding group. I enjoyed the sport and the people, all in a similar age group to myself, competing regularly and gaining second place in the North Island championship, riding of all things, my 400cc Husqvarna. Looking at the certificates I never had a national or North Island win; seconds and thirds, yes, even a sixth.

Above: Obviously very much at home on the Husqvarna. Archives.

Left: Popping mini wheelies. I 'think' three-year-old Hugh Jnr enjoyed them.

Bottom: Second, in the 1971 North Island trials championship, on my Husqvarna.

I can't blame the choice of bikes as I rode four different versions up to my cartilage removal when, due to constant pain, I was no longer able to compete.

Motocross remained my chief interest. During the three years and four months after our return from Europe, I won at least 18 national and North Island tiles. As luck sometimes has it, my most successful weekend was enjoyed just a matter of days before my enforced retirement. The 250cc

Above: A winning ride is always enjoyable. Archives.

Left: Winning one of many North Island titles. Peter Beazley.

Bottom: Ross McLaren's 400 CZ has more grunt than my 360cc Yamaha. Archives.

and 500cc National Miniature TT Championships were held at Te Aroha on March 10, with the National Motocross championship events next day at Gees Farm near Hamilton. Heavy rain preceded the Te Aroha meeting. The trick was to keep out of the worst of the greasy mud and straight-line it on the grass. This was the rear-wheel-spinning-on-full-throttle situation that I thrived on. It was a good day and I won both titles. It seemed that due to the bad weather and muddy conditions, some of the top riders didn't compete or they were saving themselves for next day's more highly rated motocross titles. My main opposition for the Motocross title, Ivan Miller, was one.

Saturday night I worked until late, cleaning and preparing the SC 500cc Yamaha. This was a machine that gained notoriety due to its weight, power and average handling, but I found it to be manageable. By 9pm I was as prepared as well as I could be for the main event of the year. This was the first national graded championship to be run on the highly successful French system: under a graded format, i.e. juniors, intermediates and seniors, with three heats counting towards the overall result. Coleman Suzuki had imported a special 400cc Suzuki and enlisted the young and very talented Ivan Miller to ride it. For three years, Ivan had enjoyed the sponsorship of Comerfords, a large motorcycle retail outlet in England. He had regularly gained top-six finishing positions in British championship rounds since late 1969. Eventually, he was selected to represent Great Britain in the 250cc Motocross des Nations championship in Czechoslovakia, where he finished second. A brilliant ride that surely showed, with the right management, he was world championship material.

Flying off a hill to win my last national title. Archives.

Commentator Bruce Weeks, Tim Gibbes, ACU President Don Tomkins, me and Ross McLaren. Archives.

This title was important to me. Almost to the date it was 20 years ago that here at the same venue, in 1953, I had entered my first ever serious competition winning all five races I had entered. Now 20 eventful years later it would be the site of virtually my last.

I hadn't met Ivan although I had been told that he suffered quite severe pre-race nerves, so all I could do was put as much pressure on him as possible. He was young and fit. I was 37 years old and anything but, with constant cartilage dislocation problems and quite severe pain from joint wear.

Not one to be left out, Janny demonstrates her skill. Archives.

I chased Ivan hard in the first race and noticed he was rather slow entering a corner at the bottom of a steep drop that turned uphill. Very early in the second race, while still on his rear wheel, I flew down the steep drop and took the inside line from him. I saw him stamping at the gear lever but the Suzuki didn't respond. A mechanical failure had occurred and I went on to win. I was enjoying the day and I chased Ivan so hard in the last race that I fell off but still finished in second place. It was a disappointing result for Coleman Suzuki as they were the main sponsor for the series.

Three days before the cartilage was to be removed from my left knee I couldn't resist squeezing in my last motocross meeting at an event near Taumarunui. In laid-back fashion I rode most of the day then took a glass and a bottle of wine and sat out in the middle of the course alone, taking in all that was going on around me. I had enjoyed the discipline of motocross above all other forms of racing and would have carried on indefinitely. Every corner, hill, jump, the straights even, could be and so often were a challenge. Always busy, and the risk added excitement. This is how I had always enjoyed my off- and on-road motorcycle racing. But this, old son, is the last race in your life, I thought, between sips of wine. Not a bad innings. Now physically buggered, there was no option and no regrets. What a wonderful 20 years it has been. Who knew what the future might hold?

Unknown to me, a clue to the answer was my purchase of a 1961 350cc Manx Norton with a rare Austrian Schafleitner six-speed gearbox for a modest outlay of NZ$450. The intended use was no more than a visual aid to assist an occasional nostalgic wallow. An ornament to fill a corner of the lounge in our next home.

The purchase took place on the weekend of the Hamilton Charity Street Race, in April 1973, the brainchild of the Hamilton Motorcycle Club.

I was one of a group of club members who went door-knocking residents on the planned course to gain their support. A big weapon in our charm offensive was the emphasis that this was a fundraising event for our local art gallery. Following the meeting I revisited the same residents. One elderly lady said she had spent the day in bed with a pillow over her head. Another claimed not to have seen her cat since.

The track was skilfully laid out on a fairly fast, interesting loop near the centre of the city. For a little excitement I entered the SC 500 Yamaha in the single-cylinder race and the main event. The night before, I hurriedly fitted a larger front brake from a road bike and a road rear tyre. Neither of these was of road race quality. During practice the front brake faded badly, but a team of enthusiastic Yamaha supporters removed the front forks and disc brake from a spectator's RD350 Yamaha and popped them into my scrambler. Without having time to consider what effect the much shorter forks might have, I lined up at the start.

At the first corner I hit the brakes hard and the shorter forks dived under the load, kicking the rear wheel high in the air. It was a novel experience for me and I'm sure for all those in close proximity. I stayed on it, bounced off a wall of straw bales and then settled in to do the best I could with what I had. My main opposition was Ken Fletcher, who became the chief mechanic for Barry Sheene during his most successful Grand Prix years. Ken was riding a well-prepared 350cc Aermacchi. Halfway through the race, when I was pushing him hard, he left his braking a little late and plunged into the straw bales, leaving me to win. I started the main race of

The Douglas, and the family on Gordon's prized historic vehicle. Archives.

the day and managed to hold sixth place in very good company, but to maintain that position required hammering the bike far too hard, so I retired.

A large crowd made the club's effort worthwhile, and over the next six years $12,000 was donated to the local art gallery. The current value is now estimated as being over half a million dollars. That night at the prize giving, Janny showed the first signs of labour. A day later, Michelle was born. Caroline and Hugh took to their new sister with love and attention. Janny's hard-working nature, pleasant personality and being a devoted mother made life very comfortable and pleasant for us all.

As the 1970s progressed, interest in classic motorcycles, those built after World War II, developed with clubs springing up around New Zealand. By the mid-'70s, rally organisers had difficulty coping with the number of entries.

Enjoying a vintage rally on the restored 1947 Triumph. Archives.

On tour with our Vincent and Watsonian Avon sidecar. Archives.

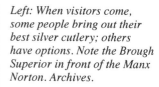

Left: When visitors come, some people bring out their best silver cutlery; others have options. Note the Brough Superior in front of the Manx Norton. Archives.

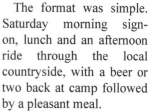

Middle: So fortunate to have the choice. After three and a half years, the BM had 80,000ks on the clock. Archives.

Bottom: Well, after organising it, I felt compelled to join in. Peter Beazley.

The format was simple. Saturday morning sign-on, lunch and an afternoon ride through the local countryside, with a beer or two back at camp followed by a pleasant meal.

All weekend we were surrounded by bikes that we had lusted after in our youth. I attended most of these rallies with Janny and all our children using our Vincent and Watsonian Avon sidecar outfit. Long-lasting friendships were established. We were on a mission of crusade-like proportions, fuelled by the re-awakening of the camaraderie, freedom and adventure that had played such an important part of being a motorcyclist in the post-war era.

Soon it became obvious that some owners of older race bikes would enjoy an opportunity to use them in a low-key event. Would the Hamilton club include a classic event at their 1974 street race? I put a fairly well-researched proposal to the committee.

Isle of Man TT riders all. From left: Bob Coleman, Sid Jensen, John Dale and winner in 1954, Rod Coleman. Archives.

Peter Murphy. A brilliant rider from the mid-'50s. Peter Beazley.

Len Perry, winner of a host of New Zealand titles, riding the much celebrated 500cc Velocette. Engine number M.T. 5 001. Peter Beazley.

After a short discussion they agreed: "Great idea, you organise it."

My spare time for the next few weeks was spent on the phone and writing letters. Eventually, some 30 owners of good bikes agreed to enter. That 1954 Isle of Man TT winner Rod Coleman, and his Isle of Man TT representative brother Bob, accepted our invitations and helped gain the support of many more, including the remarkable Sid Jensen and six more TT representatives. Enthusiasts travelled more than 2,000km to take part. All the bikes and riders were immaculately turned out. The event had been described as, and was intended to be, a parade, but it soon became a race. Fortunately, there was just one spill, when an ex-works Norton was dropped, but no damage was done. Many years later, classic enthusiast and celebrated international journalist Alan Cathcart, who was instrumental in setting up the UK's Classic Racing Motorcycle Club, felt that our Hamilton event was perhaps a world first.

Ken Mudford. Rider of factory Nortons and a Grand Prix winner. Peter Beazley.

Graham Ross, who had told me I couldn't take part in Clubman races in Whakatane and Tauranga 15 years earlier, was now an ardent vintage and classic bike enthusiast. We began discussions on how we could establish a club catering solely for classic racing motorcycles. I knew the Pukekohe circuit manager quite well and called on him explaining what we would like to do. At that time the circuit was under-utilised, plus he was sympathetic to our cause and offered us a reduced hire fee.

We had made our first step. After we discussed the basic format of the proposed event we called a meeting for June 30, 1979 to be held in the Hamilton club hall. We invited owners of racing machinery and enthusiasts with a long history of working at club committee level.

The sole purpose of the club, at this stage, was to organise a two-day national rally, incorporating low-key racing and rally-type activities with a strong social agenda. It would be a place where all pre-1963 classic machinery could take part for the enjoyment of every enthusiast. It was also envisaged that some financial assistance would be given to South Island and Australian supporters. Tentative dates of February 16–17, 1980, were set for the first meeting and the 19 people who attended made a donation to establish a working fund. A total of $79 was collected. Our second club meeting attracted 50 enthusiasts and I was chosen as one of 16 officials to lead the way forward.

Enthusiasm gathered apace. The road rally, to be held early on the Sunday morning, even had the mayor of Newmarket, Mr Bill White, wanting to join in on a Velocette, and John Dale, Rod and Bob Coleman and up to 10 more New Zealand Isle of Man TT representatives intended to take part. Several Australians were planning to fly over. Elmer McCabe, with an immaculate AJS 7R and Matchless G45. Robert 'Rob the Rudge' Hart, who had a collection of 40 Rudges. Eric Debenham, aka 'The Flying

Grandfather', was listed as attending with a Vincent, and Dennis Quinlan on his Mk VIII Velocette. In November we heard that the UK's Classic Racing Motorcycle Club had held its inaugural meeting, with 400 attendees. Now the wheels were really turning.

The first Pukekohe festival exceeded all expectations. The biggest crowd ever to attend a club circuit meeting at that venue stayed to the end, entranced by the 90-odd race bikes and 150 rally machines. There were 23 races and many of them were close-run affairs that had spectators waving programmes over the fence in appreciation. At the end of the weekend several participants confessed they had been away from racing and motorcycles for 25 years or more, but they had never forgotten, and the bug had bitten deep.

Our post-race newsletter gave a portent of the future regarding overseas guests: 'Our Australian visitors added a sharpness to each event they entered. Dennis and Eric were high in their praise of the low-key attitude of officials and the friendly atmosphere.' They were the first of many to become unofficial envoys for our club. The newsletter also continued with an ideal that the club upholds decades later: 'We wish to continue as a rally-social weekend, not, certainly not, an out-and-out race meeting. This we believe is the very essence of classic machine racing; the machines are what make the event, they are the centrepiece — factory racer, production racer, super sports or home-brewed, all are equal here. Provided the last rider across the finish line gains as much pleasure and satisfaction as the first, we are succeeding in our job.'

At our first annual general meeting, on June 14, 1980, it was announced that the register had a cash balance of $6,301.85. Not bad from a start-up fund of $79. By now

TV time at Pukekohe Raceway. From left: Me, Graeme Crosby, Len Perry, Geoff Duke, Tim Parker John Samson, Sid Kirwan, Ernie Williams, Dennis Quinlan and David Bell. Archives.

the register was expanding into a true national club, with prominent Christchurch motorcycle men George Begg and Maurice Wear holding positions on the register's committee. Soon they were instrumental in planning a similar meeting to our festival at Levels Raceway, Timaru, in November. By the end of the year we had more than 200 members and a substantial bank balance. I woke one morning and, as you do, rummaged about in the thought process and realised that we could afford to host any

Levels Raceway, Timaru. John Surtees, Tim Parker, organiser George Begg, David Bell and me on George's 7R. Archives.

Classic Register Committee at our home 1983. From left: Graham Page, Errol McCabe, Dave Philpot, Ernie Williams, Peter Butterworth, Jean Hayes, Robin Heaphy, Graham Ross, Me, David Bell, Les Callis and Tim Parker. Archives.

star of the Classic period from anywhere in the world. My pick was Geoff Duke. A multi world champion. who with his good looks and the aid of television, became the first national motorcycle star in Britain. I phoned the executive members, they readily agreed.

Surprisingly, perhaps, that was the first international call I had made. Initially, I was shouting into the mouthpiece; well, he was a long way away. His visit in 1981, with wife Daisy, set the scene for the following three decades. The presence of such an outstanding man gave our meeting national and worldwide recognition and acceptance.

The following year John Surtees, the only man to win world Grand Prix titles on two and four wheels, accepted our invitation to join us. All those associated with car, motorcycle magazines and even mainstream news wanted to interview and film him. The Classic Motorcycle Racing Register climbed several more rungs up the ladder of success and credibility. John rode fast and enjoyed competing at Pukekohe, then travelled south to Timaru to compete at our second meeting at Ruapuna. Like Geoff, John too enjoyed the social side of our activities.

I met Ken McIntosh in 1972; he told me he was building a Vincent-engined special based on Swiss Fritz Egli's lightweight spine frame. Ken was just 18 years old and looked younger. A more mature racer-engineer would find such a difficult project daunting, so I had doubts that the project would be completed.

Two years later, when walking through the pits at a national championship round at Pukekohe, I met a proud Ken and his completed race bike. Without doubt, it was the most handsome special I had ever seen. The engineering work was perfect. The styling of the tank and seat displayed Ken's artistic eye for shape and proportion. I meant it when I shook his hand and congratulated him; a gesture that sealed a close friendship that continues. At a time when the ultimate race bike, a TZ 750cc Yamaha, cost $6,000, Ken's Egli had eaten up no less than $7,000.

Having restored my 1953 Vincent Rapide, I was a fellow Vincent nut and a member of the worldwide Vincent Owners Club. Ken and I, like all Vincent owners, spoke the same language. Nevertheless it was a surprise in early November 1983 when Ken phoned asking, "Have you heard that a national championship for twin-cylinder machines has been introduced for this coming season?

"No, Ken, I haven't," I replied.

The Battle of the Twins would have rounds at the Pukekohe racetrack and street circuits at Wanganui and Gracefield, near Wellington. Our main competitors would be Ducatis, including the latest Pantah-based racers, and British twins.

"With you on the Egli, we could win it," said Ken.

"Really? I'd like to think about it. I'll call you back."

Once or twice in recent years I'd been tempted to have a few rides, perhaps to create a snapshot sample of the past, but no more than a dream to fill an idle moment. I had become a member of Joe Public. Road racing is dangerous. You shouldn't do it. First, I consulted Janny. As she so often had said before, concerning motorcycle activity, "If that's what you want to do, go ahead." I spoke to a close friend and long-term motorcycle enthusiast Tim Parker, who had recently acquired an extremely rare dismantled 1935 HRD TT Replica. Tim, a born engineer and being well immersed in Vincent folklore, volunteered his time and experience as did son Hugh.

I phoned Ken agreeing to give it a go; he listed the modifications we needed to make to put us on more equal terms with the modern bikes that were competing. The latest wheels, double-disc brakes up front and the best forks available. Fine. I would finance that and look after the running costs. Ken ordered the parts required, but delivery dates came and went several times. They finally arrived just before the event leaving us to work 18-hour days to complete it. On the Friday afternoon before the meeting, British Team Suzuki mechanic Martyn Brook called at Ken's factory for a look around. When Ken told him that I was riding the Egli he joined in and worked all night, just to be part of it. I left at midnight to get some sleep and they finally had the Vinnie running at 7am on a wet Saturday, just in time to load it and drive out to the Pukekohe circuit south of Auckland.

The clerk of the course reluctantly allowed me to ride behind the standard production class for a few running-in laps. We checked it over and everything was fine, so I let it off during our practice session. It felt good. The engine was strong, brakes phenomenal and tyres okay, but before being able to clarify my braking points, lines through corners or any source of competitiveness, the five-lap session was over.

The bike was left to cool, then willing hands checked it over. All adjustments and ignition settings seemed right, allowing us to head home for the first early night in a week.

The press had played it up: World champion making comeback. Combined ages of rider and Vincent 80 years, challenging the current top riders on their latest highly tuned machines and so on. Race day was fine, our team excited. But the big imponderable: I hadn't ridden in a road race for 17 years, the Vincent was an unknown quantity and I had completed just one short practice session. There was a large field containing national 600cc production race champion Dave Martin riding the Ducati importer's very well prepared machine. All this left me with a knot in my stomach; as the time of the race neared, I was suffering from a severe attack of nerves, mainly associated with loss of face if I got blown off. If I don't have a heart attack today, I should be good for years, I thought.

At flag drop I got a reasonable start. I found the Vincent was sluggish out of slow corners, but once in third gear it started to go and in top the old girl lifted her skirts and really motored. It was strong and stable as it thundered up the long back straight gaining on the leaders. Approaching the hairpin they sat up and hit their disc brakes. In a flash the situation was transformed. What had been a slowly closing gap suddenly became a very rapid one. I sat up and moved to the left to avoid others and hit my double discs hard. I found relief in their amazing power and arrived at the hairpin with room to spare. I'd braked too soon. By the fourth lap I'd closed on Dave Martin; as we raced past the start-finish and approached one of the fastest corners in New Zealand road racing, he slowed, I was set to enter it much faster. But David is national champ, his judgement is better than mine, surely. After 17 years of retirement and at 47 years of age, my confidence was fragile. We roared past the start-finish again. Dave sat up, I didn't and, to the delight of the cheering crowd in the packed grandstand, I rode around him and pulled away to win.

Ken had been correct in his assessment that the Egli-Vincent could win. All the team and the enthusiasts of my era and age group were absolutely delighted. There was still life in old bikes and old blokes.

The happy winning team stand behind Ken's Egli-Vincent. Ernie Williams, Martyn Brooks, Janny, me, Ken and Tim Parker. Archives.

We were in good spirits when we arrived at the Wanganui Cemetery Circuit for the Boxing Day meeting, even though the short, winding street layout would not favour the big Vinnie. These were the days when New Zealand motorcycle racing, due to promotion by Malboro cigarettes, later becoming known as the Countrywide series, was on a high attracting nationwide television coverage and international riders from around the world.

Before we began this campaign, I had promised Janny that I wouldn't ride outside my safe comfort zone. On the third lap of practice, I got a corner entry wrong and hit the protective straw bales hard; unfortunately, it was right where Janny and the team were standing. Evidently the bike and a cloud of straw rose in the air. We landed upright and intact on the other side of the road, wobbled about a bit and carried on around to the pits. The left handlebar was twisted back up against the petrol tank and the footrest and brake pedal bent. Not a good start but the team, including Janny, were more amused than critical. Fortunately, we had a spare footrest but no longer had a functioning rear brake. Dave passed me on the seventh lap in the race but under the circumstances second was fine. We were now equal on points.

Another street circuit followed at Gracefield just north of Wellington. This time the throttle slides were sticking open, an obviously nerve-wracking situation. Fitting stronger return springs helped, but didn't overcome it, and third place behind Dallas Rankin, Ducati, and Dave was the best we could do. Dave won the championship by two points from me with Dallas third.

After signalling our intentions, we managed to win the series in the summer of 1984–85 but it was close. I won by just two points from Dave Martin, with the experienced Dallas Rankin third. Actually, we were lucky to make the starting grid at all of the three race venues. Over winter Ken had carried out some development work on the engine. During a pre-race test I noticed a small decrease of power and stopped; he discovered a blockage in the low-pressure oil system. After making the necessary repairs we rode it up and down a quiet road near his factory. It seemed to run okay but was blowing smoke from the front cylinder's exhaust. I hoped it was only excess sump oil.

Leading into the S-bend at Wanganui. Archives.

The tombstones confirm that this is the Cemetery Circuit. Archives.

Tim, Hugh Jnr and I set off for Manfeild near Palmerston North. Five laps into the first practice session, it again lost power so I pulled into the pits. A litre of oil had been blown into the collection bottle. Not a good sign. I suggested we park it for the weekend. Tim is very accomplished at making his own decisions and he started tinkering. First he opened the timing chest to see if more problems had occurred there but it was fine. Then, in his relaxed and thorough way, he began removing the cylinder head and barrel. There was a lump deep in the cylinder liner that had picked up on the piston and smeared aluminium into the ring grooves, trapping the rings. The lump was caused by a camshaft seizure, during our first test session, which had spun the spindle inwards as it unwound off its retaining nut. It was late and convinced it was a lost cause, I went to bed. An automotive engineering friend lived nearby. Late that night he was enticed from his bed. The lump was ground off and the bore honed. Evidently it took Tim hours to patiently scrape away the aluminium that held the rings fast in their grooves. But being Tim he did it.

Next morning, blow me down: the Vincent was ready to go. It warmed up well at the track, running smoothly. After having had virtually no practice, I was lined up towards the rear of the grid. With a good start, I arrived on the outside of the first corner with several riders slightly ahead on the inside. For some reason they seemed to hesitate, so I gassed up, rode around them and pulled away in the lead. A misfire that had bothered us during practice returned. Then a nasty rattle began in a particular rev range. It got progressively worse but I managed to nurse it to the flag winning by a bike length, and discovered the mechanical rattle was only an exhaust pipe vibrating against a bolt head.

A few weeks later at Wanganui when removing a spark plug, the thread was damaged. A helicoil thread insert was fitted without removing the head, a story in itself. We went on to gain second to Dave. On the second lap of practice at Gracefield the primary chain broke. It blew the chain case apart, taking a chunk of crankcase with it. The flywheels were obvious for all to see. We won't be riding that today, I thought. Tim and local Vincent owners found a new chain and with hi-tech glue and aluminium sheeting, completed a satisfactory running repair. I went out and won the championship.

My last outing on the Egli-Vinnie was the Lyall Bay street race in Wellington in February 1985. The course was made up of several right-angled corners and an S-bend, which shouldn't have been a happy hunting ground for the Vinnie. But after a full practice session I found some real form and during the race, as never before, we were as one. With the rear wheel scrabbling for traction, I was in full control and ran away to a comfortable win. During the two season series using a 500cc Manx Norton, with a Les DeLacy-prepared engine, I won all the classic support events.

New Zealand's climate is such that no matter where you are, at any time, you can expect rain. On Saturday evening of the 1985 Classic Register's meeting, during early February, light rain began to fall; nothing unusual about that, but on this occasion it became a deluge later described as a cloudburst. The piles under houses on distant hills were undermined, allowing them to slide away to destruction. In the Pukekohe region, known as the vegetable garden of Auckland, on a nearby hillside many hectares of onions had been pulled and lay on the surface to dry, and these were washed into and blocked the drainage systems. Water gushed over land and roads and flooded Pukekohe Raceway and the camping area. Naturally, this once-in-a-lifetime event provided a fund of stories. Amusing and not so much fun. But being in it all together we could only laugh at our very wet selves. Parked race bikes with only the handlebars and petrol tank protruding. Our caravan headquarters half full of water with documents and even the money bags for the gatekeepers washed away. Perhaps the most surprised were the campers who had quality tents. They had no idea of how serious the situation was until they opened the zip and water gushed in.

The devastating scene, as we saw it, soon after dawn. Archives.

There will be no racing today. Archives.

The great Geoff Duke demonstrating David Bell's Norton. How very fortunate that he had not been invited to this event.

CHAPTER 18

The call of the classic Continental Circus was irresistible

With keen anticipation, I slice open the envelope bearing English postage stamps dated June 4, 1985. It contains letters from Gladys and Tom Arter, sponsor-entrants of mine during 1962, replying to an enquiry I have made some weeks earlier regarding the UK classic racing scene.

Gladys writes thanking me for my long, interesting letter about the family, and for inviting them to stay with us should they come to New Zealand. Tom has three cousins and Gladys also has relations here. They are planning a possible visit during 1986. Tom writes as you'd expect Tom would, short and to the point:

Dear Hugh,
  Received your long, interesting letter regards all your successes within classic racing. Don't expect me to be so interested in today's racing. My part in the sport commenced way back in 1930 and finished with the TT in 1976. Personally I can't understand people in their 50s considering taking the risks involved and I, as a sponsor, would not enjoy it now. Be aware of what can happen. You certainly had a good run in the '60s. I can understand doing trials riding but not racing. I have refused giving machines to some good riders over here, so cannot break away from that. Wishing you every success, but suggest you sit back and think a bit.

Yours sincerely, Tom Arter.

No grey areas there.

My renewed interest in racing in the UK stemmed from an invitation to take part in a parade lap during the 1982 Isle of Man TT races along with George Begg, former Isle of Man competitor and Patron of our Classic Register, and one of New Zealand's most celebrated riders, Len Perry. UK Classic Racing Motorcycle Club president Alan Cathcart loaned me his Matchless G50 to use on the Isle of Man. Before the TT I attended the 'Derek Minter Day' celebrations at Brands Hatch, Derek was to lead a parade of riders on each day of what was an English Classic Clubs race meeting,

The beautifully crafted, aluminium-framed Steve Roberts Special. Terry Stevenson.

I had been allocated an MZ from the British Museum. Friday was practice, warming up John Surtees' 500cc Manx Norton, and hearing the barking echo of a multitude of open exhausts was just as it had been more than two decades ago during my first visit. I was very much emotionally back down at the 'Atch'.

With good friends Alan and Sheila Jones at the Derek Minter Day at Brands Hatch. Archives.

Derek Minter, the 'King of Brands', rules once more. Alan stands behind him. Archives.

To only be a spectator in the Isle of Man was a novelty. I experienced the rush of air and ground-shaking speed of the superbikes as they flew past the Sulby Straight crossroads at over 160mph.

High on the mountain during Wednesday's Formula One race, we were willing on the brilliant New Zealander Dave Hiscock on Steve Roberts' unique aluminium monocoque-framed, Suzuki-powered special into third place. We too felt part of that remarkable history-making achievement, done on a shoestring and with the Coleman Suzuki engine brought over in a suitcase.

On the return trip to London I called at Stuart and Margaret Graham's home. After dinner, Stuart, the most modest of men, asked if I would like to see a few old cars out in his shed. He opened the door to a temperature-controlled garage. The first in line of five immaculate Mercedes was a 1969 300SL Gull Wing, next a 280SL Roadster, a 1955 Cabriolet, a pagoda-roofed 1964 280SL and a modern coupe. It seems this self-effacing type of personality — well, these things happen — is hereditary. His dad, my schoolboy hero, had said after having received the DFC for his exploits in flying a Lancaster bomber during the war: "Well, they had one over and had to give it to someone." Another was, "Oh, it must have been sent to the wrong address."

There are some old bangers in the shed. Would you like to see them? Archives.

Alan Cathcart encouraged me to consider having a 'racing holiday' in the UK. Tim Parker and I discussed the possibilities. I'd enjoyed the Battle of the Twins series, had felt confident, safe and had embraced the whole scene. We finally decided the 1985 European season would be the year.

I began a letter-writing campaign to gauge the possible assistance available with machine preparation, transport, accommodation and so on. All of my friends from the '60s offered us beds, or a vehicle and certainly a stack of moral support. Having kept in contact with Tom Arter and good friend Jimmy Boughen, foreman of the AMC race shop, I felt it worthwhile to approach them. Jim's reply revealed he now spent time in Tenerife in the Canary Islands, and was no longer building engines. However, "I still have all my equipment here, so if you're stuck of course I will give you all the assistance I can." Also, "I see Tom Arter about every three weeks when I am in England. He has not mellowed with age," he warned.

Les DeLacy and I sold our 1961 500cc Manx Norton. By complete chance it was the machine I had bought new in May of that year. It was replaced with a good 1959 G50 Matchless that Alan Cathcart found for me in England. Tom Arter's frank letter didn't deter me; his involvement would have been beneficial but it wasn't essential. All my applications for entries during August and September were received with enthusiasm. I was the first of the Grand Prix world champions from the classic era to venture into the new English classic racing scene. George Begg decided to come too and entered the Manx Grand Prix to be held in early September. He talked me, reluctantly, into joining him. His wife Freda was born in the Ballaugh village — her bedroom window had overlooked the bridge — and was able to arrange accommodation for us. Another adventure was beginning to take shape.

On our arrival my New Zealand friends Laurie and Jan Shephard made us very comfortable in their house in Brigg, near Hull. Laurie was now headmaster of a private school but this did not stop him taking part in classic events racing an early-model Triumph. The G50 was a good, genuine bike but obviously needed to be overhauled and prepared for a demanding series of races. Jim was in Tenerife but, through other contacts and a lot of travelling about, we got things done.

During those travels we called on Tom. I knocked on the door. He opened it and stood blocking my entrance and with a straight-faced sternness said: "What do you want?"

All scrubbed up ready for a night on the town. Tim, Jan, Laurie and I. Archives.

"We were in the vicinity, Tom, and I felt we should call."

Without any sign of a change of mood he offered: "Well, you had better come in then."

Why are race bikes always in pieces? Archives.

Well, everyone else does it. Archives.

Gladys welcomed me with a hug but conversation was a little on the stiff side for 10 minutes or so. A cup of tea, and a coincidence that Tim and Tom used the same strong pipe tobacco, thawed the air. Tom soon tired of my family-based conversation with Gladys and asked Tim if he would like to have a look in his shed. It was the same Aladdin's cave of AMC racers and parts that I had seen, and worked in all those years ago. The swirling smoke that emanated from their pipes and Tim's assurance that I wasn't there to win, but to enjoy the travel and re-enact the experiences, seemed to change Tom's view of old blokes going racing. Tim returned to the house with a box containing a carburettor, magneto, oil pump, engine and rear-wheel sprockets, clutch plates and many smaller, valuable and virtually unobtainable parts.

We had little in the way of engineering facilities, so Andy Farrer from Hull offered us the use of his well-equipped workshop. A test run at Cadwell Park in Lincolnshire showed the G50 was going well enough, but I was rusty. An elderly spectator who had been taking my lap times was kind enough to comment that they were amazingly consistent. Proof perhaps that I knew what I was doing and just needed to speed it all up.

This is bloody hard work. I wish the Poms had less talent. Archives.

Easy start, you have got to be kidding. Archives.

Our first serious test was a Classic Racing Motorcycle Club meeting in August back at Cadwell. The short circuit that was used with its undulations and flowing sequence of corners suited the bike and me perfectly. A busy and rewarding experience, if you get it right. I managed a win and a third place, followed by a very pleasant evening with two visiting Germans who had some rather interesting types of beer with them. Next stop was Ivan Rhodes in Derby, a great and ever helpful friend who allowed us the use of his extensive facilities to prepare for the daunting task of competing at the Isle of Man Manx Grand Prix. Ivan is a generous man: he loaned us his very, very second-hand Ford transit van. With complete confidence he said it would get us there and back. It did, but what a close-run thing. It took a box full of easy-start spray cans and many a push starts. It could only manage low gear up the mountain and one morning Tim was stopped by marshals and ordered off the road as it had been closed. After explaining he had my bike, they allowed him to carry on his ever so steady way. There were many a laugh, it was always parked facing downhill, but as Ivan said it would, we got back to Derby. Soon after it was consigned to a wrecker's yard.

The island welcomed us with wet, cold and windy weather. One practice session was stopped when a tree was blown down across the road. As my G50 wasn't ready for the beginning of practice, Andy Farrar had been kind enough to bring his quick 450 Ducati to the island as a backup bike. I covered five laps on it, one at over 90mph, which pleased him. Tim finished the G50 in time to allow me another five laps but, like the weather, my form was rather average. Now I had little enthusiasm for the project, unlike all those years ago when I was living a boyhood dream; now it was a dull, somewhat anxious, heavy load. I wrote a carefully worded letter absolving conscientious Tim of all blame should I be involved in a serious or fatal accident. It was put in a sealed envelope and given to Laurie.

No turning back, the start is in 30 minutes. Archives.

Race day was very windy with scattered showers, the worst combination. My first lap was some two minutes faster than I had achieved in practice and the second faster again in the mid-90mph mark.

Wonder if I can do a deal. The guy in the upstairs window shows interest. Mortons Archive.

Then just before the Ballaugh Bridge jump, when flat on the tank negotiating a series of very fast top-gear corners, a crunch and a screaming engine indicated a broken primary chain. A quick left hand whipped in the clutch lever and my race was over. At the time I was lying in a respectable seventh place.

Soon after, the season began to unfold in that never-to-be-forgotten Continental Circus way. To enable us to take part in the Austrian Old Timers Grand Prix and the French Bol d'Or international events, good friend Keith Arney loaned us his well-used but mechanically sound Volkswagen Kombi van. After hastily gathering the absolute basic requirements, we set out. Our first night was spent somewhere in Belgium. As we had just one blanket and one pillow between us, Tim took the pillow and lay on the cover above the warm, rear-mounted engine. I lay across the front seats under the blanket. Early next morning, in true traditional Continental Circus style, our breakfast was 'a glass of water and a look around'.

Arriving at Salzburg we met Luigi Taveri from Italy, one of my main competitors of the 1960s. He was taking part on his immaculate four-cylinder 250cc Honda. Even though it had been 19 years since we had last met, it was "Hey, Hugh, it is good to see you!" There is a lifelong trust among riders, not only due to having ridden close, hard and fast, but based, perhaps, on a sharing of the highs, lows, fears and even nightmares of our mutual past.

Top: The Kombi wagon, Tim and our two-seat hospitality suite. Archives.

Middle: My old sparring partner Luigi Taveri, Tim and a Honda four. Archives.

Bottom: Lean it over further at your peril. Werner Rehwagen.

The Old Timers Grand Prix was one of the most remarkable events in the fast-growing classic world. The cream of European race machines, cars and bikes were taking part. Most were of European manufacture, all of interest and beautifully restored. In this company, for me to have been given the Number 1 race plate was a true honour. The events were based on the Regularity Parade principle where the rider with the most regular lap times won, followed by a pleasant social and prize giving. John Surtees took part on his Manx Norton renewing his rivalry from yesteryear with Ernst Hiller on a factory-prepared Rennsport BMW. John also had the enviable, though hugely responsible, task of demonstrating a mid-'50s Mercedes Grand Prix car.

We had entered the classic support races at the famous Bol d'Or endurance race held on the Paul Ricard circuit in the south of France. After crossing the border from Germany we were stopped by a customs patrol. They checked our paperwork and then the female leader of the group saw Tim's pipe sitting on the dashboard. She picked it up and smelt the bowl. Though only speaking in French, it was obvious that she wanted to know what Tim smoked in it. His startling reply was "Camel sh--t and used tram tickets." Suddenly, they all spoke English and we had to empty the van for

Top: Wearing out my boots and fairing. Archives.

Above: Ample champers and a solid silver trophy. Archives.

a full and very thorough search.

At the time, French riders and teams tended to dominate the 24-hour championship series and the Bol d'Or was held in a festival atmosphere that attracted many tens of thousands of motorcyclists from all over Europe. It was party time.

The pits were a different world from those I had left in 1966

Massive transporters dominated the scene and every car was an expensive late model. So here we were, two modest, middle-aged Kiwis wearing shorts and T-shirts in a faded blue Kombi.

I joined the flashy, decal-laden race crews at the sign-on office. After unloading the G50 we noticed a group of French enthusiasts gathered around a 350cc Manx Norton. The group went into a huddle with their body language indicating something very odd, and quite beyond them, was wrong with the bike. Their gold watches and clothing indicated that, like many others taking part in classic events, they were not short of a few francs.

Tim and I sidled up and enquired regarding their problem. It seemed the clutch would repeatedly go out of adjustment. Tim and I felt that the thrust rod was soft and wearing away. I introduced myself and they were surprised and pleased to meet us. After removing the suspect part, Tim, with a borrowed gas torch, heated the ends to a dull red and quenched them in oil and the problem was solved. The owner of the Norton spoke English, was grateful and asked where we were staying.

"We have nowhere to stay."

With a worried frown he said, "One hundred and fifty thousand spectators will be here and there is no accommodation available within thirty kilometres." With that he pulled out of his satchel what looked like a large plastic brick with an aerial attached, walked to one side and spoke into it at length. He returned with a smile: "I have a room for you in a nice hotel. It is being repaired, so no charge. This evening I will take you there."

Tim found another owner in difficulty. This chap had just collected a 'barn fresh' Vincent and sidecar but the challenge to make it run was too much for him. Tim quietly got to work. After an hour of tinkering and a short push-start with a cloud of smoke the engine burst into life. Tim's new best friend couldn't thank him enough but happened to own a winery so we were more than pleased to receive five bottles of wine.

From the first practice lap the G50 ran well and after just eight laps we were on the pace, setting the fastest time in our class. A Michelin tyre representative called and offered us a pair of tyres he felt would better suit the circuit than what we were using; we accepted them with thanks. That evening we were shown into a very nice two-bedroom apartment, near Nice, which overlooked the Mediterranean. We gained the impression that our benefactor was a part owner of the establishment.

After a shower and shave we visited a nearby bar. After several martinis we moved on to a Chinese restaurant. Tim's schoolboy French could not unlock the mysteries of the menu. However, with help of a waiter, who possessed no English but a fine sense of humour, we settled for several dishes that appeared suitable to our tastes; the meal was superb.

Next day I won both races and set a new lap record. With John and Brenda Holder, John gained considerable success though the late '50s including winning the Thruxton 500-mile event. We enjoyed a pleasant evening with his sponsor Keith Ashton and a group of English riders, some of whom I had ridden with in the '60s. The five bottles of wine were disposed of and that was only the start.

The season finale was the English classic club's Race of the Year at Snetterton in Norfolk. Within a few laps of practice we were in trouble. As soon as I began cornering at something like speed, the Michelin-clad front wheel began pattering wildly. An Irish chap overheard me telling Tim about it. He offered us a Dunlop tyre. The straw inside it indicated it wasn't of recent manufacture, but he was quite sure it would cure our problems, and it did. At the time there were no designated quality tyres available. The headline in Motorcycling Weekly of September 24, 1985, blared: 'Hit for six'. The report read: 'Hugh Anderson's European classic season culminated with a tremendous win in the Classic Racing Club's 500cc Classic Race

of the Year at Snetterton on Sunday, to add to his three victories on Saturday and two wins in Sunday's supporting races. The ex-50cc and 125cc world champion had to work hard to battle his way through the field after a poor start. From 12th on lap one, he set about reeling in front runners Ian Griffiths and last year's winner Dave Bedlington.

After winning six races, I'm rewarded with a ride on an old truck. And that's just fine. Archives.

Anderson relegated Bedlington to second place on lap seven. The New Zealander returns home on Thursday.'

The last meeting was over and we had done well. At times, the 10-week journey had not been an easy one. Tim's work ethics, skills and commitment to having the G50 at its best not only allowed us to enjoy it, but in truth made it possible. Without his company, skills and humour, the venture would have failed. The day before we left I received an unexpected phone call. It was from Randy Owen. Randy had come out to New Zealand some 14 years earlier and with some input from me he had taken my place as the fully supported motocross rider for the Yamaha importers. He was brief and to the point. "I heard you were here," he said. "It's taken a while to find you. If you are coming back next year I can fix you up with a van and a bed. Keep in touch."

The ever helpful Les DeLacy had a little-used, much-modified 1955 650cc BSA engine. For our 1985–86 New Zealand season we decided to fit it in my 350cc Manx Norton frame. An indication of its performance was when competing in the BEARS class at Wanganui, against the latest European bikes all of larger capacity, I finished fifth. As expected, the BSA Manx did very well in all the classic races we entered.

In April I received a letter from Maxime Giraudroux, an influential member of the French Classic Racing Club AFAMAC. Two races would be included in the French Grand Prix on July 18th and 20th and the club would offer a substantial contribution to Tim's and my travel costs. So it was game on again, for an eight-week, seven-meeting campaign.

Randy Owen loaned us a Toyota van and fully loaded we drove north to our first meeting, the Bob McIntyre Memorial festival at Knockhill, near Edinburgh. Laurie now was racing a 450cc Ducati and joined us. Just as I was beginning to get going in Saturday's practice, I sensed the beginning of a slight vibration and called into the pits. Tim put an extendable magnet into the oil tank and withdrew it to find pieces of a thin shim attached. Luckily, Ducati owner Andy Farrar came to my aid once more. His little Duke went well and I scratched around the tight, demanding circuit well enough to gain third place in the Bob McIntyre Memorial event. Afterwards, the inevitable bottle of Glenfiddich came out, courtesy of club president Bill Cadger. Next day we were all suffering a bit.

Tim stripped the motor, replaced the crankshaft shim, and rebuilt it on a makeshift bench he had built from 44-gallon drums and an old door in Laurie's garage at the school. Then it was off to Montlhéry, the famous old French motodrome, built to compete against such grand counterparts as Germany's Nürburgring, Italy's Monza and England's Brooklands. It was hosting one of Europe's biggest classic festivals involving cars and bikes, an historic event more than a race, but you know how it is. The favourite for the main event was Jean-Paul Boinet, a French champion and current member of the successful French Suzuki Endurance Team. He was entered on a Manx Norton fitted with a 750cc Norton twin engine. The event was run on a 'two heats and a final' basis. I won both heats but Jean-Paul won the final by 2.03 seconds. Understandably, the big Norton engine out-accelerated the 500cc G50 from the several slow chicanes and my front brake wasn't able to cope with the demands of the day.

We returned to England and took part in two classic club events before returning to France to compete in the main event of our European tour, the French Grand

Prix support races at the Paul Ricard-sponsored circuit near Toulon. It was the first time a full-on classic race — as opposed to a parade — was held as a Grand Prix support event.

The first race was televised live and I joined Phil Read and John Surtees on the grid. Between us we held 19 world Grand Prix titles. Other competitors had come from far and near, including American Dave Roper, riding a G50 Matchless entered by Rob Iannucci's well-funded, New York-based 'Team Obsolete'.

Surtees led on his Manx from the start of the first race and I followed with Alan Cathcart third on a rare factory Paton twin. Roper made a slow start but soon caught us on a bike allegedly running 13:1 compression and 120 octane American racing fuel. He went on to win while Surtees' engine slowed with a problem. Then Alan passed me for second.

Later Alan wrote: 'I got a rude shock at the start of the last lap when Hugh Anderson out-braked me into the first corner, with both wheels sliding on his Matchless. Our bikes were evenly matched in top speed, but the Paton accelerated slightly better, which enabled me to re-pass him two corners from the end, but not until the two of us sat it out all the way around the turn side by side, front wheels pattering furiously, rear wheels scrabbling for traction and grip. I had the better line at the last bend and took the flag half a second ahead of Hugh after a nerve-wracking last lap. At 50 years of age, Anderson is still a skilful and determined racer par excellence.' John Surtees finished fourth and Phil Read retired.

The second race was run after the last Grand Prix event. It appeared to be a rerun of the first until I found myself in a desperate nip-and-tuck battle with Surtees. Alan slipped through but then Roper swept past us all and set off for the chequered flag.

Alan Cathcart's report: 'Anderson dropped back when a fuel line split on his G50, which began leaking petrol on the rear tyre, with obvious results. Doubtless the Kiwi former world champion's considerable MX experience came in useful, enabling him to cope with the resultant slides.' This left Surtees and me fighting for second place but, on the fourth lap, the Paton jumped out of gear twice, and the second time bent a valve badly enough for it to go on to one cylinder and forced me into the pits to retire. John Surtees secured second place with me third again.

Another report, from a French journalist: 'If anyone had ever thought that races with old machines were more in the nature of a pleasure outing than true competition, those people should bring themselves up to date. After seeing the two tests fought out at the French Grand Prix, everyone was able to see the worth yesterday's champions still have on the track.' Soon after, a new, worldwide association was established named the International Historic Racing Association (IHRA). It quickly found members from 11 countries and pushed ahead with the aim of presenting race organisers a package of competitive, experienced riders on authentic classic machines. The future of Classic racing at the highest level seemed assured.

We returned to England for our final event, the Classic Race of the Year at Donington Park. This was another big international challenge with entries from not just the UK but Holland, Germany, France, Spain and the US. I started from the fourth row of a full field of 40 riders in my first race, took the lead on the second lap and hoped to hold it. By three-quarter distance, Dave Roper and Bob Newby, multi British classic champion on the unique four-valve Mullarney Manx Norton, were on my back wheel. In typical style, Dave powered past at the end of the penultimate lap and Bob's very special four-valve Norton out-accelerated my G50 to the finish line. The race for the lead over the last three laps had been very close and hard fought, entertaining the large crowd. I had to retire from the Race of the Year. We spotted a small puddle of oil under the gearbox caused by a damaged seal. As we were one of the few with a standard gearbox we couldn't locate a spare. There was little time to warm the engine before the race and when the flag dropped, it refused to start.

Later we relived our adventures at a good old-fashioned Kiwi barbecue organised by Laurie and Jan Shephard and attended by none other than New Zealand superbike designer John Britten and some of our friends from France and naturally England. In eight weeks we had taken part in seven meetings and travelled the best part of 15,000km. What a great time!

Interest, enthusiasm, good health, the challenge and a strong sense of adventure allied to the enjoyment of being back, in many ways, to my youth and at each event I improved. The deep-seated pleasure of the benefits of finding the perfect line through a series of bends and the increase in engine rpm you carry into the following straight. Negotiating an S-bend where you ride from kerb to kerb and hook up with the exit, on that mark, just beyond the apex perfectly. As you reach race speed you feel the bike come to life as it writhes a little, becomes lighter and more flighty in its response to your demands. The rear tyre begins to squirm, the small surface irregularities smooth out and you know that this is as fast as you should go. That is when the true reason for racing a fine motorcycle is realised. The acceptance of lapping a second or so slower than in your youth eliminates age as a hindrance; in fact it adds to the reward. You experience the stimulation of risk without the shadow of fear.

Plans were made to return to Europe in 1987 but just 10 days before my departure a bombshell was dropped. The UK's governing body, the Auto Cycle Union, suddenly demanded overseas riders put in place their own personal accident insurance, which must cover injury and repatriation (flying your body home). It was impossible to arrange.

Laurie Shephard and I prepare for a short tour of the south of England, 2010. Archives.

I accepted an invitation, as did several others, from Australians Ken and Brenda Lucas to compete on one of his collection of classic racers at Victoria's famous Southern Classic 1987 meeting at Winton. Ken is a clever cookie. When we arrived, most of the bikes were partially dismantled and needed building. He knew that this was the quickest way to get them built and race worthy. Within the group were experts in electrics, carburation, and welding; no job was impossible. My good friend Ray Holmes from Tauranga slid off in practice and was run over by a following rider. I dropped my bike and ran to his aid. Ray got up, no probs, and wasn't even sore next day. Riding Ken's very good G50, I beat the much-fancied Corrish Ariel, ridden by Tony Gill, who dominated the Australian classic scene at that time. This speedway-derived hotrod nearly blinded me with its exotic exhaust fumes. (Whatever they were burning, I doubt that it was straight methanol.) After applying pressure for a few laps it came down to a breaking duel; he wasn't going to win that and I slipped past to win. Brenda's hospitality, with the assistance of our wives, over the long weekend was outstanding and yet another excellent example of how the enjoyment and understanding of the Classic period drew a group of virtual strangers together and allowed them to fully integrate and have a great time in every way.

In November 1987 Alan Bland from Christchurch phoned explaining he was having Phil Pick, a brilliant tuner from London, build a BSA 750cc triple engine that he was fitting into a Rob North frame to be used at the BEARS meeting in January. Alan asked me to ride it. Naturally I agreed.

BEARS racing had its world debut at Ruapuna, Christchurch in January 1983. A highly motivated talented group ran all manner of fundraising events. The publicity these activities attracted drew the largest crowds ever to attend a motorcycle meeting at that venue. Riders responded in kind and for the first time, owners of non-Japanese bikes had a race meeting of their own.

As so often happens, the Rob North-framed BSA, the first of its kind to be built in New Zealand, was finished 'just in time'. After a few laps on this beautifully built machine I was struck by the way it steered, fell into corners and held its line. We enjoyed a successful weekend winning The Best of British category. The BSA/ Norton hybrid won its class too, with Helen and Andrew Gourlay supplying a bed, food and, dare I mention it, beer — it was another of so many great weekends.

It seemed that the insurance issue with the English ACU was related to New Zealand Motor Cycling having become affiliated directly to the FIM (Fédération Internationale de Motocyclisme). Traditionally, we had been part of the English ACU system riding with a British licence, but now we were unable to compete in England's national events, only their international meetings. Neville Goss, the promoter of that meeting at Thruxton back in August 1960, when I had been broke, now had an influential position in the English ACU establishment. I phoned him and pointed out that apart from having achieved so much when riding on an English licence, I had also been a member of the British 1967 motocross team. Neville petitioned the right people and the problem was overcome.

For 1988 Air New Zealand provided me with a competitive air fare and an excess baggage allowance that included spare wheels, tools, tyres and more. Finally, I was heading back to another northern summer of classic racing. This time I was travelling

The BEARS insignia.

The BEARS programme made for close, hard racing. Steve Green.

alone and riding for two top tuners: Roger Titchmarsh, who had offered to prepare my 1959 G50, and Phil Pick, who with a sponsor built a 750cc, three-cylinder, Rob North-framed Triumph for me. The stakes were being raised in classic racing in the UK and Europe, with a host of fast new machines and hungry riders on board.

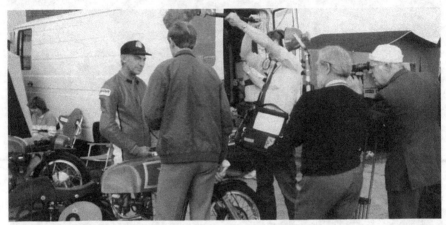

Gaining attention from the mass media at Snetterton — though not quite on the scale of today. Archives.

Managing to get through 'The Bomb Hole' nailed. Photo Peter Wileman.

Both bikes went well during practice for the Race of the Year at Snetterton. After a mediocre start on the G50, I quickly pushed through to second behind Mike Dowkes on Roger Titchmarsh's Seeley-framed Weslake twin. I closed the gap, but Mike won. A competitive field lined up for the 750cc race, seen by many as a glamour class and dominated by a group of hard chargers from southern England. Phil had done a great

job on the engine; the bike ran beautifully. I managed to make a gap and hold on for a win.

We moved down to Lydden in Kent, where a useful short road circuit had been squeezed onto an undulating hillside that normally hosted off-road car rally events. During those competitions clay was deposited on various parts of the track and though swept clean, left a hardly visible, very slippery residue. Rather frustrating as it restricted a rider's ability to crank the bike over and get on with it. Once again the bikes went well and I won all six races I'd entered and made the fastest lap of the day.

With the G50, and a rumpled Roger Titchmarsh, Snetterton 1988. Photo Peter Wileman.

Feeling confident, Roger and I attended Assen's famous Speed Week beginning on the 22nd of June. Staying with friends from the 1960s, Ab and Bea de Groot, in a nearby village meant I could sort out some carburettor issues on the G50 by roaring down a narrow strip of tar through the middle of a vast commercial vegetable operation. I was hitting 130kph, causing dozens of very startled heads to shoot up out of the greenery. The pre-event write-up went: 'Golden Oldies. Two four-time world champions clash head-on in Thursday's Historic Grand Prix: Italian Walter Villa, Benelli four, and Hugh Anderson, who returns to Assen for the first time since his Grand Prix days.'

Clearing off on the 750cc Triumph triple. Archives.

Since last riding here the circuit had been shortened, but there were only three new corners. In a few laps it all came back and I qualified third. Late in the evening, in brilliant weather we lined up for the race, surrounded by a huge expectant crowd of 50,000. A good start gave me the lead, although the howl of Walter Villa's four-cylinder Benelli was never far behind. He passed me on the third lap of 10, and slowly drew away, but then suddenly at half distance his engine began smoking. On the sixth lap it popped, leaving me to win and stand once more on the celebrated podium of one of the greatest Grand Prix of all.

An entirely different challenge was presented a week later, at Yorkshire's Scarborough circuit. This track snakes around a hill with downhill hairpin corners that have you braking from high speed to almost walking pace. There is a flat-out, long, undulating, blind, curved strip that leads via left and right turns to the finish. The only way you can pick the best route through that fast downhill section is by lining up the tops of various trees at three different stages of your descent. Many southern England classic racers avoided the place, as this was a totally different challenge to their home circuit at Brands Hatch. When Roger started the G50 for practice it sounded ominously noisy so we rolled it back into the van. A main shaft bearing had collapsed.

Our race on Phil Pick's triple, one of the Norman Hyde-sponsored British championship rounds, was late on Sunday afternoon. My only practice coincided with a heavy shower on Saturday morning and was stopped after three laps. When we were assembled on the dummy grid a rider and a woman appeared practising dance steps in front of us and obviously enjoying the attention it created. I queried who it was. "That's Geoff Johnson, he rides for Honda Great Britain, has just won the 600cc class in the Isle of Man and is on a special 1,000cc Triumph triple prepared by the series sponsor", I was told. Well, there's a challenge, I thought. This smartarse obviously doesn't take riding against us, the old classic lot, seriously. I gained a reasonable start, was a little cautious at first, due to lack of practice, but soon moved into second place and got to work. The front brakes were terrific and I soon found the fastest lines and gained on the cocky Yorkshire man. At mid-race, I overtook him under brakes in a narrow section as we passed a café before the Memorial hairpin. I hit the gas hard as I drove out close to a stack of straw bales, knowing that if the rear tyre slid away the bales would stop it.

With water streaming across the track, the Triumph triple became a handful. Photo Peter Wileman.

Enjoying the aquatic conditions on Jim Evans' G50. Peter Wileman.

Again we came to a hairpin, then tore together downhill and under a footbridge. This was my braking mark. The front of the bike bounced about, not unlike my 50cc Grand Prix Suzuki used to under heavy breaking, but it remained stable enough. Around the tightest hairpin in motorcycle racing then off around a slight curve to the right and then left and down that undulating drop into a fast left and right to the start-finish line. My mistake on the last lap was taking these two corners in top gear, being loathe to rev engines hard. I paid the price. Johnson got under me on the left-hand corner and won by less than the length of his bike. As I rode back to the van Phil Pick, our sponsor, his wife and friends were dancing about in joy. We had nearly pulled off a win for the pensioners that no one thought possible.

Fellow racer Jim Evans offered me the use of his excellent Seeley G50, and Phil Pick's Trident was available to use in the open class for the Classic Clubs meeting at Donington Park. Riding a borrowed bike can be inhibiting, but closely fought third places in Saturday's two 500cc races were fine. Even better was a second followed by a win on the Triumph in the Open class over Cornishman Alan Benallick on an eight-valve Triumph twin. He was the man to beat at the time. On Sunday light rain fell for most of the day. I won the first 500cc race going away, but struggled on the Triumph in wet conditions. After two wild slides I settled for second place and didn't go out for the second event. Jim's bike was slow to start in the second 500cc race, with the field of 35 riders long gone. In a race of just five laps and using a touch of the controlled anger from yesteryear, I carved through the field making the fastest lap of the day for all classes and took over the lead on the last lap.

The leather soles of my boots were tending to slip during the push starts so before my last meeting, at Brands Hatch on July 22–24, I glued on a pair of thin rubber substitutes. On Saturday morning, soon after, I reached the knee-and-foot-scraping stage during practice on the Triumph when the sole of my right foot caught on the track surface as I entered Clearways. Instead of sliding on the tarmac, the rubber sole gripped, wrenching my right foot off the footrest and under the rear wheel. This left me lying along the side of the bike with my left leg hooked over the seat, my head below the handlebars, knee on the road and my foot out behind the bike. Somehow I managed to get two fingers on to the front brake lever to scrub off some speed before the inevitable crash. Just when I was eyeing up which area of trackside grass to lay it down on, my speed dropped sufficiently to stay on the tarmac. When I finally brought it to rest, I needed a marshal's assistance to get up and back on it and was damn pleased to be able to ride back to the pits. That evening with Alan and Sheila we iced the swollen foot and ankle. Next day I managed two second places on Jim's bike and finished in the leading group on the Triumph.

Some of the best engineers back home in Hamilton were sympathetic towards what I was doing and when I brought the G50 engine home in August 1988, we set to and thoroughly overhauled it. Les DeLacy, as always, worked his usual wizardry on the cylinder head and gas flow. Danny Ryan redesigned and manufactured a modified main bearing housing that solved a major ongoing problem. And meticulous tool maker Neville Mickleson modified a new big-end bearing and carried out the finishing touches to a pair of new crankcase castings. I now had a very sound, reliable engine to use in Europe during the 1989 season.

Les DeLacy and son Paul had modified an aluminium cylinder head for the 650 BSA engine that I had used the previous season. During the first practice session at Wanganui on Boxing Day I felt a little subdued, however next day during the short early-morning practice, the freewheeling, effortless speed and fun was back. I passed many of the fastest in the field, including BEARS racing pioneer Lyndsay Williamson, before overdoing it and whistling up a slip road. Lyndsay was riding his Jerry Branch-tuned Harley XR1000 special, housed in a McIntosh-built Egli frame. He had a reputation as a tough competitor with an unassuming demeanour. After practice Lyndsay quietly came over and enquired what I'd had for breakfast as he would like some of the same. And so the scene was set for letting things hang out a bit.

Though only using petrol, the DeLacy-tuned BSA-Norton Special leads a field of methanol-burning moderns.

I gained a flyer of a start in the BEARS race and led for the first lap from Paul Pavletich, who was riding Dallas Rankin's slick-tyred, methanol-burning, modern Ducati hotrod. He slipped past on the second lap but I did my best to stay with him, as I knew there was a phalanx of younger fast guys behind. As I passed the start-finish towards the end, I caught a glimpse of the white flag. Great. Just one lap to go. Maybe I could hold off Formula Two champion Bill Cooney, who had pushed me all the way, for second place. I had coached him in previous years and now he was breathing down my neck on a new 750cc Ducati racer supplied by Auckland Motorcycles.

I charged on and approached the finish line ahead of him but the white flag was actually waved this time. Damn, another lap to go. Sure enough Bill passed me on the straight. Bugger, second was my place. I kept repeating it like some weird mantra. Second was my place. I allowed a gap to form as we approached the Cemetery S-bend then very early I opened the throttle wide. This gained me sufficient speed on the exit to slowly edge past Bill on his left as we approached a tight right-hander. I had an old, worn-out front drum brake. Bill had the latest twin discs. As he tried to get between me and the right-hand kerb, I leaned on him, with his front wheel rubbing hard up against my leg. It was okay, his brakes were much better than mine, allowing him to stop much quicker than I could. We came to the corner. I ducked around it and dashed off to the next, a slowish but long right-hander. I didn't move out to the left as normal, but stayed in the middle of the road waiting for Bill to accelerate past on my right. As soon as I saw his front wheel again, I rode over the front of him, got the corner and pipped him to the finishing flag. I had never done anything like that before. I rode quickly back to my car, expecting to see a rather well-built, angry Bill coming over for a 'chat'. Later in the afternoon I went to him and apologised. He wasn't unpleasant at all and only said: "I thought you must always ride like that."

I rode Alan Bland's BSA triple racer again, at the extremely popular 1989 BEARS meeting at Ruapuna. We had been testing different suspension settings and gearing, but my lap times were not as good as I would have liked. Trying too hard coming out of the hairpin the rear tyre broke away. I managed to correct it and although the bike was upright, the front wheel 'tucked under'. I hit the road partly under the bike and still holding the handlebars. As I scrambled from underneath it, I knew my hand was bad, but after just two steps it was obvious my right foot wasn't much better. I removed my glove to see the flesh had been torn away from the back of my hand, exposing a decidedly worn away main joint of the third finger. Being termed a compound fracture, a full-on hospital theatre had to be set up to attend to it. An X-ray showed two compressed fractures in my foot. Not a very clever exercise. I couldn't use crutches or walk; a wheelchair was the only option.

Janny was at the beach with Dave and June Kenah. Hugh Jnr met me at Hamilton Airport. Seeing me being pushed across the tarmac in a wheelchair touched off his sense of humour. A question of what will Mum say got him laughing more. I must have brought him up wrong. When I phoned her, Janny didn't show much concern either, firmly saying: "Hugh, the weather is great here. I'm staying for a few more days."

Back in Europe in 1989 I had my first ride for Fred Walmsley, a trained engineer turned businessman who was gaining a reputation as one of the classic world's top tuners, and who offered me one of his Seeley Mk II-framed Matchless G50 for the

Standing on the Dutch TT podium in 1989 with the 350cc class winner, journalist and author Mat Oxley.

1989 season. I rode his Seeley Mk II-framed Matchless G50 in the Historic event held during the Dutch TT speed week in Assen from June 19 to 24th. A field of 40 classics lined up in front of 48,000 spectators. The first corner was steeply banked and gave the impression of being slower than it was. I was fairly sure that from a push start it was possible to get around it without closing the throttle. Approaching it in fourth place, I rode above then past all three riders in front of me and steadily increased my lead to win comfortably. The result was well received by the large crowd.

I arrived back at Roger's on Saturday morning and immediately left for Scotland, to compete once more in the Bob McIntyre Memorial Trophy event, this time using Roger's successful Weslake-engined Seeley-framed bike. On arrival at the circuit a tousled-headed, wide-eyed Irish man approached me and asked if I had seen a chap, whose name I have long forgotten. I said "No". "Well, you'll no be seeing him tomorrow either." And with an air of authority, he walked off. It seems that the rider he referred to had, that day, won and set a new lap record. In Holland it had been 28 degrees, on Sunday morning it was a freezing eight with light rain falling. As I lined up for practice a blackboard stated that parts of the track were flooded and there was oil all around the circuit and then, believe it or not, sleet began to fall. As I had at Monza 25 years ago, I followed the lead riders and noted how our bikes reacted to the track conditions. The Trophy, in memory for a rider I had the greatest respect for, was well worth trying to win. It seems that Saturday's fast boys were spooked by the conditions and apart from a few pleasant slides and front-wheel lock-ups, using a disc brake, the winning ride passed without a problem. Oh, and as that Irishman had told me, I didn't see whoever it was all day.

BRANDS HATCH MIKE HAILWOOD MEMORIAL SUPER PRIX AND HISTORIC PARADE JULY 14–15, 1989

John Surtees and the English Classic Club combined their comprehensive resources to put together what was potentially the greatest Classic Motorcycle event up to that time. Enthusiasts from the post-war period flew in from all over the world. It was a reunion of massive proportions creating the largest crowd to attend a motorcycle meeting at Brands for some years, raising 50,000 pounds for PHAB, a charity for Physically Handicapped and Able Bodied Children. Charismatic John was highly respected, as you would expect, throughout Europe and Japan. He was instrumental in having examples of virtually every make of Grand Prix machine manufactured post-war, and many earlier models, even having a 1965 250cc six-cylinder Honda available for world champion Ralph Bryans to parade each day. They made a mightily impressive display when lined up in a large colourful airy marquee.

I had been told to expect to be riding 'something'. On Friday afternoon following practice, after John had assembled the many machines, I approached him. He put a hand on my shoulder and said, "Hugh, it's your lucky day, you'll be riding the ex-Mike Hailwood Honda four. It hasn't been used for a few years, is rather smoky and we don't know what it is like mechanically. The gear change is on the left, one up and four down, but you'll be able to handle that, won't you?" "Sure, John, where is it?" I replied. My lucky day? I wondered. If there's any kind of an engine failure my greatest legacy will be the bloke who broke Mike Hailwood's TT-winning Honda. Beating Dave Roper in the main race may not be the only challenge this weekend.

During my first ride on it I kept the engine revs as low as practical. At one point when slowing for Druids hairpin the massive long megaphones seemed to suddenly harmonise. Christ, what's that? In with the clutch and gently rev the engine; no, it's okay, now which way does the gear lever go? Up for down or is it down for down? Better think about it for a bit. By the second session I felt less apprehensive and began to realise it was indeed a privilege to be riding a machine that will always be noted in the annals of history. To fill the circuit, a staggered start was used. On our last outing John, on a 500cc Benelli, and past British national champion Roger Marshall, on a 500cc MV, came by riding hard. Temptation became my master and

On full lean at Paddock Bend during the Mike Hailwood Memorial Trophy event 1989. Archives.

Riding around Chris McGahan, the English Classic Clubs number two rider, at Druids hairpin, Brands Hatch 1989. Archives.

giving it three-quarter throttle and 10,000rpm it proved to be faster than the two Italian bikes.

All the race competitors had two races each day. At Club events, though surely this was an international, grid positions are established by the rider taking a numbered marble from a hat. I've never won a raffle in my life or drawn a front-row position. The typically five-lap races give little time to overcome a poor draw. On Saturday I gained a first and third, making the fastest lap each time. Dave Roper on Rob Iannucci's Team Obsolete's G50 had been in other heats and won both.

I was a little concerned about the Avon experimental rear tyre the company had given me. I had been in talks with the company since May 1988 about them developing a classic-specific rear tyre. They needed some convincing that a market actually existed, but relented, and asked me to help them develop one. On a cool Saturday the rear tyre had felt a little squirmy during my last two laps. It showed no wear and was smooth, just like new. Normally under these conditions you would lower the pressure to get more heat into it. But Sunday was a hot day so I raised the pressure a little and hoped it was the right thing to do for the 20-lap Mike Hailwood memorial event.

Dave Roper and I hit the front within two laps. His Team Obsolete G50 was considerably faster than mine but my knowledge of the track was greater. By the 10th lap I felt the rear tyre going again. I decided to pass Dave, just to show that I could, before it was too late. I came out of Clearways faster than him, moved into his slipstream and pedalling it through the gears without closing the throttle stayed with him. A fast exit out of Paddock and down the hill had me in a position to out-brake him into Druids hairpin. On an impulse I went around the outside and rode over Dave into the corner. As I leaned into it his front wheel rubbed against my protruding right leg. I gassed up and rode away from him. Dave blasted past me up the straight, as I knew he would, and that was the race over with. Still, second place ahead of Europe's best was okay. And a hug and reunion with Pauline, Mike's widow, finished off a good weekend.

As I had each New Zealand summer, after catching up with all the jobs that needed attending to, I carried out my activities as a committee member of The Classic Register and rode at most of our meetings. It was pleasant to enjoy them for what they were. A good day or weekend out, a social evening spent with like-minded pleasant people.

Fred Walmsley ran a two-bike team in 1990. I joined Phil Nicholls, an experienced Isle of Man competitor, on a pair of the latest Seeley G50s. Our first meeting at Snetterton in mid-May went well. I won all four races the Seeley was eligible for, and Phil was never far behind. Fred was happy. Following Snetterton, I had been invited by Suzuki GB to help out at a riding school at Cadwell Park for Suzuki owners on road bikes. On arrival we had a discussion and I was warned that my bike was fitted with new tyres. When leading a group of riders into the first right-hand corner, at what seemed like a snail's pace, I looked behind to check the situation. Immediately, the front wheel slid away. In my attempt to lever it upright I was leaning hard to the left. As it went down to my right it threw me onto the track. I heard again the rather too familiar noise of breaking bones. Dumping the bike in front of 20 pupils was not the greatest thing I've ever done, however the pain suppressed my embarrassment. The local hospital confirmed broken ribs and my right shoulder blade broken in two places. Fortunately, Laurie and Jan Shephard lived quite close.

I stayed with them going for long walks and kept squeezing a tennis ball in the hope it would help. Not wanting Janny to know, I practised for some hours writing with my left hand. Luckily, it was good enough for her not to notice.

By happy coincidence son Hugh Jnr had been sent to the UK by his company for work experience. I had arranged entries for him to ride my G50 at Oulton Park, the Dutch TT and the Super Prix at Brands Hatch. By the time the Oulton Park meeting came around, five weeks had passed since my fall. Whilst being far from pain free, I felt ready to ride. Practice went okay. I enjoyed being active again and the shoulder was holding up. Our first race, late on Saturday afternoon, became a five-way dice. As always, Bob Newby was pressing on. He won, followed by Phil Nicholls. I was very happy to finish third after pulling a fairly dramatic slide avoiding two other riders who had tangled. Drizzle on Sunday suited me fine. In the main race of the weekend I quickly moved through cautious riders up to second place behind Bob. I forgot all about the shoulder in an unsuccessful last-lap lunge to win. When I stopped back at Fred's race van, I had to lift my right hand with my left off the handlebar. When it was free, my arm went into grotesque, uncontrollable spasms. I held it to my side, hoping no one would notice. I was surprised how you can ride with virtually only one arm. Obviously, the painkillers had done a good job. Despite limited time on the bike, Hugh Jnr proudly upheld the family reputation, twice stylishly finishing second in the pre-1965 Period One class.

The Dutch Classic TT had become the major international event of the year and I looked forward to the challenge. On the third lap I passed Bob Newby and settled into a safe, enjoyable rhythm to win. Alan Cathcart, after challenging Bob for second, finished a close third. I was well pleased with having won three in a row at the venue with the highest spectator turnout in the classic racing world. Hugh Jnr had a much more interesting event. His practice was restricted by a minor ignition fault. Then the primary drive belt broke, leaving him with the 10th fastest practice lap. Nevertheless he gave the race his best shot, moving up into seventh place before sliding off on a fast and difficult corner. Naturally, he didn't want me to know that he had fallen, so with the help of officials hid the bike behind their protective wall. Janny's dad was a popular, respected man in Assen. When the officials realised who Hugh was, they burst out laughing. As they later explained, "Gerrit Oeseburg's grandson had landed at our feet."

Now it was on to the Super Prix at Brands Hatch on July 15–16. Around 800 riders had applied to enter. Competitors from all over England had left home at the end of their working week and arrived in the early hours. The main event, the Mike Hailwood Memorial Trophy race, once again honoured not only the greatest rider the world has known, but also one of its most effective ambassadors and a friend. I didn't know Mike well, perhaps few people could claim to, but we did have time together. Having been one of his contemporaries added to the importance of the occasion and increased the 'edge' I always strived for at a major event.

Hugh Jnr had entered the Super Prix and attended Wednesday's paid practice session, but decided to withdraw and help me instead. I gained the impression that the speed of riders at the notorious Paddock Bend may have influenced his decision.

The Super Prix competitors were divided into two qualifying races. I was in race one. Team Obsolete's Dave Roper, my biggest challenger, was in race two. The 'take a numbered marble out of the hat' grid selection process had me drawing a place on the second row. I got a good start and immediately hit the front going hard. Following me was Richard Cutts, one of the fastest here, but he lost it exiting Druids and broke his collarbone. Dave Roper won, with his race time just 0.06sec faster than mine. Now there was real pressure on the locals. Later in the day Bob Newby and my team-mate Phil came off at Clearways and Phil took no further part. On Sunday morning Dave Roper slid off at Graham Hill Bend, tearing the backside out of his leathers, but he was okay. I won two of the four preliminary races, Roper one and Newby one. Alan Cathcart, on Ian Telfer's standard Manx Norton, was always in the hunt, setting the fastest lap. My main rivals now were five-time British classic champion Bob Newby, American champion Dave Roper and Alan Cathcart.

The riders from the Continent and people who had little knowledge of racing there had no chance. Brands is special. It takes time to find the lines and get 'on the limit'. If at any time you are upright during a lap you are doing it wrong. Team Obsolete, owned by larger-than-life New Yorker Rob Iannucci, had brought over top rider Pat Moroney to ride a special 750cc KR Harley-Davidson. During a mixed practice on Friday I caught him, followed, then passed him and pressed on. I guess he was unaccustomed to being passed by a 500cc British single. During his first race on Sunday he came off, suffering a separated shoulder. When interviewed afterwards he said: "These guys are the fastest classic racers in the world. I've never had to ride that motorcycle that fast in my life." He wasn't joking. A serious accident caused an hour's delay and the Hailwood Memorial Trophy race was reduced from 20 to 15 laps.

Hugh Jnr, very capable with a stopwatch, was to give me pit-board signals. Our eldest, Caroline, was living in London at the time and was with us. At the dummy grid I chose a marble and, bugger me, it was for the back row! Fortunately, Bob and Alan Cathcart fared no better. But Dave was up near the front. Bob got a jump on me at the start. He cut through the field and I chased him. Surprisingly, after only six laps we were with the leaders. A lap later we had passed Dave and were sitting first and second. I checked Hugh's signal board but the sun was reflecting off it and I couldn't read his messages. Damn. I decided to sit 20m behind Bob for the time being. For some reason the 'how many laps to go' board was not being operated. Late in the race I saw one of Hugh's signals: Roper +0. That was the trigger to get serious.

I had to pass a lapped rider at Paddock Bend; I couldn't wait to get up the inside and so went around him. He drifted wider, taking me with him. Keeping the throttle nailed to the stop, I slid off the track over a ridge of gravel onto a patch of rough tarseal but managed to keep it all together. It was all on now.

I closed steadily on Bob and as we approached Druids I braked under him and made a great job through Graham Hill Bend and rode on at my full potential to the flag. On the last lap at Clearways, Bob made a mistake and Dave got alongside him, but Bob held second by 0.01sec.

Over recent years Rob Iannucci and Fred Walmsley hadn't seen eye to eye on various issues of classic machine eligibility. Written protests and counter protests had crossed officials' desks. As we stepped onto the purpose-built, open vehicle to begin our lap of honour, Fred noticed Rob walking with a laboured, heavy tread back to the paddock. Rather smugly he commented, "There goes a beaten man." For me it was a proud moment. I had Caroline and Hugh and a very happy sponsor riding with me to share the applause of the large crowd. Situations like these arise just once.

Later, Janny vented her displeasure in not having been able to join us.

On the following Tuesday evening a large group of Fred's friends and supporters gathered for our celebratory dinner. Fred, sitting at the head of the table, was in an effusive mood but I couldn't seem to get out of a subdued state. Soon I would be 55 years old. Surely competing at the top level was over for me? The burgeoning worldwide classic racing movement had given me a new lease on life. I had been there from the beginning, in the same way I had been with Suzuki in both their road and motocross eras.

I now had a clear obligation to give poor Janny a break. She had put up with so much over the years. A German doctor wanted to buy my G50. He understood the importance of this bike and how it had been developed over several seasons into a regular and reliable winner. A good home to send a good bike to. Maybe it was time to make a clean break from racing and revert to being a contented family man.

The following morning I went out into Fred's shed for the last time and sat on the bike that had been tailored to my needs. I relived the weekend and stopped to dwell once more on my feelings that moment just after winning the main race. I'd felt the form required to go to the next level had been so near, so reachable. Only a little more riding time was required to gain the elusive key of entry to that perfect place and experience again the greatest prize of all, becoming 'the other person' and 'being there' just once more. I cannot claim to having been dry-eyed as I dismounted that bike for the last time.

Robert Fawcett, of , saw fit to write a feature article headed 'Hugh Anderson, Gentleman and Champion'.

He wrote: '... 54-year-old New Zealander Hugh Anderson made a clean sweep in the world's two most prestigious historic races, making him the unofficial Classic World Champion.'

I guess that at 78, this could well be my last wheelie. The photograph was taken by my close friend Moss Smith, on his farm, while riding his rare strapped-tank 250cc Yamaha. Just weeks later, when far too young, Moss passed away.

EPILOGUE

Our father is an extraordinary man who has led an inspirational life

He is living proof that dreams can become reality with passion, hard work and, of course, talent. His journey from a farm in distant New Zealand to Europe to become a Grand Prix World Champion in just four years is simply amazing. He didn't win once but four times in an era of great danger and a time of huge technological change and experimentation.

Always an original thinker, Dad has had a significant influence on Grand Prix two-stroke racing, motocross and the NZ Classic Racing movement throughout his life. He is able to observe and analyse his abilities against his rivals, then know in detail, via his visualisation skills, what strategies to employ to win, showing a deep understanding of sports psychology, long before the phrase had even been invented.

Dad has always been a proud 'Kiwi' but representing a country obsessed with rugby and cricket, it is unfortunate that his skills and achievements are recognised more overseas than in New Zealand. His fan base there is still strong after all these years.

Dad never forgot where he came from and many school friendships remain strong and cultivated to this day. This along with all the friends he has made along the way means that someone is always popping in for a coffee and chat.

As children we were able to enjoy living on the same property he grew up on beside the Waikato River. Going for walks along the river bank with our Doberman dog, goat, sheep and cats. Lying in the long grass and discussing things that were important to us at the time. Then picking a large bunch of arum lilies to take home for Mum. Quality time that we have not forgotten. Motorbikes, horses, a backyard full of animals and an orchard full of fruit — what more could you ask for?

We are very proud of Dad's huge effort in producing this book, and hope you will enjoy reading his story as much as we have enjoyed sharing it.

Caroline, Hugh, Michelle

The year of the superchargers, 1997

A unique 500cc four-cylinder supercharged AJS, perhaps the most complex Grand Prix machine ever made in England, was brought out by Sammy Miller, the greatest trials rider in history and a successful museum curator.

Another unique machine was the Velocette Roarer, a name gained from its distinctive exhaust note and an inline twin-cylinder machine that I had the privilege to demonstrate. This was owned by Mr Velocette himself, Ivan Rhodes, who purchased all the parts of the machine that was left in the factory when it closed.

The third and by far the most successful, winning a long list of races including the

1939 Isle of Man TT, was a supercharged BMW owned and demonstrated by that most versatile of men, John Surtees.

Once again the Register gained status from having this magnificent trio demonstrating the unique sound and performance, 12,000 miles from their base. For the first time all circulating together, it was another wonderful weekend. Success breeds success; our committee was made up of energetic, successful people who worked in total harmony committed to the success of the club.

Above: Supercharged Velocette roarer. Start-up day, May 7th 1989. From left: Len Udall, Graham, Ivan and Rene Rhones, Peter Goodman, son of the Velocette founder.

Left: The cat Rastus. This remarkable animal travelled all over New Zealand on the tank of Max Corkill's motorcycle. Tragically, they were both killed in an accident not of their own making.

Gerrit Oeseburg

Gerrit Oeseburg, Janny's dad, was a man of courage and standing within the community, easy to respect and admire. I was proud indeed, over a period of time, to gain his confidence, respect, and parental love. A mechanical engineer employed by the Dutch Army, he was the maintenance chief of a vast fleet of military vehicles stationed in the north-east of Holland. Within the Dutch mechanical trade, the English language was frequently used to name mechanical parts. As I learned a little Dutch and he learnt a little English, we created a language unique to ourselves.

Gerrit had been conscripted into the Dutch Air Force as a gunner based in Amsterdam. The planes were obsolete and fragile. In the event they didn't get off the ground, he wasn't disappointed. He returned to the north-east of Holland and joined the underground. In due course he gained a place in the leadership of his area. Due to his knowledge of the area, in the dead of night, he would deliver downed pilots to another group for the next stage of their journey to the coast. He rarely came home. Sufficient food was always made available to Tinie and Janny.

After several visits, late in 1975 Gerrit and Tinie immigrated to New Zealand. We rejoiced in being a family again.

Gerrit often joined me in my workshop. During a lunch break, with a smile at the memory, he confided the following with me. A Citroën car was owned by the local doctor. This vehicle had all the required passes attached to travel freely within a prescribed area, and Gerrit serviced and maintained it. Coincidentally, when the underground newspaper was to be distributed, the Citroën was due for a service, and Gerrit made these highly dangerous, clandestine deliveries.

The second story was that towards war's end on wet and windy nights, he would, with friends, scout around the camps of the retreating occupational forces hoping to locate animals and return them to their local farmer friends. One night they found seven milking cows and carefully guided them towards home. They came to a canal. Gerrit had no idea how they would cross it. One of the group was a farmer, and as the animals gathered at the water's edge, he approached the lead cow, cupped its ear in his hand and shouted with a loud 'Hoo!'. Without hesitation it jumped into the water and the others followed. He roared with laughter, tears streaming down his face. For him it was total recall of a situation that, at the time, was perhaps an indication that the curtain of darkness was being lifted and the light of optimism returning.

The more serious work that he was involved in, he refused to discuss. A book was written, *Mobilisatie, Collaboratie, Liberatie*, in which he is mentioned. At war's end he was awarded medals attesting to his courage and commitment to the cause. Being the man he was, they were never mentioned or worn.

On joining the underground he had sworn to an oath of silence; to him it was for life. An indication of his character and pain threshold was that in his late fifties, without any form of pain relief, he had all his teeth removed, left the premises and drove himself home.

Form and learning about it

Most riders, as they progress through their early years, during a race, practice or a test session, will from time to time hit a sweet spot. Everything flows with effortless ease. These are the special moments. Understandably, when that rider pulls into the pits he is on a high — "Man, that was exciting, enthralling, satisfying" — then when he is asked questions or asks them of himself, he has little or no recall of what he has done, learnt, or in fact how it came about. For example revs, gears used, breaking points, lines on corners, tyres beginning to let go; his answers are a bit vague or "I don't know, but hey that was fun". But he did not capture the moment or understand the mood or the mental state that allowed it, as I had at Marton in December 1957. I have frequently heard on numerous occasions riders speak of a brilliant ride or a unique truly outstanding result, one they were unable to repeat.

The 'other person' that I had created knew and could recall with total precision every minute detail of every section of the circuit on every lap. Without that, you give irregular performances and do not know why. Frequently, the bikes are blamed; poor lap times justify hasty revisions of its setup, all to no avail. Questions are asked: "But it went so well last week; why not now?" However, competitors who are unable to recognise or understand the makeup of form are frequently not equipped with the ability to find fault with themselves.

For me, going to the start of a Grand Prix without a precise plan would have been unacceptable. To occasionally go out on a track and just let off steam and have fun is fine. My first opportunity to participate in a paid practice session and enjoy the freedom of not having the pressure of preparing for a race was at Brands Hatch in early 1961. After a long layoff, due to my shoulder injuries, I had the satisfaction of completing a series of laps in very competitive times.

Basking in the stimulus of good form was absolutely exhilarating, me and my 7R in complete harmony back on the limit again, and that should have been sufficient. But when I returned to my van and reflected on it, I realised that I had learnt little. From then on every time I rode a race bike it was for a reason, a purpose; the results were fully recorded mentally and/or on paper and I learnt.

Those sweet spots are form and need to be captured in their entirety. How did it come about? What allowed it? A routine is created, and repeated each time you come under starter's orders. In my life it was if you can do it once, you can do it 100 times; if not, why not? There are questions to be asked, mainly about yourself. I must admit to having taken self-criticism to the extreme. In the short term there were gains but in the long run finding only fault caused a crisis in self-confidence. A personal trait that had never been a strong point.

Good Old Days

Reminiscences about Hugh Anderson

The first time Hugh Anderson rode for Suzuki was in the 250cc race at the Isle of Man TT 1961. Suzuki also had Alistair King, Paddy Driver, Mitsuo Itoh, Shunkiichi Masuda and Michio Ichino.

Result was four Suzuki riders retired, Ichino came 12th and Anderson 10th. Suzuki management appreciated and put a high value on Anderson's 10th place. This was his first ride on a two-stroke machine. He willingly worked closely with his mechanics and had good control of the unstable Suzuki RV61 machine over the five-lap 188-mile (305km) race.

Suzuki signed a contract with Hugh Anderson in 1962. Anderson also had a contract with the English AMC factory to ride their 350 and 500cc machines.

Degner, riding a Suzuki, won the 50cc class. Anderson riding the 125 and 250cc machines did not gain such good results due to machine trouble and could not complete all the races.

Ernst Degner crashed at the Ulster Grand Prix and could not ride in the 50cc class at the German and Italian Grand Prixs. Suzuki invited Anderson to take Ernst's place at these events. Suzuki did not expect good results as Anderson, at 178cm and 75kg [actually in leathers I was just 70kg] was not suitable for a tiny 50cc racer. But Anderson was able to fold his 'king-sized body' around the machine and gained excellent results. First British Championship, third German Grand Prix, fourth Italian Grand Prix, sixth after falling and restarting at the Finnish Grand Prix, first Argentine Grand Prix, and second at the Japanese Grand Prix.

After 1962 Anderson made a stellar performance as the breadwinner for the Suzuki team. He won the 50 and 125 World Championships in 1963. In 1964 he won again the 50cc and in 1965 the 125 Championship. His number of championship victories were 50cc, eight, and 125cc, 17.

Anderson has a very mild character and never showed disappointment or voiced anger when he retired from a race due to a mechanic's error. He was called by his nickname 'Anchung' by all of the Suzuki team. He was very well liked by all the staff members. Anderson's characteristic riding form was inside leg wide open on a corner, and his red hat with 'N.Z.' and the national bird, a kiwi, painted on it.

These are our clear remaining memories of him.

The riders from the Commonwealth gained respect

Continental Circus stood for Europe's motorcycle road-racing heritage in the years when all the countries during the whole season held international and Grand Prix racing, fascinating the population. In the '50s up to the '70s some events attracted more than 250,000 spectators on race day!

Especially from the great world of the British Commonwealth. Was it then a dream to compete in the Isle of Man TT and travel week by week throughout the old continent to fight for success — and the crown, to be a World Champion!

For most of them it has been a hard life to survive. They were all great sports characters. They competed in the most dramatic era in Grand Prix racing. The sport was extremely dangerous. The variety of technology was fascinating: four-strokes against two-strokes, single-cylinder against multis, practically no regulations — in six classes from 50 to 500cc capacities. The best should win. The World Champion Hugh Anderson, for the experts, is like a bright shining lighthouse through the decade of the 1960s. His name will remain forever as a true ambassador for these great times.

Wolfgang Gruber, Salzburg
Grand Prix racing photo journalist 1960 to 1993

Avoiding the ultimate question during the 1960s

Accidents occurred at every meeting, many lives were lost. During the period of unreliable engines, too often I felt I may not survive the race. During those difficult times, I would gain a very real sense of relief when practice for a race meeting was over. For sure, I would live until the next practice session or the four days 'till the next meeting. But I never spoke of it. My consistently refined pre-race routine helped negate the effects, though there were times when I rode with what I hoped was a built-in safety margin. Some of that feeling of relief was perhaps due to being released from the intensity of my commitments.

Janny too, of course, was well aware of what might/could happen. She too, never mentioned it. Janny felt that I didn't dwell on the darker side and worked only with positives. If she was to vent her feelings, I may have irritably rejected them. It was not because it was not a valid point, but because it was much closer to the surface than Janny was ever to know.

Pukekohe Classic, February 1998

Kevin Grant and I decided to run a 900cc Ducati in the Open Class at the 1988 Classic Festival at Pukekohe. At the end of the first race on Sunday, I felt a further change to its carburettors would put us in a position to win.

I fluffed the start badly and was back in midfield. By the end of the first lap I was getting near the leading bunch and at the end of the long back straight, braked into what I thought was the lead. After rounding the hairpin I saw a bike 200m in front. Thinking how the hell did he get that far in front, I increased my pace. I went faster than ever around a long left-hander and into the following difficult slightly uphill right. Knowing the exhaust pipes were low I hung off the side of the bike more to compensate for the extra speed I was carrying. Very suddenly I was down, still holding the bars, being dragged along the road at perhaps 140/150kph with sparks and flames spewing from all the parts that were scraping and gouging along the road. "Jeez, this is bad," I said to myself just before I was knocked unconscious.

A few metres from the track there was a concrete wall; I cannoned off it back onto the track, the race was stopped, there was dead silence. My son Hugh saw it all and was the first to my side. He saw Janny coming, went to her and asked her not to go to me, as I was dead; she ignored him and came and sat with me.

A helicopter was called, a group had formed around me, I began to come around. In Hugh's words I asked him "What happened?" He told me. A minute later I asked again, he told me, but when I asked for a third time he said, "I don't know."

My first memory was the sound of the chopper, and the sheer joy of still being alive had me on a high. A paramedic came to me and began checking me out.

"Your right wrist is broken."

"Yes, I know."

"What else hurts?"

"My right elbow and left knee, otherwise I am okay."

"How did you get here?" he asked.

Feeling in a light-hearted frame of mind I answered, "Surely you could ask me something more difficult than that?"

"No," he said, "give me the answer."

And do you know I couldn't; try as I might it was a blank.

"Stick around for a bit," I replied, "I am sure it will come back to me."

I was loaded into the chopper and with Janny set off to Middlemore Hospital. Meanwhile I had been connected to a radio telephone system and the medic continued talking to me. After flying for 15 minutes or so, I remembered how I had got to the circuit. I told him and added, "I knew it would come back."

The doctor attending me seemed concerned about my upper back, chest and neck area and had extensive X-rays carried out on two occasions. It seems old fractures to my vertebrae and ribs were showing up. He questioned my pulse rate.

"Are the high forties normal?" he asked.

"Yes, I swim four mornings a week."

He walked off and left me in peace. After 24 hours I was released with the advice that to avoid severe arthritis in the future I should have a specialist attend to my broken wrist.

The orthopaedic surgeon agreed that a reconstruction was required.

I woke up with someone shouting in my ear, as they do, and saw my arm suspended by an overhead gantry affair and it didn't look good. There were four long 4mm bolts screwed into the bones above and below the fracture; a 4mm bar had been clamped to these creating a splint. A piece of wire with a toggle was poking out of my hand between my thumb and forefinger. There was an incision beginning in the back of my hand and 140mm back up my arm. An arm block had been used; there was no pain.

The arm block was removed, I waited for the pain, there was none. Next day the surgeon called and everything was fine. After four days I could go home. Great, "but what about these long bolts protruding out of my arm? I can't wear any clothes."

"All right, we will fix that."

Soon after a chap arrived with a set of bolt cutters; the 'bow-ing' as he cut through each one sent intense vibrations through the damaged area up my arm and through my body. The recovery period went well with a district nurse who, with her husband, travelled extensively by motorcycle and called frequently to change the dressings. Finally, after the promised six weeks, the day came to remove the steel work. Whilst I had always been curious about how it would be done, I hadn't dwelt on it.

They worked on the good guy, bad guy system. This was the bad guy's turn to alleviate my concern; why else would he tell me? He said, "It will be like having four babies in four minutes." I was given laughing gas, it didn't raise a smile. He produced a set of vice grips, fair dinkum, bloody vice grips, clamped them on the first rod but they slipped, he adjusted them and they clunked on hard. Then he seemed unsure if they were left- or right-hand thread. Once over that hurdle, it all went painfully well. I didn't emit a noise, but my serious attempts at levitation were thwarted by Janny and a nurse holding me down. I could give an elaborate description regarding the different kind of pain that is created by flesh wounds and the grinding of bone, but as this is not a medical journal, there seems little need.

A few weeks later I rode at the Centennial Celebration of History meeting at Assen in Holland. Who said old guys don't heal fast?

A champion

It is not only skill, but an insatiable hunger, not necessarily for public applause or monetary reward, but a development of and, in some cases, acceptance of oneself.

A huge need that overcomes any fear of injury or worse, you feel this is what you were born to do. Without achieving your goals, who are you? It is through an expansion of vision, belief in your translation and judgemental skills that make a champion, and he now knows full well the drive towards perfection is hard, cruel and never-ending. Having taken on that challenge and climbed that mountain and accepted the recognition, position, applause and accolades — indeed having taken note of and enjoyed every aspect of the view from the top — his ambition and dreams, until now the very elixir of life, like a drink left standing have become flat, the effervescence gone.

A new champion is knocking on the door and wants what you have, much more than your need to retain it. the time has come to move on and enjoy the lifelong respect that is accorded to all sports' true champions.

Shirley Alderdice with daughters Tracey and Sue. Photo by Zac from Pit Bull Photography.

Reg Hone of Tauranga was an ardent motorcycle road-race enthusiast. At road races during the 1950s he was a flag man for several clubs travelling as far as Levin to help his son, also a flag man, to carry out machine examination and control the meeting. Shirley and brother Bob attended these events with their dad. As a family, they became followers of my career. Shirley took centre stage and the family posted all the newspaper and motorcycle magazine cuttings to her.

During the early 1990s Shirley and family felt that my achievements had not gained the recognition they deserved and set about putting things right. Without my knowledge or input, Shirley Alderdice and daughters Tracey and Sue conscientiously compiled sufficient evidence to convince the Honours Board in Parliament that I should be awarded an MBE. I received it on 11 June 1994.

Thank you, girls.

Tim's boat. We have caught our share of trout and saltwater fish and shared great stories while we were at it.

The clutch had been slipping. Perhaps I have overdone the repair. Mike Clarke.

Totally in my element on Mike Clarke's Matchless Métisse; 72 years of age and enjoying one of the most pleasant rides of my life. Chris Clarke.

LIGUE MOTOCYCLISTE DE NORMANDIE

Groupe Sportif de Torcé-en-Vallée (Sarthe)

Téléphone 20

Sections de Torcé-en-Vallée et de Mézières-sous-Ballon

sport   FFM   tourisme

KANGOUROU CIRCUIT

Tim Gibbes built a circuit. This is the letterhead used by the promoter. It was here that a wasp got into my trousers. Archives.

From left: 2000 World Champion Mark Loran (Sponsors Randy and Raewyn Owen), and Australian Lee Adams, twice third in the World Championships. Archives.

Alan and Sheila Jones with the trophies I won in 1988.

Riding styles

During the pre-war era, riders sat forward in the saddle with their knees held tightly against the tank and with a firm grip on the wide handle bars. The hang-on-and-hope period. Stanley Woods, the famous winner of 10 TTs, seldom moved from that position. How the riders of the '30s managed to lap the Isle of Man at the speeds they did is remarkable.

For the 1938 season Velocette introduced a modern swing-arm frame with oil-damped suspension units controlled by compressed air; girder forks were quite acceptable when efficient rear suspension had been added.

The Manx Nortons adopted plunger rear suspension, then added undamped telescopic forks. These were likened by the great TT winner Harold Daniel to riding 'a five-barred gate'. Consequently, these Nortons became known as, and always will be, the 'Garden Gate' models.

For 1949 AJS introduced a totally revised 350 known as the 7R, a delightful machine that had oil-damped telescopic forks and swing-arm suspension. Due to it being very reliable, easy to maintain and affordable, it became affectionately known as the 'Boy Racer'.

The sensation of the 1950 European season was a new frame designed for Norton Motors by Irishman Rex McCandless, a brilliant engineer who also introduced the most sophisticated form of oil-damped front and rear suspension of the time. These frames became the benchmark of frame design for the next 15 years. Harold Daniel, obviously a man of imaginative quotes, likened the superb ride it gave to being ensconced in a feather bed, and now for all time it will be known as the 'Featherbed Frame'.

No matter the surface, it coped with it in a lazy, effortless way providing the rider with a predictable passage, under any conditions. This was a speed machine that for the first time gave the rider confidence to sit back, tuck in, put his chin on the tank and become one with his motorcycle.

In 1949 a gifted young rider from Lancashire had joined the Norton team. Geoff Duke, an original thinker, discarded the baggy two-piece leathers of the time, introducing a tight-fitting, wind-cheating, made-to-measure one-piece suit and an iconic riding style of grace and perfection that became synonymous with that Norton frame.

It was probably as a boy on a motorcycle in an arena of privilege, pleasure and learning without advice or criticism that a relaxed separation of me and the motorcycle was established. First it was Dave Kenah, at the 1959 New Zealand TT, who commented on my knees sticking out. Then in 1962 when immersed in the hotbed of British short-circuit competition where one top rider boasted of falling on more than 100 occasions. For me it was a more exaggerated knees-out, bum-off-seat, breath-holding effort. I was not the only one but it was seen by the critics as absolute heresy.

Mike Hailwood made the following comment: "Frankly, I admit I am one of the knee-sticking-out brigade. I wish I could explain why I do it but I can't. I think it helps me corner faster and at least I am in good company for Hugh Anderson and

Phil Read do it more than I do." This, it would seem, was the beginning of a new style that has continued to evolve to this day.

The Paul DeLacy 1938 500cc BSA. At Phillip Island on the 30th of January 2005 during their annual classic motorcycle meeting it rained. We won the four-lap event by 45.110 seconds from Australian National Champion Clive Harrop on an Ariel. Twelve days before the event, I had turned 69. Actually, I nearly dropped it a couple of times but Paul doesn't know.

MIKE HAILWOOD

When competing on the short circuits of England, I often rode in the presence of Mike Hailwood. Occasionally, I passed him but he passed me more often. However, his brilliance gave credibility to all those that competed with him.

During the late '50s and early '60s, Bill Lacey was seen as the best engine builder and tuner in England.

Stan Hailwood offered him terms he could not refuse to look after Mike's engines.

"I worked all hours on MVs, NSU Sportmaxes, about nine Nortons and two Ducatis. Mike was a hard rider, but I don't think he knew what a carburettor was, or anything like that. Ask him what revs he was using and he would say he hadn't been looking."

Stan was difficult to work with; after a major row the two men parted.

"I finished with Stan, but told Mike that if he really needed my help, he only had to come and ask."

International motorcycle racing during the mid-'60s and the underestimation of the Japanese industry

Working with state-of-the-art, highly complex, cost-no-object, prototype motorcycles that each year had more cylinders, higher engine revolutions, more power and gave an ever more evocative primeval scream from the scientifically designed exhausts had so many positives.

The competition on the track between the Japanese factories was a gloves-off, bare-knuckle battle. The rules laid down by the Fédération Internationale de Motocyclisme that controlled the sport at international level were minimal. The demand for top riders had never been greater; at last they had some leverage and were in a position to negotiate for, and obtain, fair payment for their skills.

This high-powered, ambitious combination created dramatic headlines in all the world's motorcycle press. Having had the opportunity to perform on this enticingly colourful stage and being held in high regard throughout the European community was intoxicating. It was not only the winners that benefited but every competitor. For those who dare to challenge life's restrictions and boundaries and were motivated by pride, commitment and the responsibility of representing his country at this, the most extreme sport of that time, it was a privilege.

During the mid-1950s when contact was made between the British and Japanese industries, the reports appeared negative, with doubt in the short term regarding the ongoing development of what were seen by some as backward designs. In general, the British manufacturers scorned them.

Early in 1960 the Japanese Motorcycle Federation invited an influential figure in the British motorcycle industry, multi world champion Geoff Duke, to Japan. Arriving on the 18th of April, Geoff visited all the factories producing motorcycles at that time. He carried out low-key tests on various models from each producer.

The 1959 production figures were: Honda 180,000, Suzuki 110,000, Yamaha 60,000.

Honda began production in 1948 with 12 workers. In 1960 Honda employed 4,000 and intended to produce 250,000 machines, 20 per cent being for export. Geoff felt that this expansion rate could not be continued, as saturation point had almost been reached in Japan.

Australian Phil Irving M.I.Mech.E., M.S.A.E.,M.I.P.E. was highly respected within the British motorcycle industry. Phil had been the inspiration and designer of the outstanding 1000cc Vincent, and wrote articles during the Isle of Man TT races under the title of 'TT Technicalities'. In June 1960 he wrote that the four-valve head configuration used by Honda, for various technical reasons, all listed, would be superior to a two-valve setup for only a limited period. Normal Honda revs were 13,500 with a maximum of 16,000, and these astronomical speeds did not have much real value so far as racing was concerned.

When the first representatives of Honda and later Suzuki came to England they were seen as being rather incompetent. That this was a totally new, demanding in the extreme, environment to them, was not generally appreciated. The fast-learning Japanese had been underestimated on all fronts.

What a difference a few short years have made. Now the fight is for worldwide market share, he who gains the best importer/distributor wins. This creates ever more pressure on the race teams as the battle front is not on the showroom floor, but fought out on the European Grand Prix circuits.

Some of the leading members of the Suzuki Grand Prix Team 1961–1967

Takeji Okano
General Manager

Masanao Shimizu
Manager

Masazumi Ishikawa
Secretary

Tatsumi Nagata
Chief Mechanic, Hugh Anderson

Tadao Matsui
Mechanic, Hugh Anderson

I've Ridden 30,000 bikes

When *The Motorcycle News* went in search of Britain's most prolific rider, they found my mate Alan Jones, a test rider for Matchless, AJS and Norton from the mid '50s to the early '70s.

Every machine produced was tested for six to nine miles. During times of peak production, Alan worked from 7am to 7pm. Alan's total distance travelled was estimated to have been close to one million miles. His favourite bikes were the Matchless CSR650 and a Norton Commando. "On my favourite bit of road, I used to take them up to 100mph then put my head down and ring their neck up to 120mph. They were terrific."

Members of the Greenwich Motorcycle Club ran the meetings for Brands Hatch management. Alan was a volunteer marshal for 20 years and 18 years as the starter. Alan's wife Sheila typed up the results that were printed out using a Gestetner. All very manual, but with the assistance of the wives of competitors, a completely professional result was accomplished. An indication of their ability was that they handled the paperwork for all race meetings including the hugely successful Britain versus America Trans-Atlantic Series.

Perhaps the most well known unpaid member of the staff was pipe-smoking Ken Phillips, the travelling marshal. During a meeting in 1962 that had been unusually free of spills, Ken riding a new just-out-of-the-box Honda police bike as a public relations exercise raised the biggest cheer when he slid off it at Clearways Corner. He worked at Brands for 50 years and lived on into his mid-nineties.

On leaving school, Alan joined the Army. After serving three years in Egypt, on his return to England he found the cold so intense he chose an indoor job at the AMC factory. At that time he couldn't ride a motorcycle. When he bought one, on his first attempt he rode straight into a tree. So began the career of a most diligent, capable rider, who when doing all those miles, came off on just one occasion.

During his work as a test rider, he travelled to and from work on one of the new bikes, a sought of extended test but with the speedo disconnected. Due in part to his nature, and his military training, even though he had to cover 27km to work, on occasion in deep snow, in 18 years he didn't clock in late once.

'In Germany, under the law, everything is prohibited except that which is permitted. In France, under the law, everything is permitted except that which is prohibited. In the Soviet Union, under the law, everything is prohibited, including that which is permitted. And in Italy, under the law, everything is permitted, especially that which is prohibited.'
— *Newton Minnow*

Alan on a Norton Commando bound for USA market.

Alan (far left) returning from a 4500km test of the International six-day trial machines.

¿Crisis?

Tsukuba circuit 24th November 1991. I was invited to Japan to take part at a meeting with a difference, an alternative option to the Grand Prix bikes. There were categories for classics, single-cylinders and a variety of non-GP machines of various capacities. I rode a local chap's G50 Seeley and won the classic event. Some people present were impressed. The single-cylinder class was gathering support in Japan and Europe. Suzuki produced this 700cc single-cylinder 'Clubman'. It was very powerful, completely smooth, steered and handled perfectly, but I thought it best to avoid suggestions that perhaps I should compete seriously on it. A comeback at 56 years of age didn't seem like a good idea (even Janny has her limits of understanding).

Slack in the chain, Steve Wynn

Steve Wynn, one of the great advocates of the big twin Ducatis, is renowned for having provided and prepared the Ducati that gave Mike Hailwood, in the Isle of Man on his return from retirement, perhaps his most famous and best remembered win.

When speaking at a Classic Festival social early in February 2007 at Pukekohe, the subject of the 50cc racing arose and in particular the 14-speed, 17,500rpm 50cc twin-cylinder Suzukis. Steve's take on it was "The first two gears are only to take up the slack in the chain."

Leading Walter Villa and Phil Read, mind the rocker box.

Battle of the Legends, Daytona 1993.

The American Historic Racing Motorcycle Association (AHRMA), with substantial support of BMW America, ran a two-race event at the popular March Classic Daytona meeting from 1992 to 1996 inclusive. President of AHRMA at the time was Jeff Smith, the British and World Champion motocross rider of the 1950s and '60s. Each year, past American champions and three or four European former world champions were invited. All the riders had similar standard R1100 RS BMW race-prepared machines all presented in a very professional manner. This was not a parade but a full-on race. In 1993 Janny and I were invited to enjoy a pleasant and rather different experience.

The legends taking part were: Jay Springsteen, Yvon Duhamel, David Oldana, Gary Nixon, Phil Read, Reg Pridmore, Don Emde, Walter Villa, Don Vesco, George Roeder, Roger Reiman, Don Castro, Bart Markel, Walter Zeller and Hugh Anderson.

Each race was an all-on affair; several rocker boxes were damaged but no one fell off.

Early in the race, as we entered the banking, I got a run on Gary Nixon. Unfortunately, my bike hit the rev limiter in fifth gear and he rapidly pulled away. Seldom are all things equal.

The social side was pleasant and Janny and I spent some time with Dick Mann, who was very much the elder statesman of the US riders at the time and for good reason respected by all. I met another of my boyhood heroes, Dick Klamforth, who riding Nortons won on Daytona Beach in 1949 and 1951. Each year he grew a beard to protect his face from the flying sand. He was just 19 years old when he won the first event.

Everyone we met were fine people, there solely to enjoy the event and the company of all those taking part.

Enjoying a coffee with Don Vesco, who went on to set the FIA wheel-driven land speed record of 458.440 miles per hour (737.788kph) in a turboshaft-powered streamliner called 'Terminator'. Photos at Daytona taken by Don Bok, Greg Yarem and Mark Mitchell.

INTERNATIONAL RESULTS

1960

Madrid, Spain	Norton	500cc		1st
Isle of Man	AJS	350cc	qualified	5th
Thruxton	Norton	350cc	lap record	2nd
	Norton	500cc		3rd
Ulster Grand Prix	AJS	350cc		3rd
Leinster 200	AJS	350cc		2nd
Italian Grand Prix	AJS	350cc		6th
	Norton	500cc		7th

1961

Austrian Grand Prix	AJS	350cc		1st
	Norton	500cc		1st
Saarlands Grand Prix	AJS	350cc		1st
Tubbergen	AJS	350cc	lap record	2nd
	Norton	500cc	lap record	1st
Madrid	Norton	500cc		2nd
Isle of Man	AJS	350cc		7th
Bilbao	Norton	500cc		1st
Italian Grand Prix	Norton	350cc		6th

1962

Silverstone	AJS	350cc		4th
	Matchless	500cc		4th
Brands Hatch	AJS	350cc		2nd
	Mtchless	500cc		3rd
Thruxton	AJS	350cc		2nd
	Matchless	500cc		3rd
Madrid	Norton	500cc		1st
Saarlands	Norton	500cc		2nd
Isle of Man	AJS	350cc		6th
Mallory Park International	AJS	350cc		5th
	Matchless	500cc		4th
Brands Hatch International	AJS	350cc		2nd
	Matchless	500cc		3rd
West German Grand Prix	Suzuki	125cc		6th
British Championship				
Race record	Suzuki	50cc	lap record	1st
	AJS	350cc		4th
	Matchless	500cc		5th
Ulster Grand Prix	Suzuki	125cc		5th
	AJS	350cc		6th

East German Grand Prix	Suzuki	50cc		3rd
Cadwell Park				
Race record	Suzuki	50cc	lap record	1st
Cadwell Park	AJS	350cc		4th
	Matchless	500cc		3rd
Argentine Grand Prix				
Race record	Suzuki	50cc	lap record	1st
Race record	Suzuki	125cc	lap record	1st

1963

Spanish Grand Prix	Suzuki	50cc		2nd
West German Grand Prix	Suzuki	50cc		1st
	Suzuki	125cc		2nd
French Grand Prix				
Race record	Suzuki	125cc	lap record	1st
Isle of Man				
Race record	Suzuki	125cc	lap record	1st
	Suzuki	50cc		2nd
Dutch TT	Suzuki	50cc		2nd
Race record	Suzuki	125cc	lap record	1st
East German Grand Prix				
Race record	Suzuki	125cc	lap record	1st
Finnish Grand Prix	Suzuki	50cc	lap record	3rd
Race record	Suzuki	125cc	lap record	1st
Argentine				
Race record	Suzuki	50cc	lap record	1st
Race record	Suzuki	125cc	lap record	1st
Japanese Grand Prix	Suzuki	50cc	lap record	2nd

1964

United States Grand Prix				
Race record	Suzuki	50cc	lap record	1st
Race record	Suzuki	125cc	lap record	1st
Spanish Grand Prix	Suzuki	50cc	lap record	2nd
French Grand Prix				
Race record	Suzuki	50cc	lap record	1st
Isle of Man TT				
Race record	Suzuki	50cc	lap record	1st
Belgium Grand Prix	Suzuki	50cc		3rd
West German Grand Prix	Suzuki	125cc	lap record	DNF*
East German Grand Prix				
Race record	Suzuki	125cc	lap record	1st
Ulster Grand Prix				
Race record	Suzuki	125cc	lap record	1st
Finnish Grand Prix				
Race record	Suzuki	50cc	lap record	1st
Italian Grand Prix	Suzuki	125cc	lap record	2nd

1965

United States Grand Prix	Suzuki	50cc		2nd
Race record	Suzuki	125cc	lap record	1st
West German Grand Prix	Suzuki	50cc		3rd
	Suzuki	125cc	lap record	1st
Spanish Grand Prix				
Race record	Suzuki	50cc	lap record	1st
Race record	Suzuki	125cc		1st
France				
Race record	Suzuki	125cc	lap record	1st
Isle of Man	Suzuki	50cc		2nd
	Suzuki	125cc	lap record	5th
Dutch TT	Suzuki	50cc		2nd
	Suzuki	125cc	lap record	3rd
Belgium Grand Prix	Suzuki	50cc		2nd
Czechoslovakian Grand Prix	Suzuki	125cc	lap record	DNF*
Finnish Grand Prix				
Race record	Suzuki	125cc	lap record	1st
Italian	Suzuki	125cc		1st
Japan				
Race record	Suzuki	125cc		1st

1966

West German Grand Prix	Suzuki	50cc	3rd
Dutch TT	Suzuki	50cc	3rd
Isle of Man	Suzuki	50cc	3rd
	Suzuki	125cc	3rd
Japan	Suzuki	50cc	3rd

* Did not finish

NATIONAL PLACINGS

1956

Tauranga Clubmans	BSA	350cc	Scratch	3rd
Tauranga Clubmans	BSA	350cc	Handicap	1st
Hamilton 100 Clubmans	BSA	350cc		3rd

1957

Ardmore Grand Prix Clubmans	BSA	500cc	1st
Wanganui Clubmans	BSA	350cc	2nd
	BSA	500cc	3rd
Marton Clubmans	BSA	350cc	1st

1958

Rotorua Clubmans	BSA	350cc	1st
	BSA	500cc	3rd
Taranaki Grand Prix	BSA	350cc	1st
Whakatane Clubmans	BSA	350cc	1st
Whakatane	BSA	500cc	1st
Levin	BSA	350cc	2nd
	BSA	500cc	2nd
Tauranga Clubmans	BSA	350cc	1st
	BSA	500cc	2nd
NZ TT Clubmans	BSA	350cc	1st
Wanganui Clubmans	BSA	350cc	1st

1959

Rotorua Clubmans	BSA	350cc	1st
Rotorua Road Race class	BSA	350cc	4th
Rotorua Clubmans	BSA	500cc	2nd
Taranaki Grand Prix	BSA	500cc	1st
Tauranga	BSA	Open Class	1st

Banned from the Clubmans Class

Whakatane National	BSA	350cc	2nd
	BSA	500cc	3rd
Tauranga National	BSA	350cc	2nd
	BSA	500cc	2nd
NZ TT Mangere	BSA	350cc	lap record
Levin	BSA	350cc	3rd
	BSA	500cc	3rd
Wanganui	BSA	350cc	2nd
	Norton	500cc	1st

1960

Rotorua	Norton	350cc	1st
	Norton	500cc	1st
Tauranga	Norton	350cc	1st
	Norton	500cc	1st
Ardmore Grand Prix	Norton	350cc	1st
	Norton	500cc	1st
NZ TT	Norton	350cc	1st
	Norton	500cc	1st
NZ Airfield Championship	Norton	350cc	1st
	Norton	500cc	1st

1961

Wanganui	AJS	350cc	3rd
	Norton	500cc	1st

1962

Rotorua	AJS	350cc	1st
	Norton	500cc	1st
Tauranga	AJS	350cc	1st
	Norton	500cc	1st
NZ TT	AJS	350cc	1st
	Norton	500cc	1st
Ohakea	AJS	350cc	1st
	Norton	500cc	1st
Tauranga Road Races	Norton	500cc	2nd
	Norton	500cc	1st
Wanganui	Norton	350cc	1st
	Norton	500cc	1st

1963

Rotorua Grand Prix	Norton	350cc	1st
	Norton	500cc	1st
NZ TT	Norton	350cc	1st
	Norton	500cc	1st

1964

Rotorua Grand Prix	Norton	350cc	1st
	Norton	500cc	1st
NZ TT	Norton	350cc	3rd
	Norton	500cc	2nd

1966

Riding a Suzuki 125cc in all classes

NZ TT Levin	Suzuki	250cc	1st
	Suzuki	350cc	2nd
	Suzuki	500cc	3rd

NZ TT Pukekohe	Suzuki	350cc	1st
	Suzuki	500cc	2nd
Tauranga	Suzuki	250cc	1st
	Suzuki	350cc	1st
	Suzuki	500cc	2nd
NZ Airfield Championships Wigram		250cc	2nd
		350cc	2nd
		500cc	3rd
Teretonga Invercargill		350cc	1st
		500cc	2nd

Appointed Member of British Empire (MBE) 1994

Inducted into NZ Sports Hall of Fame 1995

New Zealand's Motorcycling Awards
Classic Motorcycle Award 2003
Inducted into New Zealand's Motorcycling Hall of Fame

International Motocross 1967 finished 4th or higher on 15 occasions
International Motocross 1968 finished 4th or higher on 14 occasions
International Motocross 1969 finished 4th or higher on 17 occasions

During the period of January 1970 to March 1973 I won 19 national and North Island off-road championships.

Basic Classic European results 1985–1990

Won 29 races including the Bob McIntyre Memorial Trophy
English 500cc Classic Race of the Year
Dutch Classic TT 1988, 1989, 1990
Mike Hailwood Memorial Trophy
South Australian Championship
Australian 500cc Championship. Gained one second and two thirds.

I have won numerous classic races in New Zealand and enjoyed the movement from when it began way back in 1980. Those 34 years have been enjoyed so much by so many.

EXCERPTS FROM AN INTERVIEW WITH JOEL ROBERT, WHO, AT 20 YEARS OF AGE, BECAME THE YOUNGEST RIDER EVER TO HAVE WON A MOTOCROSS WORLD CHAMPIONSHIP.

What were your impressions of the recent televised motocross at Derby?

J.R.: A lot of Belgians read the British sports pages and see that many people think Geoff Smith is the best rider in the world. So I was happy to race against him at Clifton to see just how good he is. I enjoyed it immensely.

What do you feel about your reputation for being a bit of a wild character on the track?

J.R.: I am only twenty-two; when I grow old I will start behaving like an old man, not before. Could be that in Belgium we enjoy ourselves a little more than do the English.

You smoke a lot. Does this affect your racing?

J.R.: It would if I stopped. I have being doing it since I was eleven.

What about drinking?

J.R.: What about it? Everybody at home drinks, even my sister and she's only thirteen. I'd hate to be the odd man out.

Does your personality get you into much trouble?

J.R.: It depends by what you mean by trouble. Last year fireworks had us very interested. One which went off rather near a Czechoslovakian policeman brought me three days in a cell. But the policeman and I parted very good friends. Life can be hard at times in Belgium. I am from the French-speaking part, while the other half of the country is Flemish. When you go racing in the Flemish part and you are beating a local rider, the crowd will start throwing sand and things at you. If it is muddy and you fall, the crowd will push you over or hold you back until the local star is well ahead. Mind you, carloads of my supporters attend these meetings as well, and they come to my help. But at the finish if anyone has a few loose teeth, I get the blame.

**WHAT FOLLOWS IS A COLLECTION OF THE MOST MEANINGFUL COLOUR
PHOTOGRAPHS FROM MY PERSONAL COLLECTION – HUGH**

Receiving the MBE from Governor General Dame Catherine Tizard. Archives.

*With the Prime Minister Jim Bolger during the induction into New Zealand's Sports Hall
of Fame. Archives.*

Top: With Janny, enjoying photographs with a Suzuki motor company director, Masanao Shimizu, and his wife. Archives.

Middle: Race team Chief Engineer and rider. A winning team. Archives.

Left: Our Vincent and sidecar gain a definite thumbs up. Archives.

American Dave Roper in full flight. Karl Edge.

La classe de l'oncle John. *John Surtees, impressive as always. Karl Edge.*

La splendour d'Anderson. *Apart from the tyres and front brake, the G50 was standard.*
Karl Edge.

Alan Cathcart in typical full race style on his rare twin-cylinder Paton. Karl Edge.

Once more standing on a Grand Prix podium. Archives.

Above: Prize giving. A bottle of bubbly and a nice trophy. Maxine Girodroux, the organiser, directs proceedings. Archives.

Below: Enjoying Ballaugh Bridge to the max. Archives.

Where the book began. On the patio surrounded by luxuriant roses. Archives.

With my good friend Frank Bischoff. An arch enthusiast of our sport.
Photo Frank Bischoff.

I won the BEARS class at Wanganui 1987 on Brook Henry's Ducati Special. Steve Green.

The handsome, compact, powerful Egli-Vincent.

BEARS 1989. With a broken hand and foot, being pushed over the start line by Alan Bland. Steve Green.

Ken McIntosh and I 'reading' a spark plug.

Alan Bland's BSA triple on the limit. For the first time, my knee scraped the track. Steve Green.

Holding a handy lead at the 1988 Dutch TT. Archives.

Once more on the Dutch podium after a gap of 23 years. Archives.

John Surtees is happy, I am apprehensive. Archives.

Laurie Shephard and an exotic display of motorcycles. Archives.

With some hesitation, moving out onto the track. Archives.

The Mike Hailwood 500cc Honda four is a big bike in every sense. Archives.

At the 2010 Centennial Classic TT, Assen, Holland. Luigi and I enjoy our first ever meal together after all these years.

Going out on the 1966 125cc Suzuki.

Sharing the podium with a group of accomplished riders.

Below: The Bikers Classic Spa-Francorchamps 2010.

Ferry Brouwer's Yamahas at the beginning of a 250m line-up of exotic race bikes.

Enjoying the opportunity to demonstrate Ferry Brouwer's 125cc four-cylinder Yamaha.

Fred Walmsley and son Matthew with our 1989 Dutch TT-winning Seeley G50. Archives.

Brands Hatch 1989. My right knee is on the track and the right handle bar indicates the angle of lean. Yet I had never felt more in control or comfortable. Archives.

At the 1999 Australian Championships. Twice World Champion Barry Sheene and I dispute second place. Barry was third. Two years later, I qualified for the pension. Archives.

The Classic Register Festival of 1989 was the Italian year. Mr Elli is giving instructions. Archives.

Janny, our family and I enjoy the privilege of a parade lap at Wanganui in 2005. Courtesy of the Wanganui Chronicle.

Kevin, Peter Welch (photographer) and I high in the mountains. It is about 50km to anywhere. Scribbled on an outside wall was: 'There is a "dunny" in the outback, where you wipe your bum with brush; there is no one there to bother you, in the deserted mountain hush'.

Winning the Mike Hailwood Memorial Trophy, at Brands Hatch 1990 on Fred Walmsley's Seeley. Peter Wileman. Original caption from Classic Club *magazine: Perfection on two wheels. The Equaliser.*

Kevin Grant congratulating Hugh Jnr after he had won the 2005 New Zealand 350cc Classic TT. Archives.

Janny, grandson Gerrit and I after winning the 2006 New Zealand 500cc Classic TT. Not a bad effort for a 70-year-old. Archives.

The Britten, Isle of Man flag and the Red Arrows aerobatic team. Archives.

Relieved to be back in the paddock and in very good company. Archives.

The Britten and The Grant. At a vintage motorcycle display in Douglas. Archives.

Isle of Man demonstration June 2005, waving to the crowd, who responded enthusiastically. A symbolic handshake with those who know the value of history. Archives.

At the 2003 Motor Cycle Trader sponsored dinner. World champions all. From left: Graeme Crosby, road racing, Shane King, motocross, me, Ivan Mauger and Ronnie Moore, Speedway. Archives.

Two of Britain's motorcycling icons. John Surtees and international journalist Mick Woollett. Frank Bischoff.

John Surtees has obviously enjoyed his ride on The Britten. Now it is my turn. Archives.

*With Australian multi world champion
Mick Doohan on my right, I wait to start
the engine. Archives.*

*My turn is next to enjoy the privilege of
demonstrating a very special motorcycle in
these magnificent crowded grounds. Archives.*

*Riding in unison with Alan Cathcart on a pair of exotic machines at the Broadford Bonanza,
Victoria, Australia on Easter weekend 2011. An award-winning photo by Ron Weste.*

*On a long straight in the countryside, Ken McIntosh, Peter Welch and I tune in the
carburettors of Virgil Elings-owned, Mike Hailwood's Reynolds-framed RC 181 Honda-
engined machine. Ken McIntosh.*

Pop and his grandchildren, William, Gerrit, Ella and Sophie. Archives.

Ella and Sophie with swimming trophies. Sophie went on to the top of the national age group championships and gained second in the national secondary school champs. From 11 to 16 years of age, 5am starts were the norm. Archives.

Grandad's treasures. Sophie and Ella's school project, which was displayed for several weeks at the Otago Museum. Archives.

The Classic Festival Pukekohe 1988. Dave and June Kenah observe a busy scene. Steve Green.

A boy and his dog. Grandson Gerrit busy as always. Archives.

Janny and Michelle with our collection of Vincents and a bored dog. Archives.